OIL, SAND AND POLITICS

Memoirs of a Middle East Doctor, Mercenary and Mountaineer

Philip Horniblow

HAYLOFT

First published 2004

Hayloft Publishing, Kirkby Stephen,
Cumbria, CA17 4EU.

tel: (017683) 42300
fax. (017683) 41568
e-mail: dawn@hayloft.org.uk
web: www.hayloft.org.uk

ISBN 1 904524 09 5

A catalogue record for this book is available
from the British Library

Jacket photograph 'Farewell to Arabia' Camel in the Ja'alan, Eastern Oman
Produced in Great Britain
Printed and bound in Hungary

CONTENTS

MAPS AND PHOTOGRAPHS

*For Olivia, so she can read how it went; and
for Binnie who supported me throughout.*

*Lacking both the poise of an historian and the memory of an elephant,
nevertheless I hope I have managed to entertain more than offend
all those encountered on this odyssey.*

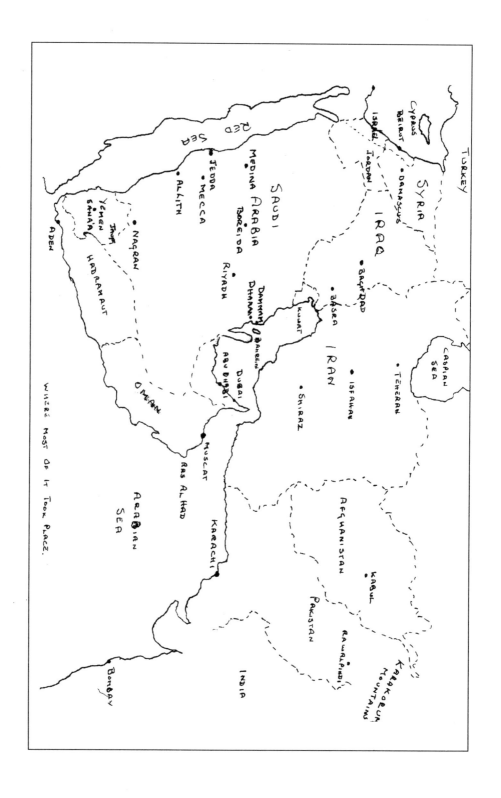

ROOTS... AND BRANCHES

When, out of 66 ancestors on my father's side, I discovered 34 were either soldiers or doctors or both, and my mother was a Nursing Sister in the Canadian Expeditionary Force that went to France in 1915, I suggest there was at least a genetic disposition that would be hard to overcome.

I have always felt it important to know where one came from - if only as a guide as to where one might be going; but perhaps it is as well not to know too much? In fact the past on either side of the family did not seem too murky....

On my mother's side a Scottish grandfather who - after emptying his bank account - told his wife (his second) that he was just "stepping outside to buy a paper," never stepped back in again. He was traced to the Calais boat train at Victoria Station, then lost.

On my father's, a great grandfather who practised medicine in Leamington Spa and was known for his diagnostic acumen - as the following shows. Summoned to the bedside of an aristocratic lady of the town, he was ushered into the bedroom and tripped over the carpet.

"Whoops," he muttered, *sotto voce*, but loud enough for the maid to hear, "drunk again."

"Yes Sir," whispered the maid, "I'm afraid she is."

Such anecdotes I heard from my paternal aunts, two of whom had achieved high ranks in the First World War. Indeed one was Commandant of Queen Mary's Auxiliary Ambulance Corps, the other commanded the Women's Transport Corps. I have lost a treasured photograph of her inspecting her 'troops' accompanied by Queen Mary. The caption beneath it closed with the following words in brackets - ("Queen Mary is the one in the big hat.") Only one of the six sisters married and she'd worked for Admiral Sir Reginald Hall of Naval Intelligence during the war, about which she was commendably discrete until her death. With the loss of a million men in the war there weren't enough men to go round. Instead the sisters taught - about the only career open to women at that time who wished to lead independent lives.

On the paternal side was a great great grandfather who set off to become a doctor but couldn't stand the sight of blood. He became a pharmacist in Watchet. I didn't have that excuse.

Father began studying medicine but his father's antics, (he led the Charlbury Riots in opposition to compulsory vaccination against smallpox in the mid-19th century), and a penchant for brandy, led to financial disaster and father perforce converted to dental surgery in order to earn a professional income as soon as possible. He was in time to join the Royal Army Medical

School group, 1908. T. E. Lawrence standing on right side of photograph with the author's father standing on his right.

Corps at the beginning of World War I, (there was no Royal Army Dental Corps in those days), and by 1915 was in Cairo. This was because of his earlier friendship with T. E. Lawrence at Oxford High School. They had gone cycling together during school holidays and I recall father telling me in the '50s, when the necessary time span had elapsed since Lawrence's death for character assassination to begin: "Huh! Say what they like - that man's stamina WAS phenomenal. We would set out each morning and by lunch time I'd be exhausted. I'd call a halt, T. E. would consult his map, name a town or village miles ahead and I'd get on a train with my bike. That evening when I got off at the agreed station... there he would be waiting for me!"

I missed the chance of meeting him on my seventh birthday. Father had written to him to say he would be coming to Cloud Cottage, but when we arrived and knocked at the door there was no reply. Father said: "Ha! Typical of T. E.! He hasn't changed, never could be bothered to keep appointments. We'll wait..." But he never came. It was the 19 May 1935 and T. E. lay dead or dying in hospital after his motor cycle accident.

In 1915 T. E. had suggested father might like to give some medical backup to his imminent foray into the Arabian Peninsula - not so far-fetched as you might think, toothache is no respecter of persons and he had learned that Prince Feisal had dental problems. In Cairo father contracted malaria and typhoid fever, at the same time. He was lucky to survive. He was shipped back to the UK and that was the end of his dreams of adventure. After a long convalescence he was posted to Sidcup to assist the late Sir Harold Gillies in maxillo-facial surgery. I think he did this quite well. I have photographs of his work and before the last war met several scarred veterans of World War I who visited us in Eastbourne and were clearly grateful to him. But then an uppity young lieutenant joined the team... and father's nose was the one that needed putting back in joint. The lieutenant's name was Archibald McCindoe... well, as we all know, one can't win them all.

So, off again, this time to a hospital in France where he met my mother. She in turn was the victim of 'shell shock', she had been in a forward dressing station near Vimy Ridge when it was bombarded... and the two of them managed to be on leave in Amiens in March 1918 when the Germans advanced and over-ran the hospital where they should have been working. So, here I am.

❧ ❧ ❧ ❧ ❧ ❧ ❧ ❧ ❧ ❧ ❧ ❧ ❧

My parents settled in Eastbourne where father established his practice in 1919. My sister and I were duly born into a professional middle class home. My parents had the attitudes and prejudices of their age, time and class. They disliked Jews and would not believe the stories beginning to emanate from Germany in the '30s about their treatment. On the other hand they were happy to believe stories of tourists running into German 'tanks', only for them to crumple as they were made of cardboard. Father refused to speak to a professional colleague after discovering that he was supporting the Spanish Republicans against Franco![1]

My parents grew apart. They felt - but they did not believe. I grew up

1910 OTC Camp, pictured left to right - T. E. Lawrence, 'Scraggs" Beeson, E. F. Hall who became a canon and the author's father, A. J. Horniblow.

---

[1] Years later when I was enjoying a mild fling with his daughter at the Middlesex Hospital this caused us much hilarity. Sue went by the unflattering name of 'Bedsprings', a reference to the ringlets in her auburn hair rather than to her athletic prowess.

reflecting their prejudices and lack of faith. An early exposure to the Anglican faith outside my home enabled me to see God as He has chosen to reveal Himself in Christ and I have a spent a lifetime erratically following in His steps, albeit frequently pursued by 'the Hound of Heaven'.

The only occasions I saw my parents animated was when they were recalling persons or experiences they had shared in World War I. At first the horrors they had both experienced bonded them but gradually each slipped into their own private purgatory. Once I saw them fiercely united in public. It was in Christmas 1938 and we had gone to the posh uncle in Tunbridge Wells who had married my aunt, (but was reputed to have served all six sisters at some time or another). We young ones were standing respectfully behind the grown ups before a formal lunch. Posh uncle raised his glass: "Well... Here's to Peace - at any price!"

"No," flashed my father, "here's to Peace with Honour!" And my mother threw her arms around him and kissed his cheek.

We took foreign holidays, went to boarding schools, and World War II started. Our respective schools were evacuated from the coast and we moved to Henley-on-Thames for the duration. My sister joined the Women's Auxiliary Air Force and went to India. I volunteered for the Army but the war had ended - probably a coincidence!

2
OUT ON A LIMB
Man can either tell a story or live a life. John Paul Sartre

When I was young I lived in the future and wished for things, some of which came to pass. Now I am old I live in the past - a 'time warp', as my long-suffering wife Binnie calls it - and wish for the things I knew then. Perhaps if things don't seem to be as once they were, they really WERE as once they seemed to be? I envy people who live in the present, it must be much less complicated.

But... stuff Sartre! I'll tell a story about the life I DID live: and what is it to live a life? First, to follow one's star. The late, great, Revd. Austin Farrer, who has been my guru for years, has put it differently - "to obey inspiration." Then, to await direction if the star is clouded. To accept suffering, to choose rightly and resist temptations. I've never been very good at that. Finally to be willing to die - not ready but willing if needs be. I can't remember if we young soldiers were willing to die, I don't think we thought about it as the war was over. I know we felt cheated that we'd lost the chance of becoming heroes and blamed the atom bomb for that. Instead we had to avoid being bored. Towards the end of my training in 1946, there arose an opportunity to do this.

There were quite a few cranks around the higher echelons of the army in the post-war years. A certain major general - out of deference to his family I cannot being myself to name him even now! - appeared one day and we were ordered to "Pay Attention!" After a load of bullshit was poured upon us, hardly from a great height as he was only 5' 2", certain of us were singled out and taken for a walk in the woods. As each one of us was sworn to secrecy it was some time before we pieced our experiences together. It soon transpired they were all similar.

Fixing each of us with a steely, monocled eye he asked: "Are you prepared to take risks?" (Hmm... yes). "Would you carry out any orders without question?" (Um... yes). "Would you kill a man in cold blood?" (Ah... depends on the circumstances). "If I ordered you to do so, would you beat me?" At which point he thrust his swagger stick into our hands. (Whoops! Sorry Sir, I think I've left something on the stove.)

No one admitted to agreeing to this last request, thus presumably denying him his 'kicks' for the day; but he followed this event by blatantly offering each of us special training in intelligence work. He went as far as recommending we should undertake an 'undercover operation' on our next posting in whichever country we found ourselves and subsequently we should submit a report on our mission to him. One friend of mine, Peter Billinge, a Kenyan settler's son, went to India where he infiltrated the Indian Communist Party and nearly got shot for his pains.[1]

---

[1]Alas, poor Peter tempted fate once too often and died in a motorcycle accident a few years later when studying to be a vet.

I opted for somewhere nearer home - Dublin. I invented a 'cover' based on the life of a Canadian friend of mine and my mother's ancestry and set off. On leave I 'hopped' a lift on an RAF plane to Belfast, then took a train south. I travelled second class, which compared favourably to English first class in the post-war period. There were two middle-aged English women in the compartment, who were determined to find out who I was; and three Irish girls who seemed impressed with my pseudo-Canadian accent. I made a note to try it more often. I found that remarks, for instance about Guinness: "Hey, is that what you call a Black & Tan over here? Like Mild and Bitter?" produced hysterical laughter rather than the kick up the back side it deserved. At Drogheda a business man got in, who joined in my education. When we arrived at Amiens Street, he treated me to a large measure of Dublin whisky which cost one shilling (5p) in the resplendent Station Bar, then took me to Jury's Hotel which was full, then to the Shelbourne, where I stayed.

After barrack room comfort this was a delight. I awoke to a beautiful morning over St. Stephen's Green. I ate a breakfast of sausage, bacon and eggs, in quantities not dreamed of in England since before the war. Even so the toast was cut short as there was a power cut. I learned that they had had no coal in Dublin for five years and had to rely on turf and wood to fuel their power stations. I then put on my Canadian disguise - lumberjack shirt, yellow tie, a white sweater with 'Monckton Ontario' written across it, jaunty white hat and camera slung across my shoulder - and set out to tour the city. I think I must have overdone the part as I was greeted with cries of: "Hiyah Buddy!" and "Where's your gum chum?" as I staggered to the top of Nelson's Pillar.

Shortly afterwards I went into a cafe for coffee with REAL cream and cake. A youngish man on my right asked me for a light and I passed my Belfast matches - bad 'trade craft'! But in fact it gave me a lead to revile the North and I was soon invited to join him and his friends where I ranted on about Canada's hopes for a North American Union freed from the British yoke.

It transpired that my new acquaintance was a 28-year-old Fascist called Angus Bruce. He had been deported from the North where his anti-Partition tactics had become overtly vicious. He hated 'Limeys' and worshiped the Nazis. He produced photographs of himself taken before the war at Tempelhof Airport, Berlin, with his arms draped across the shoulders of two Luftwaffe pilots. He was a member of the United Ireland Party whose paramount aims were to get the British out of the North and to get the Jews out of Ireland. According to him every second shop in O'Connell Street was Jewish owned.

I was then introduced to his friends, firstly Paul Skrezner, a Hungarian Fascist. He claimed to have lost his insurance business to Jews in 1945 and had subsequently been tortured by the Russians. However he was not lost in admiration for what Admiral Horthy's regime had achieved for Hungary. In fact he was just an exile with a chip on his shoulder. Next was Patrick Hagan, a fanatical Irishman who read and spoke Erse and English only when he had to. He had been deported from London in 1937 for his IRA activities, but he deplored killing and had broken with them when they started putting bombs in letter boxes. His chief claim to fame had been to try and blow up Hammersmith Bridge! This had failed because 'they'd used the wrong kind of explosives'. I could not gather what his ultimate aim was, apart from wanting to keep the old flame of hatred alight and said: "I think that's screwy!" To my surprise he agreed. It's better not to try and understand the Irish!

Next to arrive was the most prepossessing of the lot. A scholarly-looking fellow, wearing a flying jacket with the German eagle on the right breast. Hans Lofockmann, late Feldwebel (sergeant major) in the Luftwaffe had been shot down in his long range Focke Wolff 'Kurier' by three Beaufighters off the south coast of County Cork in 1944. He'd been interned. I said my elder brother had been stationed near Eastbourne with the Canadian Army in 1942 and wondered if he'd ever flown over there?

"Oh yes," he replied, "I did my advanced training in Heinkels over there in 1940."

Well, that explained some of the erratic bombing suffered by the town in the early days of the war - which included father's surgery! Lofockmann spoke half a dozen languages fluently. To him everything was a joke - including his hosts.

"The English are lucky to have the sea separating them from these lazy bastards!" was one of his winning remarks. He worked for the ground staff of Aer Lingus but most of his money came in the form of an allowance from Herr Thomsen, the ex-German ambassador who lived comfortably in the neighbourhood.

Angus' girlfriend, Connie Collins, dropped by before introductions were complete. She looked just like Ingrid Bergmann and was the niece of the late General Michael Collins. The group certainly did not lack credibility.

Next came Tony Reardon, an Irish Air Corps pilot, who had flown for the Falangists in the Spanish Civil War. He seemed more a soldier of fortune than a committed Fascist as he'd applied to join the RAF on the outbreak of World War II. He had been rejected for reasons he refused to explain.

The last to arrive made me feel uncomfortable - and scared. Jack O'Reilly, a tight-lipped terrorist with the staring eyes of a fanatic. I read somewhere this definition of a fanatic: "A person who redoubles his efforts for a cause he has either forgotten or ceased to believe in." He had gone to Berlin in 1940 and by the following year was working as a radio propagandist alongside Lord HawHaw. In 1944 he had been landed from a U-boat on the coast of County Clare with a radio transmitter. He went straight to his own home where he was picked up by the Garda two hours later. Whether this was the idea or whether it illustrates standard Irish security was not clear! But I suspect the latter, as he was taken to Dublin, promptly escaped, returned home and destroyed his radio. He was then recaptured and interned until the end of the war. He saw Germany as having been the bulwark against communism, cursed Churchill for not having listened to Rudolf Hess' plan to make peace with England so that Russia could have been destroyed and dismissed the British Commonwealth as 'a flock of sheep following a crippled shepherd.' His current activity was trying to get

German 'expertise' to help the IRA to destabilise the Six Counties. Judging from the marked lack of enthusiasm on Hans' face as he explained this I suspect he would have a hard job doing so.

It was 6.30pm before the party broke up - six hours of talk with coffee and cake as the only diet. It was a fortuitous introduction to the seamier side of Irish politics; I remember a spook once telling me: "Napoleon didn't know the half of it when he asked for Generals who were lucky... it's much more important for spies to be born that way." Incidentally, I did submit a report on my 'mission', which got a perfunctory acknowledgement - and that was the last I heard of it.

That night, Hans and I decided to go to the Abbey Theatre where we saw an excellent comedy entitled *They got what they wanted.* Afterwards we went to Berni's for supper: half the Luftwaffe seemed to use this as their mess. They were all in uniform, but without their service caps - hence were 'improperly dressed', as far as the Irish authorities were concerned. Before leaving I was invited to join them in a stirring rendition of *Horst Wessel...* oh well.

❧ ❧ ❧ ❧ ❧ ❧ ❧ ❧ ❧ ❧ ❧ ❧ ❧

Meanwhile the army was struggling to regain its peace-time composure. To certain pre-war regulars I met, the period 1939-45 had been an inconvenience that upset the even tenor of their careers, like hunting and shooting. Training conscripts was beyond the pale so this was left to young officers like myself. It wasn't easy. Most were disaffected, to say the least, but I found one could trick them into blind obedience.

One day, while on grenade practice, I slipped the detonator out of a 'No. 36' Mills bomb, put it back with the rest and continued training until one was thrown which did not explode. I looked at my sergeant.

"Oh God, a dud!" he said, paling visibly. The thought of a stiff firing pin that might slip forward as we approached was indeed alarming.

"Come along Sergeant, we know the drill," I said confidently. Armed with guncotton slab, detonator and fuse I climbed out of the trench and beckoned him to follow. We found the 'dud' with its firing lever already advanced. I put the guncotton against it, inserted the primer and detonator, lit the fuse without a tremor and sauntered back to cover whilst my sergeant's eyes remained - wide! There was a satisfactory bang.

"Right, let's carry on - next man!" I called cheerfully.

A few minutes later a thought crossed my mind - WAS the grenade we had blown up the one without the detonator? I passed the rest of the practice with sweating palms, until the last grenade had been thrown and exploded. Well, it had the desired effect - after the 'incident' the lads decided 'Sir' was someone they were prepared to follow.

I still wanted to be war-like so I volunteered for the Parachute Regiment; and finally decided I would like to stay on in the Army. In those days potential regular officers had to join Line Regiments. My reception by the second in command of the Royal Sussex Regiment at Chichester in 1948 was frosty. This was not surprising since I was wearing a battle dress made of Guards' barathea cloth, a parachutist's Dennison smock and a red beret with a Royal Sussex cap badge. After looking me up and down like a mongoose eyeing a reptile he pronounced: "The battalion is going to Akabar. You can stay behind in the depot and guard the regimental silver."

I decided my father was probably right after all. Three weeks later, still in uniform, I was being interviewed by Sir Harold Boldero, Dean of the Middlesex Hospital Medical School. Father and he had been students together. Nepotism reigned and I was accepted as a first year medical student. The Army acquiesced after I agreed to serve at least a short service commission in the Royal Army Medical Corps after qualifying.[1]

My father had to pay my student fees for the first three years while everybody else was on 'grants'. Finally, when his practice had so shrunk that he could no longer afford to keep me, it seemed as if history was about to repeat itself - but I had no wish to become a dentist![2]

It was about this time I remember coming home one day and seeing him escorting a frail elderly lady down the surgery steps as a colleague was passing.

"Ha! Doing a Bodkin are we, Horny?" he called out.

Dr Bodkin Adams was celebrated at that time for persuading terminally ill patients to remember him in their wills. Father was not amused. His income had dropped 600 per cent in the previous two years. The powers that be relented and from 1951 onwards I received a grant to cover student fees, books and cost of living.

The author pictured as a young Paratrooper in 1948.

[1] I never did; but served six years in the Territorial Army prior to that, which satisfied my conscience.

[2] He had stayed out of the NHS for the first few years and was living off capital.

3
STUDENT DAYS

In 1948 the Middlesex Hospital and its Medical School were still in full bloom. The transition from military to student life was not an easy one and on at least three occasions during that first year I nearly 'did a runner'. I partially satisfied my latent militarism by joining the Territorial Army, 21st SAS Regiment (Artists Rifles) which in those days were conveniently based in walking distance from the hospital at Duke's Road near Euston Station. Fortunately I made one or two friends amongst my fellow students who guided me, but I made more friends among my fellow TA soldiers - Jim Johnson, Toby Blackwell and Raymond Montford, to name but a few. Life as a post-war medical student was not the riotous existence Richard Gordon would later portray in his Doctor in the House series. Most of us were ex-Service, quite a few married with children.

One student became a life-long friend. David was the younger son of the missionary surgeon and mountaineer Theodore Howard Somervell. I found myself dissecting a dogfish with David. He had come straight to medical school from Bryanston but had spent most of the war years at school in America whilst his parents were in India. By now they had established a family home near Ambleside and it was there that I was introduced to climbing.

In the summer of 1949 we set off for Andorra. Why Andorra? Well, small always was beautiful; and I liked the idea of a country being governed by a council of 24 elders presided over (in theory) by the President of France and the Bishop of Barcelona - almost biblical! They had their own postage stamps for tourists to send postcards home, the revenue from this providing a free internal postal system for the inhabitants. Further income was provided by a commercial radio station but the main source of revenue was from smuggling. There were no roads, only tracks, but the elders lived in the hope that entrepreneurs would sign up to build luxury hotels - in which case they would see that the contract included a few hundred yards of tarmac. The population included a lot of Germans, lying low after World War II, and Spanish Republicans.

The Spanish Civil War had led to Andorra's present economic boom. Several large hotels had already been built between the frontier and the capital where the forecourts were filled with large American convertibles. The 'Spivs' traded in tobacco, chocolate, wine and perfume originally; but business expanded after World War II when returning French PoWs were given 'first refusal' of surplus US Army trucks. A deal would go like this. An Andorran would approach one of these 'veterans' and say: "Here's half a million francs - go and buy a truck and bring it to me - and here's 100,000 francs for your trouble."

The truck would duly arrive, the Andorran would drive it straight through into Spain and sell it for two and a half million francs to the Spanish Government.

With American cigarettes selling at 2/- (10p) for 20 and cognac at 15/- (75p) a bottle, it was not surprising that the local authorities adopted a 'live and let live' attitude to the prevailing anarchy.

So this was the country for which we were bound on the Newhaven-Dieppe ferry one morning in July 1949. The vessel was crowded but we managed to slip into first class undetected for the 80 mile crossing. We reflected on the 'travel boom' that was just starting - was it escapism? Motion after all numbs the mind. It was providing a living for a lot of people who were cashing in on it. For some it was a form of neurosis, a need to keep moving, thus avoiding the very real effort required to think. Looking around us we decided that for most travel was something to boast about to one's friends at home. On which depressing note we landed.

We caught a train to Rouen where I wanted to see the Cathedral where my father had first courted my mother. But the town had suffered from RAF bombing and the sight dispelled any romantic dreams I might have conjured up. We had intended to 'hitch hike' from hereon, a popular means of travel among the young in England which had persisted after the end of the war: but clearly it had NOT caught on in France. Furthermore we had chosen a Catholic feast day on which to start our travels so there were few lorries on the roads. I even donned my red beret... but none of the Airborne fraternity were on the road either. After two days we took a train to Toulouse.

Throughout this holiday we were obsessed with food. Rationing still existed in England and David was a big lad. As for me I had eaten my way through more than my share of rations at home and gone hungry at school throughout the war... bread and dripping (if we were lucky) or bread and 'vegetable', i.e. swede or turnip, soup comprises school suppers. So my diary resonates to the sound of menus, not music.

I ran out of money and had to scrounge off David. We caught a local train to L'Hospitalet-prés-de-l'Andorre where there were no provision shops so we had to beg some bread from a café before we walked into Andorra. The dusty track led to the Soldeu Pass through countryside perhaps best described as a 'scruffy Switzerland'. There was strip farming on the mountain sides divided by untidy low walls. We camped on the pass at 7,500 feet where there was a patch of grass. Behind a rock we found a recent inhabitant, a very dead sheep. We both slept uneasily, probably because of mild anoxia. Next day we crossed the col, over 9,000 feet, from where we had a fine view of a mountain range to south east, the lower Spanish mountains to the south west, and across Andorra to the north west, the Haute Pyrenees.

We descended to Soldeu and caught the local bus to Andorra la Vieille where we planned to buy food. It was an experience, as are local buses the world over! Overcrowded, but there always seemed to be room for one more person. At one point we stopped to let a farmer alight with two pigs he had failed to sell at market. At an isolated cottage, two sacks of potatoes were left against the door, whilst anyone walking was entrusted with the local mail.

After shopping we ate far too large a lunch before returning to our tents over the Soldeu Pass. We'd left our kit: it never occurred to us it would not be safe, and it was. But our over-indulgence left us both 'liverish' and ill-tempered. We slept badly, and it was only a large carbohydrate meal with sticky greengage and gooseberry jam next morning that led to an exchange of civilities.

Off we went to climb Pic Negres. We reached the Spanish frontier where a group of sinister-looking Spaniards were waiting at the customs posts, ostensibly for a truck delivering corn from Andorra,

"I wonder what will be hidden in it?" said David.

"Don't let's bother to wait and see," I replied and we headed off up the valley where we erected our tent under lowering skies. The storm, torrential rain and thunder, duly arrived as we got into our sleeping bags. David did the decent thing, got out and dug a trench on the mountain side of the slope to divert the torrent already flowing while I lifted the ground sheet inside the tent so that excess flowed under us. The weather cleared towards dawn and after scrambling some eggs we were away early. We reached the summit ridge and were plodding up it when we overtook a middle-aged couple. They were English. We felt deflated, here we were, making a Summit Bid, accompanying an aged suburban couple from Croydon out for a morning stroll! However honour was slightly mollified when the husband turned to his wife and said: "Well dear, we mustn't hold these youngsters up - don't you think we've gone far enough?"

"Whatever you say dear," she replied, already on her way down. They'd left their Morris Minor at the customs post which somehow we had missed on our way up.

The ridge became sharper and steeper and we were carrying everything except the proverbial kitchen sink. There were now precipitous cliffs dropping 1,500 feet on both sides. I decided this was no time to impress David with my 70lb Bergen rucksack, which we SAS chaps carried as a matter of course, and opted for a traverse, even though this meant both losing height and the chance of bagging the first peak on the ridge. We took it; and ended up under the major summit. Now we had to pay the price - a flog up a scree slope, which I recorded as: "A pretty bloody climb." We regained the ridge near the summit - and gazed down at the grassy slope on the other side! The Pyrenees are unpredictable; but it would have helped had we consulted the map. Oh dear! How many times in future would I hear that plea from an SAS man - "Never trust an officer with the map!"

We dumped our kit and headed up the last few feet to the summit, a steep climb but bliss to be unladen. Soon we were noshing chocolate, dates and biscuits at 10,600 feet. We were joined by a plump bird, a cross between a pigeon and a grouse but with scimitar-shaped, white-edged wings and a black and yellow beak. No doubt a common inhabitant but we couldn't put a name to it.

We scree-ran off the summit to a tarn about 1,800 feet below us. We were stupid enough to swim in it to cool down and just about froze to death. In fact we never really warmed up again that night and shivered miserably in our bags waiting for the sun to rise, but it was an idyllic spot and we spent the day there.

Next morning we descended to the valley. It was a rough descent and my pack beat a tattoo against my sweaty back. The sight of the tumbling stream in the valley floor made my tongue stick to the roof of my mouth! Careless of the scratch of rock and thorn we raced the last few yards and flung ourselves flat at the water's edge, scooping handfuls of icy water into our parched mouths - we'd descended nearly 4,000 feet.

"Careful!" cried David, "Don't drink too much at once!"[1]

We probably did. At last I rolled back and lay with my face in the grass, the scent of sage and thyme in my nostrils. When I looked up I saw wild raspberries growing in a crevice. Opening our packs I got out our mess tins and some condensed milk. The smell of the fresh fruit was nectar. We shovelled down spoonfuls, interspersed with further draughts of the mountain stream. It was not long before both of us were violently sick. When we had recovered we staggered down to a poor village called Porta. Here we parted next day, David to England while I made my way to Perpignan. We both felt quite pleased with ourselves. It was after alighting from my train in Perpignan that I bumped into a Frenchman and said: "Sorry, old boy!"

I was rewarded with a snarled: "Assassin de Jeanne d'Arc!"

An unforgettable accolade, and epitaph for our French adventure.

---

[1] David's innate kindness usually overcame his medical training. On another occasion when we found a fallen climber with a broken ankle, he gazed sympathetically at him and asked: "Would you like some fruit cake?"

4
AN ARABIAN INTERLUDE

Back to medical school. By 1953 the NHS was bankrupt, for the first time. A famous London radiologist, Sir Arthur Cochrane Shanks, was quoted as telling his juniors: "Gentlemen! The NHS is running out of money - no more lateral chest X-rays!"

This instruction is more amusing for radiologists than laymen, and rather like telling a lorry driver only to use top gear to save fuel. However, by 1953, I was already curious about radiology. I was 'walking the wards', and finding it difficult to maintain the enthusiasm shown by my contemporaries for clinical medicine. The thought of looking through people rather than at them was attractive. I felt like a break; and once more fate was there to provide it.

The second in command of 21 SAS, Tony Greville-Bell, had recently returned from a 'swan' around the Middle East, one result of which was a plot to second two officers from the regiment to the Arab Legion for a few months. The two selected were Raymond Montford and Toby Blackwell, but the latter was due to get married that summer and Jennifer, his bride-to-be, was unlikely to agree to a postponement while, as she put it, he 'played boy scouts in the desert'. Cue for Horniblow. Although an embryo doctor was not the ideal young officer to go, there weren't many people of our age able to drop everything for three months and disappear into Arabia. I was able to persuade Sir Harold that I could drop back six months and have the chance to do some work on heat illness. I had an ally in Dr H. L. Marriott, a consultant physician on whose 'firm' I had worked. He had studied the subject in Iraq during World War II, when he had access to the 'glasshouse' and would make the inmates run round an airfield in summer, wearing their greatcoats and carrying loaded packs! This 'study' had shown the importance of salt and water balance in the prevention of heat illness.

And so, in the summer of 1953, bizarrely, I found myself in the transit camp at Goodge Street tube station - to which I travelled each day to the Middlesex Hospital Medical School! - 200 feet below ground and dressed as a captain in the SAS. Without by my leave or thank you I was put in charge of 44 wild, be-kilted, soldiers of the Highland Light Infantry bound for Tel-el-Kebir in Egypt. We embused, after I'd told them I was a civilian and I didn't want any trouble from them, and were driven to Stansted Airport where we boarded a chartered Avro 'York' belonging to Skyways Ltd., which had RAF roundels painted on it as the Egyptian Government, for reasons of its own, refused to allow civil aircraft to ferry troops into the Canal Zone. It took seven hours to reach Malta, then on to Fayyid where we landed about midday. Raymond and I were met by Major John Cowtan, G2 (Operations) in the HQ of Middle East Land Forces. John had had an exciting career with

Special Operations Executive during the war, being an explosives expert, and went on to become a major general and chief engineer. He was an amusing and stimulating host. He had arranged for us to stay in the mess of the 1st Royal Dragoons (as they were then, now part of the Blues & Royals), who were superb hosts. God knows what they thought of us but they were tactful in the extreme. While we were there Egyptian 'terrorists' abducted an RAF leading aircraftsman called Rigden. Raymond and I saw men of the Parachute Brigade indulging in 'wog bashing' as they called it while they carried out a 'cordon and search'. Not a sight to make us proud of our red berets.

However, after a morning's duck shooting with John - when I didn't hit a thing - we were on our way in an RAF 'Valetta' en route to Habbaniya in Iraq, which dropped us off at Mafraq in North Jordan. Here we were met by an Arab Legion officer and taken to Zerqa where we were to live in the 'A' Mess for the next few months. This was the old Trans-Jordan Frontier Force (TJFF) Mess. It was occupied by several elderly bachelor British Loan and Contract officers but had an English speaking Arab as well so that it could be seen to be integrated!

A few words about the Arab Legion - so much has been written about it and its commanding officer John Bagot Glubb already, I'll keep it short. It was raised by Frederick Peake, a 36-year-old British Army officer, in 1922, the year that King Abdulla was given an Emirate, Trans-Jordan as a consolation prize for losing out in the post-1918 'division of the spoils'. Glubb did not take over from him until 1939. During those seventeen years Peake Pasha, as he was known, pacified the tribes and established a gendarmerie, creating a peaceful society in that part of Arabia, possibly for the first time in history! Glubb had been maintaining some sort of law and order on the eastern borders with his Desert Patrol and establishing schools.

He took over from Peake Pasha and the Arab Legion grew. Until 1948 and the Partition of Palestine, Trans-Jordan's western border had been the responsibility of the TJFF, but this was a British Colonial Cavalry Regiment and was disbanded as the British withdrew from Palestine. Glubb's little army acquitted itself admirably in the hectic years that followed. But their expertise was still where the Legion had been born - in the desert: and that was where Raymond and I were to learn. It was still funded by Britain, costing the Foreign Office £9,000,000 a year, so we felt we had proprietary rights over it, feelings not shared by King Hussein and his followers!

Behind our jolly desert holiday lay a deeper plan, typical of those hatched by a fading Empire unable to accept that it was not going to be a world power much longer, (mind you, we thought it would in those days!) This was to harass the Russians from desert bases in Saudi Arabia and Trans-Jordan, when and if they swept down through Northern Iraq and across Arabia to the Suez Canal. We were to survey conditions in Trans-Jordan for this kind of operation - and, later, review escape routes from Northern Iraq.

We started like good tourists, visiting sites and shrines as well as army centres. First of these was the 3rd Regiment in Irbid, then commanded by a large, genial South African called Pat Gray. He and his wife were very kind to Raymond and I throughout our stay. Poor Pat, after Glubb's departure in 1955 he went across the Arabian Peninsula to command the Hadrami Bedouin Legion, in the Eastern Aden Protectorate, and was murdered by his own men at the time when British rule was breaking down in the '60s.

Pat took us to visit the Rutenborg reservoir, which before the 1948 Arab-Israeli War had supplied water for the only hydro-electric plant in this part of the world. It used to supply power to the whole of Palestine north of Jerusalem. In 1948 however it had been destroyed, officially by the Iraqis but 'enquiries led me to believe' the culprits were 'Jordanian adventurers'. At any rate it was senseless destruction, a case of cutting of everybody's noses to spite as many people's faces as possible. We gazed at the neglected shell under layers of undergrowth and hence began our education into the bitterness that divides Arab and Jew. This was harshly represented before us now: ruins beside us, an Arab Legion company in the old TJFF camp by the bridge leading across the Jordan into Israel; ruins of the old Palestine Police post with its married quarters in a strip of no-man's land opposite; and beyond them, watchful Israelis in their posts.

All this gave Raymond and I food for thought. Here we were, two Britons still playing 'the Great Game', planning to harass a Russian drive to the Suez Canal; and hosted by an Arab country whose interest in our project was marginal. Arab nationalism was waxing and most Jordanians were planning of 'the last round' with Israel. In the face of this ever-widening gap of interests between Britain and Jordan we found only one British officer sensitive to Arab concerns - not counting Glubb himself - and that was the Chief of Staff, General Jim Hutton. It was he who encouraged the defence of the West Bank and divided Jerusalem against Israeli attacks. Most of the British officers, certainly those on secondment, saw their role as one of supporting Britain's interests in the Middle East.

There were some glorious exceptions. Our next trip was to Kallia, on the north shores of the Dead Sea. Here we met up with 'Admiral' Geoff Douglas, also known as the First Dead Sea Lord. We had both known Geoff when, as an ex-Royal Marine, he had served in 21st SAS. "A quiet adventurer with complex needs" - there, that'll do! Commando... lobster fisherman... Laird of Lundy Island... seeker of the abominable snowman (with Hamish Mcinnes)... chief instructor at an Outward Bound School... and with large liquid brown eyes that searched... and searched... and got him into serial marriages and affairs. The story goes that he was landed before D-Day with another Marine on the Cotentin peninsula below Cherbourg. Their mission was to destroy the lock gates and hold up German E-Boats which might attack the invasion fleet. His companion twisted his ankle in a rabbit hole. They sheltered in a French farm house. D-Day came and went. The ankle got better. They proceeded with their mission. Evading the Germans they damaged the lock gates to such an extent that it took the Americans - who captured the city and harbour the following day - some weeks to get them working again. Meanwhile the use of the inner harbour was denied to the Allies... Ah well, the fortunes of war.

Right now he was a contract major with the Arab Legion, living in a tent, and responsible for a 'Navy' of two landing crafts and three pinnaces. He entertained every Friday with a huge curry lunch which he prepared himself. During the rest of the week any spare food was tossed into the residue and re-heated. Thursday was NOT a good day to eat with him. His ingenuity was not limited to the kitchen. With oxyacetylene blowtorch, metal saws and steel from the phosphate mine workshops next door - these had been looted in 1948 but were still an Aladdin's cave to Geoff - he manufactured gun plat-forms, turrets for Browning machine guns and armour plated bridges for his craft. The Israelis had some boats at the south end of the Dead Sea but, to date, there has not been a naval engagement - what an historic battle that would be! Fought 1,200 feet below sea level!

The day Geoff took us for a trip there was a stiff breeze blowing and the spray whirling into one's eyes was agonising - not surprising in view of the salinity. This was a real problem in keeping craft and weapons operational. Any working surfaces had to be cleaned daily with 'sweet water'. Raymond and I swam in it and took silly pictures of each other, reading a newspaper, leaning on one's elbow; but in fact 'showing off' was tricky as the lighter extremities tended to pop out of the water and one turned turtle.

We struck lucky with a fresh curry, the original one had gone green in the appaling summer heat after only a few days. On Friday among the visitors was Brigadier 'Teal' Ashton, who was commanding troops on the West Bank. Geoff explained that he didn't like washing much, hence his nickname 'Teal' - a bird notoriously quick off the water. With him was Colonel Nigel Brommage, commanding 2nd Regiment, also on the West Bank at the time. Nigel was a Grenadier who had 'defected' to the Arab Legion in 1948 and fought against the Israelis with some distinction. I assume the British Army had forgiven him. Here he was back again and rumour had it that this time it was at the request of King George, rather than King Hussein, Nigel having been caught in *flagrante delicto* in the library at Windsor with a Royal Princess[1] during a Ball.

Then it was our turn to visit Nigel. From his positions we could see the Mediterranean, a reminder of the narrow strip that was Israel's 'waist' in those days, before they invaded the West Bank in 1967. Nigel was a man of few words, neither did he have time for procedures. A soldier who over-stayed his leave was told to go back home - and stay there. When Raymond com-plained of constipation he was told: "Drink some well water!"

Before leaving Zerqa on this particular 'swan' I had asked it there was any-thing I could do while on the West Bank. Someone asked for information about Israeli parachute training. I suspected they were using our old drop-ping zone near Lydda. Nigel snorted when I suggested I should observe them: "What the hell for? We know they've got them. Some desk wallah without enough to do wants to get noticed I suppose."

[1] No prize for guessing who, it was a long time ago!

So he arranged to put me in a dead olive tree near the border and over-looking Lydda - or Lod, as the Israelis now called it - airfield, carrying binoculars and lots of water. "Stay there until it's dark, there'll be hell to pay if you get shot!"

Gee, thanks, I thought. There followed one of the most boring days of my life. Dropping began early and within half an hour I was sure that they not only had British parachutes and equipment but probably instructors too. Since they were jumping from 'Dakotas' I might just as well have been back in Oxfordshire where we had trained. A wait for darkness can, I assure you, be as long as that for dawn.

On with the tour - next we drove to Aqaba. The Royal Sussex had come and gone. There was just a company of Coldstream Guards with artillery support to act as a 'foot in the door' against any Israeli incursion from Eilat, just half a mile away. Beyond that was Egyptian Sinai, while only a few miles south Saudi Arabia. We 'snorkelled' to our hearts content in the warm blue water along the reefs until the horror of a Guardsman losing his leg to a barracuda some way from the shore. After that we were afraid to even paddle.

✥ ✥ ✥ ✥ ✥ ✥ ✥ ✥ ✥ ✥ ✥ ✥ ✥

It was time to do some work. We joined the Desert Reconnaissance Squadron. This had originally been formed by Nigel who had handed over command to a battle-scarred veteran called Hamdan Biluwi. He had fought with Nigel in the 1948 War and had so many metal fragments in him he would have rattled if shaken. He spoke no English but at the outset we had our Arab teacher with us, a rather plump 'townie' from Salt called Ibrahim, who did not relish life in the desert.

When I first drove into the desert I thought it looked like Dartmoor but made of stone and dirt with clumps of thorn rather than heather. Our section of half a dozen Land Rovers headed north and east all day until we hit 'the lava belt'. This looked all the world like a giant cinder heap, a line of lava boulders running north-south, ranging in size from three inches to three feet in diameter. The surrounding country was rolling with some scattered 'jebels' up to 700 feet high. It made a great defence belt.

There were two gaps through it. To the north the Haifa-Baghdad road alongside the old Iraq Petroleum Company pipeline taking oil to the Haifa refinery, now abandoned. Every 200 kilometres there were pumping stations, H1, H2 and H3 in Iraq, and H4 and H5 in Jordan. There were still British families living in these isolated camps, responsible for maintaining the pipeline, in case oil was to flow again one day. Raymond and I enjoyed showers and whisky with one of them. To the south was the old Baghdad road, now little more than a track. It led to Azraq, with its blue pools and surrounding marshes. Despite the splendid ruins of the Crusader castle and all its links with the Arab revolt, I was not anxious to be there after dark. It had a bad reputation for malaria and we had not been taking anti-malarial precautions.

During the next few days we worked our way north along the west side of the lava belt and were finally rewarded by finding a third way through to the east near the Syrian frontier. It was here that we suffered a puncture and I leapt out, anxious to show my proficiency at changing a wheel. I was firmly thrust to one side and the rest of the crew had effected a wheel change in the time it would have taken me to get one nut off! We drove into open desert, dry earth with clumps of strongly scented camel thorn. Every so often we came to mud flats, shallow lakes in winter, where the drivers could throw caution to the wind and charge over the next couple of miles. There were wells with clean, if limited, water and here we camped with the local bedu. All were known to one another. We were provided with unleavened bread - I now know what the Israelites complained about! - dates and sour milk. A herdsman introduced us to camel's milk: as his herd had not drunk for the previous 25 days, this was strong, and according to Ibrahim, would purge us. Every time I moved that evening he expressed delight and called out: "Do you need a spade now?" I fear I disappointed him. I suspect I was too dehydrated.

Next evening when we stopped Hamdan took me to supper with the local headman. His hospitality conformed to legend - a 'mensaf', goat stuffed with chickens on a bed of rice. I learned to pass tit-bits to the guest on my left, roll rice into balls - and pass one of the goat's eyes smartly on to my neighbour! Before drinking mint tea as a *digestif* I had water poured over my greasy hands - to be honest, up to my elbows, I had got into such a mess.

Next day was my mother's birthday (she was to die within the year) and Daquilullah, my driver, and I took a DRS Signaller to a hilltop near the Saudi frontier where he transmitted birthday greetings in Arab Morse code, to Arab Legion HQ in Amman, whence translated greetings were passed on to the Post Office in London - she got them too, if a little garbled. (Shades of "Send three and four pence am going to a dance.")

So far we had done little save tour the desert. Now we planned to impress Hamdan with the value of re-supply by air. We had arranged this with the Arab Legion Air Force before leaving Amman and right on time a de Havilland 'Dove', piloted by Captain Ali Hussein, swept overhead just as we finished laying out DZ markers. Back he came and down tumbled our supplies. The operational aspect of the exercise was now somewhat spoiled by Ali waggling his wings and landing on the mud flat - where we all gathered for a tea party.[1]

The next step in our exercise was to rendezvous with another troop of the squadron but they never turned up. I decided we should try our hand at desert navigation - Raymond's experiments with a sun compass had so far been none too successful - he had recently positioned us somewhere in the eastern Mediterranean. But I was confident of Daquilullah's ability to find his way anywhere. The weather changed. The sky turned blood red, black clouds

[1] Ali was a Circassian, as fair as myself: in fact when he came to London that autumn and I introduced him to Jim Johnson in that well-known Chelsea watering hole 'The Antelope' the latter refused to believe he came from Jordan until he recited an Arab poem to him. Alas, I believe Ali got involved in politics and died in mysterious circumstances.

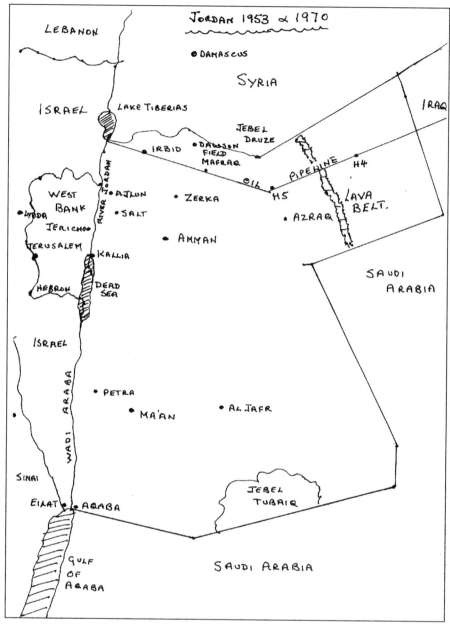

massed to the west and it rained - in August! Ali had already flown himself back to Amman as we set off for the police post at Al Jafr away to the south west. We had not gone far when a dust storm hit us. We could barely see the bonnet and we cowered behind the vehicle. It passed as quickly as it had come, thank God. Had Daquilullah not been there I would have melted into a claustrophobic jelly.

We reached Al Jafr after dark. Here there was a prison for 'political prisoners', who were all labelled Communists, i.e. they were 'agin the Government'. The officer-in-charge dined us in his quarters, where we were served by manacled prisoners of truly villainous aspect. It was an uncomfortable experience, since we were told that these wretches would await trial indefinitely. Next day we were joined by the rest of the squadron and headed south to Ma'an and from there to a 5,000 foot peak, Jebel Batra. Here Daquilullah waited patiently at the bottom while I scrambled to the summit... well, of course, when I reached the top I found the summit cleft, the other peak being significantly the higher of the two, and separated from it by a vertical drop of several hundred feet. When I got down Daquilullah asked me: "Was there 'khazna' (treasure) at the top?"

I couldn't have explained, even in English; and 'because it's there' would not have had the same impact in Arabic! On our way back to join the squadron I am ashamed to say that we shot two gazelles - we dined well, but the one I shot was a pregnant female, and I was rightly ostracised by the men.

Next day we set off for Petra, while the rest of the squadron returned to base. When we found it was empty... well, it was midsummer. We drove down the Siq, the narrow entry gorge from Wadi Musa, to the 'khazneh', or treasury. Here Daquilullah pointed out the urn above the great facade, scarred with bullet holes, where his ancestors had fired in the hope of breaking it and unloosing a shower of gold coins which legend claimed it contained. Of course it didn't. We scrambled over the deserted ruins to our hearts' content, then decided to spend the night in a tomb.

Daquilullah did not fancy that and, as his tribe, a branch of the Howeitat, were in the vicinity I sent him home for the night. Had I known he was but recently married I would have thought twice. When he returned with the Land Rover at dawn he was so exhausted that I had to drive all the way back to Amman. We had stripped the vehicle down and I was to learn another lesson - that the combination of sun and wind dehydrate the human body before one realises it. Despite drinking copiously from our 'chuguls' (canvas water bags hung in the breeze that kept cool thanks to convection), one was unaware of sweating, so fast did it evaporate from the skin; the same process that kept our water cool, but we had a circulation to maintain!

We reached Amman in the late afternoon to find 'trouble at mill'. The Israelis had hammered a border village in response to alleged sniping and the Arab Legion had not responded. It did not take long for 'the usual suspects' to spread the word that this was because the nearest unit, which happened to be British-officered, had been ordered not to take action by the British Ambassador. I soon became familiar with this tortuous thinking, the product of frustration and paranoia on the part of the Palestinian refugees. A mob formed, unfortunately in the street up which we were driving. The British Embassy being well guarded, they chose a softer target - the British Council offices. By now Daquilullah had woken up and with a wicked grin - he had taken over driving once we entered the city - he drew to the road side, jumped out, and waved to me to follow. I took the precaution of wrapping my 'kheffiya' over the small portion of my face still exposed and tried to look riotous. Outside the offices I noticed that tonight's attraction was a lecture on 'Ruskin

Dakilullah, the author's driver, Arab Legion, 1953.

- the man and his writing'. In view of the current situation this seemed to reflect admirable *sang froid*. Came the first tinkle of broken glass and the next thing I knew Daqilullah had joined the stone-throwing mob. He saw I was standing paralysed, and thrust a stone into my hand. There were few windows left intact within range but, what the hell, I thought, might as well play the part. I scored a direct hit, which I admit was satisfying, then grabbed Daquilullah as the police appeared up the road and we made a break for our Land Rover.

The streets were now full but we forced our way back to the north and reached Zerqa without further incident. Again, British calm was maintained that night as it was decided to go ahead with the 'A' Mess Ball. Raymond and I dressed up in the latest SAS fancy dress - black tie, 'bum freezer', cummerbund and evening dress trousers - which irritated the staider officers in their mess kit. We both struck lucky that night, although older and wiser heads would have said we were both heading for trouble. Raymond made a pass at an attractive young blonde called Flavia, daughter of an Italian doctor whom we had interned when Italy entered the war in 1940 and who, as a result, had no love for the British. The doctor had been released in 1945 and had run a successful practice in Amman since. What we didn't know was that Flavia had caught the eye of the young King... well, 'being lucky' in those days did not imply 'scoring'; and perhaps it was as well that he didn't.

On my part I had already fallen for the beautiful Stella, wife of the Chief of Staff, Jim Hutton. He had swept her off her feet at the end of World War II when, from her boarding school in Bexhill, she had married the dashing Tank Corps officer and incurred the undying jealousy of her class mates. She was very beautiful and I marvelled that she was a mother of three. By now she was responsive to male advances and I suppose I was the latest face in camp!

I think Jim viewed his wife's antics with resignation, he was a busy general and could afford to have moon-struck young officers adoring his wife as long as it was 'within bounds'. Stella was cordially detested by all the other wives, save one, Carol Parsons, who in fact was the nicest of the whole bunch. Carol's husband Rodney became warden of an Oxford College.

Champagne, music and love kept me going until 3am - oh the stamina of the young! But dehydration and salt loss took their toll. Next morning I awoke and could not move. It was Friday, the quarters silent and after half an hour I managed to crawl down to the mess where I drank a jerry can of water and several teaspoonfuls of salt. What a lesson.

❧ ❧ ❧ ❧ ❧ ❧ ❧ ❧ ❧ ❧ ❧ ❧

My next adventure was someone else's fault. Lurking in the bowels of HQ was a seconded major by the name of George, whose job as intelligence officer kept him largely indoors. Doubtless tired of hearing Raymond and I boast of our desert experiences - by now we thought we were veterans - he arranged a tour in the south and agreed to meet me at an RV where I duly turned up with one of his staff officers, Emil Jumeam, a Christian Arab. We flew in a DH 'Rapide', landed and waited for three hours. No sign of George. We flew back and I dined with Emil that night. This was my introduction to urban Arab hospitality. I arrived at 8pm, apologised for being late and waited until midnight when dinner was finally served. I staggered back to the mess at 2am and at 5am was back at the airfield where Captain Ali Hussein was waiting with his 'Dove'. We searched the area, where a wireless jeep had already arrived, and after two hours found two very bogged down jeeps in the sands of the Tubeiq Mountains - just about the wildest part of the country.

Ali landed us nearby on a mud flat. The three of us wandered over to find George, who was a prep school master before the war, behaving like the very epitome of the 'desk wallah' he was. His driver was lying groaning on the ground with dysentery - he'd never driven in open desert before and I think he'd decided it was better to die. The radiator cap was loose, the radiator itself dry. Neither vehicle had sand tracks. The driver of the second vehicle, a remarkably cheerful young British warrant officer, also had roaring diarrhoea. It was his first sortie in the desert and he too had broken a cardinal rule, following George's jeep far too closely and bogging down in the same patch of sand.

Ali flew off with the invalids and signalled the wireless jeep to stay put. He returned in a few hours with food, fuel, sand tracks, water and large luscious melons, plus a bottle of Courvoisier. George and I, who had been half-heartedly continuing to dig out the vehicles, were inspired in different ways. George accepted my 'treatment' of water, salt and brandy, in that order; and slept like a babe in the shadow of an awning erected on one side of the jeep. I was galvanised into activity and got the other jeep out in half an hour, but by then it was nearly dark. George became operational and I had to sleep with a loaded Sten gun by my head - I wondered if he expected Cossacks? In the morning we got the second jeep out. George sprang into the driver's seat and promptly bogged it down again ten yards further on. Before I could shoot him, Ali returned, in the 'Rapide' this time and out climbed three drivers from the DRS! We embraced!

Then it was my turn to feel an ass. One of the drivers approached the second jeep, paused, took out a tyre pressure gauge, and let all four tyres down to 10 psi. He then quietly drove it out of the sand. It had not occurred to me that George had the tyres of both vehicles inflated to 28lbs. psi - fine on hard-going but guaranteed to stop you dead in soft sand.

Leaving George looking rather dazed in their capable hands, I opted to return with Ali. I had a date to take Stella to the movies.

❧ ❧ ❧ ❧ ❧ ❧ ❧ ❧ ❧ ❧ ❧ ❧ ❧

Raymond and I were due to complete our Arabian odyssey in Iraq but before doing so were to return to the Canal Zone for a further briefing from John Cowtan. I received instructions to call upon Glubb Pasha to collect his copy of the 'war plans', which were apparently due for updating. These he kept at his home so it was there I went en route to Mafraq. I found him somewhat distrait. He looked more like an absent-minded professor, with half his chin shot away and gentle blue eyes, than a desert warrior; but there will never be another Glubb and already he has passed into Arab folk lore. After a time his wife came in to help in the search and I was to hear the classic words: "John, I DID see the goat eating something - have you looked under the sofa?"

And there we found them, slightly chewed but otherwise all pages intact. I don't think anybody believed me in GHQ, with the possible exception of John Cowtan himself.

❧ ❧ ❧ ❧ ❧ ❧ ❧ ❧ ❧ ❧ ❧ ❧ ❧

Raymond and I flew from the Canal Zone to Habbaniya, the RAF base in the desert west of Baghdad. Very much a legacy of Empire this cantonment was known as the 'golden cage', because of its lush gardens and amenities surrounded by hostile desert. The 'inmates' were not encouraged to roam, indeed the story goes that one officer's wife spent two years there under the misapprehension that she was in Egypt. We didn't stay long but went on to the British Embassy in Baghdad where we met Anthony Parsons, then the assistant military attaché.[1] He and his wife Sheila kindly dined us, and the next day we joined the 'Hornby survey party', a group of Royal Engineers engaged in mapping the northern areas in co-ordination with an aerial survey being carried out by the RAF at the time. Iraq was still swarming with little groups of British solders carrying out projects like these, or training the Iraqi Army. Young King Feisal had just been crowned and an atmosphere of hope

---

[1] Later he became Britain's Permanent Representative to the UN.

filled the country; alas Feisal was a 'wet' compared to his cousin Hussein in Jordan, and five years later these hopes evaporated in bloody revolution.

We drove off north in a convoy of Land Rovers and three tonners. The soldiers seemed happy enough to have something to do, and included the inevitable 'old sweat' from pre-war who had served in India and knew how to treat the natives. He shouted at them in a mixture of bastard Urdu: "Hi there you wanting Panne?" and dog French: "manjy manjy," at the same time stuffing his fingers in his mouth. In fact he did, to use the ghastly modern term, 'care' for them.

We passed through Kirkuk quickly, as our Iraqi Army liaison officer warned us that the Kurds were 'restless' - when aren't they? It was a pity as ancient city is piled on ancient city so that the impressive mound at the centre of the modern city beckoned us; but it was not to be.

That night I visited the British consul in Mosul. He had recently arrived from some Eastern Bloc country and would not discuss anything unless a wireless was blaring, so used was he to being 'bugged'! The Hornby party set off up the Ruwanduz Gorge from Arbil, Raymond accompanied them while I headed north in a Land Rover with two Assyrians, soldiers of the RAF's Levies from Habbaniya. During the next few days we searched for a 'rat line', an escape route from the north, through the Hakkiari Mountains east of Amadiya. It was wild and rocky country and I enjoyed it but was delighted to rejoin Raymond after a week's separation and, according to him, had contracted verbal diarrhoea. Well, conversation with my Assyrian companions had been... limited.

❦ ❦ ❦ ❦ ❦ ❦ ❦ ❦ ❦ ❦ ❦ ❦ ❦

However one of the Assyrians, Yacu, had aroused my interest in the Yezidis. One morning I had donned a blue Aertex shirt. I understood that Muslims believe this colour wards off the evil eye. I did not expect Yacu to complain, as he was a Christian. But his point was that I would offend the Yezidis - Devil worshippers.

During the rest of our stay in Iraq I made enquiries about this sect but really learned very little. It seems that Devil worship, hated by both Muslims and Christians alike, exists throughout the Orient but is strongest in northern Arabia. I suggested that the sect, in this case, came from Yezd in north Iran, but no one confirmed or denied this. Then I learned that 'yazd' is Kurdish for Devil. I was told their 'base' was near Mosul, and one day drove, fruitlessly, around a desert, which was said to be 'Yezidi territory', where the villagers seemed more than usually reticent. Covens exist across Asia, from northern Manchuria, via Tibet and Iran to Kurdistan. On mountain tops 'flashing lights' bear witness to the 'power houses' that exist there. I thought back to Arbil, a city older than Kirkuk and like it built on the foundations of others, its walls thus rising above the surrounding plain.

After the British occupation of the Mosul area in 1918 we had apparently prevented the locals, i.e. the Kurds, Assyrians and Arabs, from slaughtering the Yezidis. Also the Turks had tried to destroy them at the end of the 19th century. Somewhere in this area was meant to be their Holy City, with a white stone tower above it, topped by a gold or brass ball. This would reflect the sun's rays so the 'flashing lights' or 'power house' is explained.

The sect was founded by one Sheikh Adi, born near Baalbek, which is described as: "the ancient city of the sun whose colossal ruins lie on the western skirt of the desert near Damascus." A certain amount of geographic licence is already present! Sheikh Adi believed in God... but considered Him to be too remote. In the 12th century Sheikh Adi went to Persia where he had a revelation and founded the cult on Mount Lalesh, which could be near Yezd? The revelation was associated with fire and I suspect got confused with Zoroastrianism.

The belief was that in God's remoteness, He created seven spirits, the first of which we call Satan. This name is forbidden to the Yezidi, who thus call him Melak Taus, or 'angel peacock'. He will rule on Earth for 10,000 years. While Sheikh Adi was on a second pilgrimage, Melak Taus took his human form, so when Sheikh Adi returned his worshippers thought he was an impostor and killed him. At this point Melak Taus reverted to his true form of a peacock and told them that Sheikh Adi's death had completed the founding of the religion, that he would return on Judgement Day and carry the faithful with him to paradise.

Just in case I thought this was going to be a simple link with Christianity - though what part was the Devil playing? - I learned that Jesus Christ was a spirit who came to Earth to wage war on Melak Taus and his 10,000 year occupation of Earth. At the Crucifixion Melak Taus entered the Body of Christ and expelled Him from Earth. The disciples took the two Mary's to find an empty tomb. Melak Taus appeared as an angel and told them that their Jesus was safe in another world. But neither Mary would believe him. So he slew a peacock in the garden, dissected it, then reassembled it with his spirit inside and flew away to become the 'angel peacock' whose symbol the Yezidis still worship today.

The temple I was searching for was said to be small, rectangular and clearly unpretentious, just niches in the walls to hold candles with a black stone serpent standing on its head to the right of the entry door. Again, there were echoes of Adam and Eve. The tower was on a nearby hill. Around the temple were a cluster of huts for pilgrims. I was told the serpent was highly polished with boot blacking! Beneath was a subterranean stream that flowed underground to the Wadi Zam Zam near Mecca. Like the Kaaba, this stream was holy to the Arabs before the birth of Islam. I began to see why the Yezidis had managed to offend both Muslim and Christian! Furthermore, in the vault beneath the temple were the 'Kolchaks' or priests who came to make black magic.

So we are left with the 'angel peacock' in charge of Earth for another 9,000 years. The Yezidis do NOT regard him as the spirit of evil but of power -

some would say it's the same thing. After 10,000 years he will re-enter paradise as the chief of the seven spirits, a good enough reason for the Yezidis to worship him now.

The seven spirits, the seven towers: these have links with the Book of Revelations. John of Patmos was writing during Domitian's persecution of the Christians after 90AD. Emperor worship had been introduced. John wrote to the seven churches in Asia Minor, which stretched inland from Smyrna as far as Laodicia. John saw seven standing lamps of gold, one of them being God holding seven stars, these being interpreted as the seven angels of the churches, while the gold lamps are the churches themselves. Seven is clearly significant.

But where did the Yezidis come from? Were they born into their faith or were they converts? I heard a tortuous tale that they are the children of Adam, but not of Eve! They had an argument about whose kid was whose. They agreed each to make an 'egg' from mud, his moistened with semen, hers with her menstrual blood. Each was placed in a clay jug and buried for three months. When they were dug up, out of Adam's came a baby boy; but in Eve's there was just dust. (This should delight the feminist cause!)

The event is said to have caused Eve to return to Adam and from them sprang the people of the Book - Arab, Jew and Christian. But this leads to a problem - if the Yezidi came from Adam alone - how in turn did they breed? The only explanation forthcoming was that they were hermaphrodites! At any rate, they were now allowed four wives to make up for it! There was also a more optimistic hint that, in paradise, there will no longer be male and female but that man and woman will be fused in perfect union.

So, back to Yacu. In addition to never wearing anything blue, he gave me two other warnings. Firstly, never use any word in front of the Yezidi that could be misheard as Satan, eg. 'shaitan', 'khaitan' (thread) or even 'shait'

Yazeedi Temples, Iraq, 1953

(arrow). The second warning was never to spit in a fire or even tread on a spent match as all fire is sacred to them. When I asked him how he had learned these things he looked sheepish and admitted he had once looked in their 'Kitab al Aswad' (Black Book).

Finally I asked him how much evil they really did. All he could tell me was that their priests were allowed to take a virgin every night. Judging by the scarcity of Yezidis, let alone virgins, I concluded that the whole fabric of their religion was threadbare.[1]

Our time was up. We returned to Fayid, made our farewells, and still in our Arab Legion kit, caused a slight stir when boarding our aircraft. At least this ensured I was not going to be put in charge of the troops again! We landed on a raw November day, to be met at Goodge Street by a horrified Tony Greville-Bell.

"What the hell do you think you look like?"

We were too tired and cold to invent an excuse.

---

[1] For a fuller and probably more accurate account of this religion, I refer you to *The Cult of the Peacock Angel* by R H W Epson, published by H. F. & G. Witherby, London, in 1928. Also *A Pilgrimage to Lalish* by C J Edmonds, published by the Royal Asiatic Society in 1967. Edmonds was one of Iraq's most experienced administrators, both as a member of HMG's Foreign Service, and subsequently when employed by the Government of Iraq from 1933 to 1945.

5
AN UNCERTAIN FUTURE

My Arabian adventure had cost me six months 'seniority' as a student so I was out of step with the rest of my year, who went on to qualify in spring 1954. Instead I sat my finals in the autumn. This put me alongside the Oxford and Cambridge students who were much brighter than I! However, I still managed to get a house job, probably because I'd edited the Hospital Journal.

I recall that the day I learned that I'd passed I went back to the flat I was sharing with three others and lay on my bed in the depths of misery. In retrospect I think it was the realisation that I could not put off practicing medicine any longer: or, more prosaically, it was a hangover induced by the lunch time session which had culminated in mayhem in the canteen. I had bought a tray of cream buns and was throwing them at the assembled students. I was brought to order by a peremptory telephone call from the Dean, Professor Brian Windeyer, who shouted: "Horniblow! You're causing a riot!"

"Yes, Sir!"

"Well, stop it!"

"Sir!"

I'd run out of cream buns by this time anyway. Six months later I was working as his house physician out at Mount Vernon Hospital. He was a good boss.

After this I went back to the Middlesex Hospital to work as a surgical casualty officer and to wonder what on earth I was going to do next. The reason for my profound depression on the day I qualified was becoming apparent... I did not really want to be a doctor. Such thoughts amounted to sacrilege. I despaired and found myself on my knees again, this time in All Soul's, Langham Place. Then, instead of retribution, came relief, in the shape of Audrey Abbott-Anderson.

We had met towards the end of World War II and had become good buddies. She had two sisters and wanted a brother and I was happy to fulfil the role. We could provide mutual support when either of us got entangled with people we wished we hadn't; or needed a partner to wile away a boring dinner party. She had joined the ATS[1] about the same time as I'd joined up and had subsequently married Douglas Grocock, a professional soldier who had spent part of the war in a PoW camp. Like so many ex-PoWs he found peacetime soldiering difficult and had spent much time in extra-regimental employment, e.g. with the Trans-Jordan Frontier Force until 1948, then in Oman, then, after marriage, in Iraq. From there Douglas and Audrey had visited Kuwait and met Dr. Angus Maclean who was working for the Kuwait Oil Company. Audrey had explained my dilemma and, as he had plans of his

---

[1] Auxiliary Territorial Service, as the Women's Army Corps were then known.

own that involved leaving KOC, we contrived a meeting.

Suffice it to say that the meeting was mutually satisfactory. Within a few months I was bound for Kuwait and Angus had taken up a post in the Neutral Zone south of Kuwait as medical officer for an American company called Aminoil.

My arrivals in Arabia were never propitious. It was September 1956 and the countdown to the Suez War was accelerating. Just a few weeks earlier 21 SAS had been spared destruction by planners who thought it a good idea to have us parachute into the Western Desert, then drive eastwards to cut the Suez Canal before the Anglo-French invasion!

So here we were on the ground at Abadan in Iran, forbidden by Arab Air Traffic Control from crossing their air space. A big yellow moon hung over the oily waters of the Shatt-al-Arab, beyond which the lights of Iraq twinkled. In those days Kuwait had only a 'kutch', i.e. rough and stony, runway and no night landing facilities. No longer could we enjoy the luxury of flying boat travel to the Gulf, with nights spent in a comfortable guest house: we sat hunched in our seats until dawn when we ungummed our eyes and tongues and flew for just twenty minutes into Kuwait International Airport with its mud huts and corrugated iron roofs.

Before proceeding any further, I think there are some questions to answer. What is Kuwait? Why is Kuwait? Even, how is Kuwait?

The first is the easiest to answer. It is a patch of desert about 80 miles long and 100 miles wide, rising slowly to about 1,000 feet above sea level in the north west where it drives a wedge between Iraq and Saudi Arabia. Most of it is flat as far as the eye can see. Kuwait City lies on the southern side of a large bay whose northern shores abut Iraq. Here the earth is packed hard, a continuation of the Syrian Desert. To the south, where it merges with a Neutral Zone shared with Saudi Arabia, the ground is softer and sprinkled with 'arfage' or scrub. There is little sand but, to quote a well-known *Daily Telegraph* correspondent: "It's got some of the finest beaches in the world." Sand and sea are certainly abundant along its east coast but fresh water almost totally absent, save in a few sparse coastal oases.

As to the 'why?' well, it depends whose side you are on. A simplistic answer is that two tribes, the Al Sabah and the Al Khalifa, were driven out of central Arabia in the latter part of the 18th century, along with a third tribe, the Al Thanis. The latter stopped off in Qatar, possibly the least attractive peninsula in the Gulf. The other two went on to settle around Kuwait Bay. But this wasn't big enough for the two of them, so the Al Khalifa opted to sail back south to settle the island of Bahrain. Which is where they stand today.

And as to the 'how?' I like the story that it was founded by Winston Churchill, Foreign Secretary in 1921, irritated, as he always was, by Arab politics. Faced by yet another border dispute, he seized a pair of compasses, thrust one point into Kuwait City and extended the other to the northern border of Iraq. He then swung it through 180 degrees and declared: "Right! That's the southern border." He then found that this point was some miles into territory that could well have been Saudi Arabian, and he had no wish to entangle with the emerging power of the Saud dynasty. So he devised a Neutral Zone, with mineral and other rights to be shared equally between the two countries.

So this was where my dilemma about my future career had landed me. The deputy chief medical officer of KOC was there to meet me. Gene Rickert was an American employed by Gulf Oil, who shared the operating responsibility of KOC with BP. Gene was a 'no nonsense' Texan bachelor, nicknamed 'Demon' for his frenetic activity in all fields of endeavour. He was liable to greet staff turning up for duty at 6.05am instead of 6am prompt with a cry of: "What's up fella? You on night shift?"

Work, I was soon to learn, started early because of the heat. Gene's bark was worse than his bite. As this was a Friday morning, the day of rest in the Muslim world, he took me on a tour of the old city. This still had its mud wall, built as recently as 1917 to keep out raiding Wahabbis from Saudi Arabia. It came down in 1957. The four gates were left standing. At one of them a preventative medicine section of the government public health department remained on duty for another one and a half years <u>after</u> the wall came down - still waiting to pounce on the unvaccinated coming from the desert!

We then headed south on the sand track leading to what was to be home for the next three years - Ahmadi. After driving about fifteen miles we passed a collection of Nissen huts on our left. "There it is," said Gene, "That's it! that's the hospital!"

The other eyebrow went up. I'd been told that work was about to begin on a 'state of the art' hospital in Ahmadi - it would be the first British-designed hospital since 1939! - as present accommodation was 'not ideal'. I had not imagined anything as bad as this. It was in fact the camp that had been built to house labourers when the oil field opened up after the war. Next to it was a village of 'barasti' (dry reed) huts, strengthened with petrol cans and old packing

Kuwait, 1957. The old city wall comes down.

cases, anything in fact that would keep out the weather.

Seven miles further on was the miracle town of Ahmadi, with its golf course, swimming pool and white bungalows with trim gardens. I was dropped off at the guesthouse and shown to my room with its central air conditioning and introduced to my bearer, Nabi Bux. I think he was the laziest servant I ever knew. He regarded turning on my bath water each evening, watching it fill, then announcing: "Hot bath ready Sahib!" as the extent of his duties. And so I had arrived in 'Pinner with prickly heat'.

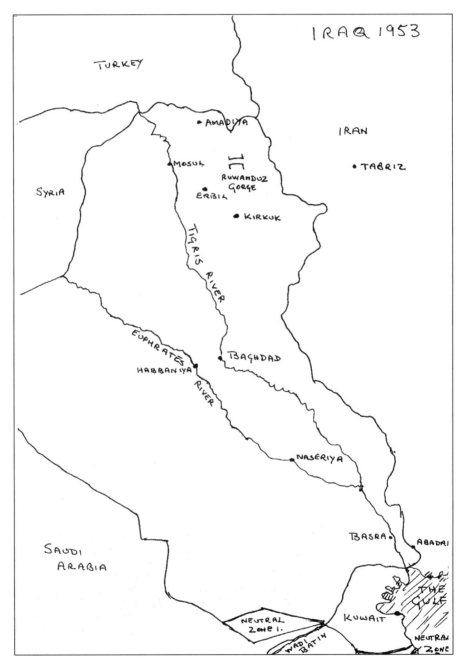

It was the custom for joint Anglo-American ventures in the Middle East after World War II to be initiated by Americans, then gradually handed over to the British to maintain: to be more precise, the Scots. In 1956 60% of the Western staff in KOC were from north of the Border. As salaries were based on home cost of living, it was also three times cheaper to employ a Britisher than an American in those days!

While the Texan pioneers in 1947 were prepared to live rough in trailer camps, the British soon started to plan a colony. "What do you guys want? Bucking-Ham Palace? This is meant to be an oil camp!" was a typical outburst from a Texan driller when he saw the first bungalows being built.

By 1956, Ahmadi, like Habbaniya, had become a 'golden cage'. Bowing to difficulties in recruiting specialised staff, the company had allowed husbands in key positions to bring their families. Some of these would spend their entire lives within the compound, travelling to Kuwait City only to board an aircraft for contractual leave - three months every two years. But then it was said that the only activities not available in Ahmadi were mountaineering and skiing - so why leave the place?

By then there were about 2,000 Western expatriates, called 'senior staff', including families; about 6,000 Indo-Pakistanis, classified as 'clerical foremen and technical staff' - to avoid calling them 'junior staff'! Even in those days political correctness had begun to make itself felt. The labour force of some 20,000 were largely Arab, although some were Iranians. Very few Kuwaitis were employed in any shape or form.

As I was replacing Angus Maclean, an Arabist, I was employed to look after the labour force and so my mornings were spent in the clinic in Ahmadi. Apart from the fact that I needed an interpreter in my early days, such Arabic I had learned in Jordan being non-medical in nature, I was also fresh from the casualty department of a London teaching hospital. But despite these handicaps I was soon reassured. The medical problems were similar. I soon learned the tricks that malingerers practiced to get a day off work: haemoptysis, i.e. coughing up blood - and Tb was rife in those days - meant an immediate referral for a chest X-ray, a further wait in air-conditioned surroundings and then, if he timed it well, a brusque call to go home and be sure to report first thing in the morning. I learned to make the patient cough in front of me into a sputum pot before anything else. Haematuria, i.e. blood in the urine was common among the Iraqis, indeed a diagnosis could be made by asking which town he came from: if the answer was "Nasseriya", in southern Iraq, testing for bilharzia was almost a formality - they all had it.

The object was too often to get a day off work - who can blame them? The Arab finds the summer heat as trying as any Westerner. A bizarre collection of aches and pains merited an aspirin and water - but aspirin tablets were plain white, and therefore no good in the patients' eyes. I persuaded the pharmacy to put a drop of phenolphthalein in the next batch they prepared - and lo, pink aspirin tables, which went down well!

But my eyes were really opened in the afternoons when I worked in the Arab families clinic. I learned that Arab girls suffered from rickets. What! With all that sun? Yes, but the trouble was that they were never exposed to it. A bedouin child at birth was wrapped in a cocoon of camel dung up to the waist which absorbed bodily excretions during the first few weeks when Western mothers are forever changing nappies. Their survival at this stage depended on their not having died from tetanus acquired when the umbilical cord was cut with a stone. Subsequently they were wrapped in the black cloth that was their uniform. Breast feeding was maintained for three years. All these factors made Vitamin D synthesis inadequate. A classic example was my driver's daughter Zara. Married at fifteen, she had to have a Caesarean section because of her tri-foliate pelvis a year later. I was amazed so many girls contrived to have normal deliveries - but I suppose youth helped, the pelvis being distensible at that age.

We had a domiciliary Tb service. Once diagnosed and the tribal camp localised, one of our British nursing sisters would visit the patients three times a week and inject streptomycin and literally force tablets down their throats - 'recorded delivery' we called it. One could not trust a patient to take tablets after they had had an injection, the latter being the cure all; but the tablets helped prevent resistance developing to the streptomycin. Every so often I would go along to review progress armed with a pair of bathroom scales, for we used weight gain as a guide to progress. One day, after drinking the statutory coffee from unwashed cups - well, cups washed in filthy water - we bade out adieus, climbed into my Land Rover and drove off. At once there was a jolt under the front wheels. I got out to find a very dead sheep lying there, cold and stiff. I was told I had killed it and I must pay. I did, Rs.300, about £23. Of course they knew the oil company would pay in the end - which they did - nevertheless I fear our hearts were hardened... and we did not return to that camp.

However we were encouraged when, a few days later, all eleven patients arrived at the families clinic to continue their treatment, having hired a pick-up truck for the round journey of 30 miles across the desert. Soon summer would come and they would all disappear into the desert, in the remorseless search for pasture, and their treatment would cease. Maybe the clean desert air replaces orthodox medicine - I was to learn that the patients' health had seldom deteriorated when they returned to the clinic in the autumn.

Being a commercial organisation 'annual medicals' were obligatory for all employees and all of us doctors had to perform them; and they were boring. One small, shy, Indian doctor finally flipped. He failed an employee (an almost unheard of event) and when asked why he said: "Because he had grey pubic hairs."

There were other lighter moments. One day Gene Rickert invited me home 'to tea' - although coffee and blueberry pie were always served - and told me I was to accompany him on a house visit to the ruling family in Kuwait. Despite the burgeoning health service in the state, there was still a certain 'cachet' in ordering a visit from a company doctor.

"Remember Philip, whatever you do don't admire anything in the palace.

Arabs feel they've got to give it to you. If we're lucky we'll get a gold watch apiece anyway!"

Off we drove and soon entered the palace gates of Sheikh Jabir Al Ahmed. We stopped at the foot of the palace steps and were told that the patient was being summoned. Meanwhile we took a tour around the Sheikh's beautiful garden - I exclaimed at the beauty of the roses and our escort clucked appreciatively - after all the English were connoisseurs of roses he said. Then we were ushered into a room where a portly member of the family was wheezing away. Gene and I made a drama out of auscultating his chest, though it was clear from the other end of the room he had asthma. Gene administered the mandatory injection and prescribed pills. The wheezing calmed.

Gene spoke an aside to me: "I guess I'm going to be unpopular but this guy's probably allergic to the dust of all those tree blossoms near the gate. I'll have to tell them to cut them down."

There was a tree belonging to the acacia family that did seem to trigger asthma amongst expatriates during the pollen season, and they were discouraged in Ahmadi. However on this occasion Gene's advice was received impassively and after the obligatory coffee we were ushered out. I hesitated after shaking hands - but no gold watch.

We drove slowly towards the gate. Suddenly Gene stopped. Running behind and waving excitedly was our earlier escort.

"Ah," said Gene triumphantly, "here are our wrist watches!" The man drew alongside.

"So sorry," he puffed, and thrust a red rose into my hand.

We existed in splendid isolation in Ahmadi but it was not long after my

Zara with her father.

arrival that the Suez War occurred, and despite the company's efforts we could not ignore it. KOC published a daily news-sheet during the exciting days when British paratroops were storming down the canal towards Port Suez. It resolutely ignored the Middle East and regaled us with reports of trade agreements with Brazil! Whilst the war lasted the locals behaved impeccably towards us, it was rather nice to be on the winning side for a change. But all this changed once we accepted the 'cease fire' - as far as the Arabs were concerned we'd been beaten and now was a good chance to get their own back. The Americans, too, took good care to distance themselves from us, while the Indian shopkeepers put up signs saying "British customers not welcome". Then things took a more serious turn.

I was still living in the guest house. One night in December I was duty doctor and still up when I heard the dull boom of an explosion, muffled by the heavy rain that was falling and carried northwards by the wind so that few other people heard it. Guncotton makes a distinctive noise when detonated. I was in my car and driving along wet, deserted, streets before wondering whether I was doing the right thing. Too late - I could see a flickering orange glow to the north of the town. Soon I was on the sand track leading to Kuwait City and not more than half a mile along this when it became clear what had happened. An oil well, 'Ahmadi Five', was ablaze just off the road. The fire was growing brighter with every passing minute as more gas and oil swelled up from the earth. There was already a small crowd of onlookers and I walked nearer the well which was spouting fiery gas like a dragon.

On my left I saw an American shooting brake, containing five or six shadowy Arab figures, their head dresses obscuring their features and all drawing on cigarettes. Somehow they did not look like bedouins. In fact as I approached them I was sure they were townsmen, but before I got too close

An ocean-going Kuwaiti Dhow.

the driver reversed and they drove off.

Later I had little doubt that I had been looking at the saboteurs; and later still decided that one of them was Abdulla Al Ghanim!

Here a note of explanation is needed. Abdulla was the son of Yusuf Al Ghanim, doyen of Kuwait's merchant class who had negotiated the original agreement with the western oil companies before the Second World War. Indeed it was said that when the tribes first settled in Kuwait there was an argument between the Al Sabahs and the Al Ghanims as to who were to the rulers and who the merchants... and the Al Sabahs lost! Yusuf had sent Abdulla to Scotland after his schooling, whence he returned with a sharpened business brain and a Glasgow accent - the westerners called him 'Jock Al Ghanim', which he didn't like much. He became a friend both before and after his marriage to Lulua; and was also a friend of my future wife Binnie's family. He went on to become a hugely successful business man, then joined the latter day Government and became Minister of Power. But in 1956 he was a 'rebel with a cause' - and perhaps well justified!

At the time I only remember wondering how they'd got there so quickly... and decided to remain 'shtum'.

The heat was growing more intense and the place crowded. The fire department were in their element. Chaos mounted as hoses were run out from water tankers, ropes were strung around the well head and firemen crept forward behind flash screens. Over all I could hear the British supervisors bawling at their Arab firemen - in English - and shouting for George Porter (head of catering) to supply them with coffee and sandwiches - "And mind they're fresh!"

Thoughtfully I went back to bed. To finish this story; of course they didn't extinguish the fire, it needed rare expertise. This duly came in the shape of the legendary 'Red' Adair, the Texan fire-fighter, who arrived with his assistant a few days later. I watched them chomp through steak and eggs for breakfast, noting that Red lacked any hair on any exposed part of his body - no doubt an occupational hazard. It took even him some time to quell the monster, trying to blow it out with explosives, i.e. starve it of air, failed. Finally he was able to 'cap' it by drilling an oblique shaft into the well's shaft and pouring cement into it.

❧ ❧ ❧ ❧ ❧ ❧ ❧ ❧ ❧ ❧ ❧ ❧ ❧

I mentioned George Porter above. When his wife had to return to the UK due to poor health, my boss, Dr John Guthrie, Chief Medical Officer, of whom more, much more, later, thought it would be kindness if I moved into his permanent married quarter to keep him company. This was a happy move as far as I was concerned. I enjoyed a luxurious life style and George's company. His stories of the early days in Kuwait kept me fascinated.

In 1947 demobilisation flooded the job market. Many men had tasted tropical warmth and domestic servants in the Middle and Far East. Others were restless. Shrewd heads in the City hinted that Kuwait's future was bright. So out they came to support the 300 or so American drillers who were opening up the Burgan field. They landed in a 'Dakota', after a trip lasting several days from London, on a sand strip outside Kuwait, as often as not in sweltering heat. Here they were welcomed by an ex-RSM, in the dulcet tones of such men, and bundled into an open lorry which took them to a tented camp some twenty miles to the south. Here they dumped their kit, had their first meal and wrote home... as George said, many letters must have started like his - "Dear God, what have I done?"

Further south was the drilling camp at Wara (meaning 'behind' or 'beyond', rather a suitable name) close to an Arab village where Bedu were starting the slow and often demoralising process of settlement. As far as the eye could see was flat brown desert with a 150 foot pimple, Wara Hill. It was a hutted camp and must have been similar to a frontier town in the Wild West 70 years earlier. Many of the drillers carried revolvers and were of mixed Red Indian or Mexican stock, prone to shave their heads like Cherokees. There was no cooling in those days and a popular method of getting ready for bed was to empty a bucket of water over oneself and one's cot and trust that sleep would overcome one before the overpowering heat reasserted itself. They would work 24 hour shifts, then have twelve hours off, during which they would play poker for eight hours, supported by whisky and sandwiches, a bucket in the corner of the hut providing relief for their bodily functions. Occasionally the sex urge drove a few of them to seek solace from the ragged, dirty girls in the village. The consequences were sometimes fatal - no enquiries were made if a man had gone to the village and never returned.

The principle of 'hire and fire' worked. Men began to conform, or left. The arrival of the first wives was the death knell of this colourful era; but still the transition to a more stable community was rough! Ahmadi was being built and the first dance was held in a hangar. Just about every man in the company was on parade, spotless in clean shirts and reeking of after shave. Alas for good intentions. Within half an hour the five ladies were being escorted home by their anxious husbands while everyone else got down to the normal business of brawling and smashing the furniture.

Near our present hospital was a Nissen hut that had once housed the Magwa Club. Drinking was of course the main occupation and George told me of the two American drillers who had left in their pick-up truck after a liquid lunch to return to Ahmadi. Driving down the sand track the passenger nudged the driver and said: "Hey Bud - take it easy, there's an aeroplane in front."

"Aw shut up and go back to sleep, you're drunk!" was the not unreasonable reply. Next minute there was a splintering crash as they sliced the tail off a de Havilland 'Dove'. When they staggered out of their truck they found the pilot of the aircraft, sobbing hysterically on the ground nearby. It transpired that he had been en route to India to deliver the aircraft to a Maharajah, had developed instrument failure and drifted off course to the south; then, with fuel tanks nearly empty, he had made a near miraculous forced landing on the only track he could find. The lawyers had a fine old time arguing who was going to pay for that crash!

6
SUN, SAND, SEA - AND OIL

B
ut all this was history. Now the giant American construction company Bechtel had arrived to build a refinery at Mina-al-Ahmadi, the harbour down on the coast; and there I went to work in the mornings in a spanking new clinic. Jessica Patience came with me, a superb example of the nursing sister Scotland produced in those days - and hopefully still does. Sister Patience was of statuesque build and had a voice which, when raised, could shatter a glass at twenty yards, and she was the anchor of the clinic.

We were also responsible for emergencies on the jetty so had to be ready for cases of 'heat illness' brought ashore from tankers, as well as diving problems. Although the waters of the Gulf were shallow, sometimes company divers were called upon to work for prolonged periods below water, albeit at moderate depth. It gave me an excuse to attend a course at the Royal Navy's Diving School back in Gosport! Here I learned that I suffer from something called 'negative buoyancy', which means that I tend to float ten feet below the surface rather than on top - something to do with having heavier bones than I should have for my overall structure!

There was a decompression chamber on the jetty where divers suspected of contracting 'the bends' were placed, re-compressed to the depth at which they had been working, then gradually 'brought to the surface' by reducing the pressure. I was summoned to see several suspected cases while working in Mina, but as the 'patients' had been diagnosed by diving colleagues they erred on the side of caution. Some of the cases I did see were, I suspect, suffering from hangovers.

Heat illness was a real and terrible threat at that time. Tankers had no cooling facilities aboard except for their meat storage space. In July when tankers - and I am talking about as many as 500 a month - were returning laden down from the Gulf the prevailing wind was from the north west, i.e. a following wind that reduced relative air movement to zero. British tanker crews were still served - and indeed, I was told, demanded - hot treacle pudding for lunch on these days, so it was hardly surprising that ships sailing south east from Basra and Abadan should reach Kuwait with cases of heat stroke aboard. All sweating had ceased, the body temperature exceeded 106F (41C) and there was mental disturbance - these patients had succumbed to intolerable heat stress and their vital brain stem centres had melted.

Thanks to the aforesaid Dr John Guthrie, we had equipment for treating heat stroke - metal-framed tables with a similar canopy, made from rods which were perforated so that the recumbent patient could be 'showered' from all directions with cool, not cold, water pumped through the hollow tubes. At the same time fans were directed at the patient. This produced 'physiological cooling' of the patient, unlike earlier attempts to cool them down by plunging victims into an ice-cold bath. All that did was to cause intense peripheral vasoconstriction, if not death from shock, i.e. they actually retained heat rather than lost it. Despite our efforts fourteen men were beyond medical help that summer of 1957, including a seventeen-year-old cadet who died on his first Gulf voyage.

While on this subject, I might as well describe the second heat illness - heat exhaustion. This has synonyms such as 'miner's cramps', and is characterised by salt deficiency. Classically muscle cramps are regarded as the earliest symptom but I learned to look for mental depression as the harbinger of the illness - cramps, giddiness, nausea, exhaustion and headache all follow if untreated. Expatriates were prone to this, before they became acclimatised, i.e. the sweat glands learned to selectively re-absorb salt, because they drank too much beer and failed to eat salted peanuts with it. We urged employees to take added salt, whether it be on their food or with their beer, and enteric-coated salt tablets were placed on tables wherever food was served. Of course the campaign went pear-shaped - I saw office workers in their totally air-conditioned surroundings solemnly swallow half-a-dozen salt tablets before meals. Soon they would appear in the clinic with puffy ankles and cries of: "Doctor, doctor, is it my heart?"

I concluded that a healthy, well-acclimatised man needed no added salt if he eats a balanced diet.[1]

⊰⊱ ⊰⊱ ⊰⊱ ⊰⊱ ⊰⊱ ⊰⊱ ⊰⊱ ⊰⊱ ⊰⊱ ⊰⊱ ⊰⊱ ⊰⊱ ⊰⊱

Twice now has the name John Guthrie appeared. 'Al Doctor Al Kabir', the Big Doctor, as the Arabs called him, was my boss.

"Doctor, composer, writer, he died on 29 October 1986, a man who enriched the quality of living of those around him at every turn and on every day of his long life." So wrote an obituarist. John was born in New Zealand, where his father had also been a doctor and who had looked after the health of members of Scott's Last Expedition on their way to and from Antarctica.[2]

John was always torn between medicine and music. Beethoven and Schubert were his gods. But in the event his father sent him to Edinburgh to study medicine. A tall, lonely, introvert, life for him blossomed when he met and married Vivian Duncan, daughter of the Edinburgh painter, John Duncan, and herself a medical student and artist. World War II found him as an RAF Medical Officer. After the war, he studied music for a year then came the

---

[1] Some years later I saw a company of Royal Marines 'digging in' in the Kuwait desert during a four day sandstorm with a shade temperature of 120F. Not a man was incapacitated in these searing conditions, thanks to their superb NCO's who insisted on 'demand drinking' and compulsory feeding. This meant three meals a day, salt added to taste - and an average of 36 pints of fluid per man every 24 hours. OK - so they were fit and acclimatised; but what a performance!

[2] John once told me his father had seen a page of Scott's diary in which he wrote, presumably at the time when Oates left the tent for the last time - "And about bloody time too!" Certainly his heroic self-sacrifice was in vain as the party had already run out of food and fuel. John supposed his father had destroyed that page.

chance of a job in Kuwait. Both he and Vivian were dubious but he told her, about the experience he had gained at the RAF Base in Shaiba, South Iraq, during the war: "Come on! I can guarantee you sunlight to paint in! And at least my piano won't suffer from damp."

So they arrived into the chaotic world George Porter had described to me. Vivian worked in a children's clinic for the embryonic State Medical Service at first while John struggled with the twin burdens I came to know so well: keeping abreast of daily health needs and planning for the future require-ments of an ever-expanding monster which regarded expenditure on medical facilities as a diversion from the serious business of producing oil. He still found time to compose songs at the piano.

In 1942 their daughter Deirdre had been born. When she arrived for the Christmas holidays in 1956 I had already seen a photograph of this Junoesque creature, aged fourteen, clad in bathing suit and clutching bow and arrow in her self-chosen role as Diana. As a dedicated 'poodle-faker'.[1] I could hard-ly wait to meet her. John and Viv had already welcomed me into their home where their Indian servant Felix - who adored them both - was always ready to pour me a cold beer while I waited for them. Angus Maclean, now work-ing for John Paul Getty down in the Neutral Zone, was a frequent visitor and spent a lot of his time disagreeing with anything I said. He had married at the end of the Second World War, had a son, Justin, then divorced.[2]

Well, after that I won't say I lived for school holidays, but certainly Deirdre's presence added spice to life. We swam, sailed, danced and partied the nights away. With such artistic parents it was hardly surprising they had produced such a wild child of nature! These were the days when 'heavy pet-ting' was tolerated and we managed to stop at that! I would like to think that it was both respect for her youth and her parents that held me back; or per-haps I knew in my heart of hearts that I would never be able to control so wil-ful a person whose carefree irresponsibility would overwhelm me. But at the same time I knew I had struck lucky, even when she exasperated me. I sus-pect it was a case of two selfish people whose hormones were attuned to each other.

While John had discovered Federico Lorca and was busy setting his poems to music, Deirdre had discovered Spanish dancing, which she exhibited, at the drop of a hat, at the numerous parties John and Viv held in their house during the school holidays. This developed into dancing on the table at other people's parties. Unfortunately such behaviour was misinterpreted as an 'invitation' by certain Lebanese and Iranian hosts... and I found myself on one occasion having to defend her honour with a well-aimed boot up the arse of an amorous Persian. But Deirdre sailed through it all without turning a hair.

During term time I had made friends down in Kuwait City, for Ahmadi was already proving claustrophobic for a bachelor. The managing director of KOC, Sir Philip Southwell, was a keen sailor and early on had got permis-sion to adopt the name of a defunct sailing club on the Thames and resurrect it on the shores of Kuwait Bay. Sir Philip was greatly admired by KOC staff.

---

[1] An Anglo-Indian term for a man who chooses to chase girls rather than game!

[2] Some 40 years later Justin was to marry Deirdre, after her own colourful series of mar-riages.

Kuwait Harbour, 1956.

Certainly he had their interests at heart - as they had reason to thank him for, when they retired, the company pension plan was generous. He was proud of 'his baby' and, in the late fifties, invited Ian Fleming to write the history of KOC. It seemed a surprising choice! However, management directed me to dine with him one evening in the Yacht Club and, having read the earlier James Bond books, I was prepared for his snobbery. He had found 'Pinner with prickly heat' a bore, and was desperate for any spicy stories I could tell him to enliven the tale. I did my best.

For instance I told him the tale of the beautiful Persian girl whom I had anaesthetised in the families clinic while she underwent minor surgery. I was administering ether and at one point removed the mask to check her respiration. As I went to replace the mask I saw a large pink worm crawl out of the corner of her mouth! Like so many locals she must have been infested with ascaris worms. When anaesthetised the pylorus relaxes; so the worm had decided to make a break for it and head upstream for the mouth via the stomach and oesophagus rather than take its usual course down to the rectum. But still, it was not enough and Fleming withdrew from the assignment.

The Cumberland Yacht Club, to give it its proper title, was a great boon and blessing. Located in one of the company's original pre-war two storied houses, one could eat, drink and sleep there.

One day in May 1957, while workmen were busy tearing down the walls of the city, I drove from Ahmadi to collect a yacht crew - Anthony and Anne Acland. He was Second Secretary in Her Britannic Majesty's Political Agency at that time. He and Anne lived in an enclave called the Bebehani Compound, a square surrounded by Arab houses falling into picturesque decay. The Bebehanis themselves, like many of the city's leading families, were of Persian extraction. We drove to the club and Noor, our Indian boatman, rowed us out to one of the 'X' class yachts moored offshore. There was a light breeze and soon we were slipping quietly through the waters towards

Kuwait harbour. It was peaceful away from the roar of traffic as the city awoke from its siesta and commerce resumed. Anne stretched herself along the deck and composed herself for sleep while Anthony and I congratulated ourselves on having overcome dull sloth and gone sailing. I gave a sigh of contentment and snuggled down with the tiller in the crook of my arm. A burst of gunfire shattered the early evening calm. We sat up smartly and looked shoreward. Nothing had changed.

"Must be kids shooting at birds," I said.

"Yes," said Anthony, "or someone's practising on the range."

I looked at him. "What range?" I asked.

There was another, longer fusillade. It sounded suspiciously like a machine gun firing.

"Yes, what range?" enquired Anne. The firing redoubled in intensity.

"It must be manoeuvres," said Anthony firmly, giving me a conspiratorial wink that Anne could not see. Both of us glanced covertly seawards where we knew a number of British merchant ships lay in the anchorage. Anne followed our gaze.

"Do you think perhaps..." she began tentatively, when there were a series of heavier thuds from the shore.

"Those weren't made by rifles," I said, a trifle unnecessarily.

"Do you think perhaps..." Anne started again, "it might be a good idea to sail out towards those ships just in case there's any anti-British trouble going on?"

"Nonsense!" said Anthony, "if there'd been any danger of that we'd have heard about it in the Agency."

"Oh yeah," I said under my breath; and then out loud, as I put the tiller heard down and pointed our bows seawards. "All the same, I think if might be better if we got away from this spot - I think we're in the line of fire."

My guess wasn't far wrong. There had already been one or two whispers above our mast and now came the full blown whine of a ricochet. This was followed by two distinct splashes in the water between us and the shore - and they weren't fish jumping.

Duty re-asserted itself.

"We'd better to back," announced Anthony, "I ought to ring the Agency."

We went about and headed for Shuweikh. The firing seemed to have reached its climax and by the time we had reached our moorings all was quiet again. Noor on the other hand was beside himself with excitement when he rowed out to collect us.

"Much shooting sahib, all policemen running, many tanks in streets," he said.

"Yes, but WHY? What's happened?" we all cried.

"Not knowing sahib."

We scrambled ashore and ran up to the yacht club. Anthony went straight to the telephone and got through to the agency. Nobody knew anything.

"We might as well see if we can get home," Anne suggested.

We drove cautiously back, stopping to peer round each corner first. There was no more firing. We reached the Jahara Gate where there was a troop of armoured cars, covered with small boys. This was a reassuringly familiar sight. Everybody was chattering and pointing southwards where we could see a pillar of dust and smoke arising from among the houses. Near the Bebehani Compound Anthony jumped out and approached a group of well-dressed Kuwaitis standing outside a large house.

"Ah! There's Abdulmutallib, a friend of Anthony's, he always knows everything," said Anne confidently. He lived up to his reputation.

"Chap's off his head," said Anthony when he climbed back into the car. "Keeps shouting - 'We've dealt with them as they deserve.'"

"Who's dealt with whom?" asked Anne and I simultaneously.

"It's the Yassins - they're a branch of the ruling family. Apparently they've been asking for a bigger share of the family income and the Ruler wouldn't give it to them. They started getting quite nasty about it so this morning the Ruler sent Abdulla Mubarak (Head of Public Security) to their house with an ultimatum - leave the country in twelve hours or else. They chose the 'or else', barricaded themselves in with about 100 servants and what we heard was them shooting it out with the army which Abdulla Mubarak brought in when the ultimatum expired - he's had a fine old time!"

"I bet," said I, "all he needed was a 25 pounder and he'd have launched a battalion attack against the house!" Words spoken in jest: but I later learned that the army HAD loaded a 25 pounder gun; though wiser counsels prevailed before it was let off.

We reached Anne and Anthony's house. Geoffrey, their Indian cook, was enjoying an attack of hysterics. There had been great excitement in the compound during our absence. One two pounder shell from an armoured car had ricocheted through the upstairs room of an adjoining house, full of sleeping Arab women. No one had been hurt but we could hear the faint wails of the women as one by one they collapsed in exhaustion. In another house a shell had passed through the bedroom of a Frenchman, also asleep. He must have lunched well for when he awoke later he had heard nothing untoward and accused his cook - a friend of Geoffrey's - of knocking a hole in the wall to let thieves in. We had a late supper that night as Geoffrey burned the first one! He then cooked the savoury in kerosene. He had another attack of hysterics and departed to bed. In the end I stayed the night. Dear Anne and Anthony, they were always so kind to me, their house was an oasis to which I probably repaired too often for their liking!

There were two interesting footnotes to this tale. I discovered that, once loaded in fact, a 25 pounder gun of that pattern could NOT be unloaded. It so happened that next day a future friend, Colonel 'Tam' Pierce of the Royal Artillery, landed to take up a post as gunnery instructor to the Kuwait Army. He was a surprised man when he stepped off the plane to be greeted by a Kuwaiti officer with a request to discharge this cannon somewhere harmlessly into the sea before he was allowed to go to his new home to bath and change. He duly did so and then went to his new home which was one of the old KOC town houses - and next to the Cumberland Yacht Club.

An account of this family skirmish appeared in the following day's *Daily Telegraph*. It was gripping stuff, too, though one might have been forgiven for thinking it described a full blown civil war. However as the correspondent was in the bar of the St. George Hotel in Beirut at the time it is hardly surprising.

❧ ❧ ❧ ❧ ❧ ❧ ❧ ❧ ❧ ❧ ❧ ❧ ❧

All this driving up and down to Kuwait inevitably led to accidents to my smart green Chevrolet. The first was when I was returning along the new coast road one night and a donkey strayed out into my path. He died a quick death but made an awful mess of the front of my car. Leaving the wreck there I eventually got a lift back to Ahmadi. Next day I set off for the nearest police post to where I had left the car, having persuaded a Kuwaiti friend, Ibrahim Al Mulla, head of the government's oil checking department in Ahmadi, to come along with me. This friendship was, incidentally, looked upon none too favourably by the KOC authorities in those days; and when I took him and Khalifa Al Ghanim, Abdulla's cousin, into the Hubara Club for dinner one night the other diners managed to make my guests really uncomfortable. I was reminded of the days in India when a sign outside a British club was reputed to read "Dogs and Indians not allowed."

Anyway on this occasion Ibrahim proved a god send. We went to a police station where nobody knew anything about the accident. But there was a forlorn policeman standing beside my battered car so we tried the next police station up the road at Fahahil. Here it was clear my fame had spread before me. As soon as Ibrahim had explained our errand to the policeman at the door he turned and shouted inside: "Here is the killer of the donkey!"

Policemen spilled out to examine the murderer. I was led inside where Ibrahim, enjoying my predicament, did nothing to soften their feelings towards me. We sat down to await the arrival of the investigating officer. Here luck was on my side. He turned out to be an Indian; and Ibrahim, like many Kuwaitis infected with Arab nationalism at this time, courtesy of Gamal Abdul Nasser, resented the presence of Indians in positions of responsibility in his country. (English 'experts' were a necessary evil for the time being, but they could not see why it was necessary to employ Indians at all, except as 'coolies', and especially in government service. The fact is that the country wouldn't have run without them!)

Anyway, Ibrahim put on his most insulting drawl, acquired during his recent two year stay in England. He prayed the officer to hurry up with this trivial matter; and added as an afterthought: "I have an appointment with His Highness."

The Indian police officer was rattled. He took down a very brief statement, then announced that the matter would be handed over to the traffic police in Kuwait.

"That's fine," said Ibrahim as we left, "that's the last you'll hear of it."

But he reckoned without the owner of the donkey. It was common practice for villagers to turn their more decrepit animals - and this one certainly had been! - loose to graze near the new coastal highway in order that they should suffer the same fate as 'my' donkey. They then claimed the full value of the animal under Sharia Law - at that time it ranged from Rs.16,000 for a human being to Rs.500 for a donkey. I was summoned to the traffic police. There I met a large Adeni named Hassan Raja. I never discovered what function he had in the government, but next time I saw him he was an executive in the electricity department. I suspect he was a political activist, *persona non grata* in the colony, whom the Kuwaitis had granted asylum. Fortunately for me he was out to demonstrate his authority and talked the donkey owner out of his claim - for which I was duly grateful.

Meanwhile my car had been towed to the Al Ghanim garage in Kuwait - they had the General Motor Company agency - and duly repaired the vehicle. Marzook Al Ghanim, another son, was the manager and told everyone he was going to fit a cattle plough on the front in case I tried to repeat the performance.

The next accident caused less damage but was more frightening. It was during the next summer holidays and I was returning, with Deirdre, from a formal dinner party at the Aclands. We were travelling round the new dual carriageway that had been built outside the city when we were overtaken by a lorry. My eyebrows went up when I realised he was in the other carriageway! He slowed down and I lost sight of him. Next minute there was a crash as he decided he'd better join the traffic stream on the right side of the road without, unfortunately, noticing us as he did so. We ground to a halt, the car several inches narrower than before, both of us mercifully unhurt. As I started in at the Lebanese driver of the lorry, a car drew up and a suave figure descended. In perfect English he offered assistance, and introduced himself as Aziz Al Ghanim - another cousin! Again my car was towed away to the Al Ghanim garage and Aziz escorted us to the local police station. He gave my statement to the duty sergeant who laboriously scrawled down details.

I became aware that the room was slowly filling with policemen, gazing in awe at Deirdre. Earlier that evening she had poured herself into an electric-blue evening dress that was more than just off the shoulder... the penny dropped. I took off my tuxedo and draped it around her shoulders.

"Thanks, I'm not cold," she said brightly and made to remove it.

"Shut up and wear it!" I growled. She looked at me in puzzlement, then at the gawping policemen and slowly understanding dawned in her eyes. She gave them all her most dazzling smile, they responded sheepishly and one by one slunk out of the room. We were released.

"I always dress up, I never dress down!" was one of Deirdre's favourite cries; and indeed she lived up to this motto. Some time after the affair of the electric blue gown, when I was working in Kuwait City and had a villa there, we went to an Agency dance where she appeared in Spanish style. (She was destined to become 'Avis Rara', a Scottish flamenco dancer in Spain - and managed to earn her living in this role before her first marriage.)

We were still 'together' and afterwards repaired to my bungalow. She undressed in the bathroom and joined me... some hours later, it was time to drive her back to Ahmadi. We got up and I heard her switch on the bathroom light; promptly followed by a scream. Now, if Deirdre screamed, it was serious. I grabbed gun and 'longi' and shot out of my room. She stood naked and frozen in the doorway. I looked past her and saw her dress, with its multiple lace petticoats, lying on the bathroom floor and heaving as a hundred or so cockroaches tried to escape the light. Alas, she had dropped her dress over the floor drain which led to the septic tank in the garden. Have you ever tried to shift cockroaches from lace petticoats? Dawn had broken by the time we had finished.

"Good party?" enquired Vivian, as we tried to creep in undetected via the kitchen, where she had been making tea.

"Rather!" cried Deirdre cheerfully, "apart from cockroaches in the loo!"

One has to give it to her. What could her mother deduce from that? Later Marzook Al Ghanim told everyone he was extending bumpers down both sides of my car.

A month later I was returning from the hospital late at night, tired and ill-tempered. I could hardly believe my eyes when I saw the lights of an approaching car on MY side of the road. He kept steadily on until at the last minute I braked, hit an oil patch, and turned through 180 degrees before he hit my rear bumper and spun me off into the desert. A police car soon stopped. I gazed with mounting horror at the eyes of the Bedouin taxi driver who had hit me. The upper halves of both cornea were covered with the 'pannus' of trachoma, the fibrous scarring that spread like a film over the eyes of sufferers, eventually blinding them. It was improbable that he could have seen anything but the glare of my lights. We were joined by another car, driven by a KOC 'character', Tommy Tucker, the Marine Superintendent down at Mina. A huge man, well known and indeed loved by his employees, he grunted his approval as I pointed out to the already friendly policemen that the taxi driver was blind!

"Oh yes, many of them are," he said calmly. "But then they can buy their driving licences and their medical fitness certificates. However this man is a Saudi - so I'll charge him."

I heard no more about the case. My car went back to the Al Ghanim garage. Marzook told everyone he was fitting reinforcing bars to my rear bumper; but more important he agreed with me that whereas green may bring luck to the Irish it would be better to re-spray my car a different colour. It became cerulean blue. I never had another accident in Kuwait.

❦ ❦ ❦ ❦ ❦ ❦ ❦ ❦ ❦ ❦ ❦ ❦ ❦

The seasons passed - slowly when it was hot, too fast when it was cool. With ten inches of rain the winter of 1957 had been the wettest in living memory. As a result grass in the desert grew taller and greener than ever and camels appeared as if from nowhere.

It struck suddenly. One morning in late June I arrived at Mina clinic to find it looking like a plague house. Patients were lolling against the outside walls wherever they could find shade and inside I had to step across recumbent figures to reach my office. There were already about 70 sick there and it was not yet 6.30am. I gazed around wildly, seeking inspiration and thought: "If this lot is admitted to Magwa Hospital there'll be no room for anyone else!"

Sister Patience came to the rescue. She came out of the treatment room like a galleon in full sail, clasping a huge bottle of aspirins, followed by Khadir and Ahmed, her faithful Persian sweepers, each carrying a bucket of water and a cup. Two of our Indian orderlies were already noting pulse rates and temperatures of each patient before she reached them. She saw the look of dismay on my face - this wasn't the way we dealt with things at the Middlesex Hospital - and said firmly: "It's the only way. I'll bring you their chits to sign in a minute. Anyone with a cough I'll refer to you. The rest I'll fill up with water and send home. Do you think four days off work will be enough?"

"I hope so," I muttered, "but for God's sake tell them to report back here if they develop a productive cough."

Visions of Arab labourers dying like flies from bronchopneumonia filled my mind. But we were lucky. How ever many died elsewhere, we had only one death directly attributable to Asian 'flu among our patients and he died in hospital.

Up at Magwa, 'Big Joe', as Yusuf Khan, our Afghani labour boss, was back in his element, erecting tents. He had once worked for the Imperial Russian Circus in India, where it survived long after the defeat of the White Russians. We had nearly 300 patients there, twice the normal bed establishment. For three weeks the epidemic raged then quietly it began to subside. I suppose the greatest danger to which the labourers were exposed was dehydration, due to high fever on top of the high summer temperature. I felt more than a twinge of guilt at night as I slid into my air-conditioned bedroom and thought of the wretched patients lying in their 'barasti' huts with no relief from the stifling heat. Surprisingly enough they recovered quicker than the Europeans and were back at work before many of them. Thank Heavens the epidemic hit before the humidity of August was on us.

❦ ❦ ❦ ❦ ❦ ❦ ❦ ❦ ❦ ❦ ❦ ❦ ❦

Early in August the north wind dies away, followed by a few weeks of calmer weather and a gentle breeze from the south. This is the westerly fringe of the monsoon, by now sweeping north from the Indian Ocean and bringing acute discomfort. While the temperature may drop a few degrees, the humidity increases three or four fold. The moisture-laden air creeps up the Gulf to Southern Iraq and is known as the 'date-ripening wind' - giving little comfort to the perspiring locals.

That year I had called upon Ahmed Al Ghanim, oldest member of the family, and in the course of discussing the weather (Arabs share this obsession with the English) I remarked that people expected a good date harvest as it was so humid. He replied: "They're all wrong. It will be a bad date harvest... I feel it in my bones." He was quite right; and as he was either 101 or 102 it was unlikely he was guessing.

That summer I had been asked to take on a 'summer bride'. This was not some kind of lottery prize for jaded bachelors but the term used for staff who undertook to 'house sit' for families who had gone on leave. Some of the latter preferred to have bachelors rather than other families with children 'on the housing list'. I was lucky enough to have sailed with Jack Newlands the previous winter. He bequeathed me his house (this was before I moved in with George Porter) for the summer months, complete with Pakistani servant Abdul, a spaniel, chacaw, gazelle and hedgehog. Abdul was soon infatuated with Deirdre and plied her with unlimited 'pakoras' - which she adored - and also enhanced her hour-glass figure.

Jack Newlands had been a professional Gurkha officer who had retired at the time of partition and come out to Kuwait as a 'white coolie'. KOC had collected quite a colony of men like him, who had held responsible posts in India. Britain had found it difficult to absorb some 4,000 'old India hands' in 1947. Britain's climate drove many of them back east with commercial organisations, others inspired Noel Coward to write the Indian Army Officer. Those who came out to Kuwait in the early days were quartered in a hutted camp down at Mina-al-Ahmadi, where, Jack told me, the corridors rang at night to cries of: "Boy! Chota Peg! Jilti Hai!" On their doors they fixed cards with their name, rank and regiment. One corridor boasted no occupants of less than Field Rank - until a young humourist of less exotic background arrived and wrote: "Private RASC" on his door.

Time passed; those unable to make the transition from sahib to store-man move on. Others, like Jack, carved out administrative niches within KOC's organisation - for nowhere does Professor Parkinson's law apply more than in an organism forced to out-grow its strength by external pressures; and how those pressures increased, once Anglo-Iranian collapsed and all BP's eggs were in Kuwait's basket! Jack administered something called management research who, for example, investigated why - at the time I arrived in Kuwait - there were three 'officers' in personnel; but three years later there were nine - when the company's staff were shrinking. Well, as a fellow TA officer, Tony Royle once asked, why did the army need 120 brigadiers ten years after the war when it had reduced to 30 brigades?

Apart from entertaining Deirdre I could now entertain others! One was Jameel Araf, an assistant editor of *Akhbar Ilyoum*, a weekly Cairo magazine. Jameel was a powerfully built Egyptian with a forceful personality and the traditional journalist's partiality for Scotch. He had come to Kuwait to try and get a visa from the British Political Agent to enter Muscat and Oman (as it then was). The rebels there, under their leader Emir Talib bin Ali, had mounted a serious insurrection against Sultan Said bin Taimur in Muscat.

Under the existing treaty we had with the Sultan, all visitors needed a permit from the UK Government. Not surprisingly, Jameel was making very little headway - in view of Gamal Abdul Nasser's attitude towards Britain.

Jameel was all reason: "Sure we realise you must go to the assistance of the Sultan, you have a treaty with him. But what is there wrong in letting me see what is going on? I will merely record what I see - and the British cannot object to me writing the truth?"

"Well," I answered slowly, "in the first place I don't think it is our government which would object to you visit. But I think the Sultan himself might have something to say about it - Cairo Radio hasn't exactly been praising him lately. Our visa control apparatus simply works on his behalf."

Jameel roared with laughter: "You're as bad as your diplomatists Doctor Philip - you know bloody well the Sultan will allow anyone you say into Oman!"

"Even if that was true - and mind you, I'm not saying it is - all you really want is British protection while you're there," I countered.

"Why should I need British protection in an Arab country? They are my brothers, we speak the same language."

It was my turn to laugh: "Not yet they're not, I wouldn't give you much chance of survival wandering about Jebel Akhder by yourself. They're wild people. Isn't it true that the Egyptian Army had more men killed by the Sinai Bedu in the 1956 War than by the Israelis?"

He considered this one for a moment. "Yes... it is true. They are savages. But you will be safe once you are with the rebels."

"Ha! I suppose you've got a safe conduct pass from the Independent Government of Oman in Cairo?"

"Ha yourself!" he cried, avoiding a direct answer. "So you admit the existence of a free republican government? That surely proves that the people of Oman are fighting for their freedom against the despotic rule of the Sultan?"

"Who is undoubtedly an Imperialist hireling," I ended for him cheerfully. By now the level in the Scotch bottle was falling fast.

"Look, let us look at the facts. Under the Treaty of Seeb which was made in 1920 something..."

"Which has never been recognised by anyone save your government and the Sultan," Jameel interposed.

"Touché," I agreed, "but it IS recognised by our government, that the Sultan is ruler over Muscat and Oman, which includes the Jebel Akhder. Everyone was quite happy with this for 30 years, so why not let negotiations start from there?"

"Happy?" said Jameel scornfully, "How do you know they were happy? You want to know why there was no trouble until a few years ago? Because it is only now that the world realises that John Bull's teeth are becoming soft and oppressed people can say what they like without being shelled and bombed by your gunboats and aeroplanes!"

There was a nasty element of truth about this. But how could statesmen of yesteryear, who had bound us in treaties with ramshackle tribal sheikhdoms and the like all over the world, have foreseen that Britain's power would have been crippled in less than 50 years by two debilitating world wars? I tried to explain this and ended: "Say what you like, the Pax Britannica may not have been much, but it was at least Pax."

"It was a reactionary, totalitarian, regime." said Jameel loftily, "A British colonial governor was as much a dictator as Adolf Hitler. it was thoroughly

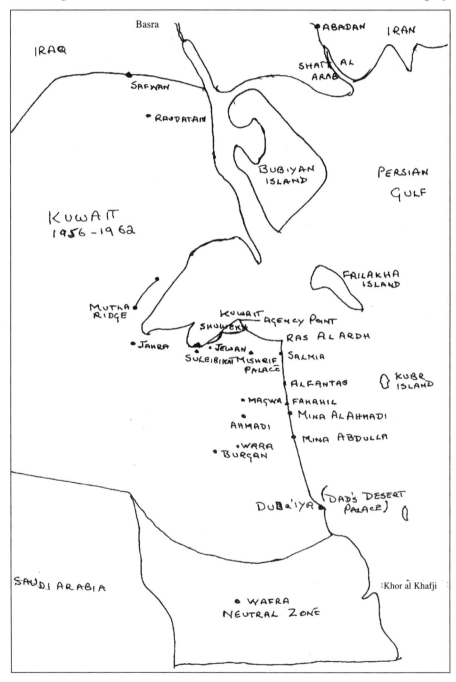

dangerous and repressive - only the British could have wielded such power without behaving like such a tyrant."

"Thank you for that," I said a trifle lamely.

He shrugged his shoulders: "It is nothing - in a few generations you will forget you once thought you were born to rule the world. Like my people will have forgotten they were once slaves, thanks to Gamal Abdul Nasser."

"You really believe he is good for Egypt?" I asked.

He shrugged his shoulders again: "Without him there would be no hope. Look at my country! The land owned by fat 'pashas' who did nothing but extort rents from their 'fellah'! Whole villages riddled with disease - like trachoma so they couldn't see to read and write even if they were taught: bilharzia sapping their strength, malaria their blood. Illiteracy - not enough schools nor teachers."

"If you're so short of teachers, why are there 700 in Kuwait?"

Jameel's eyebrows went up: "Why not? We cannot think only of ourselves. All Arabs have the right to learn and it is our duty to help them. If there are no teachers, then we must train more. Now everything in Egypt is changing - men and women can hold their heads up again. It is natural that we want all Arabs to share the wonderful feeling of achievement that comes with progress and inspire them to do the same!"

"Which includes advising them to kill British soldiers in Oman with land mines?" I asked.

"It is a war against oppression," he said simply.

"And if Talib should win - do you really think there would be less oppression?"

"It would be different. Arab has always oppressed Arab; but that is no reason why British should oppress Arab."

"I must say I agree with that, but I still cannot condone the way Cairo Radio incites the mob."

There was a really funny serial story being beamed to North East Arabia by the Cairo propaganda machine at that time. It was a sort of *Mrs Dale's Diary* with an RAF officer and his wife in the leading roles. Their dog Coochy was an important member of the cast. Here's a sample extract:

Wife: "Hello darling, had a good day?"

Husband: "Splendid thank you my dear - bombed and machine-gunned three wog villages. It's amazing how easily their houses collapse under high explosives. And you should have seen the children scatter when I strafed them with my machine guns!"

Wife: "Oh well done darling - that will teach them a lesson! I hope you destroyed the wells too?"

Husband: "Every one - there won't be anyone living around there for a long time!"

Wife: "Oh but darling, I've been so worried today, Coochy has been sick, wouldn't touch her lunch. What are we going to do?"

Husband: "By Jove - she's bad is she? Let me have a look." (Sound of whimpering dog) "Yes she is. There is only one thing to do. We must fly her back to England at once. There's a transport plane standing by with food and medicines to take to some starving people who are meant to be on our side. Doesn't matter, I'll order it to be unloaded and then the plane can fly Coochy straight to London!"

And so on, to the proverbial nausea. It may sound nonsense to us, but it was really quite skillful: an exiled Omani wandering near the RAF airfield at Sharjah might well see a moustachioed pilot religiously walking his dog every evening: he might see aircraft being unloaded and taking off, apparently empty: he would not expect to see any wives, they should be in purdah...

But to get back to Jameel. He laughed as I spluttered.

"Look Doctor Philip, haven't you noticed something about us Arabs? We know that the British did not bayonet children in Port Said last year. I was there as a war correspondent, as a matter of fact, but no one in Egypt will believe it. But Arabs in other countries will want to believe it. If we say that your soldiers are murdering women and children in Oman, the Omanis may laugh, but people in Egypt will believe it. It's a game for us - we like to imagine such things are true, but we can only do this if it is happening somewhere else. We couldn't play the game if we said it was happening at home. Our eyes cannot deceive us but our hearts can! Don't take it so seriously!"

I must have looked a bit glum.

"Look, let us be practical. You will win this round in the Oman, you want to and so you will - though God knows why. But what will you do when you have put the Sultan firmly in the saddle? Will you warn him to behave better in future? To build schools and hospitals for his people and not just prisons? To help his people?"

"I hope so," I said sincerely, "though I myself have no idea of the problems he has to face."

"Well... we'll see," said Jameel, "but if you want my opinion you'll do nothing. It's time you learned whom your friends are, then you'll not be so frightened of offending them."

"Yes, it would be nice to know whom our friends are..."

"Why the Arabs of course!" cried Jameel, "Once you make a sincere effort to help us, we will accept you! But how can we when your every move is calculated to bring prosperity to your merchant princes? When every treaty you try to negotiate is aimed at embroiling defenceless Arabs in some new move of the Cold War?"

We drank some more whisky. The adrenaline exhausted, we became maudlin. We talked of Utopian days when liberal progressives from Britain and Arabia would walk hand in hand, when the desert would blossom, when every Arab would eat off Derby china and every Englishman would wear an Egyptian cotton shirt... 'booqara fil mishmish'... 'tomorrow when the apricots blossom'... well, why shouldn't men talk like that?

Back at Mina Clinic the Asian 'flu was forgotten, but the humidity was worse. Another British doctor had arrived to assist my Indian colleague and myself, so I thankfully handed over the senior staff sick parade to him and devoted myself full time to the labourers. 'Dusty' (what else?) Miller had served in the Royal Navy during the war and turned up on his first morning in spotless white short-sleeved shirt, pressed white shorts, stockings and white buckskin shoes. Sister Patience and I were impressed; but 'Father John', as John Guthrie was called behind his back, decreed that shorts were offensive to Muslim Arabs, so he joined the rest of us in crumpled white long trousers and long sleeved shirts, looking like wine waiters after a tough day in the Hubara Club.

The oppressive weather induced an increasing number of malingerers to 'try it on'. In more reflective moments I couldn't blame them. Who the hell wanted to slave away ten hours a day in this heat if one could spend most of the morning in the air-conditioned waiting room of the clinic, with an iced water fountain at hand? Some of these emotions must have transmitted themselves to my patients. The ones I saw early and sent brusquely back to work raised a submissive hand in farewell, as if to say: "OK - so this time you win."

Others who had contrived to get well down the waiting list and avoided the consulting room until nearly lunch time would break for cover and run as soon as I opened my mouth to bark: "Moutamaridh!" (malingerer), at them and grabbed their 'sick chit' to write 'fit'.

But the ones who came in mid-morning found I was in a conciliatory mood after coffee. They had missed about three hours work and were well enough satisfied and able to sympathise with me for wasting my time! Sometimes they would almost shake hands after I'd written the dire word 'fit' on their chit, (they'd lose half a day's pay).

When the waiting room got too crowded and different nationalities came into physical contact there was friction, usually between Palestinians and Lebanese; sometimes between Arab and Indian, though this usually ended in stalemate with both parties shouting in their own languages, unable to appreciate the eloquent insults of the other.

One morning the hubbub was louder than normal. The door burst open and Sister Patience rushed in. "They're killing each other out there. They'll break up the clinic. Go out and stop them!"

Under her steely gaze I was on my feet and out of the door before I had time to think. Two Arabs were wrestling on the floor, another two held a bench in a threatening manner, waiting to bring it down on the head of the unlucky combatant. Around them several others were scrapping in the more desultory Arab style - pulling at each others' shirts and slapping ineffectually at each other. Arabs deplore hitting each other with closed fists.

I shouted: "Stop that!" and no one took the slightest notice - in fact two of them pointedly turned their backs on me.

"Go on," urged Sister Patience.

"Not likely," I replied, "Isn't it coffee time?"

Jessica gave a snort of disapproval but I walked firmly into the treatment room shouting: "Suspend all treatment until further notice!"

This was quite superfluous, patients and staff alike were jammed in the other doorway watching the fight. We pushed our way into Sister's office where I slammed the door with relief.

"Well, do something," she said lamely.

"I shall ring Public Security," I said loftily. I did so. We sat and waited. Within a few minutes the noise outside reached a crescendo, then faded... there was the clash of nailed boots on the floor, the door opened and a large, swarthy, officer, clearly of African origin, entered, giving a perfunctory salute and a wide grin.

"All finished!" he announced.

Sister Patience rose to the occasion. "Thank you so much - do have some coffee - black or white?"

Which must have been the origin of that particular joke, but then Sister Patience was never at a loss.

⁂ ⁂ ⁂ ⁂ ⁂ ⁂ ⁂ ⁂ ⁂ ⁂ ⁂ ⁂ ⁂

In the hot weather, the sea proved a godsend; it would have been too easy to remain in one's air-conditioned quarters and just venture out for the Friday night film at the Hubara Club. Even so, it was preferable to be in or under the sea than just on it. Sailing in such light airs was akin to being on an eye-level grill, for apart from the sun's direct rays, there was an even brighter glare reflected off the surface. The solution was to go on a launch trip.

KOC provided two diesel launches for staff to use, free of charge, and manned by the Marine Department. Abdul, a delightful Iraqi, skippered the larger one. He had been in Kuwait for 20 years, half of them with the company, and had three children as neat, clean and bright as their dad. But the authorities would not grant him Kuwaiti nationality; alas, in those days it was less desirable aliens who could acquire it - at a price.

We would get away early on a Friday morning before it became really oppressive. Father John was a great enthusiast for these trips and would see to it that we were well provided with food, beer and fishing tackle. Huge cold boxes were placed on the foredeck beneath the awning and for the first half hour one felt deliciously cool up there in the breeze: after when cold beer was needed.

There were three offshore islands, Kubr the nearest was 18 miles east. All were uninhabited save by myriads of sea birds, mostly Caspian tern. The Persian Gulf Lights Authority maintained a light tower on Kubr Island to aid tankers bound for Mina. In the aftermath of the Suez War Ibrahim Mulla told me that in Kuwait city the word was that the light would be used to guide British midget submarines into Kuwait Harbour... presumably to sink British shipping?

It took two hours to reach Kubr, the time being spent watching dolphins under our bows or the small flying fish on our beam. John insisted on playing 'liar dice' - at which he was extremely bad. If the tide was high, Abdul could put our bow practically on the beach. It was part of the ritual landfall to walk round this sand hummock with its sparse scrub before getting down to the serious business of snorkelling.

It was too easy to laze over the coral and end up with a severely sun-burned back; but the lunar landscape beneath one with its canyons, peaks and giant 'toadstools' trailing weed in the current was hypnotic. There were yellow fish with gentian fins and green ones with red dorsal spines. Hermit crabs stared up at the strange, bubbling, intruders, ready to dart back into their shells if one made a sudden movement. There was always the fear of shark or barracuda but, although we saw them occasionally from the boat, happily they shunned the shallow waters off the island.

The most dramatic sight would be rays flopping ponderously along the sea bed, with 'wing spans' of up to four feet. When frightened they would stop and 'shimmy' on the bottom until they were covered by sand, invisible save for their bead eyes watching upwards. An unwary swimmer who got too close could have his fingers slashed to the bone by their barbed tail. But the commonest accident was to tread on a sea urchin. Their needle-sharp spines would break off and fester in one's heel and had to be painstakingly extracted fragment by fragment.

After lunch we would fish. The Arab crew would be happy, and successful too, ground-fishing off the stern; but we preferred trawling as it provided a breeze while sailing slowly round the island. We would lay out three or four lines over the stern and the first cry of: "I've got one!" was usually due to one line snagging another.

Spinners varied from expensive fish replicas to a polished kitchen spoon - the latter tending to be more successful. At times we would motor through water alive with jumping fish and swooping sea birds, without even a nibble. A catch would come when one least expected it. The commonest trophy was a 'queen fish', black and silver with a prominent dorsal fin. They made good eating but could be quite a job to land. Apart from thrashing about on the end of the line they would sometimes go deep and snag the line round a rock; or else the hapless creature would be attacked by dogfish as it was hauled in and the carcass shredded until it came off the hook.

The home run at eventide was in many ways the best part of the day. The air cooler, the sea calm and stretched like a turquoise quilt to the horizon where it met the sky in an indigo blur. To the west was the black line of desert below the fierce orange glow of the setting sun. Abdul kept the engines throttled back and we huddled on the foredeck, relatively muffled up, watching the lights of Mina brighten in the dusk. As we passed the jetty it was the signal to rise and pack up the debris of a day really 'away from it all'.

In the summer of 1958 I went on leave for three months. Deirdre and I had rowed. I met and even got engaged to a French girl called Pascale. It didn't last the summer. I went back to the Middlesex Hospital to have my tonsils out, not recommended at my age. I'd been put in a side ward but was last on the list. It was the night of the Hospital Ball and I was bundled into the general ward by day staff anxious to be off gallivanting. I have always been difficult to 'put under' and suspect I'd had heavy sedation. At any rate I didn't wake up until long after midnight and the roisterers had returned in playful mood... to be precise some junior doctors tied my feet and my hands across my chest with a large lily in them. When I did finally awake I assumed I had been Laid Out... I got an apology in the morning!

I then went to the Riviera for two weeks convalescence in the villa Jim and Judy Johnson had rented for the summer with son Rupert and nanny Daphne. I crossed Jim in the air as he was due back at Lloyds after he'd taken a long weekend with the family. A week later Judy was feeling mildly nauseated with a looseness of the bowels. I diagnosed gastro-enteritis, a mistake for which daughter Lottie (born nine months later) has never forgiven me. One evening I took Daphne ('Tata' to the children) to Monte Carlo casino; and won twice on '17 Rouge'. All I can recall now is the intense hatred on the faces of the 'blue rinse brigade' who hung around the table.

That summer four of us - Paddy Paddock, the senior BP petroleum engineer working with KOC, John Walters and his wife, Jean - chartered the ketch *Thuella* from Salcombe. One of John's claims to fame was that his cousin, also John, was SNOPGY, or Senior Naval Officer Persian Gulf, a mere Commander; today he'd have been at least an Admiral! He had three frigates under his command. Our cruise was chiefly notable for the fact that, out of nineteen days at sea, we saw the sun twice - an English summer at its best? On our way from St. Malo to Guernsey our auxiliary diesel engine seized up - of course when we were on a lee shore in rough seas with a contrary wind that was dropping. For reasons which escape me I started squirting lubricating oil from a can into the air intake... whereupon the engine fired... and kept running as long as I kept squirting. Well, miracle or not, it got us safely into St. Peter Port. There we managed to snag one of the underwater cables left by the Germans in World War II with our anchor; and needed a diver to free us.

When we set off home the forecast was bad; but we had a deadline. The Walters became incapacitated by seasickness, Paddy and I lowered the mainsail and we beat hopelessly against the northerly wind under storm jib. Shortly after midnight, Paddy fell backwards in the cockpit and put his knee out. By dawn we were a bare 25 miles from St. Peter Port. I put about and ran back in a few hours. Paddy went to hospital, then joined the Walters on a flight home. I managed to find another yachtsman who was able to help sail her home. As the local Guernsey paper reported: "Ill fortune dogged the Thuella."

I had grown accustomed to dramas whenever I flew in the Middle East. On one occasion, flying to Beirut courtesy of Lebanese International Airlines in a DC3, crossing the mountains west of Damascus we ran into rain and the cabin roof started to leak. Without turning a hair the stewards came down the aisle issuing ground sheets to the passengers. On another occasion, flying over the Bakhtiari Mountains in another DC3 of Iranair en route to a medical conference in Teheran the co-pilot appeared wild-eyed in the doorway to announce that they had done all they could but they were unable to gain enough height to cross the mountains - so sorry but we were all going to die. He turned and disappeared back into the cockpit. We shifted uncomfortably in our seats and forbore to look at each other - very British.

The steady roar of the engines continued. Minutes passed, the mountains beneath grew no closer. The cockpit door flew open again - by the wonderful skill of our pilot we were going to be saved after all! No explanation was ever forthcoming for this bizarre display - a wager perhaps?

In July 1958 I was returning to Kuwait in a BOAC 'Constellation'. The pilot announced that we were being diverted from Baghdad because of an incident and would land in Basra. Here we were kept on board while we were re-fuelled in a hurry, then took off for Kuwait - apparently the captain would not risk the few extra miles without filling his tanks. I noted the passenger next to me break into song as we took off: he then told me he was an Iraqi, domiciled in Kuwait, and would not expect to have lived had he been caught in his native country. It was 14 July 1958, King Feisal, Emir Abdulillah and Nouri Al Said had all been slaughtered in Baghdad that morning. I never cease to be amazed how everyone seems to know about 'coups' in Arabia except us. We landed safely in Kuwait.

During the next few days other employees were routed back via Iran but wives and families were not allowed to return. Ibrahim Mulla met me and said there were 1200 'red devils' in Bahrain. In town the rumour factory was at full tilt - there were British paratroops in Ahmadi. H. H. Emir Abdullah, the ruler, had met Gamal Abdul Nasser in Damascus and Kuwait was going to join the U.A.R.

7
ITCHY FEET

Well, it all settled down and, as the weather cooled I realised I was becoming bored and restless - I even applied for a post as a trainee administrative medical officer in Leeds! By the time I was ready to be interviewed the post had been abolished. Amateur theatricals began to take up an inordinate amount of time. I cheered up a little when I heard that Douglas Grocock was to replace the British military liaison officer. Douglas and his wife Audrey would be a boon to social life; but then Sheikh Abdulla Mubarak insisted he would only have Tam Pierce, who had taught gunnery to the Army two years previously.

In December we had a meeting of the Persian Gulf Medical Society, now termed the 'Gulf Medical Society' in deference to Arab sensibilities; still, no Iraqis were allowed to attend. Nevertheless 65 doctors joined in an inaugural banquet at Sheikh Fahad's (Minister of Health) Palace where we waded through fourteen whole sheep. I had an American couple billeted on me from Aramco. He was engaged in trachoma research, she an ex-Broadway star who taught me the 'chacha'. I gave a lecture on 'Medical hazards in building an oil refinery': even I didn't think it was very interesting, and an oblique compliment by Viv Guthrie: "You could make reading from the London telephone directory interesting" - confirmed this. A lecture on Tb by the state specialist, an Egyptian of great charm and very co-operative with the KOC Medical Department, was the first nail in the innate superiority I felt towards non-western doctors... and which in time led me to accept the fact that many of my Arab colleagues were significantly brighter than me! We spent time in the American Mission Hospital, which had been established at the turn of the century. While we all respected the pioneers of this institution and Dr Lou Scudder, the present medical officer in charge, KOC doctors were slightly narked by the proud boast that no patient ever died in the Mission Hospital. That was because any patient who was showing signs of impending death was immediately transferred to Magwa so that we could take the blame!

The refinery was now 'on stream' and Mina clinic had accordingly run down. John transferred me to Ahmadi and, while he was on leave, I was summoned by the 'Demon', the hyperactive Gene Rickert. Until then I had spent the afternoons wandering around local Arab villages where our employees and their families lived, doing what I told John were 'public health surveys'.

"Philip, you're gonna do the radiology."

"No Gene I'm not."

"Yes Philip you are." End of message.

I knew my lame excuses would not wash with him. So for the next few weeks I 'sat in' with our Australian radiologist who was off to London to take his Diploma in Radiology; then I was let loose.

Well, I've always believed in the apprentice system and by the time Michael Strachan returned six months later I was enjoying what came to be my career; and I was allowed to remain his 'assistant' until it was time to leave KOC.

Remorselessly the time was approaching. In the spring I went skiing with the Aclands who were about to return to London; and as the Cumberland Yacht Club had already moved to Mina, there was now even less reason to visit Kuwait.

Again the flight to join the Aclands in Kitzbuhel had proved interesting. I was flying in a 'Viscount' of Middle East Airlines out of Beirut. Having re-fuelled in Athens it was due to fly to Zurich but contrary winds forced it to fly to Rome to refuel again. Once airborne the captain announced to cheering passengers that their arrival in London would not be delayed as he was now going to fly direct there... bad luck for him, I was the only passenger scheduled for Zurich, which he soon learned from me!

After ski-ing I flew to Rome where I was honoured to give Sister Patience away on her marriage to Leonard Keevil, an engineer with George Wimpey, who had been building a second jetty. First they went through a civil marriage, in Italian, then we went on to the Church of Scotland where they were 'properly married', as Jessica put it. There were few witnesses and after the bride and groom departed I took myself, still in what I considered my smart suit, to *Il Trovatore*. The entire audience were in evening dress, and I was banished to the gallery! Imagine that in a London theatre in the '50s.

Then it happened. Patience was rewarded. I was invited to join the Joint British-Pakistan Karakorum expedition as medical officer in June 1959. John and Vivian were as excited as I was. Initially I applied for six months leave but L. T. Jordan, the Texan general manager, was no fool. He was aware that no expedition to the Himalayas would take that long! So I had no choice but to resign. Nevertheless 'L. T.' not only provided the expedition with all the medical supplies we needed, authorised the training school to crate it and had the company aircraft fly it to Karachi but even allowed John to invite me back for a three month locum appointment as a radiologist after the expedition.

All this, in addition to his parting words: "If I'd been your age feller - I'd have done the same thing!" A big man in more ways than one was Leyland T. Jordan.

My departure from Kuwait coincided with Angus Maclean's departure from Aminoil. This post had not provided him with the freedom he sought, per-haps to roam among the Arabs? I never knew - but now he reappeared as 'assistant general manager administration' for John Paul Getty's oil company at Mina Saud, not much further away than Aminoil and still in the Neutral Zone. And he accused me of wanting power!

Just before he left Aminoil we were involved in a drama. One Thursday afternoon I had driven Deirdre down to the Neutral Zone to a deserted beach. We had been 'skinny dipping' and were stretched out on our towels. One thing led to another. I became aware that the pounding in my head was noth-ing to do with raised blood pressure but was the sound of a diesel engine and turned round to see a fishing boat about five yards off shore with three Kuwaiti fishermen gazing intently - indeed I would say malevolently - at this 'exhibition'. There was enough of a swell to give rise to breakers, otherwise I think they might have landed; and had I lived I would have had a hard job explaining what had happened to John and Viv. Sheepishly we crawled under our towels. The fishing boat drew away.

Having sworn a solemn vow not to take risks again we drove along the foreshore to the creek where Aminoil had their base. This was a World War II tank landing ship which acted which acted both as a base for operations and accommodation for western staff. Angus had invited us to drop in on our way back to Ahmadi. We gave him a (highly censored) account of our mishap and ᵤₜer a strong drink we regained our joint composure. Angus agreed that we had been lucky the sea was rough enough to prevent them landing!

It was dark by the time we left but the coastal track was not hard to follow and soon we were skirting round the perimeter fence round Sheikh Abdulla Mubarak's desert palace on a cliff overlooking the sea. We were approaching the gate on the north side when a figure staggered into the middle of the track and waved us down. It was one very large, very drunk, American. He collapsed across the bonnet of my Land Rover.

"Oh shit!" said Deirdre with feeling, "What a day!"

I jumped out. In the security lights on either side of the gate I could see the buckled gates themselves and inside the compound a bent pick-up truck which had rammed the guard hut. Scattered in the sand outside it were half a dozen of the Sheikh's guards in varying stages of consciousness but all groaning and clutching their heads or limbs. It seemed incredible but yet clear that our American had failed to 'hang a right' when the coast track reached the palace gate and gone straight on.

It was a time for a quick decision. It could only be a matter of minutes before one of the guards recovered enough to spot us - and their attacker. I raised his head. He looked at me blearily and said: "I gotta get home."

"Where's home?" I asked.

"Khafji," he grunted. That was right where we have just come from. There was no time to waste. I helped him to the back of the car, and unceremoniously bundled him in. I then did a fast 180 and set off back the way we had come. Our passenger kept groaning: "Those guys were out to get me..."

In dawning horror I realised that we were absconding with a man who had just beaten the living daylights out of six of Abdulla Mubarak's sentries... I pushed the accelerator through the floor board.

We reached Khafji and Deirdre was out of the car and up the gangplank in a flash. I gently restrained our passenger who decided he needed to throw up: which he did fortunately outside the car. He smelled like a distillery. Angus appeared on deck, took one glance and, within minutes two brawny, sober, Texans were frog-marching the man up the gangplank.

"Right!" said Angus, reverting to his role as Commando medical officer with Lord Lovat, "You two get the hell out of here. Deirdre's told me enough.

Get back to Ahmadi as quickly as you can - but take the Wafra (i.e. the inland) road. When you get there go straight to John and Viv's and tell them you went straight there after you had a drink with me."

There was nothing to argue about and off we went.

It was several days before we heard the full story. "Tex' - would you believe? - turned out to be a chef. He had only been with Aminoil about six weeks and that Thursday he'd been given a 'day off'. He'd borrowed the pick-up, having announced he wanted to see what went on in the 'big city'. Judging by the cluster of bottles of Jack Daniels found in his cabin he probably went well supplied with liquor. Presumably he'd found the 'big city' uninspiring as his first reported sighting by Public Security was when a pick-up truck was seen going fast around one of the sand roundabouts outside the old wall - in reverse. Later reports had him driving over flowerbeds in Ahmadi, then weaving down the tarmac towards Mina where he stopped another car and shouted: "What's my f.....g ship doing out there?" pointing to a tanker berthed alongside the jetty.

The driver of the other car had the sense to shout: "That away!" pointing south and drove on, to report a lunatic was loose. It must have been shortly after this that we met him.

With commendable speed Angus got Tex sobered up, packed up and sewn up. He was on the first aircraft out of Kuwait next day, an Iranair flight which took him to Teheran. Angus, with his fluent Arabic, went to the head of Public Security, one Colonel Abdul Latif Thuweini - of whom more later - and told all. The incident was declared closed.

The epilogue came later. Tex disappeared once he had landed in Teheran, despite being provided with a through ticket to Dallas. Enquiries revealed this was not surprising - he was already wanted for murder in Texas.

8
TO THE KARAKORUM

I left Kuwait on 11 June 1959. It was a dull overcast day, made even more unpleasant by a 'shamaal' - the hot desert wind that can blow out of the Iraqi desert at this time of the year, bringing dust and sand that fills every crevice, even getting into the folds of a shirt in a closed drawer. It was not conducive to nostalgia. Nigel and Joyce Owen drove me to the airport. I sensed both were envious, they had been expatriate doctors for many years and the suburban atmosphere of Ahmadi had got to them too. At the airport I met up with Gerry Murcutt, another wandering colonial who was employed at that time as the site engineer for the Ruler's new palace on the sea front. Gerry's tales of the Great Ground Nut Fiasco after the war made a youngster like myself reflect on the wise man who had once said that the British Empire had been acquired in a fit of absent-mindedness; or perhaps incompetence?

My departure to Bahrain coincided with the return of the Deputy Ruler, Sheikh Abdulla Mubarak, so I shared a Guard of Honour and a military band. (Little did I guess at the time how often I should be called upon to repeat this exercise in the future.)

As I boarded the aircraft and waved, albeit sadly, to my friends, I knew I was doing the right thing - for, as one of our Pakistani surgeons, Mahmoud Ahmed, had said: "Ahmadi's fine if you just want to sit around and have a few drinks."

Bahrain was hot and humid. The enervating atmosphere of the island, compared with the 'buzz' of Kuwait, reflected its lowly position in the oil tables. Physical activity was reduced to a minimum. I stayed overnight in Speedbird House, BOAC's transit hotel in those days, never renowned for its standards of service or cuisine. After a hot and sticky night, I boarded a BOAC 'Britannia' next morning bound for Karachi.

Thick cloud cast a yellow pall over this miserable brown town which had been forced from a fishing village to become Pakistan's first capital seventeen years earlier. Here I had my first taste of military influence - a Pakistan Army captain met me at the aircraft steps, shouting: "Welcome Doctor Sahib!"

He rushed me through customs with my feet barely touching the ground, exhibiting the genial contempt that the military had - and probably still have - for the civilian authorities. Outside was a World War II jeep and driver who whizzed us off to the old RAF transit camp at Drigh Road - apparently untouched since 1947. I saw for the first time carts with pneumatic tyres pulled by camels; cars drawn by horses; the huge old black shed at the side of the airport, built to house the ill-fated R101 Airship; and what my escort, Inayat Khan, called 'Spiv Street', the haunt of smugglers and 'get rich quick' boys, steadily undermining the economy of their new country. (As late as 1998 I concluded that no one was actually <u>paying</u> income tax.)

So, into the dusty camp, where the commanding officer had ordered all the bushes to be torn up - to what purpose I wondered? Perhaps he suffered from asthma and had heard that certain trees could trigger an attack! Most of it was empty, but this after all was a vast camp built in 1942 at a low ebb of Britain's war in the east with the Japanese poised to invade and we might well have found ourselves fighting to maintain a toehold in the sub-continent. Today, the Pakistani airmen were smartly turned out and the officer's mess spotless. So was the club with its swimming pool and squash courts - the latter staffed by professional coaches - all needless to say called 'Khan'. I enjoyed sleeping that night under a huge ceiling fan.

Next day was still cloudy and humid but Inayat took me sight-seeing as the flight bringing the rest of the expedition members was delayed. We saw a host of crocodiles, a cotton factory and a molasses factory. Passing the shore-based naval establishment, PNS Dinawar, I was surprised to see a Union Jack flying from the yard arm - had someone forgotten to take it down in 1947? Hardly, if anything it should have been a White Ensign! No explanation was forthcoming.

In the afternoon I was taken by 'bunder boat' to Karachi Yacht Club on an island in the harbour. This was a social centre for expatriates but an active sailing club as well. They had 'Fireflies', lively little dinghies, and I noted how the local sailors all had flat stomachs; whereas the sailors in Kuwait, used to the heavier X craft, seldom had to 'lean out', hence were rather portly. Here I met Vinny and Marge Pollard, who kindly put me up in their flat when we returned in August and the heat was shattering. He was manager of the Pakistan Oxygen Company. She had parachuted into Albania during World War II and looked ready to do so again at any minute. An air-conditioned bedroom was still a luxury at that time. My abiding memory of government quarters was of ceiling fans and lavatories that didn't flush.

Life for expatriates was relatively good in those days, for Karachi had grown from minor port into sprawling town - it could never be a city - of two and a half million people, most of them Muslim refugees from India. (By 1999 this had grown to nearer ten million.) Looking back in history how rarely it seems that refugees benefit - in the long term. Karachi was terribly poor. There was no tinned or frozen food available even for those who could afford it; and I cannot recall seeing any car larger than a Morris Minor. Expatriates relied for 'luxuries' on whatever friends brought back with them from leave.

Majors Tony Streather and Peter Varwell, respectively leader and administration officer of the expedition, both members of the Gloucestershire Regiment, arrived that evening; and we went straight to the Officers' Club where we met up with Willy Brown, an old friend of Tony's from post-war days when Tony had been ADC to the Governor of the North West Frontier Post. Willy had been commanding the Gilgit Scouts and in the latter months of 1947 had led a rebellion against Indian attempts to take over the whole of Kashmir. The result of his efforts can be seen today in the continued existence of the Northern Area, where the largely Muslim population are administered by Pakistan. Willy left the Army but stayed in Pakistan for some years in business. On one occasion he was set upon by vengeful Sikhs when he was visiting Calcutta and left for dead. However he survived and eventually retired to Scotland where he raised horses before dying in the mid-80s.[1] Tony, meanwhile, had stayed on in the Pakistan Army until 1952 when he had finally transferred to the British Army.

Other members of the expedition flew in during the next few days and by 17 June the advance party was ready to leave. The social life of Karachi was already beginning to pall, I recall a reception at the BOAC manager's house to celebrate both his wedding anniversary and the award of OBE. Everyone, apart from us, wore dinner jackets. We wore KD, i.e. tropical uniform. (I had 'invented' one of my own, an Anglicised Kuwaiti field officer's uniform with an Iraqi forage cap.) The only 'local' guests were Parsee families. I sensed any one of them could have bought any one of us ten times over. We returned to a 'scratch' dinner in the mess of consommé, cold lobster and gin.

Next morning we took off at 8am, having been allowed to use the Pakistan Air Force VIP rest room - where the loo worked! We were aboard a Bristol 'Freighter', one of Britain's many disastrous post-war aircraft; on the subject of its load carrying capacity, an RAF pilot was quoted as saying: "it would have difficulty in pulling the skin off a rice pudding."

We had wished a squadron or two of them on the Pakistan Government who in those days were still too polite to say "no thanks" to their erstwhile rulers.

Since we were a party of twelve, with all our kit, we were probably near the aircraft's weight limit so we were forced to fly at low altitude; and once we had turned away from the mouth of the Indus with is mangrove swamps and offshore islands where the smugglers lurked, our flight took us over the broad brown Sind desert - frankly boring.

Deafened and desiccated we finally reached the old RAF station at Chaklala, on the outskirts of Rawalpindi. This was now the HQ of the PAF - and if imitation is the sincerest form of flattery, then the RAF should be proud: apart from the slightly darker skins of the airmen, we might just as well have been the Queen's flight landing at RAF Northolt. There was an old 'Dakota' fuselage, its tail propped up so that it was level with the ground and a rubber mat beneath the door, on one side of the airfield. It was still being used for training paratroops and, with its RAF roundels still faintly visible, it brought back memories of 1946.

We were divided up between various officers' messes and I was lucky enough to draw Probyn's Horse, founded at the time of the Mutiny, which the US Army Training Mission had tried to re-name 'the Fifth Cavalry' - with little success. Their regimental cap badge incorporated the Prince of Wales' feathers but, in deference to Pakistan's status as a Republic, the tops had been cut off so it now looked like a 'W'. The regimental lines were spotless as was

---

[1] In 1998 his widow published the diaries he had kept at the time of the insurrection under the title *The Gilgit Rebellion*.

the khaki drill of the soldiers and the whiteness of anything immovable in the camp; while the lush greenery of the whole cantonment area refreshed eyes grown weary by hours of gazing at desert.

I was ushered into the officers' mess where the duty officer sprang from his leather armchair and cried: "My dear chap - have a dry gin! You must need it after that awful flight!"

I never drink a pink gin with pearl onions today without remembering that occasion.

It was a mess night and I was in awe of my surroundings. The shining mahogany mess table must have been sixty feet long, the regimental silver sparkled, portraits of Lord Birdwood and Probyn himself gazed benignly down on us, while the Colonel regaled us with tales of the Mutiny - clearly the Sikhs and Pathans of Probyn's had been on our side! - and the 1957 reunion when ex-British officers had been flown out to join in the centenary celebrations. Around us were lean brown statues who only moved on the command of the mess 'havildar' - the command being little more than the flicker of an eyelid! These waiters wore red 'pugrees', tight white jackets - what we would call 'bum-freezers' - with red 'dickies', red and blue cummer-bunds, white trousers and - gym shoes!

After dinner we retired to the Ladies Room - not that there were any present on this occasion. Here, portraits of King Edward VII and Queen Alexandra gazed down at us, just as benignly: but all was not lost in a haze of Victoriana for alongside them was a signed portrait of Princess Alexandra who had visited the regiment just two years previously. On a table, lay Country Life and Horse & Hound, albeit somewhat out of date, a silver cigarette box two feet long, and a silver leopard. On the wall above it was a plaque commemorating the 1957 centenary of the regiment's birth. How

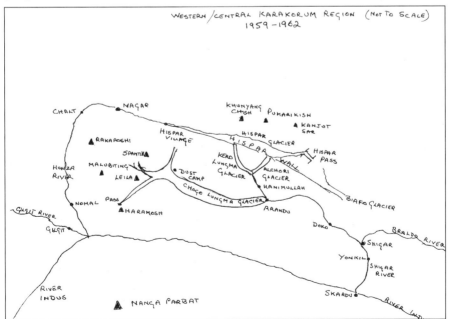

long, I wondered, could all this last?

Dinner was served at 10pm (breakfast lasted until 11.30am) but we were still in time to attend a dance at the 'Pindi' Club. Here we were guests of Colonel Omar of the Guides Cavalry. On our arrival he ran down the steps and embraced Tony with a cry of: "You old bastard - how are you?"

It was a Gala Night, the first day of Eid Al Adha, the Muslim feast celebrating the aborted sacrifice of Isaac by Abraham. I doubt whether such a Gala Night would be tolerated today... even at the time I felt both uncomfortable and sad. Why were young Muslims attending a dance, totally alien to their culture, on such an occasion? There were a few elderly English people clinging to the walls of the ballroom like limpets. A small band, wearing dinner jackets of course, played 1940s dance tunes for a few brave souls who shuffled round the floor roughly in time to a fox-trot. Then the band broke into a 'jive' and a young Anglo-Pakistani couple took to the floor. The girl was as graceful and sinuous as a siren and managed to put as much sex appeal into a kick of her heel as a western stripper reduced to her G-string: 'nautch girl' met 'bluebell girl' and the combination was spell-binding.

So this was the epitaph... the memsahibs in their picture hats with their 'pukka' sahibs had gone, Islam was taking over - but the defiant offspring of the two worlds danced to a jazzed up version of Noel Coward's *The Party's Over Now*.

Next day we left for Peshawar. We travelled in open jeeps on the Grand Trunk Road. On the way we passed the monument to Nicholson, one of the 'titans' of the Punjab in the last century, who died in the assault on Delhi in 1857.[1] We went via Abbotabad. The cantonment reminded me of Ahmadi! Hardly surprising in view of the number of 'old India hands' recruited by the Kuwait Oil Company after 1947. The neat rows of bungalows, orderly streams and trees, seemed somehow fragile when compared with the brown plain of the north Punjab and the tantalising glimpse of snowy mountains far to the north.

Then we came to the Indus, swirling and turgid from the summer thaw in the mountains, and crossed the combined road and rail Attock bridge.

"Ah," said Tony, "now we are in God's own country - the North West Frontier Province." He waved at the watchful guards of the Baluch Regiment who occupied the massive Mogul fort built to protect the crossing.

Indeed the country did become less arid though I would not have thought our Maker would have regarded it as the jewel in His crown. We passed thick groves of mango trees - I learned there were 75 different varieties. So to Peshawar, where we went straight to the Political Resident's house, where Tony had once served as ADC to the last British Governor; and were served tea and cakes on the lawn. The present PR, Major Mohammed Yusuf, was of course a friend of Tony's, and the latter had brought him a selection of gramophone records for his family - Mozart being head of the list. Then to the UK High Commissioner's, a pleasant man called Harrison, who put us up for the night in a building for all the world like an English country house. Among

---

[1] In 1999 I took the opportunity to climb the hill on which it stands and found it defaced. I suspect this had been done shortly after Partition as there was a sign near the foot of the hill, dated 1950, which warned anyone caught defacing 'historical sites' would be punished.

those summoned to meet us were a CMS priest and an English lecturer from Islamia University, and I wondered at the good relations that still existed between us after the bloodshed at Partition. Before retiring I glanced through the visitor's book in my bedroom and was surprised to see that just six months previously my bed had been occupied by one Julie Vaughan Hudson, who had been one of Prince Philip's cortege on his recent visit.[1] I sent a rude card off to Julie complaining about the lumps she had made in the mattress.

Next day it was - 'Carry on up the Khyber!' The pass starts about ten miles west of Peshawar and our road took us past the airport, Peshawar University and Islamia College. At Jamrud, where the Sikhs built a fort during their occupation in 1836, we entered Tribal Territory and Tony began to mentally foam at the mouth. We stopped at a village for tea where he, inevitably, knew someone; in this case an ex-officer of the Chitral Scouts whom, in my ignorance, I deduced had either Polynesian, Arab or Spanish blood; possibly all three. He was in fact partly Tibetan! He was also an active smuggler and arms dealer.[2] He proudly showed us Sten guns, Lee Enfield rifles and Luger pistols, all manufactured on the spot and indistinguishable from the originals: but Tony told us that the chances of their barrels bursting when fired were as great as in Kipling's day, when only 'Gezails' were being copied.

We were hurried on our way, which was unusual for a Muslim community. Getting away was usually the problem. But Tony explained that there was a feud brewing with a neighbouring village as to the ownership of a house on the outskirts and that the shooting might begin at any time. We concluded this was probably a tale to tickle the tourists... but then in a land where every male carried a weapon it is not surprising that 'lead poisoning' is common. Compare this situation with that of Switzerland where indeed every male has a rifle - but it is kept locked up at home under normal circumstances!

So the road wound upward alongside the old camel track and the railway, completed in 1925, but with a service now reduced to one train a week up to Landi Kotal on the Afghan border. Once we had passed Shagai Fort the narrow pass widened and the scenery became boring - one can absorb just so much rock. The regimental plaques at Shagai were well cared for (as they were in 1998 when I visited again). Near the frontier we came to the anti-tank 'teeth' built in 1942 in anticipation of a possible German thrust into India. Well I thought, it gave the troops something to take their minds off the war raging east and west of them. The bazaar at Torkhan was not very exciting - aluminium pots and pans, cheap jewellry, sweet meats and cakes, crawling with flies, and fruit. We drove all the way back to Rawalpindi that night, it was a long day.

Next day we were up early for the flight to Skardu, again in our trusty Bristol Freighter; but this time we had scenery worth flying low for - a bit too low at times. I thought our wheels would touch the brown, knife-edged ridges we crossed. Soon we edged round the west flank of Nanga Parbat, its summit 10,000 feet above us. I wondered where Mummery's body lay and

[1] Julie's brother Bryan was one of my close friends at medical school, and his wife Gillian subsequently became Kathy's godmother while I became godfather to their elder daughter.
[2] By 1998, smuggling had been nationalised and was run by the Army, Chinese goods being 'imported' via Afghanistan.

recalled Herman Buhl's fantastic solo ascent just six years before: he too alas had died two years ago previously, on Chogo Lisa. Then we were in the Indus Valley and followed this to Skardu. Warned that we should expect a bumpy ride, we certainly got it, but by now I was nearly comatose, having dosed myself with Avomine.

We landed and transferred our kit into two Bedford trucks. I photographed this activity and got a rocket from Jawed Akhter Khan - our liaison officer who was there to greet us. He gazed at me sternly and said: "This is a sensitive area. Photography is strictly forbidden."

I think these were the first and last cross words he ever spoke to me. He was to become Kathy's godfather - despite the fact that he was a Muslim.

We bumped off along the 'kutch', i.e. rubble, road to the Government guest house. The hanging branches of the trees beat a tattoo on the tops and sides of the trucks. We had to cross a river, not the Indus itself but a tributary, over a rickety bridge, and survived by driving at full pelt. There were audible sighs of relief when we reached the opposite side. The bridge actually collapsed later that night!

The rest house was a new building of the traditional 'dak bungalow' design with a wide verandah and an outside kitchen from which we were served curry and spinach - I still have a taste for 'sagh'. That evening we were invited to watch a typical frontier polo match on the 'Maidan' where there are no apparent limits of space or rules governing behaviour. Charging straight into one's opponent or hooking his stick to dismount him were fair play.

Next day, 21 June, I visited the local hospital. Dr Raschid was not a happy man.

"I am posted to this backwater because I have no political 'clout' with my superiors in the Pakistan Medical Service." (His use of English vernacular was impressive.)

Had he had any clinical interest in his patients he must surely have been satisfied, at least in the short term. There were cases of rampant goitre, due to lack of iodine in both soil and water, Tb, trachoma, osteomyelitis, typhoid fever, fractures, kala azar - all were rife. Of course, he did lack much of the medication needed to treat these conditions - but any clinician in a London hospital would have been green with envy.

He asked me about the health services in England: "I suppose it is the same in your villages? All the money is spent in London?"

I was glad to disillusion him on this point! We walked under the fort where the Indus, in flood thanks to the summer thaw, had brought a whole section of the bank crashing down. We tried fishing for trout and the local black fish without success; but gorged ourselves on the mulberries that grew in profusion on the bank.

Next day we sorted kit. In the evening we dined with the Political Resident for the Northern Region and were somewhat embarrassed to find our host and his friends in dinner jackets while all we could raise were clean sweat shirts. The Raj's boot was clearly on the other foot. We dined off chicken, rice and salad, already a pleasant change from the curried bones, spinach and chapattis that were the staple fare in the rest house. I sat next to the airport manager. Like so many government servants he bore a grudge against 'the establishment' - in this instance, against the PAF who were not averse to smuggling contraband such as drugs, and had offered him bribes to overlook it. He had refused them - hence regarded his promotion prospects as blocked. Nevertheless he enjoyed being in Skardu as it enabled him to save money for his family.

❦ ❦ ❦ ❦ ❦ ❦ ❦ ❦ ❦ ❦ ❦ ❦ ❦

On 23 June the expedition set off. Tony had got the porters in hand and off we went to the river bank, with 150 of them in tow. We paid them Rs.4 per day for carrying 60lb loads for a 'pirau', i.e. a fixed stage march of about ten to fifteen kilometres, usually to the next village. They had to provide their own food. We crossed the Indus on 'Alexander's barge', a large dugout ferry. Near the bank the water was calm but when our paddlers had propelled us into mid-stream the current whipped the barge around and we spun off downstream for fully half a mile before they regained control and landed us on the far bank. Here we refreshed ourselves from a fresh water spring as it was already hot, before setting off up the hill to the jeep track.

And so we trudged over mud flats until the valley narrowed and the track narrowed to a lane, and we came to the village of Yonkil. Here I was presented with a bunch of flowers by a child: how charming, I thought, but I quickly learned that I had been identified as 'the doctor', no doubt by some well-meaning member of the expedition's advance party. The child took me to his house, a two-storied mud building, and I climbed a ladder to an upper room where his mother lay, pale and sweating under a pile of rugs. I was told, through an interpreter, that she had abdominal pains and no periods - a common enough presentation of disease in the Third World as I had already learned. Having established that she was not pregnant I placed my stethoscope on her distended abdomen and heard precisely nothing. But my action clearly impressed the crowd of women who by now had joined us.

The practice of 'bush medicine' was, alas, alien to this product of a London teaching hospital. There were no X-ray or laboratory tests to hand and my experience of local disease was zero. Had she been wasted and coughing Tb would have headed the differential diagnosis. Chronic bowel infection or infestation seemed possible: had I been able to identify the organism or parasite, treatment would have been futile - re-infection would have recurred within days. So I gave her some indigestion medicine and hoped we would return another way.

Many of the women now began to show me their goitres - multi-lobulated lumps in their necks, arising from their iodine-starved thyroid glands. Again, faced with chronic disease, there was nothing an itinerant doctor could do. Outside I was confronted by the men of the village with their badly infected eyes, ears and feet: for the latter I was able to paint the sores and crevices in their feet with gentian violet - I had learned in Kuwait that 'white medicine', be it tablet or lotion was regarded as ineffective - but here was a dramatic demonstration that something could be done. This was my cruel introduction to 'expedition medicine'. One needed a heart of stone and the skin of an ox to face the wretched sick of the Himalayan valleys.

Outside in the fresh air again we were invited to watch a local polo match. This was even wilder than the game we had seen in Skardu and the absence of rules anathema to my public school-bred views on sport. Apart from the fact that the 'pitch' was open-ended and enclosed laterally by stone walls that were only 50 yards apart and a hazard to horse and rider alike, the players slashed, hacked and drove headlong at each other, the 'chukka' being largely irrelevant.

As evening fell it was time for the 'tribal dancing' as Tony insisted on calling it. To my uncultured eye it had much in common with that I had seen on the shores of the Arabian Gulf - shuffle, shuffle, hop - but here it was the village maidens who danced and not the men. Muslims indeed they were; and I have concluded over the years that the precepts of Islam have a stronger hold over Muslims the further one gets from Mecca - but the natural grace of the women of these valleys has to find a natural outlet and for them it is through dance. The shuffling of their feet in time to pipe and drum was repetitive and boring, but the graceful movements of wrist and arm that accompanied it were hypnotic.

Village morality was strict but again the rules of Islam were stretched in these isolated communities, both three day and three year marriages being deemed acceptable.

We bedded down that night in the village school, to have erected our tents would, it appeared, have been an insult to our hosts. The younger villagers were loathe to leave us in peace and a group of them began to sing, uncertainly at first. Then, to my amazement, I began to identify words: "Ing tong ing tong ing tong ing tong ing tong tiddle aye po," repeated again and again. I started up in my sleeping bag: "It's I'm walking backwards for Christmas!" I cried out.

"Belt up and let's get some sleep," grumbled a few voices. But I was enthralled, could this be the source of one of the Goons' greatest hits? If so how on earth had words and music crossed half the globe from this remote Karakorum Valley? I recalled that Spike Milligan had been born in India of a military family, and hadn't both Peter Sellers and Harry Secombe served there? I interrogated the singers through a sleepy interpreter but all I got were shy smiles and shrugged shoulders. They said: "It was just a song that had always been sung." I fell asleep, dreaming of the expressions on the faces of Spike Milligan *et al* when I played my tape recording to them.

A few days later we caught up with our advance party and I shared the news of my fascinating ethnic experience with them. To my distress I became aware of averted eyes and suppressed giggles. Eventually Jim Thomas,[1] Fleet

---

[1] Nice one Jim. We kept in touch for some time after the expedition but then he was killed attempting to land on a carrier, a fate that befell many naval aviators in those days. He was a good companion and a source of strength whenever the going got bad.

Air Arm pilot and expedition humourist, came clean. He admitted to having spent the evening before our arrival in Yonkil teaching the song to a group of lads and impressing upon them the need for total secrecy as to its source when they met the main party the following evening.

We continued our approach march in a north westerly direction. From Yonkil to Doko across a stony desert where we were struck by a sandstorm - not what I had expected in the Karakorum. Then we came to some hot springs, enclosed behind mud walls providing privacy for both male and female bathers. Sergeant Mike Quinn overdid his stay in the hot water and I found myself treating a mild case of heat exhaustion - excessive sweating on the walk (he always carried too heavy a pack), a dry burning wind that aggravated convection loss from the skin, followed by prolonged immersion in water above body temperature were too much for his body's heat control system. Salt tablets would have made him vomit but I was able to barter cigarettes for some powdered rock salt which I mixed with 'jungle juice' (tinned lemonade powder) and laid him under a wet towel in the shade. He soon recovered. Meanwhile one of our number managed to break the wooden ladder getting into the hot spring - more cigarettes were paid for this. It was here at Doko we saw our first lammergeyer circling over the huts which were covered with what I thought were Queen Alexandra roses. Well, there was no one ready to contradict me among the brutal and licentious soldiery (my late mother's description of the military.)

And so we came to Arandu. It had taken us five days and the help of 160 porters to cover the 72 miles from Skardu. Here we set up base camp at the foot of the Chogo Lungma glacier in what appeared to be an idyllic spot with lush grass and shady trees. The particular serpents in this Eden were flies, which tormented us from dawn to dusk. I was grateful for my 'kheffiya'. "No flies on those Arabs," remarked Jim. We rested at Arandu for a couple of days while parties prepared for their summit attempts. Like Gaul, Tony divided us into three parts.

On 30 June my party set off up the Al Chori glacier. This runs northwards up towards the great Hispar glacier. At 5 am on 2 July we awoke to an ominous sight. Across the glacier to the west at an altitude of about 30,000 feet a 'front' was racing towards us at about 70mph. It would have been a good time to hightail it for base camp; but we didn't. In fact we were in little danger down in the valley but the rain began 24 hours later and continued for 56 hours.[1]

Before the storm struck, Jim Thomas and I struggled across the glacier to a campsite where another party had settled the previous night. Crossing glaciers is a foretaste of hell for those of us who fear it: whichever route one chooses through the tumbled mass of ice, rock and slippery stones - it's the wrong one. I slipped and swore, swore and slipped, finally loosing my temper altogether when Ali Mohammed, one of our Balti porters from Skardu, a kind and gentle man, offered me a helping hand. The end result of this was to make me feel even worse.

[1] Subsequently we learned that this same storm struck the Anglo-German Batura Mustagh party who were already high on the 25,540 foot peak. Dr Keith Warburton and four other members of the party were killed. I saw the memorial stone erected to them in the European Cemetery in Gilgit when I returned there in the summer of 1998.

We reached camp to find the others still abed. In theory they should have moved and we should have occupied their tents. But the rain had started, they weren't moving so it was back across the moraine as the rain grew heavier. Back in camp our porters erected a tent, which leaked. However Jim and I crawled into it. Four porters just wouldn't fit into the other tent so we struggled to build a 'cave' for two of them; they were curiously grateful. Back in our tent Jim and I brewed a casserole of steak and onions from our 'compo rations' - no luxuries for mountaineers in those days. We crawled into sodden sleeping bags and listened to a dull, almost incessant, rumble. We wondered whether it was flood, thunder or avalanches. In any case I was scared but the night passed.

Dawn brought no respite from the torrential rain. We cached food and tents, pulled on soaking boots and continued the unpleasant scramble up the glacier's lateral moraine. By now mud and stone falls made progress slower. The morale of the porters sank lower and still they had been unable to light a fire to cook their own food and rejected our offer of oatmeal blocks. The misery induced by wet cold was overwhelming - even my crotch was wet. Around midday we reached a cluster of stone refuges used by shepherds when caring for their flocks on the high summer pastures. They leaked; but the porters had had enough.

Fred Jenkins, a middle-aged army padre with a wealth of alpine experience who regarded me, with my dubious experience of climbing in Wadi Rum, Iraq, and one visit to Zermatt, as a loose cannon, then persuaded me to stagger on a bit further while the porters huddled in the huts. The flooding grew worse and my ankles were beginning to scream at the constant strain induced by the sloping moraine. We did not get far; but the return journey was lightened by glucose tablets, hot tea and a slug of whisky - which showed Fred to be a practising Christian after all.

Alexander's barge.

Back to the sodden sleeping bag. This was proving to be a right and proper introduction to Himalayan climbing, which has been defined as: "50% logistics; 40% uncomfortable walking." I was waiting for the 10% climbing in superb weather.

Well... the rain did stop, 56 hours later. After this somewhat abortive reconnaissance we started to dry out and returned to base camp at Arandu. There I found my doctoring 'skills' were finally required - and as I was to learn time and time again, the 'skills' required of me were in veterinary surgery and dentistry.

My attempts at fixing a broken goat's leg in a plaster of Paris splint were as hilarious as they were ineffective: a couple of sticks strapped on with elastoplast lasted a bit longer. Then Robin Platt, our senior sapper officer, presented with a dental abscess. This duly responded to hot mouth washes and penicillin injections. The locals were less lucky - I extracted left upper and right lower molars from two of them. Both teeth were in a parlous state but came away with their roots. An old man with a carious lower molar refused a local anaesthetic - an advanced case of needle phobia. Then came the challenge of the day.

The Lambadar's (head man) younger brother, had, I was told, been gored by a bull a few weeks previously. Could I sew up the cut? With the nonchalance I knew was welcomed by naive patients I prepared an 'operating table' of cardboard compo boxes. But this insouciance was soon shattered when the patient arrived, supported on either side by his friends, a woollen shawl around his trunk, and lay down. When the shawl was removed and his shirt lifted I was horrified to see a tear across the whole of his lower abdomen down to and through the peritoneum, exposing coils of glistening white bowel. How the bull had managed this without perforating a single loop of bowel remains a mystery.

At this point the second expedition doctor, John Clegg, who had been with Tony on Kanchenjunga four years previously and became Professor of Anatomy in Liverpool in due course, arrived on the scene. He showed his officer-like qualities by a cursory inspection of the wound, followed by a curt nod to imply 'Carry on sergeant'.

It was a mammoth task. The wound being several weeks old the opposing faces of skin, fascia and muscle were all showing healthy signs of healing 'by secondary intent', as I believe my surgical colleagues like to call wound surfaces which have grown a protective covering. How there had been no infection remains a second mystery. Well... suffice it to say that after spraying the scene with local anaesthetic, scraping the wound surfaces, and several yards of catgut, silk, and nylon he was cobbled together. I didn't dare let him stand up, but saw him safely carried back to his hut.

By 7 July the weather had improved and a small party of us set off up the Kero Lungma glacier, an eastern tributary of the Chogo Lungma. The effects of the recent storm were only too apparent, huge avalanches across the paths made life even more difficult for our porters and their 'rests' grew more frequent. I was fascinated by the way they smoked their cigarettes. For what I assumed were religious reasons - and I have previously remarked, the tenets of Islam are held more strictly the further one is from Mecca - they would not allow the cigarette to touch their lips. Instead it was held between thumb and forefinger, the lighted end within the bowl formed by their two hands and the smoke sucked into their lungs from between the thenar eminences.

We reached a handful of huts called Hanimullah about noon and camped on a plateau above them, on a carpet of flowers. We lunched off omelettes and 'pirattas' - the latter being a concession by Tony to our sophisticated western tastes. he would happily live on a diet of chapattis. I listened to the climbing talk - that of enthusiasts recalling minor incidents in the lives of slight acquaintances - but projecting them as dramas in the lives of intimate friends. I suppose this is the way we chaps like to impress each other. A less polite expression is 'bullshitting'. Fred Jenkins kept aloof, perhaps because of his age. Somehow he did not carry his Christian calling convincingly. Alan Imrie, a captain in the Hampshire Regiment and probably our best climber, complained bitterly to me, in private, about Fred's smart kit and equipment and his apparent unwillingness to put it to use! Despite a glorious blue dusk the day ended badly. It was mutton Scotch style for dinner, surely the least attractive item in a compo box.

Indigestion aside it was a quiet night and another glorious dawn; but this presaged two ghastly days of 'moraine bashing' as we laboured our way up the glacier to camp beneath what we called 'organ pipe mountain', because of the towers that rose towards its summit, and which we had chosen as a suitable objective for our party.

My abiding impression of the Karakorum is tumbling glaciers - not only the joint-wrenching, foot-blistering stony ground - but also the sharp crack of falling stones; the roar of debris sliding down the icy walls and in the silence that followed the gurgle of streams below the ice.

We camped on a plateau above the lateral moraine, again carpeted with flowers and enhanced by juniper bushes. We practised crevasse drill and abseiling. During the next few days we indulged in 'Himalayan wandering'. The weather was erratic, the snow unpredictable. Someone quoted:

> The rocks that roughly handle us,
> The peaks that will not go,
> The uniformly scandalous condition of the snow.

And soon we were all at it. On one occasion I was with Robin Platt and Abdul Ghani, one of the three Pakistani officers on the expedition, descending a slope, when we sank, one after another, into the snow. We couldn't sit, we couldn't slide, we just sank. Then cloud descended and we were in a 'white out'. Robin managed to claw himself downwards to a rocky outcrop from where he threw us a rope and he managed to haul us down to his platform. From there we could just see the glacier floor below. Then it seemed to boil. Great columns of swirling mist arose from the moraine and enveloped the surrounding peaks. Until now it had been still, then came the

The Hispar Valley 1962

Khinyang Chish Camps

Bitinmal — Base Camp

Nagar

1 Khinyang Chish (26,762 feet)
2 East Peak

Distaghil Sar (26,000)

Pumarikish (24,580 feet)

Kanju Sar (25,466 feet)

Hispar Village

Hispar Glacier

Hispar La

Hispar Wall

0 2 4 6
Miles

Camps 1&2
Recce Camps.

wind, ripping the clouds over our heads to reveal patches of vivid blue sky. Slowly the valley cleared again and we could see our orange and green tents. Thank goodness some kind soul had taken my sleeping bag in!

Another, better, experience was to follow. Alan Imrie, who was having problems with blistered feet, suggested a gentle scramble to see how they were progressing after my ministrations. It was soon clear they weren't and he hobbled back to camp leaving me to climb alone to a ridge from where - lo and behold! I saw ibex feeding and a ranunculus growing in the snow! I had discovered the ultimate contentment; just sitting and looking at mountains.

Fred continued to wait for 'Alpine conditions', as Alan rather cruelly put it; but Robin Platt and George Chapman, another Gloucester officer, went off and climbed a handsome peak - still called 'Gloster Peak' on the latest maps, it lies on the south side of the Hispar glacier.[1] Peter Varwell had become aware of the tension developing between cautious Fred and the more gung ho younger members of the team and took it upon himself to climb with the padre.

On 15 June Allan, George, Abdul Ghani and I set off across the moraine for 'organ pipe' mountain - this name does not survive on the maps! We managed to lose Abdul Ghani on the way and by the time he re-appeared on the wrong side of the glacier it was nearly 1pm and we had a hard climb to reach a camp site before dark. It rained heavily during the night but this had cleared by dawn and we set off for the summit, dumping our kit at the foot of the final snow slope. At the top of this we roped up for the final rock spire. Abdul Ghani decided to stop. He made no bones about having been 'press ganged' by the military authorities to join the expedition as the third Pakistani representative and only wanted to get home as soon as he could.

---

[1] George Chapman went on to do bold things with 22 SAS, then succumbed to the marriage bug when on attachment to US special Forces and married a widow with four children. Who dares wins? He stayed on in the USA so I don't know.

We traversed across the face to a chimney that looked promising - and proved to be rotten. This was George's first technical ascent. He followed Alan and then stuck. I climbed up to him and hammered in a piton, and placed his foot on it.

"Thanks," he said calmly and continued climbing. He remained calm as I slipped on the next stage and hung on my belay in the chimney for some minutes while bits of rock fell off. I called up to Alan: "Do you think this is safe?"

"I didn't come 6,000 miles to be stopped by loose rock!" came the stentorian reply. But a few minutes later, with the lining of the chimney tumbling past my ears like soot from a sweep's brush he had to admit defeat, only some 30 feet from the summit. It took us four and a half hours to get back to our camp where Abdul Ghani sat sulking. It was no good trying to explain to him that he would never have made it. We drank pints of tomato soup: this, together with the fact that we had found bear tracks near the tents on our return gave me, at least, a restless night.

Well, we'd had our summit attempt, so next morning, after an early lunch we returned to base camp.

Although we had scarcely over-stretched ourselves on our climb I, for one, felt tired and slipped several times on the track. I suspect a first Himalayan climb can sap more nervous energy than I cared to admit. Anyway after a couple of idle days I was up and anxious to be away again. But perhaps the best outcome from our foray was the proof that I had cured Alan's blisters! I confess that serendipity had played the major part. After days of fruitless dressing and antibiotics, both local and systemic, I had - in desperation - put him on massive doses of Vitamin C. The effect had been little short of miraculous. Within 48 hours healing was complete. Why this should have been so I still don't know. Our diet should have contained adequate amounts but I surmised that the body's requirements for ascorbic acid may increase under the dual stresses of cold and altitude.[1]

Anyway, George Chapman and I set off to explore the rest of the Alchori glacier and were duly chuffed to discover mistakes in the maps we were using, made by the Germans in 1954 and also, to find snow leopard's tracks. Actually we passed them twice. On the way up George said: "Don't worry it's quite a small one."

On the way back he looked at them thoughtfully. "Perhaps he's bigger than I thought. Come on, we'd better get moving."

They were indeed bigger but it was not until some days later that Tony pointed out that of course they get bigger as the day wears on and the snow melts.

On 20 July we set off for Arandu. Either we were getting better at it or the rain had smoothed it but the moraine seemed easier. We reached the village of Domak where we met up with Tony's party who had had a more fruitful time than us, having bagged three 20,000 foot plus peaks on the South Hispar wall, naming them Sugar Loaf (startlingly unoriginal), Engineer Peak and

[1] Nearly 30 years later I proposed to study the body's requirements for Vitamin C on Everest; but of all the loads that reached base camp by yak the box containing my research equipment was the only one whose contents were smashed. Heigh ho.

Major Rajah Jawaid Akhter Khan, Pakistan Army, 1959, who was murdered in 1971 in East Pakistan by his own soldiers.

Gloster Peak - such was the influence of our two Sapper and three Gloster members.[1]

They were not better climbers than us but Tony's leadership was probably a bit more thrusting than Fred's. Anyway, back to Arandu next day. On the way I failed to concentrate, yet again, slipped, fell about six feet and banged my head on a rock. I was never a natural mountaineer. We shared camp with the flies who seemed to relish the Barney's 'punchbowl' I puffed at them from my pipe. (I still had my teeth in those days and could clench my pipe between them in the best colonial officer style.)

On 23 July eight of us set off for the Chogo Lungma glacier and our main objective, the mountain called Malubiting. Despite intermittent rain showers we made good progress and pitched camp on a sandy hillock covered in fuschia. Peter Varwell assumed his most forbidding glare as the Lambadar demanded wages for a two day 'pirau' instead of one.

"Ek!" growled Peter.

"Do!" growled the Lambadar.

This could have gone on for the rest of the day but a violent rain shower drove the Lambadar under a rock for shelter. 1-0.

Next day we reached the head of the glacier and set up 'Dust Camp'. This title needs no further explanation. En route we had passed a glacier pool in which Peter, George and another major, Tom Hardman, swam. I excused myself on the grounds that if I died of cold they'd have no doctor. It was from here that I took a photograph of the south side of the glacier. A second photograph reflected the glacier pool. Both pictures subsequently showed a figure clasping a stick, inverted in the reflected

---

[1] Interestingly enough all these names have survived, certainly on the Polish Karakorum map, 2nd edition, Cracow, 1973.

Above and below, left side of both pictures, the Yeti!! on the lowest 'tongue' of snow

view, which I claimed was a yeti.[1] From this unpleasant camp we saw
Malubiting for the first time; and closer, the mountain called Leila. Whoever
named this beautiful peak must have known the Arab legend of the doomed
lovers, Leila and Majnoon.

For the next few days we were fully occupied stocking forward camps. It
was always a relief to get out of dust camp which seldom belied its name -
unless the seemingly perpetual west wind dropped. My companion on the
'carries' was usually Peter Varwell whose love of sailing and mountains was
only exceeded by his love of hunting. (Our friendship was rekindled some 20
years later when daughter Kathryn found herself in the same house at
Sherborne as his niece Sarah Pybus, who was her 'minder'. Thereafter we
climbed and sailed a lot over the next 20 years. In 1959 our tent conversation

---

[1] Later I sent these photographs to London Zoo, who returned them with a polite note saying
there was a 'figure' beyond the glacier but it was impossible to identify its nature.

revolved around Jorrocks - my sole source of knowledge of the hunting scene.)

During this time I was obsessed with Leila - harken to this: "26 July. A beautiful morning. Leila blushed behind diaphanous cloud whilst the light cast a green hem around her garment of snow." Well there are fewer complications in a love affair with a mountain than a woman!

By 29 July we were ready. At 4am we were up and breakfasting off (tinned) ham and eggs. Undaunted, Tony followed this with ginger pudding - those readers who remember 'compo rations' must surely be impressed. We were packed and away by dawn and at 7am had reached the ice fall that fronts the Malubiting glacier. This we ascended without problem and soon we were overheating as we plodded up the glacier itself. The sky became that darker shade of blue that people who have not climbed high can believe is real; but cobalt it is. We reached Camp One two hours later where we found Fred, Tom and George just back from reconnoitring a route up the next ice fall that led to the south east ridge of Malubiting.

"It'll go," said Fred confidently. George winked at Alan. We were all getting sunburned by this time and I advised the climbers to apply lanolin to the skin - presuming this would 'nourish' it - rather than rely on the dubious properties of glacier cream (then available) for occluding ultraviolet light.[1]

Tony and I escorted the porters back to advanced base camp that evening and the following morning struck camp and moved up to camp one. En route I fell into a crevasse and recorded: "Not frightened; but I made a bloody great hole."

Meanwhile the others had put Alan and Jawed into camp two at 20,000 feet. This was not just a diplomatic choice for a summit pair; Jawed, thank God, showed real promise as a climber, was keen and fit, and as the future showed was capable of 'going high'.

Next day Tony and I went up to join them. Both Fred and Tom became boot-faced when Tony announced he was taking me as his number two on the rope but with the quiet authority we had all learned to respect by now he turned to them and said: "It will be up to Fred and Tom to support them on the descent."

"Right," said Fred at once, "You take 'em up, we'll bring them down." Tom nodded. Honour was satisfied.

It took us four hours to reach camp two. I began to develop my own reactions to altitude - I felt dizzy when I bent down and worse when I straightened up. I saw black shapes floating across my retina when I gazed at distant peaks - and there were plenty to see, the Mustagh Tower, Masherbrum, K2 - the panorama was magnificent and the fine weather we now had looked set to last.

Alan and Jawed returned after a successful reconnaissance of the south east ridge. That afternoon it was too hot in the tents so I washed with snow and compo soap, the latter being notorious for not producing a lather even in a hot bath! However it was a good substitute for pumice stone. Next morning we

---

[1] In retrospect I suspect lanolin helped fry the skin; and probably explains why I spent a lot of time in the 70s and 80s having skin cancers removed from my head and neck! Sailing in the Gulf all summer in a pair of bathing trunks could not have helped either.

breakfasted at 5am and the four of us prepared to leave - but it was snowing. So much for even short range weather forecasting in the Karakorum. But by 7am it was lightening and Tony decided we would push off anyway. Enough snow had fallen to make progress painfully slow. Jawed and Alan led, Tony and I acted as porters. After four hours slogging up to our knees we managed to get on to the ridge - the view made it almost worthwhile! We looked across at the great white hulk of Haramosh and down into a wooded valley 10,000 feet below us. We pitched camp, wished Alan and Jawed *au revoir* and descended down our fixed rope in a 'white out'. We'd been lucky to reach the ridge in time.

It was 1.30pm by the time we reached camp two. The other four should have been there but there was no sign of them. We had seen two climbers leave camp one at 9.30am so we were worried. Altitude and tiredness were taking their toll. I had a splitting headache but Tony decided we must carry on down and look for them. Happily we soon saw Peter and George climbing towards us through the mist. It transpired there had been a minor mutiny at camp one, Fred and Tom had decided the weather was too bad and assumed we would have stayed in camp two. Peter and George had disagreed. OK, neither of them had the mountain experience of Fred and Tom but climbers who stick to Alpine lore will seldom climb Himalayan peaks. I hope this does not sound as if I am decrying the 'classical' experience of Alpine climbing, but the Himalayas are the proverbial 'whole new ball game'. The frustrations are certainly greater.

The night was disturbed. I was awakened about am by strangled cries and by the light of my torch saw Tony clawing up the tent wall. I called out: "Tony! Wake up!"

He did so, fighting for breath and gasped that he had dreamed he was back on Haramosh. Later he apologised for disturbing my sleep! A very typical reaction from such a man, but hardly needed in view of his horrific experience on that mountain in 1957.[1]

Without kit we climbed back to the ridge in two hours, in swirling mist, but were still afforded a fine view of Nanga Parbat when we arrived. The weather now looked ominous, a dark front filling the south west horizon. We spotted Alan and Jawed at the foot of the rock base of the peak.

"They're late," said Tony abruptly. Peter and George joined us and together we set off for the top camp where Alan and Jawed had slept, only about 500 feet further up the ridge. From here we could see they were now climbing much faster, in fact within the hour we heard a cheer and saw Alan waving his ice axe. They had made the east peak of Malubiting. He disappeared as they set off along a ridge, hidden to us, to the west summit.

Tony led us under the bergschrund below the ice face by which he thought they would descend - it was a more direct route and with the use of ice screws would provide a rapid descent. He was concerned about the weather and was already planning to evacuate the high camps rather than try to put more climbers on the summit. It was not long before a shower of snow on our

[1] Ralph Barker's *The Last Blue Mountain* chronicles the tragedy of the Oxford University Haramosh Expedition Tony had led in 1957 when Bernard Jillott and Rae Culbert had died.

heads heralded Alan and Jawed's return. They too had decided to call it a day and descend, satisfied to have the east peak under their belts. We saw them safely down and returned to their camp. Tony and I then descended to camp three to prepare a brew and food for the others. Between us we managed to spill three saucepans of water before getting the tea made - such are the effects of fatigue and anoxia. Camp three was at about 22,500 feet.

By the time Tony and I had stopped snapping at each other it was 6.15pm and the other four arrived. Alan and Jawed were exhausted. We saw them fed and watered, then descended to camp two, where we found Fred and Tom, overtly solicitous for our well-being. This was just as well as we were well and truly knackered by then and could not face food but swallowed pints of coffee, Ribena and tomato soup. I was reminded of Howard Somervell's comment on returning from the high camps of Everest in 1924: "I'm told I drank seventeen cups of tea - but I can hardly believe I was that abstemious."

Next morning dawned gloriously. So much, I thought, for our weather front and Tony's forebodings. Peter and George descended to camp one while Tony and I made up for lost time by eating sausage, bacon, beans, steak and kidney pudding from 7am to 9am. Meanwhile Tom and Fred went back up to help Jawed and Alan down. We descended to camp one with the help of Assad and Mohammed Hussein, the giant we called 'John Ridd', after the character in *Lorna Doone*.

I was able to visit the latter in his village, Hissar, near Skardu, in 1999. His memory had largely gone - but he recalled days spent on K2 in 1953 with Dr Charles Houston's expedition, of which Tony had been a member, and survived a storm lasting ten days at over 24,000 feet - but he could remember little else. It was nevertheless a privilege to meet such a stalwart again.

I had spoken too soon. By 1pm snow clouds were massing to the west and we just got our tents up in time. There is only one word to apply to Karakorum weather - unpredictable. I was sharing a tent with Jawed and we both slept late. I awoke feeling liverish - a family feeling caused, I suspect, by my grandfather's partiality for brandy: still, we breakfasted off oatmeal blocks, bacon and beans - Jawed went hungry as he steadfastly refused to eat any 'pork products' as a good Muslim. We packed up camp one, then Peter and I decided to climb up to the col to our north, between Malubiting and Spantik, which would have afforded us a view of the Hispar glacier. But the snow was too wet and I managed to skid on icy moraine and stuck a crampon into my arm - in retrospect, no mean gymnastic achievement. So the withdrawal from the mountain began, with tempers fraying in the wet weather. Peter ticked off Fred for not carrying a big enough load: George on the other hand could hardly be seen under his. I thought at the time, he would make fine SAS fodder. Eventually everything and everyone were gathered at dust camp.

From here on 6 August, Tony, Peter, George, Fred, Jawed and I left for the Haramosh La. We had to cross the head of the Chogo Lungma first and after three hours ground to a halt in a wilderness of seracs. While we lunched,

Tony and Fred sought a route up to the lateral moraine beneath a peak named the 'Riffelhorn' - presumably by the Bullock Workmans. Later we scrambled up a steep snow slope and found a grassy patch upon which the intrepid pair had built a cairn. It was bliss to be once more on grass, sprinkled with gentians as a bonus. George was over-tired after carrying too heavy a load, too tired to sleep he said - but I fixed this with a Seconal tablet.

Next day we trudged on up towards the La and before the weather closed in had a wonderful view of Haramosh itself, a massive snow dome unlike so many of the spires that comprise Karakorum peaks. After skirting two ice falls we pitched camp between mighty crevasses and made a mental note not to wander too far from the tent. (Pee bottles precluded most nocturnal rambles but dodgy bowels were an ever present threat.) We watched in awe a massive avalanche come down the opposite wall of the glacier below us and reach as far as the Bullock Workman camp we had left that morning...

It snowed heavily during the night but cleared sufficiently in the morning to allow us to reach the La where we built two cairns in memory of Bernard Jillott and New Zealander Rae Culbert who had died on the mountain two years previously. Fred led us in prayer for their souls which reduced Tony to tears. For those of us who had read *The Last Blue Mountain* this was hardly surprising. I cannot think of any epic save Shackleton's escape to South Georgia from the Antarctic ice, to equal it.

Tony and George then descended into the Mani valley, down which Tony had withdrawn from the mountain in 1957. The rest of us returned the way we had come, considerably faster, and made dust camp by evening. There we found mail had arrived to cheer us in our sombre mood.

It took two days to reach Arandu where tea and cigarettes awaited us, the latter being as much to discourage flies as for pleasure. In Tony's absence we pigged it on omelettes and 'pirattas'. The Lambardar saw his 'meal ticket' about to depart and became more intrusive than ever. When he demanded to use first my toothpaste, then my tooth brush, I decided enough was enough. I applied a thick layer of Anusol (a proprietary ointment used for treating piles) to the brush and then enjoyed watching him trying to part his teeth as the ointment adhered firmly to his gums! Hardly in the Hippocratic tradition: but to balance this the patient who had been gored by a bull and whose abdominal wall I had sutured appeared later and allowed John Clegg to remove the nylon sutures which were beginning to fester after a month. However the incision held... I just prayed he didn't cough before we were well on our way to Skardu.

So the expedition drew to a close... but there was one more excitement in store. When we reached the banks of the Shigar river we found we could float down to Skardu on 'zakhs'. These craft consisted of inflated goats' skins lashed together with the odd bit of timber stretched across them to make a 'deck'. Two or three to a boat we survived a rough passage downstream, albeit somewhat damp, and enjoyed competing with each other, while our Balti paddlers entered into the spirit of the thing - when they weren't avoiding rocks. Terra firma, bunks and showers were never more welcome.

9
A PUNJAB INTERLUDE

I still had several weeks at my disposal before I was due back in Kuwait. We flew back to 'Pindi in our Bristol Freighter, then, after the boring business of 'debriefing', we started repacking, helped by the last surviving British officer in the Pakistan Army.[1]

Some of us opted to go up to Murree for rest and recuperation. This hill station had known better days. We stayed in the Hotel Cecil (which finally closed in 1998) and behaved, I suppose, like any group of young British soldiers would have done - walked the streets, drank coffee and bargained for carpets, while some of us rode or even played golf! Our arrival at the links was clearly a red letter day, each player had five caddies! It was cool after the hot dusty plains. We were tired and slept a lot. Robin Platt was probably right when he remarked: "The only thing to do in a place like this is to devote oneself to the full-time pursuit of a girl!"

Alas, we didn't find any so we did not have the opportunity for 'poodle faking' like our predecessors.

The others returned to Karachi and the UK while Jawed and I went off on holiday to Swat, as he wasn't due to rejoin his regiment, the 6th Frontier Force Rifles, until September. Jawed had been at the Pakistan Military Academy with the Wali's son, whom we hoped would be an 'open sesame' for this rugged mountain state. However, it was not to be; we got the impression he had been exploited enough by his erstwhile colleagues in the army.

So we catered for ourselves, walked the hills and passed the days agreeably. Jawed, I think, represented the ideas of young Pakistan at the time. Despite being a serving officer himself he regarded the military rule of Ayoub Khan as a 'stop gap' while the country braced itself to become an Islamic Republic. My old-fashioned imperial instincts wanted him to say that membership of the Commonwealth was important - but he dismissed this as a bagatelle, Pakistan should be a member only if it suited her. This attitude was reflected by those we met, particularly the young students. The elderly were careful not to hurt my feelings and expressed admiration for what the British had done in the sub-continent!

We returned to Rawalpindi where Jawed needed to show his face and I was left to my own devices. I went to see a Fakir whom I suspect had assumed the impressive title of 'Professor' Khudabux. Having felt the shape of my

---

[1] Brigadier Rodham, known to all as Roddy, held the post of Officer in Command Army Sports at GHQ. Dear Roddy, a punctilious gentleman of the old school whom Noel Coward must have had in mind when he wrote The Indian Army Officer, lived in a suite at Flashman's Hotel. I met him again in 1962, on our ill-fated Khunyang Chish expedition, when he proved to be a source of great comfort. He retired soon after this and went to live with his sister in Woking - not a good idea? When I returned to Rawalpindi in 1998 I was relieved to find he had 'come home' and was buried in the Christian cemetery. Sue Farrington, fellow BACSA member and the authority on British cemeteries in Pakistan, took us there one cloudy morning, where we found Roddy's handsome headstone, installed by one Mohammed Istaq, stating he had died in 1973.

head he concluded I was a Canadian engineer working on the Warsak Dam project. Thus, his subsequent predictions that my first wife would have seven or nine letters in her name, that she would die aged 45, after which I would marry a noble lady of eastern birth and be recognised for my 'good works' carried rather less weight! (Though I think Binnie -her second name, Pauline, seven letters! - was relieved when she celebrated her 46th birthday.

At lunch we met the liaison officer who had been with the ill-fated Warburton expedition on Batura Mustagh the previous month. He seemed ineffectual and Jawed's comment was: "Why the hell do they have to send drips like that with expeditions when there are dozens of young Pakistani officers longing to go to the mountains?"

While applauding his sentiments I reflected ruefully that the other two Pakistani officers who had been with us, Abdul Ghani and Inayat Khan, were not the sort of guys with whom I would have chosen to go into the jungle; similarly, I think they would both have preferred to be well away from us. Tony's comment on Inayat Khan reflected his attitude to Pathans - they were 'black' or 'white': "Bad valley, where he comes from. We never recruited from there!"

Next day Jawed decided we would push on to his home in Jhelum. We caught a bus which Jawed, with the military arrogance I had come to expect, commandeered. His expedition kit (and mine) filled the back seats; and smaller travellers clung to the luggage rack, or the roof. One might have thought that Jawed's behaviour had been inherited from the Raj: but no, he was a representative of their ruling class (his full name being Rajah Jawed Akhter Khan) and the poor accepted it with no trace of resentment. Islamic society is stratified.

On arrival we dropped our kit at his cousin's house, then went to visit his uncle who was the district commissioner. I was struck by his heavily hen-naed hair - age may be respected in the east but not its tell tale signs! - and the overwhelming maleness that pervaded the house! We drank tea and sat... and sat... from time to time a visitor would be ushered in with a request or a complaint. Whether in deference to my presence or not I do not know, but most of the business was conducted in English. Perhaps it was to impress me, in which case it did, for the pleasure of hearing Edwardian English! One Ikram Hussein, late of Probyn's Horse came in and was introduced to me.

"What a splendid welcome to Pakistan you gave me! It was the best mess I have ever known! And what a splendid chap your colonel is!" I gushed.

At this point Jawed kicked my ankle and whispered: "Steady! He was cashiered for the fiddling the mess accounts - but he's related to us..."

He left the office armed with a letter of introduction, probably more like an employment order, to the manager of the British contractor, Gammon, who had formed a consortium with Mothercat, old friends from Kuwait, to build a new camp for an armoured division.[1] But most of the time was spent just sitting, gazing over the lawns, waiting for Paradise?

---

[1] Mothercat was in turn a Scottish-Lebanese consortium, born in Aden and evicted to Kuwait after Britain's withdrawal, of Motherwell Bridge and the Contracting and Trading Company of Beirut, founded by the late Emil Bustani and subsequently run by his widow after he died in an air crash. Thereby hangs another tale.

We stayed the night. Next morning Jawed borrowed a Land Rover and drove us to his village. Behind us a Skoda carried our kit. We crossed flat plains with corn waving in the breeze until we reached a hill upon which his village sprawled. Jawed's family, Rajputs, came here a 100 years ago with their followers and built his family home - now in a ruinous condition. We stayed in the modern bungalow alongside it. There were about 300 inhabitants, some farming landlords, the remainder potters - the latter being one of a few acceptable occupations for the ruling caste other than fighting or farming. The surrounding villages supplied the peasants who tilled the fields. As in Ireland there is no law of primogeniture so the land parcels became smaller and smaller as numerous (male) offspring came into into their inheritance. I had no sleep that night due to barking dogs who knew no difference between day and night.

Jawed's father, huge and stooped, had served 31 years in the Punjab Regiment and had reached the rank of captain in the old British Indian Army. He had been a contemporary of General Mirza Khan the current Commander-in-Chief. He received me politely enough but no longer seemed interested in anything outside the village. Jawed then introduced me to his mother who shook my hand in silence - then in Punjabi told us to be careful. Perhaps Jawed had told her we were going to Lahore?

She was a handsome woman with sparse grey hair but an attack of Bell's palsy had sadly left her with a lop-sided face. At least within the confines of this village women were allowed to demonstrate their existence! None were veiled and I was struck by their graceful movements, no doubt encouraged by the pots they carried on their heads - which I could barely lift when filled with water from one of the village wells.

There was a communal chapatti oven. Cows however were tethered in the courtyards of individual houses. A communal generator provided enough

Zakhing back to Skardu.

power for lighting and fans. There were no refrigerators. Food seemed to consist of interminable pilaus, curiously, and to me unpleasantly, flavoured with excessive cardamom. However Jawed said: "Still after all these years away from home this is the only food I really enjoy."

I noted in my diary I had a bathroom 'en suite' but 'no loo'. There were however male and female 'lines' behind the village to squat, with piped water to hand. I don't think any Rajput would demean himself by becoming a plumber and grappling with the concept of a flush system.

The monsoon was around. From time to time purple clouds whirled up from the south, passed over our heads and soaked us before crashing on the hills of Azad Kashmir to the north.

Nevertheless, one day we went on a boar hunt. The family rightly doubted my competence with firearms (I was a dead shot with a Sten gun at 25 yards but not much use beyond that), so put a bodyguard of four peasants armed with spears around me. The 'family' were variously armed with carbines, a .303 Lee Enfield, a Luger (brought back from the western desert by Jawed's father) and a 12 bore. We crossed the river and entered tall grass where our noisy progress soon disturbed a boar, who broke cover and headed for sparse scrub where we pursued - and lost him. But not only was honour satisfied, we had also frightened him away from the sugar cane fields and driven him towards India! Apparently there had been no wild boar around the village prior to Partition.

The time came for us to leave. I felt honoured that I had been allowed to live 'en famille' with a traditional Rajput family; and probably should have appreciated it more. We took a bus from Jhelum to Lahore where we found that Faletti's, a flagship of the Oberoi hotel chain in Pakistan, was full. We went perforce to the Braganza which excited a snort of contempt from Jawed: "Typical!"

Not, I suspect, just because it was dirty and ill-lit but also because it was run by an Anglo-Indian family. The intolerance shown toward this 'race' by indigenous Pakistanis seemed worse than the contempt that, sadly, was demonstrated by many British. But what a significant role they had played in the development of the sub-continent! Why, there would have been no railway system without them. I suspect that 'class' played a large part in people's attitudes - I've never heard anyone belittle Colonel James Skinner, founder of Skinner's Horse, for his colour; but then his mother was a princess.

Anyway, we went slumming. Jawed took me to the notorious 'diamond market', home of whores, hedonism and high life. To get there we went by rickshaw through the railway slums where workers and hangers-on of Pakistan Western Railway lived. Then past the Moghul fort and through the old city gate into the market. My abiding recollection is one of noise - no one was ready to communicate save at the tops of their voices and the streets were packed. Only the whores from Swat lining the streets were silent; they made no attempt to accost us. The noisiest were the 'smart set', rich young Pakistanis, of both sexes, out on the town. I learned that historically this had always been the quarter where courtesans and actresses were housed in elegant two storey houses, from whose balconies they could gaze safely down at the mob beneath - a 'mob' which rivalled only that of Baghdad, when it became loose, in terms of violence.

Jawed knew where to go and soon we were seated on the floor of an elegant room that would have done credit to a Georgian town house in Mayfair. I had no idea what to expect - but knew that in Jawed lay a sense of decorum that would not expose us to any vulgar indecency! And I was right. The first two dancers, Saida and her sister, were dressed discreetly as becomes 'Nautch' dancers and their display, as I had to be told, was in the classic Punjabi style. Music was provided by a stringed lyre, a pianola and two percussionists. As a concession to me they played a tune I vaguely recognised as *Que sera sera* as an encore. This prompted Jawed to step on the floor and push large denomination rupee notes into Saida's ample bosom. But just in case this led our hot blood to rise, the girls' aunt, who had been sitting in the shadows, walked behind him. So much for an Oriental 'nocte amorosa'!

Next day we reverted to standard tourism. We visited the great Bad Shahi Mosque, built by the Emperor Aurangzeb, and my knees ached after climbing the 206 steps to the top of the tallest minaret. I estimated that the Mosque of Omar in Jerusalem would fit comfortably into just the prayer ground. Size apart the overall impression I thought less dramatic than the Great Mosque of Isfahan where the strongly coloured tiles contrasted with the pale pink walls. Then we went to the Shalimar Gardens - ah! There was no sense of disappointment here. Created on a site of over 40 acres in the space of a year (1641) by the Emperor Shahjehan this is still an enchanted world of terraces, footpaths and fountains where I could have dreamed all day... Jawed had to spoil it by saying how much more beautiful it must have been before the Sikhs had looted all the marble from the pavilions 150 years ago.

"Stupid as a Sikh!" was one of the expressions he used when annoyed by an incompetent. More racial intolerance - the mutual massacres between Sikhs and Punjabis at the time of Partition were very recent, I conceded; and no doubt each side was as bad as the other. It was a wise man who said: "Never interfere in a civil war." He could have added: "or afterwards."

So to Nico's in the Mall, a coffee shop run by an Italian who had served as a catering officer in the British Indian Army. These were the days when we expected all Italians to be ice-cream vendors or restauranteurs - perhaps because they did it so well? It was a bit like being in the King's Road back in the mid-1950s when the first coffee bars opened.

And so to Peshawar: I said a reluctant farewell to Jawed who tucked me into a bunk on the Khyber Mail at Lahore Railway Station - still basking in its recent glory as the film set for *Bhowani Junction* - and we rattled off into the night. I was going to miss him.

10
INTO AFGHANISTAN

Through contacts made on my earlier visit I was able to hitch a life on an International Harvester Company truck going to Kabul. Actually getting started was a tale of Oriental exasperation - such as an incident filling up with 43 gallons of diesel then having to empty it all out again to satisfy some 'gook' that we were not smuggling anything in the tank. (In those days Afghanistan was a poverty-stricken country, hashish not being so universally popular.) But... five hours after I'd pitched up... we were off. The truck was heavily laden with wheat and the driver would not engage a higher gear than third so we literally 'ground' up the Khyber.

It was 10 September, about three months since our previous visit. At Torkhan we went through customs and entered Afghanistan. The passport official knew only one European language, German, and couldn't understand why I wanted to visit his country - the only British in the country were on the Embassy staff and flew to and from Pakistan!

Grudgingly he let me through, having copied out my entry visa (twice). I was uncomfortably aware of the presence of an armed soldier standing by our truck. Closer inspection revealed he was a Chinese CT. What was he doing here? I smiled winningly and got a blank stare in return.

The mountain scenery began to fade into flat brown desert as we progressed - slowly. Road builders... check posts... minor breakdowns, e.g. a loose valve... prayers. At one check post I saw another armed Chinese CT sentry who seemed anxious to talk, so on impulse I shook his hand firmly and said: "Good day!" The effect was totally unexpected. He turned and ran. At the next stop we ate chicken and chapattis and drank filthy water, watched by an Afghan cop who steadily consumed bottle after bottle of Coca Cola. My driver explained that Coca Cola was believed to contain an aphrodisiac. This chap was going to have a problem, I thought. I noted that his otherwise neat military appearance was spoiled by his gaping fly buttons, but decided it would allow for ease of urination as well as copulation.

We came to the Kabul Gorge. By now I was hot, tired and becoming increasingly irritated by our repeated halts at the behest of army patrols, rock falls and broken-down vehicles blocking the road. The hill we faced seemed interminable and hateful. At one halt I drank five cups of tea and still hadn't passed water since leaving Peshawar.

The change when it came was sudden and dramatic - we were at the top of the pass, the rugged landscape bathed in moonlight and the air cool. Another truck behind us stopped and the driver produced fresh melon and I my emergency supply of fruit cake. It was a celebration.

"Here we will rest. It is Allah's Garden," said my driver. It was in fact the top of the Lataband Pass at 7,000 feet. I was not about to argue. I lay on my back and marvelled at the stars, wondering whether Dr Brydon had had a similar chance to relax when he was riding in the opposite direction over a century earlier... the ground was soft and I slept.

We arose at dawn and at 6.30am we were in Kabul. My driver bade me farewell, recommended the Hotel de Kabule (sic), put me in a tonga and waved me on my way. He had not been a very inspiring companion but then he had not asked to be burdened with a passenger. Anyway I think I was still feeling the effects of our expedition - curiosity jaded and surfeited by scenery.

The Hotel de Kabule turned out to be dead rough, used by the lowest type of commercial traveller. I wasn't that broke so I got back into my tonga, shook my head and said to the driver, hoping he read his Koran: "I want a better hotel," in Arabic. It worked. Soon we stopped outside the Hotel Kabul, (I think there had been a misunderstanding initially). This was a very new, Russian-style, gleaming concrete shoe box. Inside it was an astonishing mixture of good and bad. My room had twin beds made of plywood and plasterboard, but the walls were stucco and spotless, the lino new and squeaky clean. The plywood cupboard fell over when I tried to open the door. In a cubby hole was a wash basin, with a cold tap, that emptied into a runnel in the floor that led through the outer wall. I was surprised to see from the window that there was a down pipe connected to it. There was no light.

I went to breakfast, served at a long communal table at which sat a motley crowd of Russians, Chinese and the inevitable aid workers from the west. I was served a passable omelette by an Afghan waiter in dinner jacket and black tie, whose sartorial elegance was spoiled by the filthy shirt cuffs that in turn exposed the flea bites on his wrists.

Everyone minded their own business. I heard no English spoken. Several German-speakers approached me and when I answered: "Nicht festein," they shook their heads in puzzlement. I know I look like a Kraut but I think the explanation was simply that there were indeed many Germans working across the east at that time, survivors of World War II who had found life restricting under the Allied Occupation, if not actually humiliating. In view of the slaughter among men of a marriageable age German women were ready to risk marriage to Orientals - as we were to find in Saudi Arabia a few years later. The British on the other hand stayed mainly in their old stamping grounds, whether or not they had yet gained their independence.

Anyway I went out to see the sights of Kabul alone. There was a curious mix of cultures, some streets and buildings looked pure Persian, while others would not have looked out of place in a Flemish town. Most of the inhabitants wore European dress, although early next morning I found the outskirts of the town thronged with peasants in traditional dress with their donkeys. In the main street grills covered numerous dark holes which reminded me of *oubliettes* though I suspect they were to cope with the floods that must pour down from the surrounding mountains in rainy weather; or the water thrown from windows which seemed the accepted way of emptying jugs.

I took a tonga to the Siemens shop to get my camera fixed where I met a successful English-speaking German entrepreneur who had started exporting dried apricots on a commercial scale. Then to the British Embassy, still set in its enormous grounds like those of an English country mansion, with what was once a defensible wall - clearly we had not wanted a repeat of 1872! The embassy building reflected the hey day of Empire and I enquired whether there was a vacancy for a resident medical officer. Alas, no joy; but I was able to fix a lift back to Peshawar in a United Nations truck.

Meanwhile, there was one more dream to fulfil... to see Matthew Arnold's "Bright Oxus, knowing once the speed it had in High Pamir", now called more prosaically the Amu Darya. Again I was able to hitch a lift with a member of the Embassy staff and two days later I was on a mountain top, under a leaden grey sky, gazing at a sluggish river winding through brown rushes in a flat and otherwise arid land. Ah well, there was much else to be thankful for.

Then it was time to return to Peshawar. It was an uneventful trip. There I had a last contact to 'activate'. Tony had urged me to visit Colonel Roger Bacon. He had been the last British political agent in the North West Frontier Province in 1947 and had lived through stirring times. After Partition - for him, a tight rope he'd had to walk during the subsequent Muslim-Hindu clashes in Kashmir - he'd opted to stay on and was managing a sugar factory in Mardan. He kindly sent a car for me to Peshawar and I spent a fascinating day with this remarkable man.[1]

During our day together I learned that they produced half a million tons of sugar the previous year and production was being increased to 5,000 tons a day. The sugar cane came to the mills by the narrow gauge North West Railway. The waste cane was used either by the villagers for fuel or in the boilers. The cane was crushed by rollers in six mills and the juice heated in copper tubes, treated with sulphur and carbon dioxide, evaporated until it became a syrup, then spun in a centrifuge before being dried and sacked.

After my tour he reminisced about the number of times he'd been shot at; and how, when the sugar mill was starting, he'd used an Afridi battalion to load the cane from the farms onto the railway cars. Whereupon his men started to push the wagons up the line towards Mardan, around 70 miles away. They hadn't expected an engine to be provided.

⋘ ⋘ ⋘ ⋘ ⋘ ⋘ ⋘ ⋘ ⋘ ⋘ ⋘ ⋘ ⋘

It was time to return to Kuwait. I travelled on the Khyber Mail back to Karachi, then to Kuwait aboard SS Dwarka of the British India Line.[2] I was the only first class passenger on board for the five day voyage to Kuwait and had an air-conditioned cabin. As a result I contracted the worst, stinking,

---

[1] You can find out more about him in the book *The Gilgit Rebellion* by the late Major Willy Brown.

[2] Two months later Omani rebels attempted to assassinate His Excellency Ahmed bin Ibrahim, the Minister of Interior in Muscat and Oman, fondly known as 'Electric Whiskers', aboard this same ship. Two months after that, her sister ship SS Dara, was sunk by the same rebels off Dubai when over 300 passengers drowned.

cold I have ever experienced. Through bleary eyes I watched the captain and purser fleece the wretched deck passengers at 'housy housy' each evening. I'm not sure how it was done but the British officers cleaned up every time and the Indians lost. Neither experience was elevating after three months under Asian skies.

−−− −−− −−− −−− −−− −−− −−− −−− −−− −−− −−− −−− −−−

I landed from *SS Dwarka* in Kuwait harbour in early October, carrying my precious Turkoman carpet under my arm. The customs official accepted this as my prayer mat.[1]

Getting back to work wasn't easy, even as a locum.

"What on earth do you expect?" said Vivian crossly, while she sat painting me, still bearded; and intent on showing the fear in my eyes which she was convinced I had experienced in the mountains. The outcome was an alarming squint! The picture is still on view in the downstairs loo at home.

One day I undertook to take Allen Mersh's mare our for exercise. Allen was our surgeon, another old India hand, who had come to Kuwait from the IMS. Joyce, his wife, was a fanatical equestrian. The animal had not been exercised for too long and as soon as she sniffed the open desert, she was off. Not an experienced rider I could do little but cling on and slowly turn her until she began to describe tighter and tighter circles. Then without warning she dropped dead on top of me. I managed to extricate myself, limped back to the stables and rang Joyce; to learn that Allen had just rung to tell her there was a berth for her and the mare, on the next UK-bound boat. Joyce was going to Somerset to retire. The sad end to this drama was cremating the corpse on one of the company's rubbish dumps that evening.

I still don't think it was my fault, perhaps the animal had had an underlying heart disease and I had saved the family a small fortune! Nevertheless I was treated like a pariah thereafter by the equine fraternity in Ahmadi.

A happier experience was the chance to become a film star. BP had engaged a production team to make a film called *Sweat without Tears*; to enlighten new arrivals in the Middle East and especially their tanker crews sailing to the Persian Gulf. The film followed the adventures of a 'sand prospector' arriving in Kuwait and his subsequent search for sand... A humourous approach to the subject had been ordained.

He was shown digging in the noonday sun without his shirt and not bothering to drink as: "It only makes me sweat."

The script contained some classic 'one liners'. Bending down to flick something off his shovel he growled: "Bloody gold!" before redoubling his efforts.

Then came his inevitable collapse and the scene in the clinic where he was cooled on our heat stroke table. The patient was then taken to his hospital bed where, still painted with cochineal, he was forced to listen to a lecture from me in my white coat, seated on his bed eating his grapes. On the other

[1] I had tracked this particular rug from a dealer in Murree all the way to Kabul, where I had eventually purchased it for the equivalent of £200. A few years later Harrods valued it at £100! England was a better source of Oriental carpets in those days.

side of the bed stood one of our more glamourous nursing sisters, holding a kidney dish. We spent a long time with the sound crew synchronising the 'ping!' as I flicked grape pips into it.

The closing words of my lecture: "You nearly cooked yourself!" were the cue for my colleague, John Dilley, playing the part of the hapless prospector, to drift off into a delirious sequence where he imagined he was being spiced and marinated on a huge platter.

Christmas came and under John Guthrie's direction we put on the best show ever. Doctors, like lawyers, are constantly acting. This I believe accounts for the high quality of hospital Christmas concerts. John also saw them as a chance to unite members of the department. He never missed the opportunity to appear, like Alfred Hitchcock, in any scene he could - preferably in 'drag'!

This year's theme had, as ever, political undertones. KOC had reached its apogee and was now busily shedding services, other than those directly concerned with producing oil. As many as twenty senior staff, American as well as British, were being made redundant every month.

So our theme was the 'contracting out' of the medical department, the successful bid coming from 'Kuococabana' and its Proper Rioter, Don Juan Guthrino. This gave us all the opportunity to dress up as Mexican caballeros and senoritas and sing songs about our 'adobe haciendas' in Ahmadi. Management were marginally amused.

11
MEDICAL MERCENARY

After my locum post ended on 1 January 1960 I had planned to spend the next few months skiing in Austria before seeking a training post in radiology in the spring. I'd kept an eye on the job market in the airmail BMJ and one day was surprised to see an advertisement for a senior medical officer for the Kuwait Army which stated: "Had to be a Britisher with a first class record". There was more to that effect but... well, I had nothing to lose so I contacted Tam Pierce, who was back as British Army liaison officer, in his house on Shuweikh beach and explained my interest.

A few days later he took me to Public Security Headquarters in Kuwait and I was ushered in to the presence of Sheikh Abdulla Mubarak, Field Marshal, Commander-in-Chief Army, Air Marshal of the (embryonic) Air Force, Admiral on the (non-existent) Fleet and Head of Public Security. He was also in charge of broadcasting, civil aviation, posts and telegraphs; in fact most things apart from public works, health and education. He was also deputy ruler and the ruler was his nephew. We exchanged greetings and after struggling with my weak Arabic he decided to use his Palestinian secretary, Hanni Kaddoumi, to delve beyond pleasantries. After a few minutes Hanni spoke with the Sheikh, who gazed at me and said: "Tayyib! Ruuh ill'al mustashfa!" (Good! Go to the hospital!)

It appeared I was 'in'; I had little chance to say anything more on that occasion. Hanni just said: "Don't worry, everything will be as you want."

I hesitated and glanced at Tam. He indicated that the interview was over and followed me out.

"See you later. You'll get used to it!" he said. (I did eventually).

A nervous Lebanese doctor, Georges Cocony, was summoned to take me to the Public Security Hospital. Until now there was an ad hoc medical service, Georges being the nominal boss. His main duty seemed to be breaking in Abdulla Mubarak's new shoes - desert dwellers used to sandals always found shoes a trial. The hospital was to the west of the city in the area known as Jewan. Like the name Soweto, beloved totem of African culture among British lefties, its name was a relic of the British contractors who had built Kuwait's infra-structure in the early 1950s - J1 on their maps, like 'South West Township' on the outskirts of Johannesburg. The building had once housed contractors' offices. Now some rooms contained a clinic, a laboratory and some small wards. There were a motley crowd of Northern Arab orderlies and clerks milling around.

It was more like a salesroom than a hospital. I tried to keep an impassive face. I was shown a DDT store which must surely have contained half the world's existing supplies at the time: its abuse, alas, was a typical Kuwaiti reaction of the time - we can afford it so let's spray the world! In the packed

Brigadier Mubarak Abdulla Jabir Al Sabah, OC Kuwait Army, 'The Boy', 1960.

forecourt was a brand new Chevrolet, this, I was informed, belonged to a 'firash' (messenger boy) who used it as a taxi when he wasn't in the hospital. I was introduced to a Lieutenant Mahmoud Awed - this rank was related only to his salary - he was a dresser but ran a car hire firm as well. No one could sack him as he had some hold over the Sheikh...

With my head in a whirl I was driven back to Public Security HQ where I told Hanni that I would need some time to prepare a three phase operation to militarise, extend and then rebuild a military hospital on more orthodox lines. He urged me not to be long. Another Kuwaiti trait of the time was to expect things to be done yesterday: that, and the belief that if you dreamed something would happen then it did, were the main bugbears of the two and a half years I survived in the Kuwait Armed Forces.

A few words of explanation. Until recently the Kuwait Army had been known as the Frontier Force, consisting of mobile infantry who kept an eye on the borders with Iraq and to a lesser extent, Saudi Arabia. Now it was turning into an army, with artillery, Centurion tanks and the rest of the paraphernalia that goes with it - including a flight of Westland 'Whirlwind' helicopters under contract from Bristows. It was commanded by Sheikh Mubarak Abdulla Jabir, commonly known by those working for him, as 'the Boy', not so much because of his youth but to distinguish him from 'Dad', the name given to Sheikh Abdulla Mubarak - who of course also rejoiced in the soubriquet of 'Sam'.

Sam was in overall charge of public security which was devolving into Armed Forces and Police. The latter was commanded by Sheikh Sa'ad, son of the Ruler (Abdulla Salim) by a negro wife. Whereas there was a lesser Kuwaiti Sheikh, Saleh, as second in command of the army, Sa'ad's deputy was Colonel Khalil Shuheiber, late of the Palestine Police. His cousin, Jabra Shuheiber, also ex-Palestine Police, was something like Quartermaster General in the army. But despite his colonel's rank, power lay with the next in line, Major Abdulla Said Rajib Al Rif'ai, a Kuwaiti.

This, in general terms, was the game plan - if you were a Kuwaiti you held authority over any superior who was not, e.g. another Arab or an Asian.

The pitch was further queered by a shadowy character of Kuwaiti-Iraqi extraction, called Abdul Latif Thuweini, who was also ranked as colonel and held the nebulous post of Deputy Head of Public Security, i.e. nominally second in command to Sam.

I remained living in Ahmadi for some months, commuting to Jewan in a huge Dodge. Jabra had offered me a house in the town, but as it had eight bedrooms I had to point out I couldn't afford a harem on my salary. I think he only offered me the house to impress me. Eventually I found a two roomed bungalow next to Dasman Palace, where the ruler lived, which Jabra grudgingly rented for me - it belonged to Sheikh Jabir al Ahmed, Minister of Finance, whom he thought had his hands on enough money already.

Within a month I was alternating between hysteria and despair. I had found that the 'dead hand of the Ottoman' still lingered in government circles - I couldn't indent for a waste paper basket without Sam's signature. I sat in my office amending 'Queen's regulations' in the hope of instilling some kind of order into the surrounding chaos; and drinking large pink gins with Tam and Clare Pearce in their home on Shuweikh Beach.

Came the unexpected - after all, this was near the source of the Arabian Nights. Sam wanted my recommendations for the Army Medical Service after two days. Despite the fact that I knew Sam could hardly read, translators Sami and Waleed, my 'office staff' of two educated Palestinians, slaved night and day. I was told to report to Mishrif Palace, Sam's main palace south of the city, at 8am. I got there to find he had left at 7am for a holiday in his seaside palace south of Beirut. Even Hanni sympathised with my state of despair. Together we concocted a 260 word cable which we sent from the palace. A reply came back that evening, agreeing to all my recommendations! (Except for my rank, I had to be satisfied with a mere majority.)

᳀ ᳀ ᳀ ᳀ ᳀ ᳀ ᳀ ᳀ ᳀ ᳀ ᳀ ᳀ ᳀

The magic signature opened the flood gates - although I still had no contract or salary! I allocated ranks, put them into khaki, laid down standards of fitness and started recruiting - for instance I managed to replace all my drivers with ex-Arab Legion soldiers. Sam remained in Beirut where he organised the recruitment of new doctors. Curiously enough those who came later told me that they only came because they were told there was an Inglesi in charge. I also learned that HMG had woken up too late to the fact that I'd got the job, having nominated the ADMS Aden for the post... but Sam had refused, saying the choice was his.

I was even able to start doing some medicine. I saw potential recruits after their initial assessment and found some fascinating cases. The army as a whole was expanding as fast as we were. The Boy used to say that Bedu were: "like rusty swords, all they need is polishing to become fine soldiers." Well... they needed feeding first.

Among the bizarre cases I saw were a man without a sternum: two soldiers with soft swellings, one over the parotid gland, another over his scapula, which I diagnosed as a parotid tumour and lipoma respectively. Both turned out to have been caused by hydatid cysts! My surgical friends in the Ministry of Health were suitably impressed. Then there were those with the stigmata of congenital syphilis, the disease so attenuated by generations of tribal in-breeding that it warranted a new name, 'begl', and produced snail-like ulcer tracks on the skin and a variety of nasal deformities due to destruction of the cartilage.

❧ ❧ ❧ ❧ ❧ ❧ ❧ ❧ ❧ ❧ ❧ ❧ ❧

Ramadan came in March and working hours were reduced to three hours a day, from 8 to 11am. If Sam was in the country then I had to conform and turn up for 'fatoor', ie. break fast at sunset, up at Mishrif Palace. It was quite difficult knowing how far one should adapt Arab, i.e. in this case, Muslim, practices. On the whole, the Kuwaitis expected me to distance myself from their ethnicity. On one occasion I joined in a Bedouin dance, along with some Kuwaiti officers, and was pushed off the floor by a pack of Sam's body-guards. So I would make token appearances with Tam.

Army Day, 1960, 'Sam' celebrating his marriage and the author in a bush hat.

Mishrif Palace, as befitted the home of the ruler's uncle, was regal. But it still bore the marks of a Bedouin owner. There were telephones in every room, including the bathrooms and loos, thus providing that most vital link in the Arab's life - access to news. There were no pictures on the walls - who had a picture in the desert? The modern stable, i.e. the garage, contained over 200 cars.

After Ramadan... the Eid. Here attendance on the first day at the Sif Palace (the Ruler's) was compulsory. We were on parade by 5am. Like all parades we stood and waited... and waited. Huge cars arrived, we sprang to attention, then some minor dignitary descended and we all stood at ease again. At last the ruler and Sam arrived. Once one had been seen... it was time for the off.

❧ ❧ ❧ ❧ ❧ ❧ ❧ ❧ ❧ ❧ ❧ ❧ ❧

I cannot pretend I was enjoying this stage of my life, isolated in an alien culture and called upon to produce miracles. Nevertheless it had its moments, though most of these were gruesome!

One Thursday afternoon in late March, I had been summoned to Sam's palace at Duba'iya, scene of the Texan chef debacle. It took a long time to get there, negotiating the heavy traffic on the coast road, for, at the weekend, people had little else to do save drive their shiny American cars up and down the few miles of tarmac that existed.

The palace guards were now uniformed, wearing RAF battledress and berets but with bright green webbing belts. I was shown onto the verandah where Sam was seated with his cronies. He wanted to show me his elbow. He spent a lot of time playing cards on the floor and had managed to give himself an elbow bursitis; but aspiration and a cortisone injection the previous week seemed to have cured this - I hasten to add I had referred him to a competent Egyptian surgeon for the procedure! He laughed when I advised him to play cards at a table in future.

The court jester was called, followed by a fat, pale, Lebanese servant, who was told to lie on his back, then try to sit up. He failed but continued to wriggle and squirm, causing hoots of laughter from the onlookers, Sam in particular nearly choking with laughter at the spectacle. The Boy, tense and unshaven - he too had been summoned at short notice - explained that this man ate too much, largely raw meat, and Sam insisted on this daily exercise. The jester continued to act as ring master for the spectacle which was becoming revolting.

Then Sam walked to the cliff edge, and shouted: "Now!"

This was the signal for the servant to struggle to his feet and dash down to the sea where he flung himself in, fully clothed. Then back he staggered up to the balcony which he tried to vault and only succeeded in crashing to the ground. The culmination of his humiliation was greeted with roars of delight. How could he do this, I wondered? The reason soon became apparent. Sam pulled a wad of 100 rupee notes out and pushed them into his hands. He bobbed, and scuttled off to his quarters. The party retired into the house. I made my formal: "Ay Khudma taal Umrak?" (Any service, Your Excellency?) and received the formal reply, "Abadan!" (never) and left. As I drove way I reflected - how much self respect must a guy lose to behave like that for £75?

❧ ❧ ❧ ❧ ❧ ❧ ❧ ❧ ❧ ❧ ❧ ❧ ❧

A few days later I learned why the Boy had been at Duba'iya. The ruler had clamped down on military expenditure - I learned this was a frequent event but seldom lasted long - and among items shelved was my second stage plan of extending the hospital. However - I'd got a contract! Not that it was worth the paper it was written on as it allowed Sam to dismiss me if I was, in his opinion, 'unsatisfactory in the performance of my duties'. Since I had no illusions about this I signed anyway.

Some fathead had asked during the Eid: "Where is the army?" So Sam had ordered an army parade. I took as little part in this as possible, my new doctors scarcely knew how to wear their uniforms, let alone march. I stuck them all in jeeps and begged my ex-Arab Legion drivers to make sure they just sat there. I opted to fly past the saluting base with Les Barker, one of the Bristow helicopter pilots, and just for the hell of it threw Sam a US Navy style salute that would have warmed the heart of any World War II 'B' movie producer. To my surprise he sprang to attention and returned a crisp British Army style salute, incongruous, alas, as he was wearing an American GI's steel helmet. But I could never have believed his vision was so acute. Looking down at the long column of vehicles snaking past him, I was irresistibly reminded of a child towing its crocodile across the desert.

Needless to say I was having problems with the new doctors. They had been put into flats, belonging to the brother-in-law of Abdul Latif Al Thuwaini, which could only be described as sordid; and they had been bugging me since they arrived. One of them, Nabil Abdul Hadi, was a cousin of Hanni Kaddoumi - would you believe? - and had already ingratiated himself with Sam so that he had become the palace doctor, i.e. he looked after the staff while I nominally was responsible for Sam's personal health. I preempted the inevitable by telling Nabil that I would be 'consultant' in future while he would be responsible for Sam's primary care.

I was trying to make these ten civilians at least look like army doctors and had got Sheikh Saleh to undertake their basic training - at least to learn how to salute! Nabil never turned up for this, being always too busy in the palace.

To my intense annoyance he did turn up to the drill parade one morning to tell me that the confidential letter I had written to Sam a week previously, asking for better accommodation for the doctors, had been agreed. An apartment block in Salamia, a new development down the coast, had been rented: and three doctors, including Nabil of course, had already been there and pinched the three ground floor flats. Meanwhile, Abdul Latif, no doubt sore at losing his cut from his brother-in-law, had been to the flats, removed the cards off the doors of the ground floor flats and taken them to Sam - who blew his top and said these three should not have new flats at all! Faced with this behaviour I told them they would draw lots for who lived where.

The next complaint was about 'on call' duties. Some of them had quasi-specialist qualifications e.g. the radiologist and the internist, and demanded to be second on call. I solved this by saying we would all take turns in being 'on call' - including me.

This, of course, cut both ways. Friday duties were particularly frustrating, as we agreed to see police as well as military personnel. All of them resented having to work on the 'Jumaa'. One day, as the umpteenth malingerer presented himself I lost my cool and flung a cut-glass ash tray at him. There was a satisfactory decline in numbers reporting sick after that if they knew the Inglesi was on duty. After 10 pm various shifty-looking individuals appeared whom I learned were spies. They all drove Volkswagen Beetles and gave the same name. I think they were bored.

Just as I began to think that farting against thunder was easier than this, we were called out on manoeuvres; and the aftermath of our successful participation in these brought new hope. It is ever so in Arabia. Tam and I were surprised that they started on the appointed day! I got to the hospital at 4.30am. Elias Hawa, our pharmacist, had got the ambulances kitted up, and we got the 'enemy' column off with its medical section, then hung around while the rest of the army slowly gathered into four long columns. I tacked the 'home team' medical section onto the HQ column behind the signal truck - not for any strategic reason but because I knew their 110 volt power points would fit my electric razor. The soldiers were wandering around still looking curiously unmilitary despite their British Paratroop steel helmets instead of the customary 'schmaag'.

The 'Boy' hawking, 1959.

The scenario for the next few days was that Sheikh Saleh and his troops, the 'enemy', would advance slowly south from the Iraqi border while the Boy would withdraw towards the Mutla Ridge, the prominent feature across the north of Kuwait Bay. On the final day Sheikh Saleh would attack and be repulsed in a noisy climax.

Meanwhile there was little enough for me to do. The Boy had established his HQ in an enormous white marquee that was visible for miles. Tam was also spare so we persuaded Les Barker to fly us to a spot where we could keep an eye on the comings and goings from the marquee and lunched off whisky, ham and camembert cheese - hardly what the Prophet would have expected from his warriors. But He won - we had just started our feast when an open jeep roared over to us with a steel-helmeted Boy hanging on to the windscreen in approved Hollywood style.

"Tafuddal!" he cried, "Come and have lunch!"

We managed to secrete our forbidden fruits and joined him in the jeep. We spent the next three hours drinking tea and coffee, and chatting in a desultory way. Finally lunch was announced. This was served in an even larger glistening white tent erected next door while we had been 'fuddling'. Tam assured me that the only realism on exercise would be introduced by the NCOs of his training team - and he would decide when that was to be!

That night I was due to appear in the last performance of *Blithe Spirit* which Binnie Lash was producing for the Kuwait Players at the British Council. Earlier she had cast me as Charles Condamine and this had led to our meeting on a daily basis. It soon became clear that if I were to be accepted by her family I would have to learn to fly! Her father, Paul Lash was known to all and sundry as 'Splash' following a World War Two crash into the sea. After

Army parade, 1960 - the 'hardware' (Centurion tanks) which Sam had bought without telling his uncle, the Ruler.

30 years service with the RAF he had been teaching Kuwaitis to fly since the early 1950s; but as Sam ran the Aero Club he was now busily militarising this too - in fact his helicopters were the first bearers of camouflage paint. Sam was pleased to allow me to start flying training in the summer.

But right now I had to be on stage. After lunch with the Boy, post-prandial stupor was the order of the day - and I had a cunning plan. Signalling my enthusiasm I suggested to him that I must check all was well with the 'enemy', in particular their medical support. The Boy was duly impressed by my devotion to duty and Les was only too happy to get airborne again. In his enthusiasm we flew rather too far north, in fact we were hovering over a group of huts which I recognised as Safwan, the border post with Iraq. It was only when an Iraqi solder appeared from one of them, waving a rifle, that Les believed me and we went straight up. We headed south again and soon spotted a jeep with its red crescent prominent - this turned out to be Saljuq, a Turkish doctor whom I had sent to join Sheikh Saleh's troops. He was lost - a good start. We took off again, soon found Saleh who greeted us warmly. He spoke quite good English and we discussed his role in the forthcoming exercise.

He said: "It's all a sham. I could encircle Mubarak in 24 hours!" I reminded him that "ours not to reason why..."

"And look what happened to them!" he came back quick as a flash.

After coffee in a foxhole - Saleh was a real soldier - we flew back to Kuwait at dusk; and I duly trod the boards that night.

During the net few days our only medical problems were bites from scorpions and snakes. One of the latter survived an ambulance backing over it, whereupon Mubarak (my driver, not the Boy) grabbed it and raced around threatening people with it. To my amazement he ended up by kissing it. He must have known something I didn't as it certainly looked venomous. We didn't use anti-snake serum but treated all bites symptomatically - most of the soldiers had been bitten many times before.

So came the great day. There was a severe sandstorm the previous night which had blown down all the tents. The Kuwaiti officers had responded to a dare issued by one of them and had all had their heads shaved - I didn't participate - I was pretty bald already. Sergeant Elderkin, one of Tam's staff, chose to further disturb the night with a series of thunderous explosions in the interests of 'night training'. Next morning dawned cloudy but the wind had dropped. At about 8am the guests started to arrive, hundreds of sheikhs and their hangers-on. Abdul Latif turned up dressed as an army colonel - just to annoy the Boy, I assumed - then Sam in his field marshal's uniform topped with this US Army helmet. Nabil told me later that he had been walking around the palace all night wearing it.

The show started. Saleh's troops attacked and everybody fired their blanks. We demonstrated 'casevac', our medics carrying 'wounded' on stretchers to a helicopter. This went down well with the crowd. Sam then marched to a parapet and stood there, field glasses glued on the approaching enemy. This was the signal for Adolph Morath, an internationally-known photographer, and his attractive young assistant wearing a blue dress, to take photographs of him. A short dress is not recommended for desert wear: each time she bent down to hand Morath a different piece of kit - everyone stopped firing. Finally Saleh's men withdrew and everybody cheered. There was then a demonstration of field firing and Centurion tanks went charging across the desert like their ancestors on camels.

Suddenly I heard a sharp bang behind me. I looked around to see a soldier clutching his mutilated thumb, which he'd blown off with a detonator. Corporal Ibrahim, an ex-Arab Legion dresser, bandaged the stump quickly and efficiently. We had him in our helicopter in a trice and Clive Wright flew us at zero feet through the driving rain, which had just started, to Suleibikhat Hospital. Here there was an infuriating delay as the staff had already turned out for our previous 'casualties' and thought we had stage-managed another. In the end I ran to find Dom Macreadie, the British hospital superintendent, whose appearance in the accident department galvanised the largely Egyptian staff from inertia to lethargy: but the surgeon saved his thumb, after making him walk to the theatre.

Our performance during manoeuvres paid dividends, I even got some leave! But better than that, we got the OK to start planning for the new hospital. Summer doldrums descended. I noted however that: "Time flies in Kuwait as everything take twice as long to get done." In July Sheikh Saleh got married. The poor lad was dressed up in a ceremonial uniform which made him look like a circus ringmaster. Colonel Jabra told me he had been told to order it specially from Germany, but he suspected it came from Syria. Sam held the reception at Mishrif Palace which was covered in fairy lights - in fact the electric wiring became so overloaded

'Dad' gets 'hep'!

that it began to smoke... so the answer? Electric fans were produced to blow air on them! Being Arabia, the idea worked.

August was dreadful that year. There were twelve consecutive days of breathless humidity. There were 220 cases of heat stroke recorded of whom nine died: this despite the government's instruction to the contractors to halt all outside work.

We had a new Political Agent, John Richmond, who, with his wife Diana and daughters Emma and Sally and younger brother, became good friends. Within a short time of his arrival he caused a mild panic when the Agency launch, which rolled like a cow in the gentlest swell, went missing. Splash was ordered to coordinate a search, and put everything he could in the air. Even Sheikh Saad took to the sky. The launch was found the following morning, safe on the north side of Kuwait Bay, its wireless out of action.

The medical service was still short of trained staff and I was shocked when there was an outbreak of serum hepatitis among the soldiers. It didn't take long to realise we were the culprits; these were the days of glass syringes and re-useable needles, and our sterilisation procedure was shoddy. I blew my top, and sacked seventeen incompetents who had been responsible for this and other negligence. It was, alas, the kind of action which met with Arab approval. Within a week Sam had collected 25 new nurses, at higher salaries, from Beirut. On the strength of the 'high' I was now on, with respect to the authority I was (temporarily) wielding, I formed up against Sam and announced that I could not accept differential salaries within the medical service; and that if he wanted it to be organised on the same lines as the RAMC then he must accept a uniform rank and salary structure. On most occasions I would have been told to pack up and get out; but as I have said I was on a 'high' at the time: and the great thing about the Arabs is they know they only have to wait until they catch you on a 'low'.

They didn't have to wait long. In my intoxicated state I'd even asked for leave, and went home for three weeks. I met up with Binnie and we went walking on the South Downs, one of the only times she ever did! Just before leaving I was up in Ahmadi, visiting John and Viv, where I met a couple of young ex-Life Guard officers, Simon Pilkington and Richard Graves, who were spending two years globe trotting on £200 apiece. They had returned from Japan on an oil tanker, landed at the North Pier without permission, hence could not obtain exit visas as they had not entered the country. The British Consul was therefore threatening to deport them to the UK. They had already crossed China, no mean feat. I was asked if I could do anything for them. Next day I introduced them to Sheikh Saad, who was sympathetic - they used all their charm as well - and issued them with transit visas. They then met the Boy, who combined Arab hospitality with Sandhurst generosity by lending them a car, inviting them to the 'beat the retreat' ceremony that evening, and arranging them passage on a dhow travelling to Bushire next day. Well done, Mr Fixit, I thought.

12
MY STAR WANES

I returned from leave to find mayhem in my absence - what else should I have expected? My warrant officer clerk Sami (Colonel Jabra's cousin)had been sacked and the acting chief medical officer, Ghassan by name, had sent the only surgeon (a Lebanese Christian) to the desert. He had approved the installation of a company in a desert camp, where 117 men were expected to live in a hut without windows. He had sent all our ambulances to the desert, under command of the unit COs.

There were two underlying factors. The medical service was a pawn between Colonel Jabra's 'Q' Division - don't forget he was a Palestinian - and Major Abdulla Said Rajab, Chief of Ops and a Kuwaiti. And why? As the NHS knows too well, medical services cost money - not only the drugs bill but even medically approved rations, with supplementary vitamins! Within the service there was also the Muslim/Christian conflict and this had been stirred in my absence.

Well, to cut it short, I persuaded Sam he needed a doctor in Beirut to look after his palace staff there - and what better man than Ghassan? He agreed. I replaced Sami with a hand-picked PA, named Jameel Barkhowi, a Muslim replacing a Christian, and together we visited all the units to whom ambulances had been 'issued' and got them back again. After 72 hours I felt I was back in the saddle - especially when Abdulla Said Rajab came to my office and asked permission to sit down! In fact he was warming up to ask me if I would please recommend a multi-vitamin product, from a company for whom he was the agent of course, to be provided daily for the soldiers. I felt relaxed enough to gaze at the hat stand behind him and pondered - why do all Arab offices have hat stands? It's not as if they toss their 'kheffiyas' on them when they enter... the Turks didn't remove their 'tarbooshes'... perhaps Arab travellers had seen them in government offices in India?

Oh yes, we compromised - no added vitamins but I recommended a milk powder should become part of field rations... and left it to him to get the agency.

❧ ❧ ❧ ❧ ❧ ❧ ❧ ❧ ❧ ❧ ❧ ❧ ❧

My career in Arabia was always guided by a woman - not always the same one and not always directly. But fate was about to intervene. Sam had several wives and several daughters but no son. He was surging towards the apogee of his power, indeed there were already mutterings among the members of the Sabah family that he was getting 'too big for his sandals'. He needed a successor... so he married again. His new bride was a winsome lass called Suad, a princess in her own right from a branch of the Sabah family living in Southern Iraq.

I met her at Mishrif Palace shortly after the religious wedding when I had been summoned to check all the medicines which Sam had accrued over the years. (I binned the various testosterone preparations). Suad was comely and bright, and only too well aware where her responsibilities lay! It was perhaps ungracious of me to suspect even then that Sam's 'entourage' would ensure that a happy event would occur before too long.

The formal celebration of the marriage took place just before Christmas 1960 and Mishrif Palace came into its own. The fountains literally 'danced', musicians and dancers from Jordan entertained the guests, and 450 sat down to dinner.

The year ended. I was more than dimly aware that this was not a job for life. Abdulla Said Rajab came up with a new wheeze - how about a mobile hospital? He had become the agent for a British company called Rollalong Ltd, of Romsey in Hampshire, who produced trailers that could be towed by Mark II jeeps (long-wheel base). At the time I could not quite see what we needed it for; but it would be innovative and anyway, it would help British exports! I mentioned it to Sam, to protect my back, and found him enthusiastic, even envisaging needing to use it himself! He seemed worried... that was my closing thought for the year.

꧁ ꧁ ꧁ ꧁ ꧁ ꧁ ꧁ ꧁ ꧁ ꧁ ꧁ ꧁ ꧁

My diary states that Sheikh Sabah was killed on New Year's Eve. I know I had gone to Suleibikhat with the Boy to arrest him one day at the end of November, on Sam's orders. He had a house in Suleibikhat. The Boy placed sentries everywhere, then whipped a Biretta out of his pocket, flung open the door and faced an empty room. We withdrew in confusion. I cannot for the life of me recall why Sam was after him or why he was finally killed. I suspect he knew too much.

꧁ ꧁ ꧁ ꧁ ꧁ ꧁ ꧁ ꧁ ꧁ ꧁ ꧁ ꧁ ꧁

1961 started with a flurry of activity. His new marriage put Sam into overdrive - he demanded I should submit plans for a new military hospital 'next week'. He was also set on doubling the size of the army. Recruits poured in from the desert. We were scraping the barrel by now, and in addition to the usual crop of crossed eyes, crossed toes, crossed teeth and syphilis, many of them had active pulmonary Tb.

The Richmond twins, Sally and Emma, were out for the Christmas holidays and one day I took them to Mishrif Palace - Sam now lived in the White Palace, nearer town, and Mishrif was used for formal occasions. Emma gazed around her and said: "It's a giant bedouin tent! There's nothing personal here at all, just somewhere to sleep and telephone."

In the cinema there was a stereo recording of some American crooner - presumably for our benefit. Sally was excited to find one room that wasn't empty. It had a beautiful round white marble table and the walls covered, literally, with French floral prints. I wondered who on earth was responsible for that? Suad? We then drove up to the escarpment, to the north of Kuwait Bay, and in a moorland mist skipped and tumbled across the desert hand in hand, finally finding an eagle's eyrie, out of the wind, from where we saw a huge brown fox under the streaming clouds. The twins left the following evening. Ah, magic moments.

The 15th January was the Feast of the Ascension of the Prophet... so we had a holiday. I've often thought Muslims are a bit shame-faced about this celebration, their tolerance of the Christian belief in the Ascension of Christ does not really extend to their Prophet... who after all was only a man... and they seem somewhat ashamed of acknowledging such an improbable event. BOAC however celebrated by landing the first 'Comet', which Binnie and I saw as we drove up to Ahmadi. I was taking possession of *Poppett*, an X-class yacht which I had bought from 'Lofty' Colenutt, a renowned KOC sailor who ran the refinery.

Together with Dr Nigel Owen we set sail from Mina-al-Ahmadi to the Sheikh's harbour in Shuweikh, between Kuwait town and Suleibikhat, where I had acquired a mooring, thanks to the Boy. There was an angry sky and a stiff south westerly was helping big rollers onto the beach. We rounded the jetty; and the wind died. We lay there, unspeakable thoughts in our minds, as we rolled and yawed, sails flapping and boom banging. A tanker loomed above us - do Panamanians give way to sail even when we're becalmed, I wondered?

"Let's give it half an hour," said Nigel.

We rolled sickeningly in the wake of the huge tanker. Then, as if it didn't really mean it, a breeze rose from the south east. With much heaving and rolling we lurched off up the coast. None of us dared speak as the wind slowly freshened and the water began to hiss under our bows. Soon we had put fifteen miles behind us and were on the crest of the flood. Then came the rain, a hard pounding that flattened both wind and sea. We drifted round Ras Al Ardh, the easterly point of the coast, and caught the race as the wind returned - mercifully from the south east again. We set the spinnaker and creamed across the bay to Agency Point, the southern jaw of Kuwait Bay. It was time to enjoy hot tomato soup, cold beer and chapattis filled with bully beef. We charged up Kuwait Bay and six hours after leaving Mina-al Ahmadi, *Poppett* cruised quietly into her smart new home.

We drove Nigel back to Ahmadi. En route we witnessed an Arabian incident. On the outskirts of town there was a lorry in front of us, packed with Omani labourers and their household effects. They were being evicted from their barasti huts, a regular event in the lives of immigrant labourers. Suddenly one of the huts caught fire. By chance there was a water tanker between us and them, and within seconds the blazing hut and its occupants

'Dad' on army manoeuvres, 1961.

were sprayed with a high pressure hose, reducing both to a sodden mass. Four minutes later seven fire engines and an ambulance arrived. They added to the deluge. Meanwhile two barasti huts on the roadside, which had ignited earlier, were burning merrily - and a solitary policeman was jumping up and down on them. Having exhausted their water, the crews of the fire engines joined him... and eventually the fires were extinguished.

❧ ❧ ❧ ❧ ❧ ❧ ❧ ❧ ❧ ❧ ❧ ❧ ❧

I had been around for over a year and alas I have found, wherever you are, familiarity breeds contempt. I was summoned to Sif Palace to see Sam, who wanted a medical report on Abdil Latif Thuweini. He had been angling for sick leave for some time, and I had been twice to his house to examine him. I found he had a chronic bowel infestation, as many Kuwaitis had. On my second visit I was disturbed by the cries of a woman nearby.

"Listen," cried Abdul, "I think she's having a baby!"

That was the end of the matter as far as he was concerned. He got his sick leave. Next one of the Boy's school chums from Beirut was sent to me with a request that I would sign a 'chit' saying he was sick and would be delayed in returning to his work. I fudged a report - to my shame - then went to the Boy and told him he wouldn't be able to trust me again since I had perjured myself. He looked at me quizzically: "Why did you think I would have trusted you anyway?"

There is this harsh side to the Arab character which still never fails to shock me.

But there was trust on Sam's part, even if it was only in my innocence or naivety. Early in February he let me go skiing for ten days. Assuming I would be going to the Cedars he offered me a chalet which he used in the

'Dad' throws a dinner!

that I wanted to go somewhere where I wouldn't hear Arabic spoken! He laughed and then said: "Right! If you are going to Switzerland you can do something for me. Speak to Kaddoumi."

Hanni told me to come to his office early next morning before I caught my flight to Zurich. He handed me a briefcase and told me that I would be met at the airport. There were no exhortations to guard it with my life. That evening I was duly met by two dark-suited gentlemen who identified themselves, took charge of the briefcase, gave me an excellent dinner and hotel room and arranged to take me to the station in the morning for my train to Zurs. This treatment was repeated on my return. As I left the departure lounge, I turned to one of them and asked: "Would you mind telling me what was in that briefcase?"

"Oh, yes, about £2,000,000 in bearer bonds."

Even had I known earlier I still don't think I would have had the nerve to have done a runner.

The weather had been poor in Zurs, skiing an effort, and the evenings passed quietly in the company of a demure American widow who rejoiced in the name of Dolly Barkhorn and wore a different pair of ski pants every day.

Back in Kuwait I was met by Elias Hawa and the sergeants but none of the doctors... in Arabia the number of sycophants greeting you on your return from abroad is a measure of your place on the tribal ladder... clearly I was not doing too well.

The best of the doctors, Rahi Takhrouri, once told me that self interest was the cause of all Arab failure, leading to lack of communal responsibility and even existed within families.

"Only as long as they think you are of use to them will they support you," he said.

"I believe this failure as you call it, is due to something more complex than that," I replied, "You ought to see how some westerners behave when the that," I replied, "You ought to see how some westerners behave when the going gets tough! No, I think you confuse symbol with fact - or fact with fiction. You lack the ability, even the intention, to consolidate your ideas. Why, you can even accept a lie as the truth and still know it is a lie!"

None of this was really original thought as far as I was concerned, but extended from the late James Cameron's observation of a similar trait in Indians he knew; and, after all, he married one.

It was Ramadan and no one was in the mood for discussion, let alone argument. Offices were empty soon after 10am, then nothing happened until the evening 'fatoor', when I would 'play the field' among various sheikh's palaces, thus ensuring an early supper. Eating was a serious business among those who had fasted all day and conversation minimal. I would gaze at my surroundings, like the huge chandelier in the Boy's reception hall, the twin of which was reputed to lie under the ruins of the German Chancellery in Berlin.

One morning I was summoned to Suad, so I made my way to the White Palace where I found her defying convention and having a coffee party for about 60 other ladies. Shown into the room I emulated my ancestor and tripped over the carpet. This produced shrieks of laughter so when I had recovered I went up to Suad, bowed and held her hand for longer than necessary... Laugh that one off to your friends, I thought. She handed me a small package with a winsome smile and whispered: "I need a test."

My mind raced. I did not need to guess that I was holding a bottle of the royal urine and that she was sure of the result of a pregnancy test but Sam was bound to ask... and I did not want to be around if it was a girl. I gave what I hoped was a conspiratorial wink and slid out. I'm sure the other 59 women knew exactly what was going on.

Meanwhile plans for the new hospital were unearthed for the umpteenth time. Contractors began sniffing around, always a sign that money is replacing wishful thinking. I had a call from Abdulla Ali Reza. a formidable presence in the Arabian business world; and he brought the Middle East director of Taylor Woodrow to see me, none other than the brother of Paddy Mayne. Almost co-founder of the SAS with David Stirling, Colonel Paddy had died in a motor crash in Ireland. As an enthusiastic young Territorial SAS officer in the late 1940s, I shall never forget being put firmly in my place by him.

"No one should ever imagine there can be an SAS organisation in peace time. To live your whole life in enemy dominated country creates tension for which you can never, never, be trained."

His brother was a gentler giant. In the end, CAT Company of Beirut got the contract for the hospital.

❧ ❧ ❧ ❧ ❧ ❧ ❧ ❧ ❧ ❧ ❧ ❧ ❧

Early in April we had a state visit from King Saud. I had gone to the airport early to meet Tam, who had been in London, trying to sort out the weaponry on the new 'Jet Provosts' Sam wanted for his Air Force. He imagined one could fit a 20 pounder cannon onto these aircraft, which I had once heard described as having: "All the aerodynamics qualities of a well-aimed household brick."

We watched a Saudi Arabian airliner unloading hundreds of crates, suitcases and servants. We wondered whether the boxes were to carry home the loot they expected to acquire. I then returned to the hospital and led the medical service convoy up to the new airfield where the grand parade was to take place next day - the army always took position the day before they were needed. I joined them at dawn. There was a strong north wind blowing and the flags were fluttering merrily. First of all King Saud drove past us; then we drove past him, apart from one Centurion tank which broke down so we had to skirt round it. I was duly muffled in my 'kheffiya' as we passed the saluting base where I noted that King Saud looked bored but our ruler, Sheikh Abdulla Salim frankly looked horrified at the sight of so much military hardware! I suspect it was then that the dire warnings of the World Bank came home to him - this sort of military expenditure could not go on.

The royal party left, sandwiches were issued all round and the runway left covered with cartons. I made my way to Mishrif Palace. I was standing on a balcony when I heard a voice say, in excellent English: "Where there is waste there will be want."

I turned to see a handsome Saudi, as I thought, behind me. Most of them were fat, degenerate and rather rude. It transpired that Abdulla Tariqi was a Kuwaiti by birth. He went on to become world famous a few years later as spokesman for the Arab oil producers. As this time he was the Saudi Minister for Oil Affairs. He was interested to find an Englishman dressed as an Arab who, he quickly discovered, spoke little Arabic, very badly! His English was fluent and I warmed to him at once. We studied the fountains spraying water into the desert wind and falling onto the concrete.

"I think we are losing many gallons of water every minute," he mused. I told him the tale of electric fans turned on to cool the overheated electric cables when Mishrif was lit up; but our sense of humour does not tickle that of the most sophisticated Arab. I sensed he thought I was mocking his people instead of sharing a confidential joke. At that moment lunch was served and I was surprised to find ourselves nearly knocked over by the rush of guards, both Saudi and Kuwaiti, to get to the food first, despite the presence of both rulers. Perhaps a custom of the desert? I noticed that King Saud was assisted to his place and that he wore dark glasses over bifocals... a reflection of his poor state of health even then.

I slipped away before the royal party and was amused to find police lining the route but sitting down and leaning against the 'triumphal arches' which rumour said a Lebanese contractor had erected in a last minute rush at Rs.50,000 each. Well, that's the kind of story told about the Lebanese anywhere in Eastern Arabia.

That evening I had a house guest, Bishop Stephen Neill, at that time head of the World Council of Churches and living in Geneva. He was returning home from a visit to the Anglican Mission in Iran where Bishop Dehqani

Tafti was now the first Persian to hold office. Bishop Stephen had gone to India in 1924 as an Anglican missionary and helped establish the post-Imperial Church of South India in 1947. A mutual friend had sent him to me, concerned for his health. I found him an attractive and impressive man, who admitted to insomnia but was otherwise sound in wind and limb. A devoted Christian, there was a remote sadness about him, perhaps because of frustration in the mission field? Or, according to the mutual friend, heartbreak in youth when he watched the only woman he ever loved marry his best friend.

He told me a story of a government officer in India who had offered a few 'annas' for every dead rat brought to him - an attempt to thwart the loss of grain due to rodents. After a time the number of dead rats brought to him steadily increased, while the loss of grain continued unabated. It transpired that a local had hit on the idea of breeding rats and selling them to other villagers for a few 'annas' less than the official was paying. Winning hearts and minds was never easy for Colonial officers.

Next morning King Saud left and in the ensuing euphoria Sam summoned everybody to the White Palace - even Suad was there along with Tam, Jabra, the Boy and Alf. There was an unusual 'brain storming' session where we all pontificated on matters about which we knew very little - patrol boats, rockets for Jet Provosts, etc. I was only there to report on some medical tests I had arranged for Suad, who happily discussed them with the assembled company - like her blood group and the fact she was pregnant!

I was bidden to stay behind, when she demanded that I bring Allen Mersh to see her. Allen, an ex-IMS surgeon, could by no stretch of the imagination be termed an obstetrician. However he was the best known doctor in Ahmadi and as such could be relied upon for discretion - something I suspect could not be relied upon among government doctors. So off I drove to collect him,

'Dad' comes home.

The examination was cursory but satisfactory, certainly as far as Suad and Sam were concerned. Allen received a gold wrist watch and a gold bracelet for his wife Joyce, while Julie was rewarded with diamond earrings. Sam looked at me: "What time is it?"

"Six thirty, Ta'al Umrak (Oh long life)" I answered.

"Ah, you have a watch," grinned Sam. That's what comes of being 'family', like 'retainer'. Knowing there was a tendency for Arab ladies, once pregnant, to sit around all day I primed Allen to advise she took regular exercise. I was not prepared for Sam's next question. Neither, unfortunately, was Allen.

"What sort of exercise?"

"Oh, walking... swimming... ping pong," ended Allen with a laugh. Well, ιι was alright for him. For the next few weeks I had to go to the palace each morning and lose at ping pong, while Sam had a swimming pool built in record time. Needless to say I was not invited to participate in <u>this</u> activity.

Finally I briefed Allen to ask where Suad was to be delivered, i.e. where Sam would plan to be in the summer.

"100%, I will be in the Lebanon," was the prompt reply.

"Well, in that case it would be better if the Princess were soon under the care of the obstetrician who will deliver her baby, certainly once she is six months pregnant."

"Fine," said Sam, "that'll give me a longer holiday."

I watched Suad make a quick adjustment to her menstrual history. In the space of about five seconds she became another month pregnant.

Four weeks later Sam and she left for Beirut. He thus ducked lunch with

Watching the military parade, 1960, from left to right, the Boy, King Saud of Saudi Arabia, Sheikh Abdulla Salim Al Sabah (Ruler of Kuwait) and Sheik Sa'ad Al Sabah, head of police and son of the Ruler.

Four weeks later Sam and she left for Beirut. He thus ducked lunch with the Political Resident in the Gulf, Sir William Luce; a meeting with the Director of Ordnance from the War Office; and actually signing the contract to build the new military hospital, although work had already started on the site near Mishrif Palace. Despite the shock of his departure I am sure he did not leave without the Ruler's permission... to whom I suspect Suad's pregnancy provided a heaven sent chance to be rid of this crazy militarist before he spent any more money on tanks and planes! What were a few broken lunch dates?

With Sam's departure the Boy could flex his muscles and certainly some kind of rationality appeared in the daily course of events. The building of the military hospital was handed over to the Public Works Department, a double-edged weapon as it turned out but at least some kind of supervision was imposed.

In May Sheikh Saleh asked me to accompany him to an army camp on the frontier where a soldier had died, apparently from methyl alcohol poisoning. These semi-permanent camps attracted 'camp followers' in addition to shops. We found two selling methyl alcohol among other things. But the shops belonged to one Colonel Yacoub and were thus 'untouchable'. Yacoub, or Abu Yusuf as he was usually called, was an elderly ex-retainer who had been granted his rank on account of his long service - I suppose he would have been a head butler in England. A hawk-nosed old man, his military role was undefined but here his shops were busy selling army rations to families. Saleh huffed and puffed but realised he could do nothing.

Meanwhile the Boy had let power go to his head. He personally flogged a couple of gun smugglers caught on the Iraqi border, then sent them to hospital to be patched up. Thus enlightenment came to Kuwait? Two years later I discovered in Saudi Arabia that thieves were still having their right hands amputated... but now neatly through the radio-carpal joint by a surgeon and under general anaesthetic. That evening the Boy called me to his palace to treat the shoulder muscle he had strained in his exertions. Two weeks later he hauled a soldier out of hospital and flogged him too, because he had been drunk the night before. This time I took him to task.

"What do you think they would say at Sandhurst if they knew you had behaved like this?" I asked.

I realised that the soldier had only been admitted to hospital because he was drunk, nevertheless I felt there was a principle at stake. Before my very eyes it seemed the Boy sank into a deep depression. I felt almost sorry for him - mine had been a cheap jibe for a man who had to live between the temptations of the West, and its attendant decadence, provided by oil; and the harsh discipline of the desert, which he knew westerners would find intolerable. Finding the Will of Allah was becoming difficult.

13

IRAQ ON THE WARPATH

In June came the Iraqi threat. As usual, I managed to be out of the country whenever there was a crisis. On the 24th Abdul Karim Kassem made a speech in which he appointed Sheikh Abdulla Salim as "Ruler of that part of Iraq called Kuwait". This was just five days after Britain had withdrawn 'protected status' from Kuwait.

I was in Ireland when the news hit me - not that anything makes much of an impact in that country. I was watching a navvy regarding the fork which he had just put through his foot. He removed it, then under my horrified gaze, poured cement into the holes in his foot. He saw my concern and said: "It's alright, Captain. Praise be to God, I seldom fester."

I began to wonder how soon my medical department would begin to fester. As it turned out I did not manage to get back until 7 July.

Meanwhile... on 26 June the army got into some sort of position on the Iraqi frontier. It appears there was the expected amount of chaos. Everyone in the medical department was issued with a gun. My driver, Mubarak, demanded an 'English gun' and got a Sten. The doctors were sent out willy nilly, Abdul Moniem Abu Sinaa (radiologist) being given a map reference which he reached only to find it deserted. So he went home to bed.

Two nights later a junior officer called Saleh Jissani sent back a message - using the name of Mohammed Eissa, his CO - that Iraqi troops had entered the frontier post of Safwan. Saleh said he welcomed this as he could start killing them... but there were really too many. They must have gone away again. The following night a rumour reached Kuwait that Iraqi troops had entered Ruardhtain. Now this was serious as KOC had its drilling camp there. But once again this turned out to be a 'ghost' army.

At 8am on 30 June Sheikh Abdulla Salim asked for British assistance and a message was sent to the Commander in Chief British Forces Middle East in Aden, Air Marshal Elsworthy, saying: "Implement Operation Vantage", i.e. provide military assistance to Kuwait. Unfortunately it didn't say what Operation Vantage - would the landings be opposed or unopposed? Was there civil unrest? The previous year we had practised Operation Vantage with senior officers of the British Forces in Aden and Kenya, my 'Oppo' being Colonel Brian Hughes who commanded the field ambulance of 29 Brigade, stationed in Kenya. There had been, even then, a wish to see the operation for real. Well, here it was - wish fulfilment.

At 10.45am the next day OC 42 Royal Marine Commando landed, 45 minutes behind schedule, in a blinding sandstorm at Kuwait's new airport and the message: "Red Cloud has landed" was sent to the C-in-C. Visibility was so bad that my helicopter pilot chum Clive Wright went out to lead them in. Work was still in progress at the airport but Jim Forrest, airport manager, took the initiative to clear workmen off the site, while Jim Addison, chief engineer in the electricity department, took it upon himself to run a power line from the town to the control tower.

Meanwhile an RAF 'Brittania' carrying marines put down on Ahmadi airstrip. This was fine for KOC's small 'Pioneer' aircraft but the heavily laden Brittania gouged eighteen inch ruts in the oily runway and came to a halt faster than the pilot had intended. As the men disembarked KOC employees were treated to snatches of conversation which they found reassuring.

"This is the place alright."

"How do you know?"

"There's fuck-all here."

And from another to his heavily-laden companion: "Got all yer officer's kit Nobby?"

"Yer, everything except his mackin-fuckin'-tosh," was the aggrieved reply.

After midnight on the 2 July the marines of 42 Commando started to dig in on the Mutla Ridge, using their mess tins in the absence of picks and shovels. The sandstorm continued and indeed worsened during the next 72 hours. Conditions could be truly described as diabolical. The marines were reputed to be drinking 36 pints of water a day. They were already acclimatised, having been in Aden, but this searing heat was something else. It says a lot for their superb NCOs that they remained at 'combat readiness' over this scorching period. I have little doubt that such a fluid intake was necessary.

I found it hard to control my tongue some days later when I was accompanying John Richmond, now our Ambassador, around the positions of some newly arrived British troops with General (The Bull) Richardson, who had taken command of land forces. A veteran of the North West Frontier and the Baluch Regiment he turned to John and said: "The men have got to learn to live on their water bottles. That's what we did on the Frontier. The Arabs don't drink much during the day, isn't that right Ambassador?"

"No," replied John morosely, "they die of kidney disease."

I was barely able to contain myself. Even so, heat stroke was our greatest enemy. Three of HM Forces died from heat illness during that summer's crisis, one at least from heat stroke, following a heavy meal and an excess of alcohol, which combined to throw further stress on an already corpulent figure. He was found dead on his bunk, his rectal temperature still over 106 degrees Fahrenheit.

• • • • • • • • • • • • •

At 2am on the night of 6/7 July I finally made it back to Kuwait. I went to Jewan Hospital first thing, then out to Jahra where I met the Boy, tired but calm. After heartfelt apologies for my absence, which he accepted gracefully, we went up to Mutla Ridge where the marines had been withdrawn after

Officers and men of Kuwait Army Medical Service, 1961.

their spell of purgatory. Thank God, the wind had dropped and with it the sand. Now 'the Skins' (Royal Inniskillen Fusiliers) were digging in. Their colonel, who had fought in Normandy, believed in digging deep. We were followed by a convoy of some twenty press cars, anxious to report how 'our boys' were suffering in the heat.

We went to the Parachute Brigade Field Ambulance at Jahra where there was an impromptu 'O' group with Eric Parry, CMO of the State Medical Service, Dom Macreadie, SMO of the government hospital at Suleibikhat, near Jewan, Brian Hughes and myself. In an astonishingly short time we decided to shut the military hospital - let's be honest it was nothing more than a nursing home - put 24th Field Ambulance staff to live in it, and militarise Suleibikhat. If only all meetings were held standing up... and limited to 'stakeholders'! To cap a decisive morning I issued the Parachute Field Ambulance with our large German-built ambulance, which was air-conditioned, along with Dakilullah, its ex-Arab Legion driver - who became an honourary paratrooper for the duration - and was seen sporting a red beret beneath his red 'kheffiya'! The soldiers managed to install a shower in this vehicle so it became an advanced heat stroke unit.

Next day Ibrahim, my orderly, took Brian Hughes and I to the KOC drilling camp in Ruardhtain, in a sandstorm. Even inside our sealed saloon car we were stung by sand particles and when we entered the deserted camp we found the shuttered rooms already filling with sand. So like seven maids with seven mops we turned to sweeping out the clinic where I put Raymond Matterne and a field section to look after the units on the frontier. Raymond was the English-speaking Lebanese surgeon who proved deservedly popular with both Arab and British troops: a polished Beiruti, he referred to the young cavalry officers as: "Such dear boys!"

We then went to visit the 11th Hussars who were sheltering beneath cam-ouflage nets in the desert nearby. There's nothing like a sandstorm to short-en tempers and by now many were getting frayed. Their adjutant, Mike Allenby, made us welcome in his 'Basha' - talk about noblesse oblige. Ibrahim squatted in the sand outside. I explained to him that Mike was the son of Field Marshall Lord Allenby who had liberated Jerusalem from the Turks in 1917, humbly entering the Holy City on foot... Ibrahim was not impressed: "Then why did you give it to the Jews?"

After glasses of jungle juice we went to the Kuwaiti Armoured Car Unit, commanded by Sheikh Saleh, where we lunched. Sheikh Saleh was the ideal liaison officer with the Hussars and the most respected, as opposed to the most feared, officer in the Kuwait Army: even in his absence I saw soldiers stand up when his name was mentioned.

Next day the Boy held an 'O' group at 7am. I suspect he felt it was the sort of thing he ought to do; but I noted: "Results? SFA." Let's face it, the Brits were in charge. I slipped away and went to Suleibikhat where I found an RAMC sergeant and one of our ex-Arab Legion clerks had set up a joint Anglo-Arab admissions unit. All appeared to be running smoothly so I left quickly. Back at Jewan I learned that His Highness had sent Sheikh Jabir Al Ahmed to Cairo to gain support from Gamal Abdul Nasser - who was already talking about British intervention in Kuwait as 'Suez in reverse', which was encouraging.

⊰⊱ ⊰⊱ ⊰⊱ ⊰⊱ ⊰⊱ ⊰⊱ ⊰⊱ ⊰⊱ ⊰⊱ ⊰⊱ ⊰⊱ ⊰⊱ ⊰⊱

As the threat of invasion begins to fade so the 'swanners' begin to arrive. Peace-time soldiering was in the doldrums. One day when I was going to visit the clinic in Ruardhtain I got a request to take a newly arrived REME Lt. Colonel with me to fix a generator that had broken down. Any excuse would do to get to the front. (In his defence he did effect a repair.) Then the operational research staff turned up. They could have just as well carried out their experiments in Aden but here was a potential combat zone. One gallant RAMC Colonel shut himself into a 'Centurion' tank with the engine running to prove that it was impossible to fight with the hatch closed as the crew would succumb to heat stroke within a matter of minutes. We had a pre-arranged signal to release him from this oven - but when the time came the hatch jammed and we finally extracted one parboiled officer just in time. He later managed to drink lemonade while sitting under a tepid shower.

I went up to Ahmadi to see how John and Viv were surviving and learned how KOC had tried desperately to distance itself from the threat. The first staff circular after British troops arrived stated that: "Foreign troops have landed."

Thereafter reactions polarised. 'Maggy' McGee, doyen of the Texan drillers, walked into the Hubara Club and announced: "I want ten goddamn sober limeys and I want the privilege of taking them home and getting them drunk."

But not all were so forthcoming. An American wife was heard to say that when the Iraqis did come the first ones they will shoot will be the families who have entertained British soldiers. On the whole the company policy, no doubt dictated from Houston, was scorned. Jokes like the following began to go the round: "Help! There are no cakes in the store."

Reply: "That's became management is working full time baking humble pie."

And: "We've got a mousegement, not a management."

Plans to evacuate families were still being made a week after the British had landed.

By the end of July bizarre events had become newsworthy. One of the British armoured cars drove across the frontier. The staff sergeant in charge had probably lost his way but summer torpor produced rumours that he'd been hijacked or that he'd been a crypto-communist etc.

Then an 'Auster' or the Army Air Corps landed on a road near Ruardhtain and managed to taxi into a stationary lorry, breaking the Kuwaiti driver's nose, among other things. Men of the 11th Hussars began to go on local leave, which meant staying in the camp of an American contractor on the seashore near Mina-al-Ahmadi. One of them, Fred Barker, interpreted 'local leave' elastically, cabled his girlfriend in England and met her in Nice. War is hell.

Hot July wore on. The Boy decided to visit the sick in Suleibikhat Hospital. British troops were in an open ward and we started a 'grand tour', with gifts of fruit being handed to each man.

"Why are you in hospital?" the Boy would ask each in turn.

"Piles, sir," came the reply... again... and again... and again. I was vastly relieved to come across a soldier who had shut his thumb in a car door. When we left the Boy quizzed me about the epidemic of haemorrhoids that had laid so many men low.

"You know it is a sign of sexual impotence?" he stated, giving me a steely look. Anxious to defend the virility of British manhood I explained that I thought it was due to dehydration in this case and the subsequent passage of rock hard stools.

Towards the end of August we had another period of bad weather with strong winds and the inevitable sandstorm. I learned from a naval doctor, Michael Glazier[1] that the combination of sand and salt from the seas off Kuwait had effectively immobilised the jet engines of our carrier-borne air-craft. Later, when the weather improved, and boredom had set in we had joint manoeuvres. These were marred by an RAF 'Hunter' suffering a high speed stall, following which it crashed into Mutla Ridge, killing the pilot.

❀ ❀ ❀ ❀ ❀ ❀ ❀ ❀ ❀ ❀ ❀ ❀ ❀

By September there were two major changes in my life. Binnie upped and

---

[1] He had been a medical student with me an subsequently practised in Dorset, where we met again many years later.

left Kuwait for the Lebanon where her parents had moved. Splash had been summoned back to the colours when the Iraqi threat first occurred and had flown dawn patrols along the northern frontier, alone in an 'Auster'. But with the arrival of the British he had been politely thanked and 'stood down' again.

Meanwhile the politicians had been busy and an Arab League Force was poised to take over from the British. It was my good luck that the medical element of this force were Sudanese and both efficient and friendly. Their CO had served with the Coldstream Guards in the western desert in 1941. I appointed him CO Arab League Forces, thus avoiding an Egyptian CO.

To mark the British withdrawal and the end of the hot weather Peter Wilson, senior government physician, and I had a champagne party at his house on Shuweikh Beach, one of the four 'grand residences' built by KOC. It was a marked success and in the ensuing conviviality Peter and I were loaded with beer and rations that the army were abandoning, indeed 'compo' became a part of our daily lives... well, the oatmeal blocks and rice pudding were delicious.

There was a slight vacuum between the British leaving their frontier positions and the arrival of the Arab League. I flew up to Safwan two days after our party (I had acquired a military flying licence, thanks to Splash) and landed on the road near the frontier post. From the watch tower I could observe deep into Iraq to the north. It was deserted while to the south the only sign of the Saudi Arabian element was three empty marquees where the 11th Hussars had been. I was told their MO had arrived, taken one look, and booked himself into the Kuwait Hotel. The Saudi Force was by far the largest element of the Arab League Force and had arrived by courtesy of ARAMCO, who had supplied them with vehicles and rations. Once in Kuwait they expected the Kuwait Army to feed and water them; if we could find them.

The following day, 2 October, General Eissa, OC Saudi Forces, accompanied by the Sudanese Brigadier Khalid and the Boy, arrived at the military hospital, just as Guy Robinson was handing it back to us. He had taken over the Field Ambulance from Brian Hughes, who had suffered a heart attack. Not a word of warning, of course. There was total chaos with half-naked British soldiers piling their kit on to their jeeps while my men were driving ours laden with our kit from Suleibikhat Hospital. I'll hand it to the Boy, he just grinned and raised his eyes to heaven. Normal confusion was soon restored.

14
PEACE RESTORED

The British withdrawal had brought me face to face with reality again. CAT Company had started work on the new military hospital in April, but the standard of work was poor. This despite the fact that the PWD were meant to be supervising it. With Dad's departure an embryonic Ministry of Defence had been created, but this had little going for it save sumptuously decorated offices! (Courtesy of Abdulla Said Rajab!) The room of the new minister looked like the original 'tart's boudoir' with its pink and blue walls. But there was no engineering department. Neither did we have a hospital architect, so the contractor went merrily on his way, laying tiled floors then ripping them up again to lay cables. When I complained this would line the contractor's pockets but make a sterile operating theatre impossible I was told: "Right! No more variation orders!" A typically Arab way of dealing with the problem!

The situation had grown so bad that in January 1962 I submitted my resignation. It was a suitable opportunity for me to get out but the Boy would have none of it. He came to the hospital with me and at once grasped the seriousness of the situation. There were no flies on the Boy when it came to confronting contractors. The next thing I knew was that the chief engineer of PWD, Chris Birdwood, and Bill Gordon, chief quantity surveyor, were on site with us and giving stick to CAT management who were sweating in their sandals. The Boy stopped all payments. Then PWD appointed a tough young German engineer as site supervisor. He wandered around, kicking down anything that didn't measure up to his standards. Thereafter the contractor behaved impeccably.

Meanwhile Abdulla Said Rajab had been posted to Cairo as military secretary of the Arab League - to the Boy's unconcealed delight. Tam Pierce had finally left to work for a powerful Lebanese, Sheikh Alamuddin - who owned Middle East Airlines among other things - in Beirut; where Suad had presented Sam with a son. I need not have worried after all.

To top all this, Bin and I were married, also in Beirut, on 16 November. The Boy, whose permission to wed I had requested out of a sense of military decorum, advised me to avoid marrying anybody! But if I had to, then the daughter of Captain Lash was 'permissible'. Alan Munro[1] kindly accepted to be best man. I flew to Beirut and together we dined at the Sursock residence in north Beirut. This splendid house of the early French colonial period was, Alan informed me, a suitable environment for me to spend my last night of bachelordom. It was an unforgettable experience.

Next day he collected me from the St George Hotel and we lunched at one

---

[1] Alan had succeeded Anthony Acland in the Political Agency. He was now serving in our Embassy in Beirut. Later he became British Ambassador in Riyadh at the time of the first Gulf War (1991).

of Beirut's best, putting the world to rights, until I suddenly noticed it was 2.50pm and I was due to be married at 3pm! Alan hailed a cab and the driver proved that the Beirut taxi driver may be the most dangerous in the world, but he is also the fastest. We reached St George Chapel in good time. The reception was in the adjoining St George Club. (Both, alas, were destroyed in the civil war some years later.)

We left for Cyprus the next day, after a disturbed night: some joker had arranged for a bottle of champagne to be delivered to our room every hour on the hour throughout the night! We stayed in the Dome Hotel in Kyrenia and spent busy days trying to reach the various Crusader castles on the Kyrenia Range. We also spent a night as guests of Colonel Frank King, commanding 2 Para at Akrotiri, with whom we had struck up a friendship during the previous summer in Kuwait. It was a busy honeymoon!

Another diversion was caused by Colonel Stewart Carter, on leave from the Sharja where he was commanding the Trucial Oman Scouts. The black patch over one eye emphasised the piratical character he was. He had been visiting an aunt's property near Kyrenia and took a fancy to the bust of a Grecian lady adorning one of the gateposts. The owner was no longer in residence. He heaved it into his car and drove off. Unfortunately he had been observed. The police caught up with him and he was put into Kyrenia Gaol. We learned the news when we visited the Harbour Club, then in its heyday, that evening. The owner of the club was sending him meals. Subsequently I was asked to appear as a witness for the defence at his trial. The British expatriate community were up in arms over the affair, while the Cypriots were thoroughly enjoying the opportunity of embarrassing a British Army officer.

I recall being asked by his defence lawyer: "Has the defendant been accused of theft before?" and, "Have you ever known him steal anything?"

He was released with a warning, after my vehement defence of his integrity. I confess this was entirely on hearsay as I'd never actually met him before; but his reputation in the Gulf was by this time legendary and fortunately I was not asked on what grounds I based my assessment of his character.

Then we flew back to Lebanon and stayed up in the Cedars as guests of a 'fairy godmother', whom I subsequently discovered was an American drug company. So much has been written about doctors accepting freebies from drug companies but neither on this nor any other occasion was I subsequently subjected to pressure salesmanship. Later in my career I _was_ offered bribes by some manufacturers and contractors but it was always the local agent trying to make good.

After a few days of blissful walking in the high woods along forest trails and ridges dusted with the first snow of winter, we returned to Beirut where I spent fruitless hours trying to get our marriage registered with the Lebanese authorities. Father John Grinstead, the somewhat raffish ex-naval chaplain who had married us, produced a Certificate of Marriage registered in the parish of All Saints.

Although Alan Munro was information officer in the British Embassy, an

'Embassy wedding' was forbidden by the Lebanese Government. The reason was simple enough - the Christian minority who controlled the country knew that they were outnumbered by Muslims, hence insisted that all Christian marriages should be registered by the Lebanese authorities in a doomed attempt to maintain parity with the Muslims. I was presented with a massive document in the local Mairie which required a seemingly endless series of signatures in different departments - each one of course costing several Lebanese pounds. Just when I thought I'd won it was pointed out that there was no priest's signature: so back to John Grinstead, who alas made the mistake of placing the Episcopal stamp of the Diocese of Jordan Syria and Lebanon under his signature.

When I returned to the Mairie and waved this triumphantly under the chief clerk's now, he took one glance at it and informed me I had defaced a government document with an unauthorised stamp for which I must pay a fine of umpteen Lebanese pounds and start again. I walked out.

Later we discovered that out marriage _had_ been registered in Somerset House, which was a good thing as the church and all its records were destroyed during the civil war.

❧ ❧ ❧ ❧ ❧ ❧ ❧ ❧ ❧ ❧ ❧ ❧ ❧

I made a final visit to Sam's palace to the south of Beirut where I paid my respects to Suad and her infant son, Mubarak (the Blessed). I know all three-month-old children can be uninspiring, particularly if they have just been fed. Mubarak however exceeded them all in serenity. I sensed that Suad was a different person; and that I was a reminder of a happier past. I took my leave as soon as decorum allowed and never saw her again. Alas, I believe young Mubarak failed to live up to his father's expectations.

❧ ❧ ❧ ❧ ❧ ❧ ❧ ❧ ❧ ❧ ❧ ❧ ❧

Back in Kuwait it was raining, when the desert assumes a sepulchral air. We were greeted by my NCOs, the absence of the doctors another reminder that my 'glory days' were past and that I was no longer regarded as instrumental in their futures. (In fact I was able to shepherd the best of them to careers in North America where, as far as I know, they prospered.) Binnie and I moved into my bachelor bungalow which, with the enthusiastic cooperation of my servant Abu Hartim - who quickly grasped that the presence of a memsahib of her nature meant less work for him - was uplifting.

The Ministry of Defence rapidly assumed bureaucratic proportions that raged in Sam's absence. I had hoped that the Boy might blossom as a result. Indeed, I was called within hours of my return to incise a nasty boil he had developed; he didn't wince, and I thought this reflected both a mental as well as a physical hardening. But the new Minister of Defence seemed ineffective. I suspected his brief was to control expenditure and little else. Abdulla Said Rajab had manoeuvred his way out of his post in Cairo as military secretary of the Arab League and was establishing his new power base in the ministry rather than in Army HQ. So the Boy kept away, became increasingly morose and dangerously unpredictable.

On one occasion I found him flogging a wretched deserter from the Iraqi Army who had been picked up by an Arab League patrol and handed over to him. We were alone and I bawled him out: "Not again! There are three British still in Iraqi hands!" (These were the three who had got lost in their armoured car and driven into Iraq some months earlier.) "This is intolerable! What the hell do you think you are doing?" I was truly alarmed as well as angry.

He looked at me and said: "Right! You make him talk! Use the truth drug!"

Now I know this is beginning to sound like a Hollywood B movie but it was not funny at the time and before the moralists among you condemn me for my subsequent behaviour, when faced with probable murder I would still opt to save a life. Geneva and its conventions were a long way away.

I talked quietly to the poor wretch, who was deeply shocked, warning him I was going to give him an injection and that he would be alright. I let go with a few ccs of IV Pentothal, till his eyelids flickered, he gave a long sigh and he slumped back against a cushion.

"Right Sir! You may now question the prisoner."

The Boy proceeded to do so, already beginning to look ashamed. For a few moments there was only the sound of heavy breathing; then the Iraqi opened his eyes, gazed around him like a drunk coming to, finally focussing on the Boy and in slurred tones called him: "A dung-eating son of a camel driver's whore." (Or words to a similar effect.)

The Boy slumped in a chair with his head in his hands. I moved fast. I flung open the door into the passage and shouted: "Get an ambulance!" I turned to the Boy.

"This has got to be hushed up." He nodded hopelessly.

"It's alright," I continued, "I'll cover for you."

He nodded again with a look that combined shame and pathetic gratitude. I felt... awful.[1]

There were lighter moments. The ruler decided that all members of the Armed Forces should sign an Oath of Allegiance to Kuwait. Not such a bad idea when one considers how many of them were of Iraqi, Saudi or Iranian descent, while almost the entire medical service were Northern Arabs. I had to set an example so I agreed to sign. But after a word with John Richmond I had a codicil added to my oath: "That I should not be required to bear arms against Her Britannic Majesty."

The Arab League Forces were beginning to trickle away, the desert was cold and wet, and time was hanging heavily on their hands. I was called to see General Eissa (the Saudi in charge). Because of the curious situation existing at that time - Saudi Arabia had broken off diplomatic relations with the UK five years earlier following the Suez fiasco - he was not allowed to

---

[1] The prisoner was tended in our hospital and then handed over to a local branch of the Red Crescent. I understand he survived.

see me. But apparently there was nothing to stop him talking to me so I had to sit behind a screen while he asked me to set up medical examinations for the Saudi troops under his command.

Well, I've already mentioned some of the medical curiosities encountered among our own recruits. I doubt if the Saudi troops had undergone <u>any</u> kind of medical induction. They were hardly flowers of the kingdom and when I subsequently reported that, out of the first ten men we had examined, four had open pulmonary Tb and three had active syphilis, further examinations were abruptly halted.

⋞⊱ ⋞⊱ ⋞⊱ ⋞⊱ ⋞⊱ ⋞⊱ ⋞⊱ ⋞⊱ ⋞⊱ ⋞⊱ ⋞⊱ ⋞⊱ ⋞⊱

Just before New Year 1962 Abdulla Al Ghanim invited Binnie and I out for a day's cruise to Kubr Island on the motor yacht. We were joined by the twins, Emma and Sally Richmond and the respective second secretaries of the British and US Embassies - Mig and Sue Goulding and Dick and Alita Mitchell. The latter were our neighbours and became good friends, introducing us to Fauré and some memorable quotes. Dick, who was soon to leave the Foreign Service for an academic life in Ann Arbor, said: "I was told that a knowledge of Arabic was the key to the Arab mind. Now that I have the key, what do I find? An empty room." (Surely he must have had Lebanese roots!)

It was a cold, rough, day. We caught few fish and ate and drank well, except for Binnie who was sea sick. When we got back to Shuweikh Harbour we found alarm bells ringing. Iraqi troop movements had been detected near the frontier and the army was on stand by. We dashed home and I got into uniform, then drove to Army HQ, still smelling of strong drink. I called on the Boy, who seemed depressed and more than usually uninspiring, and I hoped this wasn't the face he was putting on for the troops. In fact I told him so and he braced up. He asked me to put our mobile hospital in the desert as soon as possible, back to its old pitch near Jahara.

As I left his office I bumped into the young Kuwaiti officer who had replaced Abdulla Said Rajab as adjutant, a product of the Egyptian Military Academy and no lover of white faces - or even pink ones, the name which we preferred to use among ourselves in those days. He smelled my breath as he squeezed past and hissed: "Typical!" with a contemptuous sneer. I could not think of a riposte even if I'd wanted one.

(Ten years later in Amman I met him again, this time at the height of the Black September revolt, when he was trying to evacuate Kuwaiti officers from Jordanian Army training schools. I was in the happy position of having an Abu Dhabi Air Force transport plane at my disposal. When he pleaded with me to save the wives and children of some of them the pilots demurred. They had enough fuel to reach Beirut unladen and intended to fly high; and the aircraft was not pressurised.

"Sorry old boy, can't help," I said cheerfully.)

We were on the road at dawn and spent the day shunting trailers and generators into position, hindered by wet sand. Just when we were nicely 'laagered' the Boy arrived, took one look and decided it was a suitable site for his advanced HQ. Wearily we hooked up and moved off to find another site. We did, and 24 hours later we were 'stood down' again. A familiar story for those who have experienced men at war.

❧ ❧ ❧ ❧ ❧ ❧ ❧ ❧ ❧ ❧ ❧ ❧ ❧

We had married in the sure knowledge that our time in Kuwait was coming to a close. I had been invited to join a joint Pakistan-British Army expedition to the Karakorum in the summer of 1962, thanks to Jawed Akhter, and I was thinking that I should take my professional career, probably as a radiologist, more seriously. It looked more and more as if we would find ourselves back in England in the autumn of that year. But it was politic in my circumstances, an employee of an Arab host by his grace and favour, not to resign outright; but to suggest I needed further training and would of course be happy to return... the alternative was to get the sack!

This nearly happened when I encountered a Kuwaiti officer kicking a Pakistani lorry driver whom he thought had cut in on him at a roundabout. I jumped out of my car, grabbed the Kuwaiti and flung him aside before helping the Pakistani to his feet and advising him to get out fast. Fortunately for me the Kuwaiti officer was Persian in origin. (In those days as many as a third of commissioned officers were from the other side of the Gulf, which reflected on their higher standard of education.) This meant that they were treated as second class citizens by their Arab counterparts - ranking them lower than me in the pecking order! Thus any complaint against my admittedly high-handed behaviour was unlikely to succeed. We exchanged insults.

"You're meant to be an officer, not a peasant!"

"At least I'm not an English peasant!"

The Pakistani meanwhile regained his vehicle and drove off without a backward glance.

Our last few months were pleasantly social and reminiscent of the dying days of the Raj. We entertained and were entertained. We put on a revue called *Spring Fever* which broke with tradition in that our closing number was by Palestinians led by my chief pharmacist Elias Hawa, comprising dances of rural Palestine and the Lebanese Mountains. I regarded this as a breakthrough in Anglo-Arab relations! John Richmond, our liberal Ambassador, allowed one of his diplomatic staff, Frank Trew, to go on stage and make a fool of himself along with the rest of us. I had five weeks to go.

I nearly didn't make it. For a long time I had been flying one of the 'Austers' that the embryonic Air Force had at the outset. They had graduated to 'Jet Provosts' by now and, despite Splash's departure some months earlier, the new chief instructor had let me continue flying, after checking me out.

On this occasion I took off and immediately noticed I was one wing heavy.

In fact, as I tried to climb I had to hold the stick hard down to port while full throttle barely kept her on level flight. I told air traffic control I was in trouble and needed an emergency landing. Of course this had to coincide with the arrival of a BOAC 'Constellation', whose captain had little sympathy for the tiny ant that lurched across his runway and finally stuck in the sand.

"What do you think this is - a bloody race track?" came an irate voice over the RT.

"Kindly follow procedure," a cultured Arab voice from the tower intervened. Thanks Abdul, I thought as I sat there sweating. Subsequently I found that three fabric panels had torn off the upper surface of my starboard wing. I recalled that if God had meant man to fly He would have given him wings: or perhaps it was just that maintenance was not what it had been when Splash had been in charge.

❧ ❧ ❧ ❧ ❧ ❧ ❧ ❧ ❧ ❧ ❧ ❧ ❧

We left Kuwait on Saturday 2 June 1962 with the proverbial mixed emotions. It had been home for Binnie for eight years and mine for six. We were both excited by the prospect of the forthcoming expedition, for she had been accepted as base camp manager during my correspondence with Major Jimmy Mills, the expedition leader. Furthermore I had a surrogate mother (my own mother had died in 1954) in Georgie Schofield who had stayed with us earlier in the year and promised accommodation in London at a nominal rent so we could relax on that score. Finally I had been accepted as a postgraduate student back at the Middlesex Hospital in October. The future looked good.

What we had not taken into account was that Binnie was now five months pregnant! Reluctantly we agreed that this put managing base camp out of court, but it seemed worthwhile coming along albeit only for the start of the ride.

We reached Karachi that evening and were met by a German friend, Marianne, whom I had met a few years earlier when visiting Iran with my father. She was a secretary in the German Embassy there. (Embassies had not yet moved to the new capital in Islamabad). She entertained us royally with several German colleagues that evening. Next day I introduced Binnie to the Karachi Yacht Club and we had a grand sail in one of their 'Fireflies' in wroughty weather - apart from running aground on a sand spit. For Bin was never a happy sailor at the best of times and in her current state of health this experience capped her nautical career - in fact she never sailed in a dinghy again!

15
A KARAKORUM TRAGEDY

Monday 4 June dawned hot and sticky. We were up at 4am to catch the shiny new PIA 'Viscount' to Rawalpindi. Here we were met by Wing Commander Shah Khan with the bad news that Jawed Akhter had broken his ankle playing football so would not be joining us. This put a real blight on the expedition as far as I was concerned. I expected Shah Khan would replace him as liaison officer but now he too pleaded ill health.[1]

There were already three of Jimmy Mills' climbing 'students' with us - Captain Said Durrani (Sid), Captain Khurschid Khan (Krush) and Lieutenant Nisar Ahmed (Gabby) - whom he had taught two years earlier when he had been seconded to the Pakistan Army Staff College at Quetta. This meant we could avoid many of the problems an all-British expedition might have faced: nevertheless, GHQ forced another, totally inexperienced officer, Captain Naqvi, to join us and keep numbers equal. The other three promptly ganged up on him and made him liaison officer! (with its attendant administrative headaches).

This was the first chance Binnie and I had to meet the other three British members of the team. Captain Dick Jones of the Royal Fusiliers was the expedition secretary and just about one of the nicest guys one could meet. Captain Anthony Hasell of the Royal Corps of Signals bounded about with all the enthusiasm of a scout master with his first troop; but he was not the sort of person one could be cross with for very long! Major Jimmy Mills, Royal Army Service Corps, our leader, did not arrive for another couple of days, having had to extricate himself from his job with Northern Command. He was a firm, gentle, and intelligent man whom I trusted instantly.

I have always regarded Shipton and Tilman as Britain's greatest Karakorum Mountain explorers - even though both abandoned them for the Southern Hemisphere when they became too popular. Each made memorable statements: "Himalayan climbing is 90% logistics," and "The greatest hazard of Himalayan climbing is bedsores."

Now Jimmy joined them with his reply to my question as to why he climbed mountains: "Because it achieves nothing, does nobody any good, and hopefully nobody any harm."

Soon we were to prove them all right. As all good travellers still did in those days, we went to Flashman's Hotel. It was just a series of bungalows linked around a central dining room and bar and still showed signs of 'pre-Partition panache'. You could drink draught Murree beer, Carew's gin and a curious local whisky that tasted strongly of ginger. The staff comprised grimly imperturbable Punjabis, mostly ex-soldiers. (By 1998, when I paid my last

---

[1] I learned some years later from Tony Streather that Mike Banks had given Shah Khan a hard time on Rakaposhi in 1956 which put him off British officers!

visit, the place was moribund and due for closure, but not before its kitchens had awarded me a peculiarly debilitating gut infection.)

We visited GHQ where the splendid Brigadier 'Roddy' Rodham was still Army Sports Control officer and rushing around enthusing hockey teams. He still knew nothing about mountaineering but gave us 100% support.

We spent the next four days packing, unpacking and repacking equipment and stores. Binnie was in her element, while some of us found it frustrating. On one occasion Sid catapulted himself through the window of the room where she and I were packing the medical kit with a cry: "We're going to the top!"

Without waiting for an answer he leapt back out again. "You'll have to watch that chap!" said Binnie gravely.

Sadly, we did. Six months later, and very little to do with me, Sid was seconded to 22 SAS Regiment in Brecon, where, not surprisingly, he made his mark and managed to lose my prize suit of 'winter cold wet weather warfare' gear, which I had lent him when he arrived, cold, wet and shivering at the mews house in Paddington where Binnie and I were living in February 1963. The Kuwait Army, never short of funds, had issued it to me!

After his training Sid returned to Pakistan and joined their Special Forces. In 1965 when war broke out with India, Sid was launched on a hare-brained parachute operation across the frontier. He was soon captured and tortured. This probably rendered him impotent. He subsequently married a well-born lady of his tribe (the Durranis were among the nobility of the North West Frontier). The marriage was a disaster. Sid died soon afterwards, as Krush put it: "Of a broken heart."

I am sure the trumpets sounded for him on the other side.

⊰⊱ ⊰⊱ ⊰⊱ ⊰⊱ ⊰⊱ ⊰⊱ ⊰⊱ ⊰⊱ ⊰⊱ ⊰⊱ ⊰⊱ ⊰⊱ ⊰⊱

At last it seemed as if we were ready. Then began the tedious business of getting flights to Gilgit. These were dependent on the local weather. As the town lies in a bowl surrounded by mountains it was frequently 'clouded out'. With the limited amount of traffic in and out of such a remote area it was not economically viable to install expensive navigational aids. So one learns to be patient. Ideally we needed two flights on the same day - PIA 'Dakota' for Binnie while the rest of us plus kit travelled courtesy of PAF's Bristol 'Freighter' squadron.

We were lucky. We only had to wait a day. This gave us a chance to visit the hill station at Murree, deliciously cool after the steamy plains. There, we took tea and cucumber sandwiches in the gardens of the Hotel Cecil and watched the sun set over the serried valleys below.[1]

Next day I kissed Binnie goodbye and said, with studied nonchalance: "See you in Gilgit this afternoon!"

With Roddy's exhortations ringing in our ears, we left his stout figure waving us off from the tarmac at 7.30am. I wangled a place in the nose where I

---

[1] This grand old establishment survived until 1998. On our return home from Gilgit that year Meryon Bridges and I walked through its silent, empty rooms, full of ghosts, but intact. It had closed the month before.

could look down through the perspex floor and had a superb view of Nanga Parbat. On this occasion, unlike our 1959 flight to Skardu, we flew on north when we reached the Indus, creeping over a ridge or two before landing in Gilgit with three bumps: but we were heavily laden - five tons of kit and equipment, let alone us - and the airstrip is 10,000 feet above sea level. So no skin off the noses of our aircrew! Sid, however, could not resist a crack to the captain: "I hope you're going to record all three of those landings?" (Sadly they were all killed in a flying accident near Rawalpindi a month later.)

Captain Zulfikar, adjutant of the Northern Scouts, whose guests we were during our stay, met us. 'Zulfi' was a charming, competent officer who was to prove invaluable during our time in the Northern Territories. Immediately after lunch it was back to the stores, to re-pack our kit, from air freight to jeep freight. At about 4pm my heart leapt - aircraft engines! And lo and behold in came the PIA 'Dakota', complete with Binnie. Zulfi had arranged for us to stay in the old Gilgit Scouts' guest bungalow, down on the banks of the Indus; as he put it: "Away from the coarse soldiery!"

It was certainly a romantic and secluded spot. The absence of water in the bathroom was a minor handicap, with the Indus on our doorstep. This provided us with an interesting experience. Due to the early summer 'melt' in the mountains the river was in full flood, and laden with mica. Hence, after washing, both our clothes and skin wore a silvery scum - not very fetching!

We spent a couple more days getting organised. Jimmy, with the lessons of Rakaposhi in mind, when the Hunza porters had proved invaluable, took the opportunity of hiring four of them for high altitude carrying.

At last, early on 12 June, our advance party boarded a jeep and we were off. It was raining. I kissed Binnie goodbye and left her in the Northern Scouts mess where Zulfi promised to get her on the first available flight. The weather remained bad and it was nearly a week before she got a flight back to 'Pindi and then Karachi, where Marianne cared for her until she got a flight home. Fortunately I was unaware of all this at the time as we struggled over broken tracks, landslides, porters' strikes, and all the other burdens sent to try expeditions.

In fact I was to hear from Binnie just once during the next two months - and that by chance! GHQ had registered the expedition address with the Pakistan postal authorities as: "c/o the Mir of Nagar," it seemed that no one in the postal department had heard of him - despite the fact that he, together with the Mir of Hunza, were the leading figures in the Northern Territories. So all our incoming mail was dispatched to the 'Dead Letter Office, Lahore,' from where Anthony Hasell eventually recovered it on our return. It proved bad for expedition morale, especially mine.

There was no Karakorum highway in those days. We reached Nomal within an hour and Chalt in time for lunch. By then we had crossed a flooded river and the road grew steadily worse. We had to rebuild a bridge that had been washed away; then clear boulders off the track into the river, sometimes several thousand feet below. When the track grew steeper we had to push our overloaded jeep. It took fourteen hours to cover the 68 miles from Gilgit to Nagar, where we collapsed into the guesthouse at 11pm, spitting dust.

Next morning we met the Mir, a jolly little man in a European suit, looking rather like a prosperous Devon farmer, anxious to help and speaking quite good English. Alas, the same could not be said for his Wazir, a stubborn, pedantic old man, who not only racked up the porters' wages but also forced us to dismiss our Hunza porters, so bad were his relations with his neighbour. We were to miss them, the only porters with high altitude experience in the region. We never established good relations with our Nagar porters: in fact, whenever our spirits needed a lift, we sang a dirge: "All Nagars are bastards!" to the tune of "Hi diddle dee, an actor's life for me!"

Sid and I led off at last. We started with the usual horrendous glacier crossing, then an equally hair-raising walk along a mountain path in the dark and pouring rain until we found a campsite. The rest of the advance party joined us for a sodden night, not enhanced by drinking luke-warm tea laced with mica from the Hispar River. Another wet day followed but at least we found a fresh water spring at the next campsite. I thought of Binnie, no doubt still stuck in the Scouts' mess and hoped she had plenty to read. She and inactivity have never gone well together.

The next day dawned clear and we set off cheerfully up the narrowing gorge. We lunched off sardines, cheese and Marmite, before crossing a wire bridge to the south side of the river. I recorded in my diary; "Not too frightened."

So we came to the village of Hispar and chose a campsite. The owner of the meadow demanded advance payment for the damage we might do to his grass. Even at the time I could not blame him; theirs is an existence more than a life.[1]

Next day we sent some porters back to Nagar and hired more from Hispar. This attempt to pacify the natives was not really successful - the locals were marginally more troublesome than those from Nagar - especially one 'city' boy who had briefly worked in Lahore and let us all know it. He would have been an excellent shop steward!

We set off again, with the inevitable crossing of the Hispar glacier. This was ghastly but I had been conditioned by the Chogo Lungma three years before so the slipping, sliding and cursing were soon over. Two days later we reached Bitinmal, an idyllic campsite - or so it seemed after crossing the Khunyang glacier on the mountain's west flank, surely the worst in the Karakorum? (It always is, until you reach the next one.) Here we set up camp. Anthony and I made a dam and a swimming pool. We shared the site with 40 odd yaks but they weren't very interested in us. Karachi Radio began to broadcast special weather forecasts for the expedition - one of the perks of being with the Pakistan Army - and the weather was beautiful. Alas, it didn't last long.

[1] When I revisited the village in 1998 with Krush, along with Meryon Bridges, we found that little had changed. Ten years previously the Aga Khan had sent help; but a rock fall had destroyed the new generator and the clinic was derelict. No doctor had visited for years and the last orderly had left eighteen months previously. The guesthouse was roofless. Of the 44 porters we had hired in 1962, all but two were dead.

"A strong reconnaissance and an attempt on one of the two summits of the Khinyang Chish/Pumarikish complex." Thus, the object of the Pakistan-British Forces Expedition had been defined.

So, although from our campsite we could now just see the peak of Khinyang far above us, and two inviting ridges extending towards us in south westerly and south easterly directions respectively, we were still bound by the first objective. Next day, Jimmy and Sid set off to look at the south west ridge from the west, i.e. the Khunyang glacier side, while Anthony, Krush and I set off further up the Hispar glacier to have a look at the next two 'inlets' coming in from the north, the Pumarikish and Jutmau glaciers.

On 18 June we had a pleasant walk to the mouth of the Pumarikish glacier where, deducing from photographs taken by the intrepid American couple, the Bullock Workmans, some 60 years earlier, and Eric Shipton's report on his travels with Tilman just before World War II, there should have been a gorgeous campsite on the west side - and here it was! Bitinmal was a grassy hollow, complete with forget-me-nots and a stream. Because of Krush's presence we opted for the same food as the porters, mostly dal and rice. I enjoyed it, but Anthony went a bit quiet.

Next morning was again fine and the three of us set off to climb on to the south east ridge from its eastern flank. It was covered with flat, but tilted stones that tipped down when one trod on them. Even dressed as we were, in gym shoes, shorts and shirts, it was sweaty and irritating work. We finally reached the ridge, just as a 'Sabre' jet of the PAF roared over, presumably taking the aerial photographs we had been promised back in 'Pindi, (where I eventually saw them on my return; and jolly useful they might have been!)

There was a peak to the north so off we went in the snow, without goggles or ice axes. Perhaps it was the altitude that made us mistake the ridge for a tennis court? From the top we had a fine view of Pumarikish but Khinyang peak was still hidden way up the northern end of the ridge we were standing on. To the south across the far side of the Hispar wall, I could see Spantik, bringing back memories of 1959. Then it began to cloud over and for the first time that day we showed sense and descended fast to camp - a series of falls and slides, ending up with torn pants and shoes. That night I couldn't sleep, thanks to the pain in my eyes, which I realised was due to mild snow blindness. Amethocaine eye drops stopped them hurting and I made a note to be more careful in future. Next morning the rain was back. We flogged across the Pumarikish glacier, descended the east side, then toiled up the Hispar again until we found another campsite. The rain turned to snow. Next day we turned up the Jutmau glacier and walked about four miles up its west side. Unfortunately this glacier did not have a lateral moraine - which usually made for easy walking - so we had to descend to the moraine itself. The snow continued and as I was wearing my snow goggles it was a nightmare journey.

We slept on snow that night, fondly imagining we had gone where no man had trod before - until Anthony found an empty milk tin the following morning with the marking 'CRJU - E428' on it. Possibly a relic of Shipton's party, although I thought we were further north than he had gone. The snow continued. We found a 'hanging curtain' or rock at the head of the Jutmau, effectively blocking a route up either the east side of Khinyang Peak or Pumarikish; but the clouds broke that evening, affording dramatic views of Pumarikish and Kanjut Sar, away to the north east. The snow came back and I crawled into my sleeping bag and listened to the current test match on the BBC's World Service.

So far you will have noted we had not even seen the summit of Khinyang Chish, let alone a possible route up it. Both Anthony and Krush were lie-abed sluggards in the mornings so next day I followed a hunch and was up at dawn then belted across to the middle of the glacier, to be rewarded by the sight of the peak, before cloud again enveloped it. I spent the rest of the day struggling in soft snow with one of the high altitude porters, Mohammed Ali - variously known by us as 'the Yeti' or 'the Hispar Kid' - trying to find a way out of the snow basin to the east of Pumarikish. Like the sailor who joined the navy to see the world and saw only the sea, we saw only snow and ice, most of the latter vertical. I collapsed in my bag when we got back while the good Mohammed fed me mulligatawny soup.

We left camp next morning with few regrets. Anthony and I did some 8mm filming behind the others, taking turns to curse each other for choosing the worst possible route down the moraine. Back in the Hispar we travelled fast towards the Pumarikish glacier where we found the porters had set up camp and Krush was ready with hot coffee. Well, we were a better team than when we had started out, even if we had not achieved much: at least we knew we would not be attempting either Khinyang Chish or Pumarikish from either of the two glaciers we had visited.

Next day we arrived back at Bitinmal in time for a late lunch of tinned salmon - quite a treat after porters' rations. Jimmy had engaged Saccone and Speed as our caterers, a pleasant change from army compo. Jimmy and Sid had rejected the south west ridge above us but the the ridge to the east looked more promising and they had established a camp at 16,000 feet. I darned my trousers and treated the porters with the worst coughs. I still wonder how many were tuberculous.

Next day Jimmy and Anthony went down to meet the main party while Sid, Krush and I transferred base camp further up the Hispar nearer the base of the chosen ridge (see map page 83). Our new camp was another pleasant meadow but it lacked water in the immediate vicinity. However I managed to build yet another dam, a drinking point, a swimming pool, and a self-flushing loo - not all at the same site but within reasonable distance. I have often thought that my main contribution towards Himalayan expeditions, apart from being a cheap high altitude porter, was as a dam-maker. That evening the main party arrived. We had a riotous evening, helped by Saccone and Speed's liquid supplies, and I erected the medical tent. Business was about to begin.

By 27 June our new base camp looked like a junk yard and it was snowing continuously. The Meade tent I had as a medical tent was the same one I had used in 1959 - I recognised the patches. I got Anthony to cut my hair (I had some in those days) and wrote to Binnie, promising to call by Austin Reeds to have it 'squared up' before I saw her again.

Meanwhile I faced a week of 'basecampitis' while the rest flogged up the ridge stocking camp one. Mountain climbing in those days was like living on a treadmill. I wasn't sorry, our recce had tired me more than I cared to admit. I treated the porters for chronic complaints, only hoping that the ineffectiveness of my 'cures' would not become apparent before we left. The snow had turned to rain and each day seemed greyer than the last. Jimmy was still with me and we concluded that, unless there was a radical change for the better during the next ten days we would be wasting further time and money. That's the Karakorum for you.

Our mail runners crossed somewhere on the Hispar glacier! But they brought a letter from Binnie posted in Beirut - where she had stopped off to stay with her sister - and another from Colonel Conway of the RAMC whom the Kuwait Army was trying to inveigle into joining them - on a one year contract! I wrote back telling him not to be daft - and never heard from him again. I'm sure he didn't need my advice. That was the last letter I received throughout the expedition.

On 4 July at last there came a break in the weather. It was a moonless night so there were a million stars above us. Venus glowed over the Hispar, and then the sun shone. I flogged off up the hill to camp one, to find chaos reigned. Anthony had hinted on an earlier visit that: "There was no one in charge," and it was only Jimmy's arrival that saved the day. The porters sensed that, as we paid deference to him, they'd better do the same. Up till then the porters had slept in our tents, rather than erect their own, and they had dropped their loads anywhere along the ridge, while Sid seemed sunk in gloom. I think the weather was as much to blame as anything for this but Jimmy decided that we were expecting too much of inexperienced porters and we set to fixing ropes for the next camp.

This was on the crest of the ridge above the Pumarikish glacier and very airy too. I built an ice loo on the west side. I had learned in 1959 the importance of carrying a wooden loo seat in the mountains - though to be honest it was advisable to wear a safety rope if one was to relax at stool. The view was wonderful. One early morning the Hispar glacier was lit by a weird light from the misty sun and looked for all the world like a giant orange eiderdown. Anthony found that one of our porters, Ayat Ali, had been a linesman in the Northern Scouts and the two of them laid a field telephone line down to camp one - which worked faultlessly, more than can be said for most radios.

Morale rose and soon we were on our way up the ridge in search of a site for camp three. We reached the first main obstacle which Anthony had christened 'the Bull's Head' from our early observations. It involved a steep descent on the far side and I spent miserable hours belaying Jimmy and Dick while they negotiated a route fit for porters. This led to 'frost nip' in my big toes. Jimmy had provided us with plastic American duck shooting boots, which he had discovered while in Alaska with the Parachute Brigade expedition in 1956 and subsequently swore be.[1] The theory was that even if one sweated into them the impermeable plastic meant that your feet swam in warm water. Perhaps the theory held if you were chasing duck - but it didn't if you were standing for hours on a rock at about 18,000 feet in driving snow! It took 1,300 feet of corlene rope to fix a safe passage down 500 vertical feet of rock.

Our troubles worsened. We had lost a whole sack of rope on the walk in and now we found we needed even more for securing a route round the next obstacle - the 'Ogre', as Anthony cheerfully termed it. The weather was steadily worsening and, once past the Ogre, a nasty slippery route on its east face, about 3,000 feet above the Pumarikish glacier, there were still a few miles of steep ridge before we would reach the summit. It began to look as if our expedition was destined to be a reconnaissance only. Jimmy decided we should push on as far as time, weather and supplies would allow. He remained cheerful and enthusiastic, which was more than I was, and said we were privileged to be exploring one of the last great unknown 'massifs' in the world, a tougher problem than Rakaposhi, and 'the last great mountain'. I think in fact that, at 26,572 feet, it was the highest unclimbed mountain in the world at the time.

We put a couple of tents on rotten snow on the side of the Ogre and went back to camp two, where Naqvi had just arrived from camp one with the last loads. He was suffering from altitude sickness (we were at about 17,500 feet) and so, alas, was Dick - who despite his phenomenal fitness, had developed a persistent headache that only resolved if he descended to base camp. Poor Dick, he struggled on while I dosed him with APC tablets.

To add to all this half of our porters reported sick that evening. Since as high altitude porters they received Rs.5, instead of three, a day, plus their food, whether they worked or not, there was no great incentive to shoulder a load: but today they were complaining of snow blindness. As they persistently ignored our advice to wear snow goggles - and as I pointed out to them I should know after my own experience on the reconnaissance - I put amethocaine drops in their eyes and gave each of them a tube of sulphonamide eye ointment; but added a rider to my humanitarian concern - the next man who reported sick with snow blindness would get a 'malingerer's chit' rather than a sick note, i.e. he wouldn't get paid that day. It worked.

By 18 July we were at last in a position to climb to the snow dome, at over 20,000 feet beyond the Ogre. We had collected enough odd lengths of rope to let porters pass this obstacle on what Anthony had christened 'the Nymph's Traverse'. I found it hairy, but then I'm not a nymph. Heavy snow meant that Jimmy, Dick and I had to take turns in kicking our way up the Bull's Head. By the time we reached the tent on the Ogre we were tired and we stopped for

[1] See his book *Airborne to the Mountains*.

lunch. Dick just lay in the corner of the tent. I asked Jimmy if he intended to push on to camp three proper, i.e. beyond the Ogre at the foot of the snow dome and he snapped back at me: "Of course! Why the hell not?"

I thought at the time this was out of character for him. We finished lunch in silence then set off across the Nymph's Traverse. This was about 400 yards long and at one point required one to crawl under overhanging rock. Anthony, Sid, Krush and Nisar Ahmed had roped it; which was lucky as I managed to slip off almost as soon as we had started. Jimmy and Dick were leading, then Gabby, then me. We got across safely and found Sid and Krush waiting for us. They had prepared a tent platform for the definitive camp three. Meanwhile Anthony and Nisar Ahmed appeared out of the mist above us. Anthony called out cheerfully: "There's enough room for a football pitch on top of the snow dome!"

He estimated it was about 800 feet above us and the ridge looked straight-forward after that - as far as he could see in the mist. This sounded like our first break in a long time.

Jimmy and Dick set off in the steps made by Anthony and Gabby - and dis-appeared into the mist. Jimmy called over his shoulder: "Follow us! We'll site camp four on top!"

I can't say I was hot on their trail as I was knackered. My slip on the tra-verse had not been dangerous, as I had been clipped on to the fixed rope but the fact that I had been incompetent was weighing on my mind. Krush stirred me into action and we set off up the steep slope.

It was at 2.20pm that Krush shouted behind me (we were not roped): "Something's fallen! Something yellow! On the right!"

I crawled to the very edge of the ridge and looked down. To my horror I saw two ice axes lying on the snow above the cliff that dropped 5,000 feet sheer into the Pumarikish glacier. Krush joined me and together we lay in stunned silence. Then Krush muttered: "That yellow thing - it must have been one of their sleeping mats... I couldn't see anything else in the mist."

We crawled back to the footsteps leading up the ridge. These were about twenty feet from the edge, and slowly we descended to the tent platform. When we looked back it was to an empty ridge, with a piece of snow about 200 feet long, 30 feet across and about two feet deep bitten off and dragged down the east side of the ridge. At the upper and lower edges of this 'defect' were the footsteps left by Anthony and Gabby that morning, followed by Jimmy and Dick... only theirs didn't come out at the top.

Later Anthony, Sid, Krush and I went back to the Nymph's Traverse where we had a better view of the face down which Jimmy and Dick had fallen. There was no sign of them, just the silent vertical cliff.

"Come on," cried Sid, "let's get on down there!"

Anthony and I looked at each other and shook our heads.

"I'm afraid there's no hurry," I muttered.

Anthony and Gabby stayed that night in the tent they had set up at camp three while Sid, Krush and I set off back across the Nymph's Traverse. At the crept back to camp two. Once there Sid and I wept in each others' arms. We had to accept that Jimmy and Dick were dead.

⋘⊳ ⋘⊳ ⋘⊳ ⋘⊳ ⋘⊳ ⋘⊳ ⋘⊳ ⋘⊳ ⋘⊳ ⋘⊳ ⋘⊳ ⋘⊳ ⋘⊳

I cried myself to sleep that night, surrounded as I was by Jimmy's kit and the letters ready to despatch to his wife Jeanne and daughter Clare. Despite a double dose of sleeping pills I awoke at 3.30am with the wind sighing round the tent. I usually hate the sound of wind but this was gentle and at once there arose the thought that this was a visit from the spirits of Jimmy and Dick. The cynic would say this was the rambling of a tired and oxygen-starved brain: the true believer that it was proof of the after life. I think it was the mercy of God shown to a sinner. At any rate I slept comfortably after-wards.

At 6am I set off for camp three with three porters. Krush opted to join Sid and Karl Stauffer (an American geologist who was with us) in searching the Pumarikish glacier for traces of Jimmy and Dick.

It was still snowing. In fact it snowed for 80 hours without ceasing. It took us two days to clear the upper mountain. On the third day we waited, inter-minably it seemed, for the porters at camp one to come up and help clear camp two. Suddenly they appeared through the snow, exhausted by carrying huge loads of food up through the thick snow! I made them carry it down again, together with a load of kit from our camp, to the bottom of the basin - where until this day I suspect there is a large cache of food and consumables deep frozen under a cairn. This was not so cruel as it sounds since it was one long skid down to the bottom. I was never clear as to whether the porters were just thick or sim-ply took no notice of the orders given to them.

That evening we reached base camp to find Sid, Krush and Karl back from the Pumarikish glacier. In heavy snow, with ice and rock still tumbling down the sheer face, they espied a strap sticking out from the avalanche debris. They dragged out Dick's rucksack. Further search would have been both fruitless and

Khunyang Chish, Camp 2, looking towards Hispar Wall.

rucksack. Further search would have been both fruitless and hazardous. They collected stones and made a cross nearby.

We settled in the mess tent and finished off the rum that night. It was still snowing. Two days later Krush and I left camp. There was a thick mist. Anthony and the rest waved us *bon voyage* as they settled to the miserable task of clearing our kit and equipment from the mountain.

On our descent through the valley we were cheered by the fields of white and yellow flowers, dog roses, and bird song, that we encountered. We reached Hispar that night, Nagar two days later. There I arrived first and was kept waiting to see the Mir. Krush arrived, and good Rajput that he was, tore strips off the Wazir for such behaviour. Back in the guest house three priests from Burn Hall, Abbottabad, revived me with whisky and solicitude. I never knew their names.

Next morning we rode off on hired horses to Minapin. It was at last a beautiful day and we plucked fresh apricots from the trees as we passed under them. But I got stiffer and stiffer. That night we stopped at the house of the late Captain Babur Khan of the Gilgit Scouts, whose widow and daughters made us welcome and treated us royally.[1]

"Such a relief after the sullen grasping Nagars," I noted in my diary.

The following day we entered Hunza where we might have taken delight in riding down wooded lanes, apples and sweet water on every side, had we not been conscious of the sad tidings we carried. At Chalt we spent a hot night in the guest house.

The following day we changed horses. The good 'chowkidar', Shakoor Khan, assured me my beast was docile... whereupon he galloped seven miles to a severe break in the road, where, thank God, he stopped. Across the break waited a jeep of the Northern Scouts so, to my intense relief, my days as a horseman were over. Not so Krush, even though he was a 'tanky'.

In Gilgit Zulfi met and embraced us, then 'ordered' us to attend a farewell dinner for the commanding officer of the Gilgit Scouts, after which Hunza dancers (male) distracted us with a Chinese war dance.

Next day I was lucky enough to get a seat on the PAF plane with the retiring colonel (some hapless junior being off-loaded). Krush stayed on to prepare for the arrival of the main party. A Scouts piper playing *Will Ye no Come Back Again* followed by *Auld Lang Syne* further dampened my spirits. Willie Brown, last British CO of the Scouts, would have been proud of him; but it reduced me to further tears. In this heightened emotional scene, I even had a floral garland hung round my neck.

At Chaklala (Rawalpindi's airport) a jeep whisked me off to GHQ. There an ashen-faced Roddy greeted me.

"What in God's name happened? Are you really the sole survivor?"

It was my turn to look stunned.

"No, no, it was Jimmy and Dick!" I muttered.

The mystery was soon solved. GHQ had put an effective security clamp on the tragedy but the wording of the signal from Gilgit to GHQ announcing my

---

[1] Babur Khan had been the first subedar to be commissioned in the Gilgit Scouts during the 'troubles' prior to Partition and played a leading role in the establishment of Pakistan's subsequent rule of Azad (i.e. free) Kashmir. See *The Gilgit Rebellion* by the late William A. Brown.

Camp 2, Khunyang Chish, 'The Ogre', 1962.

Pakistan-British Army expedition returning a.m. PAF flight, 28 July."

Had the word 'one' been substituted for 'sole', perhaps the interpretation would have been less dire?

I spent the next few days at Flashman's, dealing with the aftermath. The Post and Telegraph department had one more arrow to fire, after dumping our mail in the Dead Letter Office. Now they managed to misdirect a telegram I sent to Binnie, at her parents' house in Tankerton, Kent, near Whitstable. I can only assume the clerk thought 'Kent' was short for 'kentonment' and that I couldn't spell 'cantonment' properly. So he searched for a likely cantonment called Tankerton and found one in Tasmania. Fortunately an alert Aussie clerk in Darwin intercepted the cable and returned it to 'Pindi Post and Telegraph, with the comment: "Try the UK, Sport." Or words to that effect. Thus, she did not receive this message until the evening of the following day.

The telegram read: "Expedition curtailed stop alive and well stop no letter received this month due to postal interruptions."

She had gone to the post office to answer this at the same time that the BBC and the *Evening Standard* announced: "British officers killed in avalanche."

It was a blessing my cable arrived just before this. Next morning I was relieved to get her telegram: "All well here stop nine letters sent stop can't wait for you to come home."

Things quietened down. I saw the Commander-in-Chief (General Moussa) and received a sympathetic message from President Ayoub Khan. Meanwhile Anthony was having trouble back up the road. He needed to hire pack horses to carry our kit from Chalt. The road from Nagar to Gilgit was broken in fifteen places.

So on 2 August I flew back. I was having trouble with my guts and frost-bitten toes, but the latter were tickling nicely - a good sign - and it was a relief bitten toes, but the latter were tickling nicely - a good sign - and it was a relief to get out of the hot and sticky plains. Zulfi continued to be a tower of strength. When he eventually got to Gilgit, Anthony grasped him with both hands and cried: "We'd never have got here without you!"

No truer words. His vehicles and men, rations and financial support were irreplaceable: above all his friendship.

⋘ ⋘ ⋘ ⋘ ⋘ ⋘ ⋘ ⋘ ⋘ ⋘ ⋘ ⋘ ⋘

A week later we were ready to fly. Another Bristol 'Freighter' lugged us back to Chakala. There, Anthony espied a giant USAF four engined transport on the other side of the airfield. He looked at me enquiringly: "Well, there's no harm in asking!"

I listened in disbelief as he asked the captain where he was off to next.

"Orly, France," was the laconic reply.

"I suppose you couldn't take our expedition kit with you?" asked Anthony innocently.

"Sure, why not? Speak to my load-master."

And with that he turned on his heel and walked across the tarmac. Our financial problems melted - ten tons of equipment flown free to Europe.

⋘ ⋘ ⋘ ⋘ ⋘ ⋘ ⋘ ⋘ ⋘ ⋘ ⋘ ⋘ ⋘

We said our farewells. Anthony returned to Hong Kong, myself to Kent. From there I telephoned the USAF base at Orly and asked if they had any aircraft coming to England, in particular to the RMA Sandhurst where the AMA stored its equipment. My contact was a Pfc.

"Sure - where's the nearest air base?"

"I think there's one at Bracknell." I said hesitantly.

"OK, leave it with me. It's not much of a load and I've got a Charlie 130 flying to Norfolk tomorrow. I'll task it to drop your load off on the way. I'll call you back with an ETA."

He did. I was stunned. This, I decided, was how America got great. Where else in the world today could a private first class make decisions like that? Why, it was the way Empires were built! Subsequently I wasted more time trying to persuade the RMA to send a three ton truck to collect our equipment from Bracknell and take it back to their store.

Our tragedy ended, at least, on a high note.

16

A YEAR IN BRITAIN - LESS A MONTH IN YEMEN

Georgie Schofield, bless her, had lent us a mews cottage behind Paddington Station and it was to this that Binnie returned from the Middlesex Hospital at the end of October with the newborn Kathryn. Here we spent the bitter winter of 1962/3 while I struggled as a post-graduate student of radiology, also back at Middlesex. I was studying for the diploma in medical radio-diagnosis, which involved quite a lot of theoretical physics. In this I was helped by Stewart John, a BOAC engineer we had met in Kuwait along with his wife Suzie who became one of Kathryn's godparents, the other godparent being Gillian Vaughan Hudson, Bryan's wife.

Jim and Judy Johnson came to dinner one night in the mews. He explained that he had been approached by 'influential people' both in and out of the Conservative government of the time, to raise a mercenary force to support the Royalist regime in Yemen. In October 1962, there had been a coup d'état, following the death of the Imam Ahmed, and his successor, the Imam Al Badr, had been double-crossed by a group of young Egyptian-trained officers, who panicked and called in Egyptian support. Badr escaped to a cave in the mountains to the north and in the aftermath a senior officer, named Sallal - who had not been involved in the coup - became president. This republican government was really a puppet of the Egyptians who proceeded to stir up even more trouble in the adjacent British colony of Aden. As a result, to Al Badr and his princely relatives, never kindly disposed to the British presence in nearby Aden in the past, this now seemed a better option; and so covert intervention on their behalf was undertaken.

It came about that one morning in May I found myself landing from a BOAC Comet in Aden. In the words of a merchant captain, who called Aden 'Eudaemon' (the blessed) many centuries ago: "It was formerly a city when the voyage was not yet made from India to Egypt and when they did not dare sail from Egypt to the ports across this ocean but they came together at this place."

Times had changed. I was accompanying Colonel David Stirling as his baggage handler-cum-medical attendant, but posing as a hack from 'International Television News' - a non-existent organisation as far as I knew - while Colonel David did at least have his own TV company to represent. Somewhere between the aircraft steps and immigration I lost David, who had a knack of disappearing, remarkable for a man well over six feet tall, and I went through customs alone. I noted that our hand baggage, containing certain items of hardware which I would have had difficulty in explaining, had also disappeared. I took a taxi to the Crescent Hotel where the Anglo-Indian manager was a bit snooty as I had failed to book a room in his emporium.

I spent some fruitless hours telephoning around, to learn that everybody had gone away for two weeks. David I assumed had his head down in the High Commission where he had been invited to stay. I joined the Gold Mohur beach club and spent the afternoon swimming within the shark barrier - trying to get fit for I knew not what. I also engaged a qat-chewing Yemeni taxi driver on a full time basis for a ridiculously small sum. He insisted I try some qat myself. After what seemed several hours mastication I had cramp in the masseter muscles of my cheeks but no mood change. Perhaps it is an acquired habit? It tasted like sour holly leaves and not even my pulse was affected.

After a few day I moved out to a shed on an island in the harbour which our old friend Jeff Douglas had converted into a humble dwelling supplied with water and electricity from the mainland. Jeff was on leave. I was awaiting a move from above and was beginning to get bored. I found the colonial attitude of my fellow British pretty insufferable - all street signs in English, with badly written Arabic translations underneath. It was arrogant and thoughtless. Then the weather went sour, both temperature and humidity rocketed up and I developed prickly heat for the first time ever.

David appeared on the beach and told me to 'stand by'; for what he did not explain, but I prepared to get sucked into the slip stream. We went to dinner at the High Commission that night where I met Tony Boyle. He was ADC to the Governor, having failed an eyesight test for flying his beloved Hunters, hence was doomed to a desk job for as long as he stayed in the RAF, (it wasn't long). Meanwhile Flight Lieutenant Boyle became active on our behalf. He introduced me to a code using the Book of Psalms, which he assured me was simple but the importance of which I never quite grasped - who were we trying to outwit, apart from HMG? Meanwhile I impressed David by going for an early morning run to the summit of Jebel Shams.

"Excellent, you've had a good training run!" he cried on my return. Yes, but training for what, I wondered? I only had a month's leave from the hospital and had a creeping suspicion David envisaged me prowling through Yemen with sticks of dynamite hidden in my 'burnoose'. But I need not have worried. David had decided to take a longer view and arranged for us to meet his war-time driver and comrade-in-arms, Johnny Cooper, at that time employed in the Sultanate of Oman as a contract officer with the Sultan's Armed Forces. Two cables were sent, one advising him he needed compassionate leave due to his mother's illness, the other advising him to meet her at the notorious Speedbird Hotel in Bahrain, where I would be staying. David, of course, pulled rank and would stay at the Political Residency with Sir William and Lady Luce.

I spent the last few days in Aden pretending to be a TV producer, talking to local merchants and then getting caught up with two Yemeni lads who remembered me from the Kuwait Army and offered to take me up to Sanaa' to interview President Sallal. Fortunately David was not present, otherwise

I dread to think what madcap venture might have developed!

A final visit to Silent Valley, where contractors were busy finishing the new army barracks, ready for British troops due to leave Kenya when it became independent the following year. The contractors were still finishing them in 1967, ready for the NLF to take over!

I bade farewell to Yusuf, my French-speaking Somali boatman, Baidoon the gazelle and the three cats who had recognised me as a cat hater and made themselves scarce as soon as I had arrived on the island.

We flew around the Arabian peninsula in an Argonaut which took most of a day and reached Bahrain after dark. There we met with Johnny and it was left to me to brief him on the proposed attack on Sanaa' airfield. From the outset the success of this mission would depend on the co-operation of the Sherif of Beihan. As long as HMG played ball this would be possible but in the event the Profumo Affair broke, the government lost its nerve and the idea of an Anglo-French team of mercenaries led by ex-SAS running loose in the Middle East caused collective hysteria - and the mission was called off - officially. David however would not countenance this and I suspect there was hidden agreement in White's club one night when HMG was declared totally non-attributable but, after all... David was a private citizen.

I was not to know any of this at the time; but there wasn't a lot more I could tell Johnny until we had returned to London and then to Paris to establish 'the French Connection'. I got a rocket from Jim for flying first class from London on to Paris.

"Only spivs do that," he said caustically.

Well, Johnny got his team into Yemen, having to avoid HMG's attention as well as the official opposition, by taking devious routes; then, thanks to Tony Boyle the Anglo-French team found themselves together on Aden airport, where they snuck into a DC3 of Aden Airways and were duly deposited in Beihan. Three weeks later they were in the heart of Royalist Yemen east of Sanaa'. Once there they never did get to the airfield, nevertheless they were to make themselves a thorough nuisance to the Egyptian Army and the Republicans. About which, more later.

❧ ❧ ❧ ❧ ❧ ❧ ❧ ❧ ❧ ❧ ❧ ❧ ❧

Meanwhile my own relations with HMG were progressing. I was encouraged to take up a post in Saudi Arabia and this I duly did, after completing part one of the DMRD successfully that summer. I had been one of eight post-graduate students, the others being from the Middle East or the sub-continent and I had made myself unpopular with them by suggesting it would be a good idea if we were each allocated a room in the department for a week and learned from the radiographers how to actually take an X-ray. I suspect the reason for their unhappiness was that all the radiographers were girls, and they found it demeaning to be under instruction from such lowly creatures! But Dr Campbell Golding declared that every radiologist should be able to take a full set of dental X-rays... so the matter was settled. I doubt if any of us were capable of anything more complicated than a chest X-ray!

So I told 'Cam' I would be on my way and asked him to keep a place for me to continue my studies after a couple of years. He agreed in principle and thereafter referred to me as: "That chap who spends most of his life east of Suez."

I was taught a certain amount of 'tradecraft' by HMG's representatives towards the end of the summer. One exercise was to throw off a 'tail' which I thought I had after a brisk walk through the streets around Victoria Station - only to find that eluding two chaps in suede shoes and trilby hats had been easy enough - but I had failed to notice the little old lady with the shopping bag who subsequently described every move I had made from start to finish.

We bought Smuggler's Cottage in Lamberhurst in Kent in the early autumn where I left Binnie and Kathryn when I set off for Riyadh in October 1963. So began one of the less pleasant experiences in my life.

17

A TIME IN ARABIA DESERTA

King Abdul Aziz Al Saud, creator of Saudi Arabia, had died in 1953 and his son Saud had therefore been on the throne for less than ten years when I landed in Riyadh in October 1963.

The country had barely got onto the 'learning curve'. The exploding oil wealth of the previous decade had been largely squandered. Abdul Aziz himself had been torn apart by his Wahabi-scruples and his unsought wealth. Saud proceeded to squander the latter and managed to drive the country to bankruptcy.

I once heard it said that Libyan Arabs hate everybody - including themselves. One could say the same thing about the Saudis, but here it was more regional. There were still bedouins in the Nejd, who were feckless, arrogant - for no good reason - and disdained work. They were referred to as 'donkeys' by their more sophisticated cousins in both Asir (eastern) and Hejaz (western) Provinces. But, as my friend Dick Mitchell of the US Embassy in Kuwait had once said: "The one lesson the Arabs have taught the west is... survival."

I sometimes think it helps to be schizophrenic if one lives in Arabia. I was to see fully-equipped hospitals scattered across the desert, built by European companies during the 1950s, a consortium of Philips of Holland and Siemens of Germany called 'Hospitalia' having been particularly successful at landing 'turn key contracts'. They stood empty on their crumbling foundations, corridors and wards, theatres and laboratories slowly filling with sand. They had never been staffed. Soon I was to see attempts to rectify this in the next burst of activity. I watched an airliner land at Riyadh airport and disgorge 90 Bengali doctors from east Pakistan. With no attempt at indoctrination, they were pushed out into the villages of the Nejd; and left to rot, sharing nothing save their Muslim faith with the inhabitants. How right was Goethe when he said: "It is so easy to act, so hard to think."

❧ ❧ ❧ ❧ ❧ ❧ ❧ ❧ ❧ ❧ ❧ ❧ ❧

It was into this cloud cuckoo land that I fell on 28 October 1963, after spending a few days in Beirut and Cyprus en route. I was expecting to take over the Central Hospital in Riyadh and had collected John Guthrie's "Notes on Hospital Administration" from him when I stayed in Bellapaise. Unknown to me at the time there already was a doctor, a Syrian called Dr Sayyid Rabbagh, who was enjoying extended leave in Beirut. News of my arrival reached his ears and he high-tailed it back to Riyadh so as to be ready to greet me...

Having to pay a 46 Lebanese pound airport tax imposed by the Saudi authorities at Beirut airport was a warning of the kind of treatment to expect as a government servant! We flew to Dharan where there were immigration procedures, then a further hour's flight to Riyadh. I was taken straight to the Ministry of Health where I was greeted by the minister, a round, nervous man called Yusuf Al Hagery. I suspected he was a Hejazi, but in fact he was a Nejdi. He introduced me to his staff as the 'new director' of the Central Hospital - but known to all and sundry as 'the Shemaisi', the district of the city where it stood. It was clear from the outset that he had hoped I would replace Dr Sayyid Rabbagh while he was on leave and thus present him with a *fait accompli* on his return.

Poor Yusuf, he lived in a dream world as I was soon to learn, which included an almost mystical faith in the ability of the British to bring order where there was chaos. What he hadn't realised was that I would need a gunboat to start with! As well as a budget!

We even visited the hospital. This was another 'turnkey' disaster of the previous decade, equipped by Hospitalia. Designed to accommodate 400 patients, half of the rooms had been occupied by staff until recently - one of the salient features of all Middle East hospital designs is that they never included staff quarters. Now some hovels had been built within the perimeter wall to accommodate nurses. The central air conditioning plant was already a rusting heap and workmen were enthusiastically battering holes beneath the windows to install wall units. I counted 137 broken windows, the patients having decided to provide their own fresh air. I later heard that, when a few months earlier a member of the royal family had visited the hospital and complained about the broken windows to the minister, he had replied: "Don't worry, there's an English doctor coming to run the hospital."

Many of the rooms were locked and a cleaner was summoned who had about three dozen keys in his hand. Solemnly the minister tried them one at a time. Then I was taken to my flat. This had been occupied by the minister himself until eight months ago and he had insisted it be kept empty for the 'English Mudir', i.e. director. Most of the furniture was broken, the place filthy and I had my first experience of Saudi electricity. I made the mistake of plugging the refrigerator into a wall plug, whereupon there was a sharp bang and a lot of smoke. I learned that most electrical appliances were American, requiring a 110 volt supply but that the air conditioners needed 220 volts, and there were separate circuits for each. I'd chosen the wrong one. Thereafter I learned to always carry a voltmetre with me. The fridge was too filthy to use anyway.

As we prepared to leave two lorries arrived with some 40 Jordanians. They were reputed to be nursing orderlies, although they looked more like farm boys to me. One of them, Mahmoud, could read and write and was destined to become my secretary. There was no accommodation prepared for them so they bedded down in the hospital corridors.

That night I gazed at the ceiling and wondered what on earth I had let myself in for; or perhaps more pertinently - what had HMG let me in for!

It was, I suppose, inevitable that politicians in the UK would assess Saudi Arabia as ripe for revolution. The oil wealth had scarcely reached the masses, conditions were chaotic everywhere and all the time there were hectoring attempts, by the Egyptian government in particular, to subvert the despotic rule of the royal family - partly to eliminate the last British influence in the Middle East, partly to spread Nasser's Republican zeal. Both parties failed to take account of the massive inertia of the people. During my time in the Kingdom I only found evidence of one serious attempt to promote armed revolt. Shortly after my arrival there was an air drop of light weapons and ammunition by parachute into the desert some way north of Riyadh. Whoever was on the reception committee - always assuming there was one - failed to collect. By the time I could observe the drop zone from a discreet distance there were only a few parachutes lying limp among the desert scrub. The containers had been collected alright - by the police. That was the only evidence of insurrection I was to find; but despite my protestations that the regime was secure and prevailing chaos would continue to be the order of the day, I sensed I was a voice crying in the wilderness. The powers that be continued to believe that the fall of the house of Saud was imminent and that revolutionary forces would subsequently sweep Britain's neighbouring oil resources into limbo. Perhaps they had their reasons; and they had better sources of intelligence than mine. Nevertheless the protection of 'Britain's vital oil supplies' began to ring hollow - who else was to buy them? A British diplomat in Kuwait once coined the phrase: "You can't dig oil with bayonets." The fact that he abandoned this catch phrase when he found it was not helping his career, does not detract from its underlying validity.

I started to explore Riyadh. I was desperate for news from home so one of my first ports of call was the Post Office. This was a temple of calm in the noisy streets. An almost religious silence filled the vast hall where numerous young Saudis passed the hours when it was open in apparent contemplation of the piles of letters on the floor and counter. It transpired there was only one employee, a Sudanese called Mohammed, who could read English - or the Roman alphabet. Thus any letter with any such script on it was tossed at him to allocate to a post box - even if the post box, city, country, etc., was written in Arabic! It was a good idea to make a friend of Mohammed.

Nearby was the parcel office. This was truly an Aladdin's cave. The concept of a 'parcel post' was of recent origin in the Kingdom, nevertheless the sorting room contained an impressive number of parcels, indeed, every one that had ever been dispatched to Riyadh. I was able to insinuate myself into this holy of holies, in search of a parcel addressed in innocence to myself, and find it I did; for each parcel was allocated to floor space in strict order of arrival There were huge cartons addressed to 'His Majesty, c/o the Palace', for example, which had been there for years, presumably sent by optimistic salesmen from the outer world. There was no system of delivery, but Saudi

Arabia was a member of the International Postal Union (sic) so had to accept parcels both by air and sea. I suspect this particular hold up was confined to the Nejd. The few foreigners living there at the time had learned to run their own external mail and parcel post.

Outside was the 'Casino of Riyadh'. No, not a gambling den, but another modern ruin. Some ambitious adviser in the early days of oil wealth had introduced French as the language of diplomacy and thus contact with the outside world. The few faded notices around the city that were in Roman script were in this language, e.g., 'La Poste'. Perhaps the same optimist had inspired the locals with the idea of formal gardens to lighten the eye of the beholder. Now all there was to see were desiccated concrete ruins choked with thorns. They reflected the pitiless side of Wahabism allied with the total lack of maintenance - there was indeed no word in the language for it! Tales of sheikhs abandoning cars when the ash trays were full contained a germ of truth. There was simply no desire to beautify this hostile land.

❧ ❧ ❧ ❧ ❧ ❧ ❧ ❧ ❧ ❧ ❧ ❧ ❧

I had soon concluded that I could not 'direct' Shemaisi Hospital any more than fly to the moon. Accordingly I lined up to the minister and told him so to his face - and why. I proposed that I should be called 'technical director', responsible for introducing some kind of support for the current basic medicine being practised, while Sayyid Rabbagh remained 'administrative director', i.e., in charge, for all practical purposes. Poor Yusuf's face as he absorbed this news... he had fought and lost his power battle, which I suspect had as much to do with personal animosity as any real hope of improving standards of health care.

I went to sign my contract, seven copies, for which I had to pay 40 riyals for the stamps! I began to think income tax would be preferable - but of course there was no way of imposing it. In the nearby Ministry of Agriculture there were reputed to be over 2,000 employees in clerical and administrative grades who were only entitled to draw their pay at the end of each lunar month if they undertook not to attend for work the preceding 29 days - there was no space for them in the building!

Spreading oil wealth to the people was no easy matter.

Meanwhile... I went to the airport to collect two suitcases which I had consigned to air freight. Fortunately I had allocated a morning for this operation. To the documents I produced were added more and more papers signed by fatter and fatter men as I penetrated the heart of the building until the vaults were opened and out came my two suitcases, now bound with wire and handled as if they contained high explosives. The seals were broken and a nice little Hejazi clerk rummaged through them. He produced a box of Tampax and said cheerfully: "Ah, for madame!"

I presume this was to show his sophistication for we had been warned that such items were, needless to say, unavailable in Riyadh. I then had to return all the papers to the fat men, the last charging me one riyal for administration.

I was now almost in a position to start work in my self-appointed 'technical' role. Lacking as I did the ability to mend a fuse without help I set about building a technical team. I was not the only unguided expatriate lurking around the ministry. From time to time, 'specialists' had been recruited on an ad hoc basis and then left to rot as nobody knew what to do with them after the immediate job in hand had been completed.

Thus I found a German engineer called Schroer who had been brought in to support a German-staffed hospital some years previously that had duly foundered in the waste land. The staff had walked out in despair. A few, like Schroer, had no especial reason to return home and had stayed on in the ministry. He was a friendly soul, and was delighted to find someone who was trying to create some kind of order out of chaos. He had spent the closing months of World War II flying Messerschmidt jets which he said were more than a match for anything the Allies could put in the air - but he got tired of being outnumbered ten to one!

Then there was Nieuwenkamp, the Dutch X-ray engineer looking after the interests of Philips in the kingdom. He reacted to the idea of a technical team with enthusiasm also. Providing he didn't complain I don't think Philips minded what he did. Together with a Lebanese electrician, an Egyptian plumber and an Indian carpenter, we were ready to work!

We were at once regarded as a life line by the hospital staff. But we were not in time to save the lives of three Indian electricians from the ministry who were completing the installation of new X-ray equipment. They were working on the high tension side of the circuitry on the roof above the department when there was a bang - and there were three dead Indians. The consensus was that they had become careless handling low voltage circuits. Brought up on 220 volt circuits they regarded 110 volts as beneath contempt... but they'd got on the wrong side of some 10,000 volts on this tragic occasion.

To my horror I found that deep X-ray therapy was being undertaken, on purely clinical grounds. If it looked like it, felt like it, then it was a tumour; and duly blasted for periods up to half an hour daily or twice weekly, until the mass had disappeared, or, more commonly, the patient's superficial tissues had broken down as radiation necrosis set in. I managed to get this stopped until a dedicated radiotherapy department was built. So, sadly my first written report to the minister, typed by Mahmoud, my new secretary from Irbid, stated: "Reluctantly I must advise Your Excellency to shut the radiotherapy department and start again... "

(A panic call to (the late Professor Sir) Brian Windeyer at the Middlesex Hospital led to an introduction to Harold Ham, a fellow radiotherapist in Sydney who subsequently came to Riyadh as the ministry's advisor on this project. I decided it would be a treat for him to see some real desert and drove the five hour trip to Dhahran to meet him. Half way back I enthused over the dramatic scenery of dune and distant horizon.

"There!" I cried, "where else in the world could you see such stark beauty?"

"Alice Springs," he grunted, "I was born there." I drove faster after that and kept quiet.)

I suppose it stood to reason that the first requests for help from our technical team - it sounded better than works department - should be for help in changing electric light bulbs or turning taps off. But a challenge loomed.

Standing behind the hospital was a two storey building, a WHO project completed in 1960, which had stood empty since the contractor was paid off the following year. It was destined to be the central laboratory and within there were 72 large crates of furniture and instruments. Every week the minister would demand my presence and with his usual retinue of clerks and sycophants we would walk through the empty corridors as he opened every room and we gazed silently at packing cases - and more packing cases. At first this behaviour puzzled me; until I finally realised this was his *cri de coeur*, only he couldn't bring himself to say: "Doctor Philip, do something!"

It was time for the technical team to get to work. Schroer decided to use the power station, built six years previously by Skoda for the hospital but never used except as a loo by the labourers. Again we found output geared to 110 volt circuitry while all the laboratory equipment was 220 volt. With the help of a German contractor he managed a conversion. The rest of us turned to opening crates. In the end I found I was reduced to erecting Sankey Sheldon steel shelves, being the only one totally inept with his hands. I also found 12,000 old X-rays dumped in the reception area which I burned. I did not know about silver recovery in those days!

We got the laboratory up and running in three weeks and staff who had been scattered around other hospitals in the kingdom, marking time and doing next to nothing, were drafted in under an active Lebanese pathologist, Dr Haddad, dragged unwillingly from his private laboratory.

⋘⋙ ⋘⋙ ⋘⋙ ⋘⋙ ⋘⋙ ⋘⋙ ⋘⋙ ⋘⋙ ⋘⋙ ⋘⋙ ⋘⋙ ⋘⋙ ⋘⋙

I had decided that the flat was unsuitable for a family and found a villa owned by an employee of the telegraph office, who negotiated deals on my behalf and furnished it for £300. I would not have got anything for less than £2000. Fahad was a well-meaning landlord... I had been introduced to him by a Syrian officer in the National Guard, whom I had met in turn thanks to Nigel Brommage. There was a two man military mission advising the Guard, also known as 'the White Army', a largely tribal force raised, in the great tradition of autocratic rulers, to balance the power of the regular army. A bachelor cavalry officer, Brigadier Kenneth Timbrell, was the senior; Nigel, his deputy. We later met Timbrell in the Trucial States. I had met Nigel ten years previously when he was commanding 2nd Regiment in the Arab Legion. They were living in the Yamama Hotel at the time, the only 'international' hotel in Riyadh and superficially at least a centre of sophistication where you could drink non-alcoholic beer as a treat. I confess I spent many evenings there before Binnie and Kathryn arrived. Nigel's wife Pamela was with and busily negotiating for an ex-minister's house at a rental of a quarter million riyals a year. As the Brigadier was 'pigging it' upstairs he was not being particularly helpful to them - and Pamela, who could reduce a full general to tears, tore into him. They got their house, and moved in with their two children, nanny, and three servants. Pamela, meanwhile, was extremely helpful to me in preparing my new house and making it fit for Binnie's impending arrival. I dug their garden as a gesture of thanks.

The news of President Kennedy's assassination in early December upset the Saudi people more than I expected. I was constantly surprised at how little direct influence the Americans exerted in the kingdom. ARAMCO had been present for 30 years. My first reaction was to blame them; but later I accepted that their job was to produce oil, not to colonise. This was brought home to me by a delightful elderly Egyptian doctor in the ministry, Wasfi Omar, who had qualified at Cambridge in 1923. He was the WHO representative and once had had got to know me, he showed me the report on health services which had been written earlier that year... well, it saved me the trouble of writing my own. All I needed was a carbon copy. Alas, he retired at Christmas. Like all Egyptians he enjoyed a joke. Here is a sample of the time:

An Egyptian complained to his wife about the lack of variety in their food. Well, you got out and see if you can buy anything other than vegetables!" she cried. So the husband sallied forth into the market.

"Where can I buy chicken?" he called to a policeman.

"Join the queue over there," came the reply. He did so. When at last his turn came, there were none left.

"Where can I buy some fish?" This time a policeman pointed to another queue.

"Over there!" The same thing happened. By this time the husband was furious. He stormed over to the policeman.

"I want to murder that Gamal Abdul Nasser! Where can I buy a gun?" The policeman pointed over his shoulder.

"Join that queue over there."

I've never believed humour is universal. Our closest American friends, like Chester and Martha Davis, frequently found ourselves with a 'humour gap' that was nothing to do with an imperfectly shared common language. But jokes like Wasfi's underlined the fact that the British and Egyptians can never be angry with each other for very long!

❦ ❦ ❦ ❦ ❦ ❦ ❦ ❦ ❦ ❦ ❦ ❦ ❦

On 17 December Binnie arrived with Kathy in tow. She had learned to walk since I left the UK. We were still in the flat but were able to move to our new house before Christmas. Binnie expressed horror when she saw how electricity was provided. I was already hardened to the sight of wires lashed from post to post until they reached our house and were thrust like a bundle of knitting against the wall. The tangle was worsened by the extra 220 volt cable that

I had installed to power a hot water heater. To add to our problems our underground water tank had leaked so we had to have a tanker and pump water up to the roof tank.

One light on the horizon was the reception given to Kathy by the Sudanese servant Mohammed I had engaged. They were delighted with each other. He was a relative of Mohammed in the Post Office; and I had persuaded our landlord to add a room and shower on the roof for him. This was luxury for the bulk of foreign workers in Riyadh at the time.

Just in time for Christmas we were 'discovered' by the ARAMCO staff living in Riyadh. First, Mike Ameen, who was head of government relations, and his wife Pat. Mike, of Lebanese ancestry, had fought with the US Marines in World War II and had been severely wounded at Iwo Jima. We were to remain friends with them for many years. Next, there was Marcel Grignon and his wife Jean, with their two children Ann and Paul. Marcel was of French ancestry, his father having been a university professor in Algiers before the war. They too remained friends long after we had left Arabia. The third member of American staff, Hugh Renfro, looked after the local refinery. I noted at the time: "These are the only people in Riyadh able to live in a remotely civilised manner." (Forty years later I am still conscious that without them our life in Saudi Arabia would have been akin to a prison sentence.)

They were very kind to us. As we got to know them better, we delighted in their *bon mots*, e.g. when a member of the US State Department rang Mike to ask his advice on what King Saud should wear on his forthcoming visit to Washington. Mike roared back: "For Pete's sake put the guy in a 'thob'.[1] He looks like a whole sack of shit in a business suit."

Then there was Dick Kerin, horse-mad and ex-CIA, who, when discussing former colleagues in the agency, uttered the memorable (to me!) remark concerning the celebrated Miles Copeland: "Huh! That second hand car merchant! He was the only guy I ever knew who used the CIA as a cover!"

They lived in adjacent houses and let us use their swimming pool and squash court. But all this was to come.

Meanwhile I continued to struggle with the selection of tasks the minister threw at me. I sat on a tender board for next year's medicines. English was used as the medium, but sometimes suffered in the translation... for instance it took me some time to realise that Al Ahn and Hamid's bid to supply surgical instruments was that of Allen & Hanbury's. On the whole my support for UK firms when possible was not productive. For instance I lumbered Watson's, a British firm making X-ray equipment, with one small department in a new hospital - while Philips and Siemens swept the board throughout the rest of the country. (Watson's didn't thank me and unloaded the contract on Philips.) But I became aware that certain European firms (not British, I'm glad to say) were producing medicines solely for the Saudi market and consisting largely of chalk. My European colleagues supported me in getting these companies black-listed and we eventually overcame the ministry's policy to go for the cheapest offer.

[1] The white, all enveloping, long shirt worn by all male Eastern Arabians.

Then I was sent on a three day survey of the northern Nejd, after a period of particularly cold weather. We visited tribal camps and I concluded that infant mortality had been over 60% during recent weeks. Several children who were produced for my inspection with 'harara' (fever) were clearly suffering from measles. I hope the paediatric antibiotics I administered may have saved some of them from bronchopneumonia. I doubt if the report I submitted after my trip went further than the minister's desk. We were not yet ready to challenge the will of Allah. I was given less sensitive tasks after that - like rationalising OPD services.

One of the problems in the out-patients department was that Dr Yusuf insisted that consulting room doors were left open so that waiting patients could see that the doctor was working and not having a quiet kip on the examination couch. This of course meant that no clinical examinations were performed if it involved the patient leaving his or her chair... I persuaded him that this was not done in British hospitals and I would personally see to it that the doctors were not 'skiving'. I discovered that there was no consultant programme, rather that the doctors moved in an amorphous mass over to the OPD building when they felt like it! Surprisingly enough they responded enthusiastically to my proposed timetable, especially when it became clear that they would actually be working less hours than before and I would be responsible for this.

With this 'coup' under my belt I boldly asked permission to visit Jedda in our New Year. We were subject to the Muslim calendar, and clock, too. The latter was confusing as we lived by Arab time, i.e., sunrise was twelve o'clock. There were other times though - sun time, an amendment of this which was six hours on, so that dawn came at a reasonable hour; European time which was Greenwich time minus three hours; and Aramco time which was GMT minus four hours - true, as they worked in the eastern Province. When arranging to meet anybody it was the custom for foreigners to say: "Meet you at X hours before/after sunset."

So it was Binnie, Kathy and I set off for Jedda on a Boeing 720 which completed the 800 kilometre flight to Jedda in an hour. We were accompanied by an aged Turkish doctor of pharmacy and I spent the next few mornings with him inspecting the central medical stores - another Aladdin's cave! There were instruments that would have been out of date in a Victorian surgery while I found an X-ray tube that might well have been used by Sir William Roentgen himself. (Tragically, after I had managed to wheedle it out of the storekeeper's hands, the glass broke as I was packing it to take home.) Again, it demonstrated how unscrupulous merchants had unloaded obsolete equipment on the wretched Saudis in the previous decade; although my Turkish companion suspected some of the items had in fact been left there by retreating Ottomans during World War I.

Meanwhile Binnie and Kathryn were having a ball. We were staying with John Christie, second secretary in the British Embassy, who had a large villa in north Jedda complete with a lovely garden, swimming pool and an

Ethiopian maid called Tebba, who succumbed to Kathy's charms and gave Binnie a break. Jedda, with its old multi-storied Turkish houses, spicy smells and relative calm, was restful after the harsh modernity of Riyadh. We found Peter Mason managing the British Bank of the Middle East. We knew him from Kuwait and Beirut where he had assisted in our pre-nuptials the year before. He joined us at the Creek, 30 kilometres north of Jedda, where both bank and embassy had their beach huts and where swimming and snorkelling over the reefs were better than anything the Gulf had to offer. We also met John and Gwen Symonds. He was third secretary, and at a party John Christie gave in his garden I regret Gwen got thrown into the pool. On the whole though the rest of the British community regarded Binnie and I as 'country cousins' - strange how easily they dropped into the Hejazi attitude towards 'Nejdis'! Mind you, I don't think the swimming pool episode with Gwen helped much.

All good things have to come to an end. We flew back to Riyadh after nine days, to find it had rained non-stop for the previous 24 hours. Mohammed had been doing his best to mop up but, needless to say, the house had leaked. To be honest, it was soaked through. We stood and looked at it. After Christie's place it appeared to us a doll's house. Our unspoken thoughts were the same - we would have to find something bigger. The idea was dramatically reinforced a few moments later when we entered our bedroom and Binnie put out her hand to see if the wall was wet. It was - and it was also live. Thank God there was only 110 volts on the lighting circuit, but it was enough to throw her across the room!

On the move again. Our new house faced across open ground to the old mud-walled palace of King Abdul Aziz and a sand track led round the corner to the Grignon's 'palace' - where Kathy would have Ann and Paul to play with. The move was easier this time. I had been unofficially engaged by the United States Military Aid Group as their doctor, so called upon them for logistic support. Their trucks moved us lock stock and barrel - the latter being used to make 'siddiqui juice', of which more later. The technical team moved in after working hours and our new house was soon looking spruce - too spruce as it happened, for when I went to sign the contract with the agent, he warned me that the landlord had just turned up from the Eastern Province - where he too was a government employee - and had been so impressed with what we had done for his dowdy old house that he decided he wanted to live in it himself!

"I shall make sure he stays in Dammam," cried the agent. Just how, I wondered?

Anyway I submitted to signing a contract for four months, after that it would be 'by arrangement'. I should have known... and we had installed shelving, fly screens, fitted cupboards...

Well, we were going to enjoy it while we could. John Symonds was our first guest, armed with a bottle of Scotch. Later we were able to buy this luxury from the Saudi Brigadier in command of Riyadh district, but we did not have our feet far enough under the table at this stage. So Scotch was still a treat. However we had learned how to make alcohol from the Grignons', who gave us the ARAMCO booklet, The Blue Flame.

Briefly, one filled a plastic barrel with water, added 40 pounds of sugar and eight ounces of yeast, then let if ferment for ten days. The smell was unmistakable for those 'in the know' but fortunately these were rare in Riyadh - unlike Dharan, where illicit bootleggers had to be ready at a moment's notice for a police swoop. (I understand that even in those days management were warned of an impending raid.)

When it had fermented, we triple distilled it in a still provided by a benefactor from Dharan, over a gas stove. Eventually we were left with about one litre of nearly 100% pure alcohol. This we cut back to about 30-40 proof with Evian water (only the best!) and either drank it with tonic water as it was; or added exotic flavours, e.g., straining it through oak chips in a nylon stocking. By the time we went on leave in September that year and stayed in the Grand Hotel, Eastbourne, courtesy of my father, and made our first pilgrimage to the American Bar to taste a real gin and tonic... alas, it was an anticlimax. We were hooked on 'siddiqui'!

Final proof of our 'arrival' was delivery of the air mail Times. Thanks to Mohammed the Post, it was only three or four days late. It cost 6d (2.5p) a copy, but postage was 1s-3d - £27-6s per year.

John Symonds and I planned a desert trip for the 1st Eid in 1964, to visit Maidan Saleh, known as Saudi Arabia's Petra, but news that a diplomatic corps party 25 strong was going caused us to change our minds. This news reached us by an almost unbelievable route during John's stay - by the telephone! One of the features of our new house was a hand-cranked telephone, which we had given up as a bad job after a few days; but here it was, ringing, and, it transpired, from Jedda!

The public telephone exchange in Riyadh was a mud hut outside the old palace. I never found more than one operator in it at any time and his 'exchange' was a board dating back to Turkish times. There were between 50 and 100 plugs visible, but how many lines actually worked by 1964 was debatable.

Some time later there was an occasion when I spent an anxious hour one night with an operator called Sa'ad, whom I had befriended and given some medical care. The ultimate palace coup when Feisal finally deposed his brother Saud had taken place earlier that day. The army was on more than stand-by; and there seemed a chance that there might be shooting - if Saud failed to go gracefully, (which in the end he did). I decided to try and get a message to the British Embassy. Hand-cranking the house phone produced no answer from the exchange, so I went there, and was overjoyed to find Sa'ad on duty. I was let in to the holy of holies and Sa'ad began the tedious business of raising his 'oppo' in Jedda. At last I got through to a duty clerk in the embassy. The ensuing conversation went something like this:

"Hello, I know it's late but could you let the ambassador know there's been a coup here in Riyadh and Faisal is now king?"

"Are you sure? We don't want any scare-mongering you know."

"Of course I'm sure, but there may be some fighting, the Royal Guard are surrounding the palace."

"Oh alright, I'll let his secretary know in the morning," and rang off.

I never knew who he was - and as far as I can make out the message was never delivered. Oh well, I suppose history makes itself.

But right now Gwen was on the line from Jedda, and our visit to Maidan Saleh clearly would be 'inappropriate'.

Instead the three of us went and stayed in John Christie's house with the indefatigable Tebba while John was absent in England. John and Gwen Symonds brought their two kids and the seven of us set off south next day on the road to Yemen in two Land Rovers. This was just a sand track and we soon got lost in the dunes. This meant camping overnight on a salt flat. Next day we reached Al Lith and presented ourselves to the Mir. He made us welcome, which was fortunate as Kathryn had got loose and was charging around removing the bolts from the rifles of his guards! He advised us to camp in a wadi nearby where we found a river, hot springs and green grass. There was as usual a serpent in Paradise; when dusk fell we were eaten by mosquitoes. Next day we swung north again over a high plateau that looked like Kenya but with no wild game. We were on a camel track which we discovered from the driver of a passing truck led to Mecca. He seemed to think it quite normal for a party of Europeans with three children to be going there. We camped on the open 'veldt' and gazed at the plethora of stars above us. No mosquitoes that night. Next day we returned to Jedda.

Back in Riyadh we met a young English teacher called David Phillips who was teaching English at the University. Kathryn transferred her attentions to him, especially as it transpired that Paul and Ann Grignon were really a bit old for her to play with - although a few years later she would insist on 'Paul and Ann' stories before she went to bed at night. She would sit for hours on David's knee while she went through her picture books with him.

I decided it was time to see the Eastern Province. Thanks to ARAMCO I spent a week in their guest house in Dharan. The minister had asked me to look at the hospital in Dammam where our sea baggage was still languishing in customs. As there was still equipment for the central laboratory there as well - it had been there for the past eighteen months - there seemed to be several birds to kill with one or two stones.

It took me six hours to drive the 315 miles across the desert. It was interesting to compare Dharan with Ahmadi, probably the two biggest 'oil towns' in the world. Ahmadi reflected the dying Imperialistic urge to create a permanent city while Dharan was above all temporary. I sensed the American residents felt somehow guilty at making gardens in someone else's country. It was the difference between Simla-on-Sea and Butlins. But this did not apply to the Aramco hospital and its health service. In 1964 these were...

superb. (Perhaps I was in a permanent state of shock after my experiences with the state health service at the time!) Indeed there were those in high places, i.e. in the parent companies, who voiced their concern that Aramco was becoming a health service for the kingdom - with a couple of oil wells on the side. Certainly every Saudi I met would have killed to get himself and his family into Dharan Hospital should the need arise. Their 'outreach' programme impressed me. Every Saudi employee and his family were entitled to the company's health care. The following incident typifies its excellence.

I accompanied two of their district nurses on their 'rounds', both highly competent health visitor/midwives from California. We went to call on a family in nearby Al Kobar where a mother was having trouble with her latest newborn. Janet, one of the two nurses, was near despair. Despite several hospital admissions and regular home visits the boy continued to have diarrhoea and vomiting as soon as he was taken home. The child's father was threatening to take the baby back to the desert where a tribal 'medicine man' would apply 'wasm', ie. apply a red hot iron the offending part of the anatomy, in this case the belly. The mother was no fool, she - like so many undernourished women of the villages - was feeding the child on the best Aramco-provided powdered milk, and religiously carried out the sterilisation techniques she had been taught. This time Janet asked to see her prepare the bottle and actually feed the child. The mother did so, impeccably. The last thing she did however, before placing the teat in the baby's mouth, was to roll the bottle in the sand outside the door... the way her mother and grandmother before her had always cleaned their kitchen utensils. I expected to see Janet go through the roof. Instead, in the careful, idiomatic, Arabic these nurses had to learn, she explained that this hereditary method of cleaning was so important that it would be better to do it first... then go through the boiling and antiseptic wipe processes later.

Whatever the moralists will say, it worked. I left Dharan with profound respect for the way Aramco worked. 'Enlightened self-interest' was all the rage and was shown to be practical.

I managed to get our sea baggage and the laboratory equipment released. One of the problems was that there were insurance charges involved - and insurance was 'haram', ie. forbidden, under Islam. I undertook to reimburse these and produced my laundry bill from the Aramco Guest House, asked to have it stamped by them and said that that would cover the amount. When the customs official saw the word 'Aramco' he shrugged his shoulders, gave it back to me and released the goods. I found I had some authority in Dammam Hospital, why I am not sure but I suspect there was skulduggery going on in the stores division and they thought I was a ministry spy who was on to them. At any rate they fell over themselves in providing transport to take the cases to the railway station, and the next day, leaving my car with a driver, I returned to Riyadh in the comfort of the train. This railway had been built at the behest of King Abdul Aziz as a concession to modernity. Alas, it was already obsolescent by the time it was completed and by now scarcely used by the public. But it served a useful service for transporting freight from Dammam to Riyadh, where the line terminated.

Our new house was too good to last. The owner did return from the Eastern Province and after four months we were homeless again. But by now we had Aramco magic at our disposal. Mike Ameen found a Hadraumi with a house in the Malaz district - where he, the Grignons and the Renfros now lived - and negotiated on our behalf. Apart from being overawed by Mike, I think Ahmed, our new landlord, was a thoroughly decent man and was unfailingly helpful. We moved into a spacious villa with a large walled garden and impressive iron gates, once again helped by US Army transport. The only problem we faced there was when a Saudi built a new villa up the hill and tapped into our water pipe. I'm ashamed to say that I went out one night with a sledgehammer and crushed his pipe. *Force majeur* worked, he laid a new line somewhere else.

Opposite us was an impressive new two storey house and within a short time of our arrival we had neighbours. These were Chester and Martha Davis who became and remained two of our closest friends. Chester worked for an American Intelligence Agency (not, I hasten to add, the CIA) although with his physical resemblance to Sean Connery at a similar age it would not have been 'inappropriate'. Chester had Welsh-Lithuanian ancestry and was prone to profound mood swings; when the dark clouds descended we all - Martha included! - left him alone. They had met in Istanbul when Chet was a US Marine on security duties and Martha a member of the embassy staff. Since their marriage they had served in the US Embassy in Amman before returning to Washington. Riyadh was their next appointment. For the first time since our arrival life seemed to be tolerable!

Our new villa was a success. Away from the smog of the city it seemed cooler and the absence of humidity allowed us to install 'desert coolers', 'Saharawiyas', as the locals called them. Essentially they were electrically powered 'punkas' (Indian fans). A metal frame enclosed a small tray filled with water which was pumped up a couple of feet on to a straw mat on the side that faced into the room. The water trickled down it and a fan blew air through it, thus moist, cooled air was provided inside the room. We preferred these to air conditioners, I suspect they were healthier and they were certainly far cheaper to run. But of course their effectiveness depended on the low humidity encountered on the high Nejd plateau. Our garden flourished, Mohammed the Sudani was happy - in fact the only time I saw him unhappy was after he returned from a stoning ceremony, when a couple caught in adultery had been condemned to death. (The wife had been forcibly married to an elderly man and had run away with her boyfriend but both had soon been caught.) I assumed that the gentle Mohammed had been shocked by the barbaric deaths he had witnessed; but no, he was upset by the fact the crowd used big stones while the Koran stated that the stones must be no bigger than would fit into the palm of a man's hand.

We even began to entertain. One memorable evening we combined with

Chet and Martha to have a Scottish dancing evening on the roof of their house. Binnie, who was something of an expert, instructed the first eight Americans in the art of the Eightsome Reel. The music started and off they went. What she hadn't taken into account was that they were all well laced with our 'siddiqui juice', the strength and quality of which had not yet become a byword in the community. At the end of the first circle each let go of their partner prior to reversing - and eight dancers flew outwards as if impelled by a centrifugal force to collapse in giggling heaps around the roof.

Work had settled also. The technical team was proving a success and no longer needed my supervision - if it ever did! One Friday the minister insisted on taking me out to visit a village clinic. He used his private car and asked me to share the cost of the petrol with him... Dr Yusuf was a mass of inconsistencies and contradictions, I think this gesture was to show me that he did not exploit his position and reinforced it by making me put my hand into my own pocket. In fact, it proved a valuable visit, as I found the clinic was ill-equipped by any standards, e.g. there was no steriliser, no chair for the patient to sit on when with the doctor, no pictorial wall chart for eye testing. As a result I was able to spend some constructive weeks drawing up furniture and equipment lists which became standard for village clinics.

Then British staff began to arrive. Hardly the flood I had been promised, more of a trickle. First there were three delightful nursing sisters of what even then I called 'the old school'. Dr Yusuf wanted to scatter them around the hospitals, fondly believing they would act as catalysts for nursing excellence. I considered I was more realistic in insisting that they stayed together, preferably in the smallest unit possible. There was the ideal centre opposite the Ministry of Health building, where the Germans had 'come a cropper' a few years earlier. I sensed Dr Yusuf's misgivings, that we were revisiting a cemetery of his earlier hopes. But I pushed ahead. The building was in fact ideal - a three storey structure with some twenty beds, operating theatre, small laboratories and X-ray room plus good out-patient rooms. There were even staff quarters! Well, it had been designed by Germans for Germans. On my optimistic days I saw this becoming the 'jewel in the ministry's crown'.

Trouble started almost at once. Since the Germans had left, a motley crowd of transient staff had allowed furniture and fitting to rot - where downright vandalism had not actually occurred. I withdrew the technical team from the Shemaisi, which upset Sayyid Rabbagh.

Then a British gynaecologist arrived. This was the cue to create the first women's hospital! He was a charming but elderly man who had worked in the Sudan Medical Service, which he had left before independence and had then worked for the NHS in Yorkshire before retiring to Gibraltar.

Alas, we were soon struck by the 'German disease'. The nurses could not tolerate their living conditions - the drains blocked, electricity failed, water was cut off, the sterilisers fused... The list was endless.

Dr Yusuf complained to one of the nurses: "I thought you British were Empire builders! Why can't you put up with these problems?"

The nurse answered: "Dr Yusuf, you can put us to live in a tent in a desert and we would work for you and our patients. But we can't live in a sewer."

The truth was that the building and its contents were no longer fit for use as a hospital and demolition was the only answer. My fellow British saw out their one year contracts and quietly left.

Life went on. Mike Ameen introduced us to a friendly young Saudi lad, who had been educated in the USA, as many of the young men now 'coming of age' had been; and upon whom the hopes of the country, with all its frustrations and vicissitudes were to rest. His name was Salim bin Laden, his father being the country's biggest road building contractor. The family owned a large garden and date grove in a wadi some few miles out of Riyadh where we were invited to spend hot summer afternoons under the shade of the palm trees with the sound of running water. We were soon shocked to hear that a private company plane on which he was travelling had crashed in the desert. For some days there was no news; then the wreck was found and Salim alive within it. Not long after he gave a Thanksgiving dinner for his survival out in the desert. There must have been 200 guests, both Saudi and foreigners. We were treated to the full 'mensaf', roast camels stuffed with sheep stuffed with chickens stuffed with eggs, all on a mountain of rice. 'Allah kareem'.[1]

Nemesis struck in a curious form early that summer. I was summoned by a bell at our front gate - we were in our fourth house by now! - Mohammed was out so I opened the iron doors myself. There stood a rather too obvious Englishman. He was actually wearing a black jacket and striped trousers with a Homburg hat in his hand. I then recognised him as Jeffrey Douglas, late of the Royal Marines, 22 SAS and one time First Dead Sea Lord. I greeted him joyously but his sombre manner alarmed me. It transpired he was on a serious mission.

You will have gathered that I was not in Saudi Arabia entirely at my own behest but had undertaken to keep HMG informed of any tit bits of information I picked up while on my daily rounds.

In the middle of the 20th century, MI6 - or SIS, Special Intelligence Service, to use its correct title - was a much more clandestine organisation than it became in later years. With its hard core of university graduates, academics in many cases, it had a tight-knit hierarchy that did not approve of recruiting doctors: that was, somehow 'beyond the pale'. This did not stop station officers abroad from using fellow nationals of every calling to obtain information; but doctors, like priests, should not be directly employed. For instance, how could doctors be classified? 'Technical' intelligence officers? Well, a physician or surgeon was hardly a technician. 'Professional intelligence officers', then? The reaction of colleagues was predictable.

"And what the hell does that make us? Bloody amateurs?"

In the event I think I can best describe my role for those two years as 'hanger on'. Certainly I never felt part of an inner fraternity - if indeed there was one - and had no personal contact with the service other than through the station officer in the Embassy: though permitted to recruit my own agents, both

---

[1] It was Salim's next younger brother, Osama, who became notorious some forty years later as a terrorist.

national and local.

Accordingly, I had been briefed by a young man in London on the elements of secret writing. Armed with paper and chemicals in my wash bag I had set off for Arabia. I had patiently composed letters to a fictional aunt and added cryptic messages - there were few nuggets among the dross. Now it became clear that all was not well.

"We've had you sitting here for nearly a year now - and what have you sent us? Absolutely nothing! We can't go on wasting money like this." Jeff was not pompous by nature but he was trying hard to be. I expostulated at length. I had sent numerous messages, and what had I had in return? Not the proverbial sausage! Binnie was fed up with green dye that was beginning to stain the loo after my attempts to decipher messages that might have been hidden in my mail.

Well, this sterile exchange went on until it became clear that something was amiss. The penny began to drop, I think it was the mention of the green dye... Jeffrey looked at my chemicals and a look of horror dawned on his face. It transpired that London had inadvertently sent me off with the chemicals they should have retained for decoding my letters and retained those I should have been using to decode theirs. 'Q' had blundered! Even I had doubted the need for this clandestine, possibly archaic, form of communication in a country where literacy was at a premium.

Another disaster soon followed. To inscribe 'SW' (secret writing) on my letters required the use of a special sheet of paper that acted like carbon paper and transcribed invisible writing. I had been advised to store this in an old magazine left carelessly on a shelf... One day Mohammed, in an outburst of activity, decided the magazine was well out of date and slung it, with the rest of the household rubbish, over the garden wall. (The municipality had not got round to refuse collection in Malaz district.) By the time I realised what had happened, the goats had eaten it. Thereafter I was asked to give any messages to a man in the British Embassy in Jedda. He in turn had me appointed as Honourary Consul in Riyadh - which involved dealing with the first of the early British tramps, or back-packers, who had imagined they could wander around the kingdom on a shoestring. By the time they reached Riyadh they were penniless and hungry. I arranged exit visas for them and transport to their original point of entry - usually Dammam.

Travel out of the kingdom was tricky. Obtaining a return visa was our first obstacle but that summer we decided to visit Kuwait. We drove to Dharan in a sandstorm. On the car radio we heard that an MEA 'Caravelle' had crashed in Half Moon Bay on its approach to Dharan airport from Beirut, killing everyone on board. There were nineteen 'Aramcons' on board, including some of their 'top brass'. There was widespread hysteria in the American community as MEA refused to release a passenger list - possibly because one was not available?

In this taut atmosphere we waited for four hours, until a 'Dakota' clattered in out of the murk. We flew across to Bahrain where we had to wait another seven hours for the Kuwait Airways flight which had been delayed by the sandstorm. In the early hours of the following day we landed in Kuwait, 24 hours after leaving Riyadh. Kathryn took it all in her stride, bless her. We stayed with Hugh and Dee Wilkinson in Suleibikhat, almost next door to where Binnie had been brought up in the early 1950s.

Our few days break in the relaxed atmosphere of Kuwait were cheering. We saw Abdulla Al Ghanim, who kindly lent us an Opel 'Rekord'.

"Sorry, Philip, but you're not having a big car - not if I'm going to get it back in one piece!" He had a good memory: and it was good to meet him again. Poacher turned gamekeeper, he was shortly to join the government as Minister of Electricity. I visited the military hospital, finally completed - but still not open. The Ministry of Defence, PWD and the contractor were still wrangling about prices.

We sailed, swam and danced. It was good to be back, one of the few occasion when it did pay to revisit old haunts.

Back in Riyadh and at work. Dr Yusuf had finally despaired of my ever undermining Dr Sayyid Rabbagh and had transferred me to the ministry where I shared an office with a pleasant Palestinian, Khalid, and a Lebanese who went by the unfortunate name of Abu Leban, 'father of milk'. They were responsible for medical supplies. With the help of the nearby WHO unit, who were required not to make a fuss, I began to look at hospital statistics. The lack of raw data made this hopeless, so I began to visit clinics and acquire my own. I like to think that someone sometime found these useful.

The Ford Foundation were active in Riyadh and asked me to study family planning in the kingdom. In view of the total ignorance on the subject I got Dr Yusuf's permission to go to Bahrain for a few days where Dr Bevan, a senior physician, was able to direct me in something like the right direction.

In September, just before we went on home leave, Ahmed our landlord planted four palm trees in our garden. Half a ton of sand was dumped outside our iron doors, which made a splendid playground for Kathryn. The four enormous holes he dug for the palm trees did not - she fell into one and was extracted with difficulty. By now life was more civilised for Binnie. Chester had a car and a driver, who took Martha and Binnie shopping. Later, the two of them started to drive themselves; forbidden, of course, but they travelled by crafty sand tracks and parked unseen by police or Mutawwa, the religious police who ensured they were properly dressed and off the street at prayer time. Chester and I had given up playing badminton in his front yard. It was too hot.

We spent a month back in England, during which time I hired a yacht and sailed the Solent with Jennifer Blackwell and Dee Wilkinson - who kept me in order - while Binnie took Kathy to her parents, now living in Wiltshire. Our first week was spent in the Grand Hotel, Eastbourne, courtesy of my father. The Palm Court Orchestra made a sobering contrast with our recent experience. But, while I was sailing father had a stroke and by the time I got back he was in hospital. He was failing and when asked by his doctors, who were known to me, how much I wanted them to strive... I held his hand and said goodbye. He died peacefully but alas, with tears on his cheeks. His sister, my aunt Edith, who had shared a flat with him during his final years, and I arranged the burial and I returned to Riyadh ten days later. Dr Yusuf shared my sorrow compassionately.

◈ ◈ ◈ ◈ ◈ ◈ ◈ ◈ ◈ ◈ ◈ ◈ ◈

So for our last months in Saudi Arabia. Several British families had by now arrived and I helped found a 'pirate Church', which held services in the USMAG offices on a Friday morning, away from prying eyes. Christians of all denominations attended and I was sad when our Roman Catholic friends withdrew after a few months, on the instructions of their Bishop in Aden. I started teaching English to some young Saudis from the military academy, whom, I was interested to learn, were taught only Hebrew as a foreign language - the language of their enemy. I suspect the real reason for this was that it was a lot easier for them to learn, with its common roots!

Jennie, an English district nurse arrived, who was to introduce the concept of health visiting - difficult if there was a man in the house. Dr Yusuf wanted the two of us to join him on a visit to Wadi Zamzam, south east of Jedda, where there was a lunatic asylum. I say he wanted us to see it, but as ever, he was in two minds - shame at the backwardness of the treatment balanced by his duty to try and improve it. In the event the two of us went accompanied only by a driver.

The asylum was in fact a series of huge caves in the mountains, approached on foot for the last quarter mile from a sand track. The floors were of clean sand, the temperature equable, the whole place lit by oil-soaked torches tied to wall brackets. The inmates were naked. Male and female caves existed, but there appeared no bar to them mingling. Orderlies were distributing food on aluminium plates when we arrived, meat or vegetables on rice, all of good quality. We were obviously objects of curiosity but Jennie showed no fear when a man put out a hesitant hand to touch her dress. No one spoke, but there was a low constant murmuring. I suppose there must have been hundreds of patients there. Along one wall an orderly was washing the face of one of them from a drum of clean water. Nearby there were stone toilets behind blankets, again scrupulously clean.

Whether it was because it was lunch time or our visit, everyone seemed to be on the move, aimlessly but contentedly. A call to prayer was our cue to shake hands with the orderlies, there must have been one for every ten patients, and leave. Back out in the fresh air we pondered what we had seen. Neither of us could complain about what we had been shown. It occurred to me that, despite enforced nudity, dignity was maintained; and care and consideration shown. I think Dr Yusuf was a little shocked when I told him this.

Changes had occurred in the British Embassy. Jim and Philippa Treadwell had arrived - he as first secretary. Our friends, the Christies and Symonds had left, and Jeffrey Douglas had arrived, this time to stay for a tour. So we still had access to a house in Jedda. Apart from Dr Yusuf, the rest of the Ministry of Health had lost interest in me so I was very much my own boss.

In the spring the disturbing influence in my life reappeared, to wit Jim Johnson. By this time, the mercenary operation in the Yemen, which I had lightly touched on, two years previously in Aden, had rattled along and was now flourishing.

18
A SMALL WAR IN YEMEN

Jim arrived on our doorstep in Riyadh in the spring of 1965. The Anglo-French operation had increasingly required the tacit consent of the Saudi authorities so he had to visit certain dignitaries. We then flew off to Nagran, near the Yemen border, to see the local governor, Mohammed Sudairi. Dr Yusuf had granted me permission to visit Asir Province and report back on health affairs... but on no account to go near the Yemen frontier, a view endorsed by the British Embassy. Well, the frontier was ill defined. We crossed by jeep and first called at the northern HQ of the Royalist Forces of the Imam Al Badr, at Markaz Al Sherif, spread among caves and wadis. Another visitor was Bruce Condé, who occupied various roles on behalf of the Imam, ranging from soldier of fortune, public relations mogul, to post master general. Another resident was a German engineer engaged on building a bunker for the Imam, which would have done credit to his previous Leader, and would house the Royalist Radio Station. There was a unit of the International Red Cross nearby, clearly marked as non-combatant, and it was here I met a young Swiss lady radiographer, who was producing superb quality X-rays in a tent, with a small mobile apparatus and a dark room made from the packing case in which the X-ray machine had been delivered, turned on its side, and with an army blanket as a 'light trap'.

All this activity however attracted the attention of the Egyptian Air Force, and we were strafed by a couple of Iluyshin bombers which made desultory attacks with light bombs and machine gun fire at anything that moved. As they tended to arrive after lunch they seldom had any targets. Most people had their heads down - 'Egyptian PT' it was called.

After a couple of days we drove on deeper into the Yemen, to the valley where the French mercenaries were encamped. This had a decidedly more military air, which was hardly surprising in view of the professionals we encountered there. Their commander, Commandant Louis, an ex-Legionnaire who had fought everywhere against everyone who was an enemy of France, typified them. He had parachuted three times back into Dien Bien Phu before the final surrender, had escaped from his Vietnamese captors, hid with the Montagnards, returned to fight in Algiers, then gone to the Congo, from where he had been recruited for this venture. Indeed there was now a 'two way traffic' in mercenaries between Yemen and Congo, according to the conditions and terms of service offered. A cynic would regard this as typical of the mercenary mentality. Not true, these men were not young savages but men with responsibilities in France, who knew no other trade than war, who recoiled from barbarism and as often as not left one 'paymaster' for another not just because the pay was better but because the Cause was better and the leadership more competent. There were forty or fifty of them in the camp, preparing for the annual Royalist attack on Sanaa' - which never actually took place!

One of them, a Belgian called Philippe, who had been perforce a soldier in the Congo since adolescence, now joined us as we continued south to the field headquarters of Prince Mohammed bin Hussein, the Royalist leader in the Jauf, from whence the attack on Sanaa' was planned to start.

We drove across an empty plain where we saw a remarkable sight. In the middle of this trackless waste were two trucks, which had contrived to have a head on collision. Judging by the crumpled body work this must have happened at some speed! Behind each vehicle we could trace the sinuous tyre tracks as each vehicle tried to avoid the other - or had the drivers been playing chicken?

"Here we are! In the heart of Royalist Jauf!" cried Jim as we entered the mountains again. Another series of caves were to be home for the next few days. Here we met David Smiley, who was... the senior British officer in the field. I was going to write 'Commander of the Royalist Forces in the field' but in truth he was little more than a military adviser, ignored more often than not. He certainly had the right credentials, ex-Blues, a World War II guerrilla fighter in Albania and, until recently, Commander of the Sultan of Oman's Armed Forces, who had successfully defeated the rebel insurrection in the late 1950s. But Oman had to all intents and purposes been a British Protectorate in those days with an infrastructure that smacked more of India than Arabia. Yemeni tribesmen were as wild as they come, untamed by any colonial power, even if oppressed by the Turks, and owing allegiance to their own sheikhs and emirs - as long as it suited them. The miracle of T. E. Lawrence seemed to me that he was frequently able to persuade more than one Arab to do the same thing at the same time. David Smiley was no T. E. When the time came for us to head towards Sanaa' we left by truck at night, Jim and I in front with the driver, the back packed with armed tribesmen. David appeared alongside us, to see if there was room for him. We heard Emir Mohammed shout from his vehicle and arms stretched down from the back of his truck and hauled David unceremoniously inside.

We visited one more Royalist position and attended a parachute drop of arms and supplies to them. We had hoped to visit Johnny Cooper and his team, who were some way west of us. Johnny had spent nearly two years in Yemen by now, following his successful infiltration in the summer of 1963 when he had carried out two ambushes on the Egyptian Army. But it was time to return, both Jim and I had limited time at our disposal and 'swanning around' like we were was inviting trouble. (That I was to encounter on my next visit!)

❧ ❧ ❧ ❧ ❧ ❧ ❧ ❧ ❧ ❧ ❧ ❧ ❧

Back in Saudi Arabia there were no more 'break-throughs' in the field of health and I managed to secure a post back at the Middlesex Hospital as a registrar in the X-ray department, thanks to Dr Campbell Golding, whose patience I must have nearly exhausted! With Martha and Chester we visited Iran, where Chester had worked in the US Embassy previously, and visited Teheran, Isfahan and Shiraz, where I had been with my father in 1959. In Persepolis, Binnie and Martha tried to make stone rubbings of the monuments using grease-proof paper. Apart from being illegal it didn't work. Then on our way home we visited Beirut and Rhodes with them. (It was on Rhodes that Chester was mistaken by the locals for Sean Connery, a mistake we exploited whenever possible by hailing him as 'Sean' across the street.) We hired a yacht in Rhodes and sailed to Lindos, where I made a hash of anchoring in the bay; eventually, to the crews' disgust, up anchoring twice in an attempt to find a safe haven. That night, as we sat down to supper in the cabin, Chester said with a sigh: "Dear Diary - tonight I dined at the captain's table."

On our return trip we hit the 'Melteme', a fierce local wind, which reduced Binnie to a gibbering wreck, while Martha sat stoically as we plunged and pitched through the storm.

"This is what my grandfather taught us was having fun," was her wry comment. Not for nothing was there Blackbeard's blood in her veins!

Chester only cracked when we were safely back in Rhodes harbour and I sailed across the bows of a Greek cruiser upping anchor.

"It's alright, steam gives way to sail!" I called.

"Yeah - but I doubt if the Greek Navy agrees with that," Chester responded. I went about.

Looking back on our time in Saudi Arabia, I recall a story, which crystallised my feelings about two, seemingly, wasted years. A westerner was standing near an airport alongside a Bedu as an aircraft roared over head.

"There- isn't that wonderful?" asked the westerner.

The Bedu shrugged his shoulders: "Why? It was built to fly wasn't it?"

I can't help feeling that was the sort of smart-arse reply the Bedu thought the westerner would like to hear.

Again, we were lucky on our return to London as regards accommodation. My friend Tony Arnott, with whom I had lived as a medical student, was at that time working as manager for Lord Howard de Walden's estate in the West End, which included Harley Street. One of the tenants in No. 72 had a lease on the top two floors which she wanted to rent as her husband, a colonel in the Royal Marines, had been posted abroad for two years. Tony persuaded her to grant us a sublease; so we ended up renting 2,000 square feet of W1 for £15 a week!

So it was back to the Middlesex Hospital X-ray department, Campbell Goulding still in charge. He continued to teach us regularly in his weary way. There were only three of us trainee registrars now, the other two destined for more fame than I! Tony Carter had been set for a career in neuro-surgery but a minor physical handicap put paid to this so he transferred to radiology. Peter Armstrong was defying social convention of the time and living with his girl friend in a hospital flat![1] They were certainly a stimulus to me as I struggled, unsuccessfully, to keep up with them!

Meanwhile Kathy went to nursery school and Binnie discovered the delights of living next to Marylebone village. We became a popular 'stop over' for 'Aramcons' en route to and from the USA.

⪻⪼ ⪻⪼ ⪻⪼ ⪻⪼ ⪻⪼ ⪻⪼ ⪻⪼ ⪻⪼ ⪻⪼ ⪻⪼ ⪻⪼ ⪻⪼ ⪻⪼

In 1966 that disturbing influence in my life persuaded me to return to Yemen, to escort a new military commander. Bob Walker-Brown was an experienced regular soldier who had served with SAS in World War II and knew the desert from his days with the 8th Army. I confess that a month's salary as a mercenary officer (£500) had something to do with my decision to ask Cam for some leave. Life in London on a junior registrar's salary (take home pay was £118 a month) was confining.

We reached Royalist HQ in the caves without trouble and then set off for the Khaulan where a party of British mercenaries were based under the command of Mike Gooley, another ex-SAS officer. En route we encountered a patrol of 'dissident' tribesmen who blocked our further passage. By 'dissident' I mean that, while fundamentally supporting the Imam rather than the republicans, this was their territory, and they intended to extract some 'Danegelt' from passers by. They stood in an extended line across the sky-line and looked threatening. We went forward with our Yemeni escort and parleyed. My Arabic was not good enough to follow this. Then I noticed one of them had quite horrific conjunctivitis, pus dribbling from the corners of his eyes. I nudged my escort and muttered: "Tell him I'm a doctor."

Normally this is the very last information I ever wanted to be known in Arabia Deserta. I would masquerade as an engineer, an electrician, a meteorologist, anything to avoid being flattened in the rush to be 'cured' of impotence, headaches, backache, etc. So this was a measure of my anxiety! I applied liberal quantities of sulphonamide ointment into both eyes but only after irrigating them with lavish amounts of lignocaine anaesthetic. The effect was, needless to say, dramatic.

"The pain's gone!" the patient cried. Our problems faded like snow in the summer sun and we were on our way.

"Well done!" said Bob as we drove off.

"Yes - but we've got about 20 minutes before the effect of that anaesthetic wears off," I replied. We drove as fast as possible.

That evening we came to a wadi where we hid our vehicles and took to

[1] Tony went on to become a successful neuro-radiologist in the USA while Peter, after a long spell in the same country, returned to become Professor and President of the Royal College of Radiologists.

camels. Apart from saddle soreness, seasickness is the other complaint one suffers. But at last we reached our objective.

Again this was a rocky hillside with caves, which half a dozen mercenaries shared with their Yemeni hosts. Mike Gooley took us under his wing and next day we rode off to have a look at the elusive Sanaa' airfield, target of the Royalists for three years but still un-hit. This time we rode donkeys, not only more comfortable but less conspicuous, for the closer we got to republican territory the less committed to the Royalist cause were the tribesmen. Indeed Ahmed, my companion hissed: "Adoo!" (enemy) at an alarming number of tribesmen we passed. But we came to a village on the escarpment that was solidly Royalist and it was here we stopped and were shown to our 'seats' on the mountainside overlooking the Sanaa' plain and from which we could see the airfield from where the Egyptian Air Force were operating. I doubt whether they saw us but inevitably the locals decided to show off and opened up with their 81mm mortar, at more than extreme range.

While this did nothing much to discomfort the enemy, it upset the 'hive' and next minute we heard the whistle of incoming shells. I had noted one or two of the locals standing on one leg. I thought this might express excitement: but "No," one of them explained, "it makes me a smaller target when they fire back."

Bob, being a real soldier, dived into the nearest bomb crater, while I scampered alongside the totally useless protection of a ruined wall. We suffered only a few shells but I managed to collect a fragment in my foot. When quiet was restored I hobbled over to where my donkey was tethered and was shocked to see he too had collected a shell fragment, right in the buttock. I had only one shell dressing with me. Not entirely out of compassion I applied this to his rump - in the hope that he would agree to carry me out of the target area. This he did, not before time as we were less than a mile from the village when we heard the whine of jets and three Egyptian Air Force 'Mig' fighters swooped down from the direction of Sanaa' to fire rockets and cannon shells into the wretched village. I was relieved when Ahmed told me that no one would be hurt, the people had their caves nearby, which were bombproof.

It was on our return ride that I played my only aggressive role on this battlefield tour, I blew up an Egyptian RDF beacon with an eight ounce slab of guncotton. My tutor, the late Ken Cross of 21 SAS, would have been proud of me. He, too, believed guncotton to be the aristocrat of explosives, unlike the plebeian 'Semtex' and plastic explosive.

We rode hard, recovered our camels and rode even harder for we feared that the little hornet's nest we had stirred up might lead to the discovery of our vehicles, which were only camouflaged from the air. But we were lucky, we arrived after nightfall to find all quiet and set off back to Nagran, where a solicitous Mohammed Sudairi made a fuss of the 'wounded Hakeem'. My injury was minimal but a more unpleasant aftermath was the attack of hepatitis that followed three weeks later.

So back to Middlesex. A friend in the pathology department warned me that my liver function tests were 'horrendous'. Be that as it may, it was not until autumn that beer tasted good again and I decided I was cured. Chester and Martha came to visit in the summer and we stayed in Antibes, but I was very much a passenger and returned home early. However I was able to pass the examination for the diploma in radio-diagnosis that autumn. I began to cast bread upon the water... I soon got a bite.

The chief medical officer of the Ministry of Overseas Development, Patrick Dill Russell, asked to see me. We had already met in Riyadh when he was on fact-finding mission for the Ministry. I suspect my experiences there had something to do with the Ministry dragging its feet when it came to providing staff. It was Patrick who urged me to pursue a career in radiology whatever temptations crossed my path.

"Otherwise you'll end up like me," he would say morosely, as he pushed another pile of directives across his desk. From him I learned that the new ruler of the sheikdom of Abu Dhabi had asked HMG for a Director of Health. This was the term in vogue for a director of medical services, expressing the hope that health did not always have to come out of a bottle or a needle.

A few months earlier Sheikh Zeid Al Nahayan had ousted his brother, Sheikh Shakhbut, from the 'throne'. HMG had connived at this Palace Plot by providing a RAF plane to carry Shakhbut off to Iran initially; subsequently he went to live in Beirut. The pilot of the aircraft, Squadron Leader Jim Timms, was to gain quite a reputation for flying Middle East rulers to exile; indeed a joke going the rounds was that, on hearing Jim had landed in their country, rulers would pack an overnight bag.

Shakhbut was a splendid if autocratic desert ruler, who, like King Saud, foresaw the pain and demoralisation that would accompany improved living standards for his people when oil wealth spread across the desert. He kept his wealth under his bed. Zeid, whatever his sympathies for his brother, knew the tide could not be held back. For all that, I subsequently noted that Shakhbut had in fact initiated nearly every project completed during the first years of Zeid's reign.

Oil and politics mix, and I was not surprised, once I had expressed an interest in the post and demanded I should be allowed to fly out and see for myself, that BP immediately offered to pay my fare when HMG hesitated. The last thing BP wanted was to have to repeat their experience in Kuwait and build a mammoth hospital for their employees. They wanted a government health service yesterday. So early in December 1966 I found myself en route to Bahrain aboard a BOAC 'Constellation', back in first class after lean months in the NHS. In the back of my mind were visions of Abu Dhabi gained from an awful TV programme on the country that some US company had just made about: "Abu Darby - Land with a Future" which showed among other things an American Mission Hospital in Al Ain, part of the Buraimi district, some 100 miles inland from Abu Dhabi island. This was run by Dr and Mrs Kennedy and was firmly rooted in the mission strategy of leaving patients to help themselves whenever possible and charging them for whatever medical care they received. A scene showing the good Dr Kennedy injecting a prone, fully dressed, Arab patient through his clothes into his buttock did not fill me with hope. Neither did further scenes of Ahmed Obeidly, head of the Palace office, romping in the sands with his friends, a large red Buick bogged down in the sand behind him, instil much confidence in government circles.

I spent another night in the dreaded BOAC Speedbird Hotel. Walking to my room I noticed a pair of shining boots standing to attention outside a door. The door opened as I passed and a portly Englishman, with 'police' written all over him, took the boots in, then walked off down the corridor in front of me, hands behind his back, eyes darting left and right. I waited for the barked: "Now then, what's going on here?"

Tony Hooper turned out to be one of three ex-Palestine Police officers recruited for Zeid's burgeoning state. All had spent the intervening twenty odd years since the collapse of the British Mandate in various far flung outposts of the British Empire but, as these became increasingly scarce, were now available for short term contracts with new clients. One of them, Arthur Clements and his wife Derry, became our neighbours. Arthur was responsible for security, and became known as 'the spy'.

Next morning into the inevitable Dakota, and off down the Gulf, passing over the Das Island and its offshore rigs, before bumping over the 'gatch' runway that was Abu Dhabi's airport. I had arrived.

⋖⋗ ⋖⋗ ⋖⋗ ⋖⋗ ⋖⋗ ⋖⋗ ⋖⋗ ⋖⋗ ⋖⋗ ⋖⋗ ⋖⋗ ⋖⋗ ⋖⋗

I was greeted by a Palace official, my passport removed, and I was ushered into the back seat of an enormous red Buick. I recognised it as the car bogged in the sand that we had seen in the TV documentary. It now stubbornly refused to engage any gear save reverse. So we proceeded backwards down the rutted track to the Palace. It was a portent of what lay in the future.

19
ABU DHABI, 1966

rriving in Abu Dhabi is like landing on the moon. These were the words of Archie Lamb, Britain's Political Agent, when I went to call on him next day. Apart from my surprise at there being a hotel - in which I had been put to stay the previous night, I found no reason to disagree with this statement.

The Beach Hotel, as it was called, had been completed in a rush soon after Sheikh Zeid's accession. It was still barely functional - but there was already a bar for the journalists, entrepreneurs and assorted riff raff inevitably pouring into this potential gold mine.

Apart from this the only modern buildings in town were three banks, all British. Outside, the oil companies (Abu Dhabi Marine Areas for the offshore concession and Abu Dhabi Petroleum Company for that onshore) had built their headquarters at opposite ends of the foreshore. The latter had provided quite extensive staff quarters. Most ADMA staff lived out on Das Island. Inland the Abu Dhabi Defence Force were busy expanding their camp. The only links between them were sand tracks, there was no tarmac in sight.

Also within the town were the 'seats of power' - namely, Al Hisn Palace, where Sheikh Zeid had his; and nearby the Political Agency, where Britannia had hers. Sheikh Zeid called this, a little whimsically, Bait Mortumid, the 'house of the one I can lean on'.

Therefore it was not surprising that I first visited Archie Lamb to get my orders! HMG intended to fill key director's posts in the government with their protégés, either fellow British or Sudanese (at this time the Gulf still had more than its fair share of 'old Sudanese hands' in the Diplomatic Corps) and did not want any of us making waves - either politically or financially. In essence, there was little difference between a colony, a protectorate and a protected sheikdom when it came to the daily grind of local government. HMG had been content for the past 100 years to let life in Abu Dhabi drift along, providing there was no interference with her interests in the region. Now, the explosive impact of oil wealth made a firmer approach necessary; and how better than by appointing government officials who could be trusted to tow the 'party line'.

As for the Abu Dhabians themselves... well they faced a situation liable to induce schizophrenia! Centuries of stagnating in a barren land where survival was nigh on miraculous, malnutrition and infection commonplace, and tribal feuding almost light relief, were suddenly whipped away and a golden future appeared where 'do as one wilt' was on offer for all. It is hardly surprising that their behaviour alternated between cringing shame at their ignorance and ridiculous pride in their good fortune - as if it was due to their own efforts. I was duly briefed as to the terms of contract I should request, including salary - £5000 a year tax free was the going rate for a department director in those days - and told to come back for a drink later.

Then I marched off to the palace, where an amused Ahmed Obeidly, the ruler's secretary, jotted down details of my requirements. Clearly he had heard it all before. A Bahraini by origin, he had worked for both BP and the British Political Agent at home in Bahrain, before being appointed to his present post after the August coup. A womaniser, large and jovial, his urbane sophistication impressed nervous visitors like myself - and irritated the locals.

He disappeared into the inner sanctum, then reappeared to invite me in. Sheikh Zeid was in his late forties and full of charm that barely masked the hardened desert warrior. As I struggled to make myself understood in my bad Arabic - I think he understood little more than I was able to understand him - I was impressed by his modesty. There was none of the bombast I feared. When I spoke of the difficulties I would face in recruiting staff, he understood. (Later Ahmed was to express wonder that I did not bring nurses from Sweden, after all, we could afford to pay them!)

I was trying to explain the concept of rural health care in vogue at the time, the so-called 'hub and rim', a referral hospital surrounded by clinics, when Archie Lamb walked in, unannounced.

"Shugul katheer! Wajd zein!" (Lots of work! Jolly good) he greeted Zeid. Archie had told me how hard it was to persuade the Abu Dhabians of the need to work; so I was not surprised to hear Zeid's sigh of exasperation at this urging. I was dismissed, Ahmed being told to make 'all necessary arrangements'.

Right from the start I think I was a disappointment to him. Before bringing in a load of nubile Swedish nurses, I insisted on finding a hospital administrator. Here I had my first stroke of good fortune. ADPC had working for them an ex-RAMC warrant officer called Harry Napier, who had run the Iraq Petroleum Company hospital in Kirkuk, along with Dr Bill Baines, by then the IPC's chief medical officer back in London. Harry was a 'natural' for the job and was quickly released from his humdrum administration post to join the 'Ministry' of Health - if so grandiose a term may be excused for what was a virtually non-existent organisation. There was in fact a somewhat shady Syrian doctor, and a Pakistani, a registered medical practitioner as the old Indian Medical Service would have called him, called Abdul Majeed.

The Syrian, Dr Mohammed Suleiman Keilani, had been 'head-hunted' from Dubai on the strength of a lucky stab at an Abu Dhabian's piles. The Keilani clan are probably still renowned in the Arab world but prone to the vicissitudes of ill fortune that can attack the wealthy, i.e. he was exiled from Syria at the time. A morose, grey haired man, with an embittered wife, he had trained in Germany during World War II. Clinical studies in Heidelburg had been increasingly interrupted by the nightly visitations of the RAF; but somehow he had qualified and returned home in the aftermath. Politics had driven him to Beirut where there was little chance of success for a Syrian exile so he found his way to Dubai. There was little opportunity there either for a would-be surgeon in this backward sheikdom, and the chance of moving to Abu Dhabi, where the oil was beginning to flow was irresistible. He had been appointed chief medical officer by the Ministry of Health, Sheikh Hamdan bin Mohammed Al Khalifa, just weeks before my arrival.

Herein lay the seeds of the problem that was to poison my first year's work in Abu Dhabi. I was appointed as Director of Health by Sheikh Zeid; but Sheikh Hamdan was my boss. In addition to being Minister of Health, he was also Minister of Education, Public Works and Broadcasting. It was all a bit redolent of Kuwait; and as far as he was concerned he already had a doctor in charge.

The Pakistani was less of a problem, in that he was not an 'MBBS' and was content to keep a low profile running the sole clinic in town, a mud-walled villa with his office and a treatment room. I spent a week in the country and left with my head reeling. No sane man would have accepted the post: but then, as Max Beerbohm wrote, only an insane man takes himself seriously.

Working as a grace and favour private GP in the town was a splendid relic of the Raj, Dr Desmond Macaulay. A long serving member of the Indian Medical Service, he had drifted to Dubai in the aftermath of Partition where he had worked away for little reward save an adequate supply of Scotch. He had overseen the creation on the sheikdom's health service and the building of the Maktoum Hospital, at that time the only one in the Trucial States. Relations with the ruling family, the Maktoums, became increasingly strained and when Abu Dhabi hit the jackpot, Sheikh Shakhbut had been persuaded to employ him as the first state medical officer. Shakhbut's notorious parsimony prevented anything more than a clinic being built - Shakhbut foresaw better than most the perils of sudden oil wealth for his people - but Zeid quickly removed him when he seized the 'throne', at the same time granting him a house and permission to stay in private practice.

Desmond was a burly Irishman who seldom smiled and gave me little encouragement when I called to see him. I left after an hour, barely sober, and concluded that for him as for many others of that ilk, their world had ended in 1947. I could not help but compare him with his brother officer in Kuwait, Dr Eric Parry, who founded and cherished their state medical service for ten years before returning to Liverpool as an assistant professor of anatomy.

The afternoon before I left I got embroiled in a press conference in the Beach Hotel. I have always succumbed to the temptation to show off on these occasions. As I was one of the few 'white faces' available for comment I should not have been surprised when the correspondent asked: "How much do you think it will cost to set up medical services here?"

"Oh, about ten millions pounds," I answered casually, and added, "But of course that's in confidence."

It was hardly surprising that Peterborough's column in the *Daily Telegraph* reported a few days later, under the heading 'Medicus Arabicus' that: "Doctor Philip Horniblow will soon be undertaking a ten million pound development project for the Sheikdom of Abu Dhabi, where he has been employed by its ruler, Sheikh Zeid. Dr Horniblow has the advantage of being a fluent Arabic speaker."

I never learned the source of that last blatant lie! It certainly came home to roost. My Arabic remained poor to the end, a source of amusement to some and embarrassment to me. What the article did not quote was my reply to the inevitable, if hypothetical, question that followed: "It's a wonderful prospect isn't it? How challenging!"

"Arse-aching, more like," was my morose reply: and how accurate a forecast it was.

⊰⊱ ⊰⊱ ⊰⊱ ⊰⊱ ⊰⊱ ⊰⊱ ⊰⊱ ⊰⊱ ⊰⊱ ⊰⊱ ⊰⊱ ⊰⊱ ⊰⊱

I was back in London in time for Christmas *en famille*, then came a hectic time packing our belongings into sea freight, air freight and for storage: subletting our flat; and all the time 'networking' with the Ministry of Overseas Development, the oil companies and sundry folk who knew the Trucial States. I was also looking for staff.

Below our Harley Street flat were the consulting rooms of several of the great and the good in the medical profession, among them Dr Frances Gardiner, Dean of the Royal Free Hospital Medical School. On the staff she had a senior registrar in obstetrics and gynaecology, called Dr Mitzy Kasbarian, whom she recommended to me as a likely pioneer for the desert. Mitzy was my first, though by no means the last, contact with the Armenians - shakers and movers if there ever were ones! Sadly I was in no position to offer her work at that time and she went to a private hospital in Kuwait.

On 19 January 1967 we were airborne once more for the Gulf and back to the Beach Hotel, which was to be home for the first few months while our own was built. The hotel was managed by the O'Briens, a genial Irish couple who retained their sanity in an environment where their electricity supply depended on worn out generators, water was an occasional luxury, and sewage was as likely to flow back up the pipes as down them. Their staff of Indian servants lived in squalid shacks behind the hotel and behaved erratically. Despite this, the O'Briens kept cheerful and I shall always remember their cries of "Bon Appetit!" as we sat down to yet another meal of tinned turkey.

There were no houses for government employees, except for Eric Thompson, the director of finance who had a prefabricated villa on the beach. Behind it a Lebanese contractor, Albert Abela, was building a dozen villas for departmental directors. Binnie and I got the first to be completed. Surrounded by sand we needed a wall if Kathryn, four-years-old by now and showing signs of being a latter day Freya Stark, was not to be lost forever. A wall we duly got, thanks to Varhan Pirhanian, another Armenian, who was Abela's site manager. I hope Sheikh Hamdan paid for it. In the event it acted as a deterrent, but didn't stop her going out to visit a camp of Baluchi labourers nearby from whose barasti huts she would return smeared with ghee, honey and sweets which the wives and children pressed upon her. She suffered no ill effects.

While Binnie coped with all this I tried to set up a health service. Where to begin? Both common sense and received wisdom dictated that public health measures were paramount. Water was being piped down from the wells in Al Ain, where Zeid's half a dozen villages abutted three more in the Sultan of Muscat and Oman's Buraimi oasis. Sewage disposal there was none. Food hygiene did not enter into life. But it was important that the people saw something being done. Despite Shakhbut's notorious tight purse strings he had purchased a dozen pre-fabricated huts for a hospital - from the UK firm Coseley, who had supplied the buildings for the American Mission Hospital in Al Ain. Only two of these had been erected, the rest were slowly rotting in their packing cases on the beach. (There was no harbour, everything imported by ship had to be off-loaded into lighters, then dumped above the high tide mark on the foreshore - tides in the Gulf were minimal.)

Of the two that had been erected about a mile outside town one, set on a small knoll, was occupied by Dr Keilani while the other was a few hundred yards away and became my office. With the help of a Lebanese contractor, Victor Hashem, whose company ATTO had been marking time since the days of Shakhbut, waiting for the 'big time', and Coseley, we were able to get the other huts erected in some semblance of order. There was still no water or electricity - and no more staff.

But, as is often the situation, the first job was to get rid of some of the staff who were already there. Up in Al Ain a Sudanese called Abdul was running a clinic on the ground floor of a building in the town. He had produced documents from Heidelburg University Hospital stating he was a qualified doctor. It hardly seemed likely. His fate was sealed by two events that occurred on the same day. He treated a solder in the Abu Dhabi Defence Force who had a septic foot with a dressing soaked in neat Dettol - the poor lad nearly lost his foot. The same day a letter arrived from Heidelburg stating that Abdul had indeed worked in the hospital - as a porter.

Even then I had some difficulty in getting him dismissed as the local sheikhs still loudly supported him. I couldn't help feeling that one reason for this was his wife. Apart from his forged medical degree he had brought with him from Germany a buxom blonde. However, the combined attacks of myself and the British CO of the ADDF, Colonel 'Tug' Wilson, proved sufficient to have him dismissed. (Despite this he had the cheek to get himself, and his wife needless to say, invited back on holiday the following year by one of the locals.)

It took longer to get rid of Dr Keilani. I kept an open mind on his surgical abilities until the day came when he told me that he would not require the services of an anaesthetist when the hospital was functioning. "They only interfere with my work - I prefer to use local anaesthesia." This hardly suggested we were going to practice major surgery. In desperation, I suggested to Hamdan that we needed a medical representative in Beirut to oversee the treatment of Abu Dhabians we referred there - especially Tb. To my relief he agreed; and Dr Keilani was out of my hair.

I looked elsewhere and came up with one Archie St Clair Robertson, a Scottish graduate who had worked through World War II in the RAMC. He had gone to Canada, as so many doctors had in the aftermath of the war and lack of a future in the UK, but had then found his way to Arabia. He was working at a private hospital in Saudi Arabia, which did not inspire me with confidence; but he had glowing testimonials from his Alma Mater. Thus I learned the hard lesson; that only current testimonials are significant.

He duly arrived and quickly demonstrated his undoubted surgical skills in the clinic. Alas, he was a prey to the demon alcohol. He was found one night incapable of operating and he had to go. I had the unpleasant task of telling him but in a curious way this earned Sheikh Hamdan's gratitude. Zeid had told him to terminate Robertson's services and deport him at once. Hamdan, who had had contact with British people on Das Island, genuinely respected them, and the prospect of sacking a middle-aged surgeon, drunk or not, was not an attractive one. Hence his relief when he heard I'd done the dirty deed for him. But he'd learned that white men could be sacked and HMG was not going to do anything about it. Like an alsatian he got the taste for biting.

Next to go was the Director of Education and our neighbour, Harold Spencer, an old India hand with duly prescriptive ideas that did not always go down well with the Abu Dhabians. They were yet to learn that wealth was no substitute for hard work when it comes to acquiring knowledge or even western 'know-how'. Harold sealed his fate by giving a speech in fluent Sanskrit on the occasion of the anniversary of Zeid's accession to the throne, which few could understand, but which made the rest think they were being patronised.

Recruiting other staff had its more amusing moments. Even before my arrival the health department had placed an advertisement in the Daccan Herald, a South India newspaper, for all sorts of medical staff. The response was overwhelming. I spent afternoons pouring over the replies begging for work as orderlies, dispensers, technicians, sweepers - any role in fact to give them an opportunity to escape grinding poverty. As it was an English language newspaper, most of the applicants were Christians, and their stories heart rending. Part of me wanted to employ the lot, but pragmatism prevailed: and there were enough delightfully incongruous letters to keep me entertained. For example, one man, who wanted to be a dresser, ended his letter: "I am a clean living young man who plays football and cricket. Furthermore I urinate standing up."

Finding doctors was to be a real problem. Here I had to trust to the Good Lord for guidance, as *curricula vitae* are notoriously easy to forge.

Sometimes friends and acquaintances helped.

Quite early on I had a message from our old friend from Kuwait days, Abdullah Al Ghanim. He had an Indian head clerk whose son was working in a Mission Hospital in Bahrain and none too happy with his job or its prospects. Abdullah asked if I would recruit him as a favour, assuring me of the father's integrity. So I did, after duly approving his CV. Thus it was that George Mathew and his wife Valsa came to Abu Dhabi.

I had warned him that I wanted him to run a clinic in Al Ain, following the departure of Abdul the Sudanese with the peroxide blonde wife and that conditions would be primitive. They were. In due course I drove them across the 100 odd miles of desert, conversation slowly dying as the remoteness of their situation sank in. I deposited them in an apartment of one of the few two storey buildings in Al Ain, having rented the ground floor as a clinic.

They stuck it out. In addition to the problems of simply existing in such circumstances, poor Valsa - probably the only unveiled woman in Al Ain at that time, apart from Marion Kennedy, the American missionary doctor - had to contend with the advances of the Palestinian staff of Sheikh Zeid's office. The fact that she did so without jeopardising her integrity or George's position was praiseworthy.

Public health concerns I have already mentioned, and I was lucky enough to recruit an Egyptian doctor, Oswald Menassa, as medical officer of health. Oswald was, unusually, a Roman Catholic, at least by baptism, and was working in Qatar when I heard of him. Although oil money was not yet trickling down to government employees the salary scale was enough to attract him and his arrival eased me of worries about food handlers, emptying of septic tanks, etc., subjects on which I was woefully ignorant. Oswald spoke English well and was a charmer so I should not have been surprised when he talked the PWD into allocating him one of the director's houses, with three bedrooms - despite being a bachelor.

Housing for staff was one of my biggest headaches, as the Abu Dhabians could not see there was a problem - if you were a sheikh you had a palace, if you weren't you camped wherever you could. Both Zeid and Hamdan were nonplussed when I said I could not staff the hospital - by early summer the Coseley huts had been erected - unless I could offer housing for the medical staff. After bashing my head against the wall of incomprehension I finally got a deal by which our brother-in-law, Gordon Jones, who was a partner in Design Construction Group in Beirut, designed a housing compound of good quality two and three bedroom houses outside the hospital wall. I later decided Hamdan had only conceded to my request when he thought I'd made a deal with Gordon to split the profit on the contract. We should have been so lucky - the houses were built virtually at cost - Gordon took one per cent and I doubt if Victor Hashem cleared much more for his company.

Gordon and his partner Tony Irvine, had also designed the original St Andrew's Anglican Church, which was on the beach next to the ADPC offices and housing compound. Shakhbut had always been interested in religion and

Zeid was no different. He granted land to the Anglican Diocese of Jerusalem, and subsequently attended the inauguration of the completed building when Bishop Campbell MacGuiness of the Church in Jerusalem and the Middle East presided.

Afterwards Zeid told me: "That's a good way to worship God!" He had enjoyed the chanting.

Later we were fortunate to have Archdeacon Ralph Lindley, then David Elliott as chaplains during our time in Abu Dhabi. Inevitably there there 'interregnums'. During one I recall taking Evensong one winter's night with a congregation of... one. Mathew Varghese, my Indian storekeeper!

Mention of the hospital wall reminds me of another headache. When Coseley and Atto were erecting the huts that were to provide accommodation for a 50 bed hospital with X-ray, laboratory, pharmacy and outpatient facilities, they spread over several acres. Around them was open desert. Security was non-existent. I had to fight for a boundary wall and guarded gates; I saw this as essential for patient protection, little realising how it would help retain the furniture and fittings! Once we started to admit patients - and that had to wait until the following winter as there was no electricity or water provided - I became aware that we would need an inexhaustible supply of bedding. Once a patient knew he or she was to be discharged they would take mattress, sheets, blankets and pillow to the boundary fence and chuck it over to waiting relatives. When I caught one of them at it and remonstrated I was put firmly in my place: "This is the property of Sheikh Zeid - not yours! And he would want us to have it! He is our father."

Tribalism died hard. At this stage the lack of education was the other stumbling block. Harry Napier, recalling successful projects in Iraq, promoted a cull on flies, which increased seemingly by the hour.

"Iqtal hatha thubab!" (Kill that fly!) was the rallying cry and a flood of Japanese fly swats were issued to all and sundry, together with posters exhorting the populace to keep the place clean. On them was a picture of a grotesque fly eating and defecating on a lump of meat. But like so many good intentions the westerner introduces to the Orient, this was due to back-fire. Mohammed, my delightful Abu Dhabian transport supervisor, came to my office, having checked to see Harry wasn't listening and whispered: "The people are saying, 'Thanks be to God it is not us villagers but those sinners in the big cities who are afflicted by those monstrous flies'." Content that their little ones didn't matter.

Before the hospital was operating on Abu Dhabi Island, Zeid had insisted there should be one in Al Ain. His heart was always there rather than on the coast. I was ordered to take over a mud-walled palace belonging to the third brother, Khalid, in the area called Muweiji. To say facilities were primitive would be an exaggeration; they were non-existent. So we did the best we could and installed beds, relying on the stamina of the patient to survive. Malaria was a seasonal hazard and George Mathew made the first scientific analysis of the problem. Among his remarkable observations was that mosquitoes could be borne by cars from Al Ain to Abu Dhabi, then could lay their larvae in the dew that condensed at night on the metal rims of the tyres.

Zeid himself told me he had noted mosquitoes did not breed around wells that had pumps; these always leaked oil, covering the water with a thin film that prevented the larvae maturing. He asked why we could not eradicate mosquitoes? Was there not DDT now available?

In my enthusiasm to show him what could be done with 'Western know how' I got hold of a crop spraying aircraft which duly arrived in Abu Dhabi and when the weather conditions were suitable, i.e. a still, humid, dawn, the pilot flew to and fro across the whole Buraimi Oasis, spraying the whole district with DDT.

Of course it turned out to be a disaster. Sultan Said bin Taimur, of Muscat and Oman, complained bitterly that his people had been asphyxiated by poison gas, demanded compensation, financial of course, from Sheikh Zeid, and got it. Sheikh Khalid's bees, of whose honey he was proud, were all killed. But the mosquitoes seemed immune and the incidence of malaria was unaffected, according to Dr George. So much for the quick fix.

Sometimes I was called upon to practice some medicine myself. By this time in my Arabian career I had learned two things: that my first 'native' patients would inevitably be suffering from some gross deformity as the result of an appaling injury suffered years previously and for whom amputation would have been a blessing. While among expatriates, my first patient would be a household pet, usually a dog dragging its leg as the result of a paralysing infection. In neither case could I offer anything save sympathy, and was duly 'written off' as yet another reject from the British medical establishment. My lame excuse that I was a diagnostic radiologist as well as a health administrator cut no ice at all.

What I had learned in my time in Arabia could sometimes be useful. Like the time I saw a British soldier bitten in the forearm by a camel. Camel bites could be lethal, unlike love bites, although even these were more liable to secondary infection than dog bites. He and his mates were treating it as a bit of a joke; but I had seen galloping sepsis spread from such an injury. One just has to look into a camel's mouth when it is chewing the cud to appreciate that its mouth is a foetid, green, pool of bacteria. I called an aircraft from Sharja, and he was flown to the RAF hospital where the bite was widely excised under general anaesthesia; and his arm was saved.

On another occasion I was asked to see what was thought to be a severe case of chicken pox in an Indian gardener. After my experience in Kuwait I had no doubt it was smallpox. By good fortune an old colleague from the KOC, Dr Bill Thom, was working in Dubai as public health officer and between us we managed to isolate the disease and carry out a massive programme of vaccination. There was some resistance to this, once more the possession of a vaccination certificate duly signed and stamped was regarded by many as a kind of talisman. Many were obviously forged, the bearer claiming they had been vaccinated at the American Mission Hospital or in

Muscat. But we allowed no exceptions; all were vaccinated on the spot.

After all this excitement - what did we do to relax? Like most British expatriates in the tropics, we swam, sailed, played tennis and golf - a golf course with its 'browns', 'sandways', and clubhouse is considered an essential development - and had picnics on the beach and in the desert. Neither Binnie nor I were ball players so it was the beach we sought for relaxation. Tug Wilson, whom I have already mentioned as commanding the ADDF, had commandeered an old barge, which lay on the sand at the entrance to the creek on the east side of Abu Dhabi Island. It provided shade, a kitchen and a fridge and it was here that chosen expatriates forgathered on Fridays. He also had charge of the Ruler's motor yacht, a rather posh dhow, on which he invited selected guests. Tug was a small, irascible little man, with all the hang ups common in 'vertically challenged' people. He wore the badge of an RAF airgunner which he had acquired during World War II, after which he had transferred to the army, whence he had finally arrived in Abu Dhabi under the previous ruler Sheikh Shakhbut - possibly as a consequence of a failed marriage. He was generous almost to a fault, but his inevitable pomposity was asking to be pricked. Hence a rather cruel joke we played on him, in the uneasy aftermath that followed the June 1967 Israeli War.

Public services being so largely in the hands of the expatriates it was easy to persuade the manager of the Telegraph and Telephone Company to concoct an apparently genuine telegram reading as follows: "To, Wilson, Defence Force Abu Dhabi. We invite contingent ADDF Gaza Strip soonest expression Arab solidarity also prevent possible Iraqi Algerian take-over stop President welcomes your personal presence stop Abdul Hakim Amer." (The latter was commanding the Egyptian Army.)

We further arranged for this to be delivered by an army messenger after Friday lunch when enough beer had been drunk to blunt Tug's mental alertness. We nearly succeeded in having a 'stand to' - but then he thought he'd better see Zeid first; and as he sprang into his staff car, one of the perpetrators, Charles Wontner, who was also his adjutant, confessed. Tug took it well.

Next to the barge ADPC had a small beach area with some 'Fireflies' which I was allowed to sail; and introduced Kathy to the sport. She never took to it.

Meanwhile one of those steamy tropical romances developed between Tug and the wife of one of the ADPC employees. I shall call them Pat and Jane Carter and I had known them in Kuwait days when they had been with Qatar Petroleum Company in Dukhan, and we had exchanged sailing regattas with them. Tug became impassioned of Jane, a lissome blonde liable to turn any man's head, and things came to a head when Pat was away on duty elsewhere. When he returned I was chastised for not telling him what had been going on behind his back... he considered me an old friend. But the situation grew murkier. A Welsh major arrived on secondment, one Roddy Jones, and he and Jane took to each other like scrambled eggs to buttered toast. Their other common interest was horses. Tug was on leave at the time. When he returned and the news of Jane's fling reached him, he reacted predictably. While he stamped up and down in our house, clutching a glass of whisky and threatening keel hauling at least for the errant major, Binnie acted counsellor while I searched out his second in command, the inestimable Peter Macdonald.[1] The original tower of gentle strength, he took charge... Within days Roddy was whisked away by HMG to an intelligence job in Oman. Sadly for both perhaps, Pat and Jane divorced. All very Somerset Maugham.

[1] Dear Peter, World War II prisoner following his capture in Greece in 1941, he had spent his time as a POW more constructively than most by learning Arabic. As a result he had by now been in the Gulf for years and had defended Buraimi with the Trucial Oman Scouts and Zeid at his side when the Saudis were threatening in the 1950s.

20

ABU DHABI, ONWARDS AND SIDEWAYS

I have already mentioned that we needed doctors in Abu Dhabi. Politics led me to seek them in Pakistan. Pakistan, building upon Zeid's love of hawking, had nurtured relations between the two countries. He had been an honoured guest in Pakistan where he had also met some attractive ladies who were encouraged to come to Abu Dhabi to further their interests... they were chaperoned by a powerful Begum, wife of an elderly doctor, whom, it was made quite clear, I should employ.

A few months later I had a visit from a Pakistani friend from Kuwait, one Farid, now working for BP, who came to the hospital. During World War II he had been in the Indian Diplomatic service and had chosen to settle in Pakistan after Partition. We were chatting in my office when I suddenly saw him staring wide-eyed out of the window.

"What's the matter?" I asked.

"I've just seen a ghost," he answered. I followed his gaze and saw Dr Rahim trotting by.

"Ah, the Begum's husband," I responded, "Yes, he's pretty ancient but still alive. His wife is the power behind the throne, she's got Zeid's ear, runs a restaurant and entertains the rich Abu Dhabians. Her daughter Bilho and her friend Zara are said to read Islamic poetry to Zeid. Rahim was a bit cross that I didn't appoint him chief medical officer but I explained that I had one already so he settled for the grandiose title of physician with charge of out-patients." (At this stage we had little but outpatient care to offer.)

"Well," my friend reflected, "I can't mistake that walk... It was in Mussoorie that I saw him. I'd gone up there on some summer leave, must have been during that last year of the war. He was the IMS surgeon and his wife ran a real 'up market' string of call girls for the delectation of the British officers - real stunners they were most of them, in fact I recall meeting one of them..."

A faraway look came into his eyes. I didn't question him further. I told him about Bilho and Zara and a suspicion among some expatriates that they were lesbians. He guffawed, "My dear chap that sort of thing doesn't happen in Pakistan."

I glanced out of the window again and saw Zara approaching Rahim, a jacket over her arm. He thanked her and put it on.

"I certainly would hope not. Look, there's Zara now. You'll not be surprised to hear we call her Zara Baby!"

Ahmed looked and threw his head back in delight.

"I should say not! Wow! You've certainly collected them!" (He mentioned a family name.) "She used to be Zulfikar Bhutto's mistress."

Enough of this unseemly gossip. Bilho and Zara became part of the social scene and friends, adding both glamour and Eastern promise to parties. I should add that I never knew the latter being fulfiled.

Thus, it was hardly surprising that when I went to Pakistan to recruit medical staff the Rahim family played an important role. By now I had an Abu Dhabian 'minder' in the shape of Ali Shuraffa, who was our personnel officer. Ali was in fact from Ras Al Khaimeh but had lived in Abu Dhabi before the oil glut, hence was accepted as a genuine 'settler'. He was a likeable young man, educated partly in Egypt so he spoke English quite well. I had no doubt he was there to see I was not about to line my own pockets, i.e. accepting 'commissions' from those to whom I offered employment. We got on well together. We flew to Karachi and conducted interviews in the Rahim's house in the Defence Colony, which was about as 'up market' as one could get and full of upper class Muslims who had opted for Pakistan at the time of partition. It was therefore not surprising that I found myself interviewing several score of muhajirs - as these settlers were known - during the few days we were there. They stuck together; and to be honest, were rather brighter than the indigenous people. Among the most promising recruits were Nazir and Nafeesa Ahmed, a husband and wife team, physician and obstetrician respectively, who had higher degrees from the UK. I realised that her appointment would block that of Mitzy Kasbarian who was, I had learned, unhappy in her work in the private hospital in Kuwait; and waiting for a call from me.[1]

We collected a motley horde of doctors, nurses, technicians, and made our way back to Abu Dhabi. They were the founders of the health service. Meanwhile surgeons came - and went. After Archie Robertson's sad departure there was a gap until a young New Zealander arrived from the UK. He was a serious bachelor, dedicated to his work, and I cannot remember seeing him smile once during the months he was with us. He was called upon to act on one potentially lethal occasion.

Abu Dhabi harbour, 1966

[1] Eventually Mitzy came to Abu Dhabi, locumed for Nafeesa during their annual leave, then chose to go into private practice in the town. She later married a British officer in the ADDF.

Zeid had gone wandering on the beach, unusually for him. He was probably looking to see how the 'corniche' was progressing - this was one of the prestige developments in progress before sanitation, sewage, and other boring items were in place. He managed to cut his foot on some coral. Now coral cuts are nasty, not as nasty as camel bites, but still nasty. Coral after all is a living organism and the microbes excite a rabid inflammatory response in human tissue. To make matters worse, it was his left foot; and the lymphatic system in this leg was already compromised by a bullet wound he had received in the left groin during a tribal skirmish in the Buraimi oasis, which had effectively abolished lymphatic drainage from the leg.

There was widespread panic among the palace staff. To Zeid's eternal credit, he insisted on being admitted to our hospital and being treated by our staff. Our New Zealand surgeon behaved professionally and instituted what would now be termed 'appropriate therapy'.

Meanwhile every crook and creep in town tried to take over. Offers of air ambulances, surgeons, flooded in from Beirut and Cairo. Zeid kept cool. He had a painful swollen leg but he left his care in our hands. Subsequently I accompanied him to London when the acute phase had subsided and he saw various super specialists, all of whom, I'm glad to say, had the sense to do nothing save proffer advice to avoid a repetition of the near disaster.

Not long afterwards our young New Zealander resigned, shortly after he had been awarded a pay rise; but truly he was not the man for the place and time. Ahmed Obeidly had by now left the palace and gone to run the London office, in the days before there was an embassy. He found us a Harley Street physician, Tom Wade, who became our London liaison officer and with his help we found another surgeon.

Duncan Hamilton was a real 'colonial retread'. An ex-RAMC wartime surgeon, he, like Archie, had sought a career overseas after World War II, and had worked in Aden and East Africa. The epitome of a character from Doctor in the House, this rugger playing, hardworking, hard drinking Scot was I hoped the answer to my prayers... providing the drink was not a problem. I tackled Ahmed repeatedly. He remained calm.

"Philip," he said, "I've seen enough doctors here and in Bahrain to know the difference between a heavy social drinker and an alcoholic. Duncan is a social drinker." I believed him, because I wanted to; and in fact he was probably right. But in a Muslim country like Abu Dhabi, feelings were raw and sensitive under the remorseless pressures of wealth and greed. The label 'Drunken Duncan' was affixed... and stayed.

Despite the success of the surgical unit he set up, the end was nigh... And it came at an evening 'Majlis' in the Palace when Zeid proclaimed to a large gathering, after one had complained of his treatment at the hospital: "What can you expect of a man who is drunk day and night?"

He then turned to look at me. I was about to expostulate that I trusted his work, and that furthermore he had repaired Binnie's upper lip just days before and if I trusted him - why not others?

I was sitting next to Ali Shuraffa, who was translating for me and he hissed: "Shut up, it won't do any good!"

He was right of course and it probably saved my skin for a few more months.

❧ ❧ ❧ ❧ ❧ ❧ ❧ ❧ ❧ ❧ ❧ ❧ ❧

The problem of dissatisfied patients grew as our services developed. From having had no medical facilities at all less than ten years previously, I was now expected to provide the same service as patients would receive at the Mayo Clinic. I began to think of our hospital as a 'please the people centre', as the months passed and more and more patients came demanding treatment overseas. I set up a medical board, which slowed the flow of clients coming to my office. At least overseas treatment was funded by the Palace office and not a drain on my budget. The medical board had a tough job to do and was of course regarded by many as a means of stopping them getting the treatment they needed and which I had failed to provide.

A classical case in point was the man with backache. (I hope that sounds familiar to my colleagues in the UK?) Abdulla had undergone thorough investigation including X-rays and had been diagnosed as having a musculo-skeletal disorder requiring physiotherapy. We had a physiotherapy service by now, provided by an expatriate wife who was UK registered - at this time many of the paramedical staff I had managed to recruit were oil company wives. This of course was not good enough - it required effort on the part of the patient. Despite the medical board recommendation that he should persist with his treatment, he shouted loud enough and long enough in the majlis to get a free ticket to London and was referred to Tom Wade for further care.

Six weeks later he was back in Abu Dhabi. I was at the 'majlis' (audience) the evening he returned and sat writhing in my chair as he stood and declaimed to the multitude: "Ta'al umrak!" (a formal salutation), he shouted to Zeid: "I thank you - I am cured - after just one injection!" The murmurs of the crowd began.

"Now I am like a young man again!" The murmurs became louder.

Zeid looked at me. "What have you to say, Horrenblor?" (This was as near to my name as he ever got.)

I swallowed hard and bit my lip. "Nothing, O Long Life," I was able to croak, "I am glad he is cured."

I wasn't really. I had learned from my own sources that Abdullah was indeed cured: and after 'just one injection', of a virulent dose of 'clap' he had acquired from a Piccadilly whore. The injection was a massive does of crystalline penicillin.

Those lower in the social order who required treatment overseas went to the Lebanon or India. Dr Keilani handled the cases sent to Beirut, many of whom had Tb. and were treated very well at a sanatorium in the mountains. The lower orders went to Bombay where there was a liaison office and patients again received good care. One was a policeman who had contracted leprosy, which I had mistakenly diagnosed as cutaneous Tb. Fortunately there were still leprosariums in India at this time and he was treated success-fully.

Meanwhile Zeid's interest was as ever in Al Ain. Sheikh Khalid's Palace, while providing him with a good little 'earner' as regard rent from the health department, had gross limitations as a hospital. Patients were still undergo-ing surgery in the American Mission Hospital run by the Kennedys; and George Mathew was hampered by lack of any support services. Once more I came into conflict with Zeid.

The Abu Dhabi-Al Ain highway had been completed by four different con-tractors and the capital was now linked to the Buraimi Oasis by tarmac - albeit a pretty shoddy job, despite the efforts of the British consultants, rejoicing in the name 'Arabicon', to impose British standards. It had been a tough project, the road passing over 'subkha' (salt flats), drifting sand, and through unstable dunes. Nevertheless it was a vast improvement to the desert track that I had first negotiated in a Land Rover in 1966. The Abu Dhabians of course revelled in it and drove their huge American limousines and Mercedes up and down it at breakneck speed, often just for the hell of it. The outcome was predictable. In the first six months over 100 people were killed in pile-ups or cars spinning off the road. It was now that I first coined the term 'Booboo Land', when it was suggested that this death rate could be reduced if I built a clinic every ten kilometres where a surgeon should be sta-tioned to treat the brain damaged victims.

The surreal part of this recommendation - which I was told came from Zeid himself - was that it was based on an accurate assessment of the major cause of death. Once more my attempts to explain that neuro surgeons did not grow on trees; and that it might be cheaper to impose a speed limit were treated with disdain. Once more the transition from camel to Cadillac was proving a hard lesson to learn.

But Zeid was right in wanting a modern hospital in Al Ain; and I was charged to provide one. The news got around pretty fast. One of my early dealings was with an Abu Dhabi merchant who had links with an Australian company. His British 'go between' was the son of a former CO of mine in the TA and he did not enamour himself with me by offering me a bribe at break-fast. The Abu Dhabi merchant was already doing good business with the health department by providing medicines so I did not run the risk of a knife in the back by rejecting the offer. Handling bribes in Arabia was always dif-ficult, you are damned if you accepted them - you became a donkey, in the words of the Arab proverb - or damned if you didn't. In this case it was sad, as the company had provided good pre-fabricated hospitals to the US Forces in Vietnam. But a bribe over breakfast was more than I could stomach!

I went up to Al Ain to discuss the matter with George Mathew. We decid-ed the devil we knew was the best option; so recommended Coseley again. We chose a site on the north side of the village. Zeid was not happy. Once more I had to undergo humiliation in the majlis!

"What sort of a man would choose to build a hospital on a main street with noise - cars - smoke?" was his cry.

"Majnoon!" came the orchestrated reply from the elders, i.e. a madman.

To give Zeid his due, when he did get round to building his dream hospital ten miles out in the desert some twenty years later - so that only those with cars could get to it - it was a magnificent building. But by then there were virtually unlimited funds available for such grandiose schemes. At the end of the 1960s oil royalties were paper-thin across the development field.

But I stuck to my guns. Zeid got his own back by stalling on a decision at to whether to go ahead on the project. Meanwhile I had got into further trouble, this time with HMG.

There was a firm of UK consultants working in Al Ain; one of whom died under what could be termed 'mysterious circumstances'. A dead Brit was an embarrassment at the best of times and with the possibility of foul play hanging over it I chose to play Sherlock Holmes - or more aptly, Dr Watson. Death by poisoning was possible so I went to what served as a morgue as soon as I heard about the case and armed with a syringe and a wide bore needle, thrust it into the upper abdomen - just below the xiphi-sternum for the purists - and sucked - or aspirated, to be more technical. My plan was to send specimens to a toxicology laboratory, the nearest at the time being in Bahrain. Alas, I produced nothing save puncture wounds in the abdominal wall. I had learned that one cannot aspirate fluid from collapsed organs.

But the case came under the jurisdiction of Her Britannic Majesty's coroner; and he in turn still practised under the Indian Penal Code. To be more precise, that of the Bombay Presidency. This may sound odd, but the Gulf States had been administered from Bombay until Indian Independence and even by the late 1960s, certain responsibilities remained with the political agencies. (These were to finally disappear, along with the political agents themselves, within a year or two.)

So there was I subjected to a right dressing down from HM's coroner for assaulting a corpse, tampering with evidence, etc. Jim Treadwell, who was political agent by now, spoke up on my behalf and I was let off with a warning. The verdict of the court was 'death by misadventure'.

⋘⊳ ⋘⊳ ⋘⊳ ⋘⊳ ⋘⊳ ⋘⊳ ⋘⊳ ⋘⊳ ⋘⊳ ⋘⊳ ⋘⊳ ⋘⊳ ⋘⊳

After months of frustration I was seated in George's house one evening chatting with Valsa. George had been summoned to the old palace in Al Ain. We heard his Land Rover draw up with a roar; he rushed into the villa shouting: "He's agreed!"

Despite all the trappings of government apparatus, at the end of the proverbial day it was Uncle Zeid who decided what was and was not going to happen.

It is easy to be critical of him in retrospect. Some of his ideas were indisputably naive, like the brain surgeons stationed along the Abu Dhabi-Al Ain highway; or his question to me, when the need to replace and extend much of the hospital on Abu Dhabi island was apparent: "Why not use the doctors' houses for a new hospital? They are much better quality than those huts you are using."

Trouble was, I never quite knew whether he was winding me up or not. But he was under real stress in those days, surrounded by people intent on feathering their own nests at the expense of his truly beloved land and people. On the night of the Queen's birthday - always a big event in Britain's dwindling dependencies - he attended the Political Agency as guest of honour (so the rest of us had to make do with soft drinks). When the time came for him to leave he beckoned to me to follow. What have I done wrong now, I thought? Back in his palace he took the unusual step of dismissing all his followers save his Bedouin guards, sat me down and explained how unhappy he was with all the foreigners pouring into his country - especially the northern Arabs who could so easily influence his people. He drew special attention to the health department, where, inevitably, I had to draw on foreign staff to fill almost every post. He made it clear that he did not want any more Egyptians, Lebanese or Palestinians employed.

"Jib Al Hinood," he said firmly, ie. 'bring Indians'. India had historically been the manpower source for the Trucial Coast, thanks to the link with the Bombay presidency. It was only recently that Pakistan had been established. I hope my Pakistani friends will not be insulted when I state that the brains of the sub-continent were, by and large, left behind in India at the time of Partition, Pakistan having been created as a haven for persecuted Muslims. This was the 'joker' that Pakistan could always play when negotiating with Zeid. But we were also in the heyday of Nasserite Arabism, and it was difficult for Zeid to swim against this second tide - even though Arab interest in his sheikdom was purely mercenary.

Personally I was happy with this instruction. Despite my pro-Arab stance in most things, it was easier to work with Indian staff of all grades in the health field, for we had shared the same curricula for decades. But there was a snag. A recent palace edict stated that we should employ Trucial States nationals wherever possible; failing that, from other Arab Gulf States; failing that, from other Arab nations. Only if we were still unable to fill a post was I then empowered to recruit beyond Arabia.

I decided I must hold my tongue in front of Ali Shuraffa, who had by now gone to the government personnel department as its first director. I was between a rock and a hard place. I chickened out and appointed a recruitment committee to handle new appointments. Not surprisingly they opted to advertise for new medical staff in Cairo, in accordance with the instructions of the Civil Service Commission. Sorry, 'Ta'al Umrak' (your long life).

This in fact took place after I had gone to Beirut with Mohammed Al Hurr in January 1968, when it was essential that we recruited some Arab-speaking technical staff. Mohammed came from a village on Abu Dhabi Island and was Hamdan's secretary in the HQ that housed PWD, Health and Education. A humble, decent little man, he had worked on Das Island for Hamdan who was then Shakhbut's representative. The evening we arrived in Beirut we were sitting together in his hotel room discussing the British announcement that we were to withdraw from all our dependencies east of Suez by 1971 - this despite the fact that a senior British politician had just four weeks earlier visited Abu Dhabi and assured the people that Britain would stay as long as she was wanted to ensure the stability of the protected sheikhdoms. Despite his limited education Mohammed had acquired a good knowledge of English from his contact with the oil men on Das. I looked up and was both surprised and touched to see he was sobbing. The Pax Britannica was no myth as far as he was concerned. The only other time I ever saw him aroused was the day we went on a launch trip together to celebrate an Eid, the climax of which was a barbecue on the beach. It was like a 'hog roast', although of course it was beef and goat we were consuming, not pig. The Abu Dhabians were reeling around, led by Mohammed, tearing off chunks of meat and cramming them into their mouths, shrieking with delight as the juices trickled down their chests. I was the only Englishman there and I was shocked - until I recalled that, had they been Westerners, such behaviour would have been due to alcohol. A 'meat orgy' did at least have an explanation; until the coming of oil, meat was a rare luxury.

I digress. As we were recruiting laboratory staff in particular we had brought Suzy Aprahamian with us to Beirut. She was one of the many local wives we had recruited for the hospital as she was a qualified laboratory technician from the American University Hospital of Beirut. Berj, her husband, was a qualified civil engineer from Beirut, although both of them came from Jerusalem originally. Berj worked for the British consultants Arabicon, who, in the early days of development, had just about every major project in their sticky hand, and were sorely stretched as a result. Enter the Armenians!

Thus with Suzy's help we interviewed candidates for the laboratory - and they weren't all Armenians! It was also an opportunity to hand pick some Arab doctors. I must add that Dr Keilani - who had no reason to like me - was instrumental in seeing that we did not collect any political troublemakers. This was not easy, many of those we saw were Palestinians for whom jobs were like gold dust. We also collected two qualified pharmacists, one of whom, Bassam Abu Ghazaleh, became a life long friend.

While in Beirut I took the opportunity to drop into the British Embassy in their elegant mansion on the Corniche. I asked to see a second secretary as I had some information I would like to share with him. I was duly wheeled into an office where I faced a stern individual, who made an immediate impression on me by writing with both hands at once; that is, by continuing with whatever task he was undertaking when I entered and then noting what I had to say with the other hand. My information was hardly sensational, concerning as it did the transfer of some £6,000,000 out of Abu Dhabi from the palace account to the BCCI in Beirut. The response I got to this titbit was

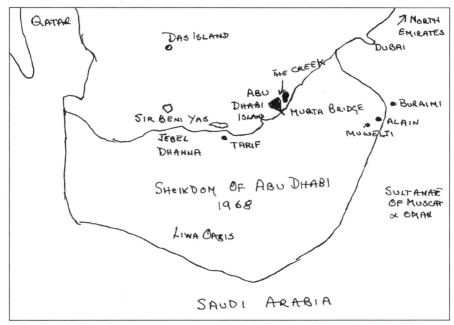

a shrug of the shoulders and a: "So what, it's his money."

I confess to being a bit disappointed at his reaction, but at least I'd got it off my chest. I was coming to the conclusion that, as we prepared to leave the Gulf, we wanted to leave a squeaky clean reputation behind us, there should be no tales of 'British Intelligence' continuing to mastermind Arabian affairs after our military departure. Nevertheless on the ground the Game was still being played with enthusiasm. By 1970 there were four different intelligence agencies at work in Al Ain. I can only assume that 'extra time' was being played, as it was hard to see whom they were spying on, except each other. "Change and decay in all around I see..."

We returned to Abu Dhabi, well satisfied with our visit. where I kept my sanity by doing a few hours screening in the X-ray department every week. I'd recruited a radiographer from the Pakistan Navy, Chief Petty Officer M. A. Butt. He was hardworking and loyal to the best of my knowledge. When we first opened, X-rays were all the rage. There was the splendid occasion where it seemed all the women on the island wanted an X-ray, not just because they wanted to know if there was anything wrong with them, but because there was a widespread myth that the magic rays actually improved well being, and might even help them get pregnant. Mr Butt would stand no nonsense. While I screened behind locked doors he would fight them off out-side. The noise was distracting but I got used to it.

Back in my office my secretary would have a list of urgent tasks for me. My first secretary was Archie Lamb's daughter, competent as she was I was glad when she left as she spilled the beans to her father on many occasions - for instance when I was trying to persuade Zeid to take on Clyde Leemaster, an American I had known in Kuwait where he had been personnel manager for Aminoil, as head of personnel. I believed his enthusiasm for all things Arab would be a binding force between the Europeans and Arabs in government service. This did not fit in with HMG's plans to appoint a sound British administrator.

And, as it transpired, they were absolutely right. Clyde was far too emotionally involved with the Arab world and the plight of the Palestinians in particular. He was also a homosexual, which was the final straw as far as the Abu Dhabians were concerned. I realised I had blundered. Clyde left and my reputation was another few notches down the pole.

My last secretary, Mrs Todd, was a sensible lady married to a senior British officer in the Air Wing, and was a gem. She had a sense of priorities. For instance one day I returned to find a German engineer seated in my office. He was from the company building the water distillation plant. He came quickly to the point.

"Do you want us to put fluoride in the water?"

"Yes," I replied firmly.

"How much?" he asked.

I stopped my self asking how much did he think, excused myself, and dashed in to Harry Napier's office.

"Quick, Harry, where's some information on fluoridation of water?"

"Well," he replied, "we've got the results back on the tests we did on the wells in Al Ain, six out of twenty of them contain twenty parts per million sodium fluoride." He looked bemused. "If you know what that means," he ended lamely.

I wasn't sure that I did either; but I knew that fluorosis was rife among the natives living near these wells. I had seen it on X-rays of the dense bones that develop and in their rotten dentition. Too much fluoride can be worse than too little. I went back to my office, trying to look knowledgeable.

"I suggest we add the same amount that you add to your water supplies in Germany."

"Ah, that's the problem - we don't. It is considered an invasion of the individual's rights to have a potential poison added to their diet."

I recalled having heard something like that in England, too. But I believed it was to the individual's advantage; and went for it.

"Right! Let's add one part per million!" That I thought shouldn't hurt anyone.

He left; and I was left wondering - just how many committees would have been required to make a decision like that in England?

21

ABU DHABI: A LONG HOT SUMMER

As the months passed, the annual health department budget grew from some BD70,000 (Bahrain dinars were standing at a little less than the pound sterling) into millions. The effects were felt. Equipment now arrived in bulk. The Abu Dhabi office in London chartered a 'Skymaster' to deliver it. These where the days when Allen & Hanbury's, among other British firms, were still manufacturing surgical instruments. What a sight that was when it disgorged its contents on the new tarmac runway! Duncan Hamilton now had the means and ways to undertake major surgery; for we had that rare thing, a blood bank, 'on the hoof', in the shape of the British Forces stationed in Sharja. I paid BD5 a pint, and bless them, we were never short of volunteers - there wasn't much else for them to do in the closing days of Empire.

We had managed to recruit an anaesthetist from Beirut, one Pierre Fahmy. A wily survivor, he ingratiated himself with me, while my Indo-Pakistani and Armenian colleagues warned me to beware. Certainly I have found Lebanese Muslims to be trustworthier in general than fellow Christians! We had a Scottish matron, Kim McManus, several British sisters - mostly wives of husbands in the government and private sectors - paramedical and nursing support. It almost looked good.

But there was a paradox developing at the same time. For the first time in their lives Abu Dhabians saw illness - providing it was not life threatening - as a passport to overseas travel. It was inconceivable that any one of them should travel without immediate members of their family with them. The only obstacle to the system of treatment abroad was the development of an effective health service at home. So government hospitals both in Abu Dhabi itself and in Al Ain could be seen as a threat to this new-found benefit. Alas, apart from the example set by Zeid himself earlier on, when he suffered his coral cut, other members of the rich and the good set a bad example by fleeing to Europe, Lebanon and India at the first sign of an in-growing toe nail. I began to see myself as a 'flying doctor'.

When the Jordanian second in command of the police department became ill, I had to accompany him to Amman; and chartered a Fokker 'Friendship' from Gulf Air to fly him there. Jim Treadwell had replaced Archie Lamb as political agent and I suggested to his wife Philippa that she should come along for the ride - Nurse Treadwell was duly enrolled. (The Treadwells seemed to follow us around Eastern Arabia.) There followed a pleasant few days, looking up old friends, while Philippa stayed in the embassy. But this was just the start. Next I was tasked to take Hamdan's daughter to Beirut and see she was safely ensconced in the American University Hospital. Dr Keilani, with his Franco-German background, thought this was the wrong place!

Then Hamdan himself became ill. This followed a visit I had arranged for a London-based consultant neurologist to see him in Abu Dhabi. It transpired he had inherited a disease from his father for which no treatment was available. Hamdan had decided to take a break in Pakistan but had developed a severe vertigo when in Rawalpindi. Charles Wonter brought me a message from the palace one evening summoning me to Pakistan; and I was airborne within the hour in an ADDF 'Islander' which took me to Dubai in time to catch a BOAC flight to Bombay. Here I had a two hour wait before catching another flight to Karachi, from where a PIA flight took me to 'Pindi. Jet lag hadn't been invented by then; but I was still glad to crash out in Flashman's Hotel the next morning. Hamdan was in a splendid suite at the Intercontinental Hotel and feeling very sorry for himself. I arranged certain tests to be carried out in the Military Hospital and was able to reassure him that this was more likely to be an intercurrent viral infection than anything else.

"You mean I can't blame my father this time?" he said somewhat testily. This was unusual for an Arab, who worshiped their fathers: Hamdan and his brothers certainly worshiped their father Sheikh Mohammed. What Hamdan could not come to terms with was inheriting a neurological disorder from a disease from which his father had been cured - after his conception.

Anyway the symptoms passed off, Hamdan was duly grateful to me for doing nothing, and presented Binnie with a magnificent fur coat, made, I'm ashamed to say, from the pelts of snow leopards.

By the summer of 1969 we were ready for a holiday. I returned alone in late July, leaving Binnie and Kathy in England. I had been away for over a month and expected the worst... and I wasn't far wrong.

I had left Oswald Menassa in charge. He looked pale and thin and ready to jump on the next aircraft to anywhere. I had thought I'd made a masterly stroke in appointing him my deputy, as he was an Egyptian ad thus basically acceptable to the Arabs; he was a public health doctor so none of the specialists would feel threatened; he was corruptible in the nicest possible way; and could speak English as well as I could.

It turned out that all these factors worked against him. The Arabs thought of him as a British stooge; the specialists screamed at him for not understanding their needs; the merchants got angry as he refused to sign local purchase orders; and the European community treated him as a 'ruddy gyppo' when he put a British family in quarantine - rightly - for not having valid smallpox vaccination certificates when they arrived back at the airport from a vacation in India. Matron was in tears because of the bias against her British and Indian nurses she thought she had detected among the Arab staff. Eric Thompson was gunning for me as our overseas treatment budget had spiralled through the roof.[1]

---

[1] The Palace Office had unloaded this on me in my absence. I have already explained how families insisted on accompanying patients and it was their expenses both in Beirut and London, which were doing the damage.

Duncan Hamilton had learned that I had called his wife while I was on leave and persuaded her that I could get them comfortable quarters if only she would come out to Abu Dhabi. I hoped her presence would keep Duncan off the bottle. I'd had to use all my powers of persuasion. She was happy in Oxfordshire, and had had enough of being a colonial wife, first in Uganda, then in Aden. The day Duncan learned what I'd been plotting he blew his top, cancelled his operating list and returned to his hotel room in a sulk. Next day he appeared in my office smelling of strong drink.

Finally, the resident architect of the hospital consultants we had finally managed to engage, had fled to Beirut in hysterics. It looked like it was going to be a summer of discontent. At the root of the problem was - money. Zeid had a cash flow problem. Government expenditure was spiralling as the Abu Dhabians found to their cost that having an awful lot of money is not the same as having unlimited money. Expectations had exceeded reality. For instance, with the help of the PWD bosses, Abdul Shakoor, a Sudanese, and Dudley Cowderoy, we had short-listed possible consultants to design a permanent hospital months before; and chosen the firm of Watkins, Gray, Woodgate. They had sent George Rice out to Abu Dhabi as resident architect. While there had been much talk, there had been no progress. Like all serious development plans, it had been placed on the back burner.

A few days after my return, Zeid came back from his holiday, in time for National Day. As senior government officials we were expected to attend. There was the usual dreadful shambles at the airport, the ADDF Guard of Honour being swept aside by the mob of Abu Dhabians rushing out onto the tarmac to welcome him. John Paley, who had succeeded Tug Wilson in command of the ADDF, was a dreadful shade of grey.

"I'll never see ADDF treated like that again," he swore softly.[1]

Poor Peter MacDonald crept away in shame, while Charles Wontner, who had a detachment of the Royal Guard with him, tried to stop the crowd single-handed. Two weeks later, we learned that Zeid had appointed a development committee. Their first decision - stop all development! Their second - stop all ongoing projects that they considered non-essential! Thus, for instance, Sainrapt & Brice, French consultants, were not pleased to learn that the scheme to dredge a channel around the island was to go on hold and their dredgers left idle.

But during those critical two weeks a lot happened. Duncan thought better of having his wife out; and I managed to rent them a good villa, owned by Ahmed Obeidly, who was visiting for National Day - 6 August. This was the fourth anniversary of Zeid's 'take-over'. It was as hot and sticky as ever.

This year was marked by a strong Iraqi presence; their vice-president was introduced to government officials and made little effort to hide his distaste when he had to shake a British hand! He then went on to push Jim Treadwell out of the way at the opening of the new markets. But it didn't impress the

---

[1] John Paley had come to us from Aden where he had been Defence Attaché in the British High Commission, following our withdrawal in 1967. The Daimler belonging to our last Governor, Sir Humphrey Trevelyan, had been commandeered by the President of the new People's Republic; but before it was, John managed to put a large sticker on the back which read: "Save the Argylls!" It was apparently some time before the new rulers cottoned on.

Abu Dhabians. It was also marked by the flight of Sunni Binagar - or Sunni bin Bangbang as we used to call him. Along with Abdul Shakoor and a legal adviser to the palace - whom I shall avoid naming! - Sunni was one of three Sudanese directors recruited at the same time as myself to head up government departments. Sunni had the municipality. Thus, Ascension Day celebrations came under his wing. Hitherto he had pushed off before the event, leaving it to his underlings to make preparations, then returned in time for the big day to capture the glory. But on this occasion he'd done a runner - and taken all his personal possessions with him, as we found when we went to check his house. (Oswald moved in before anyone else had a chance!)

Meanwhile the efforts of the medical recruitment committee had begun to bear fruit - by the tree full. I had mentioned earlier that they had opted for Egypt as a source, in line with the recommendation of the Civil Service Commission and its new boss, Ahmed Shalabi, an Iraqi. (Ali Shuraffa had gone to the Ministry of Foreign Affairs.) By early August, 20,000 applications - for ten medical posts - had arrived. Harold Wynn - Wynn the Post, our neighbour - actually complained to me that postal deliveries were being disrupted by the weight of mail from Egypt. In fact it was he who had weighed the first sack and thus estimated how many applications we had received. It said something about (a) the number of medical schools in Egypt (b) the economic state of that country. How the committee ever selected ten candidates I didn't to ask. In the event only one turned out to be a 'bad hat'. The question now was - would we be able to pay them?

I was used to being between a rock and a hard place but the future of the Coseley Hospital in Al Ain was a tighter niche than usual. All work on it had stopped even before I went on leave earlier in the summer. I knew Zeid wanted it, but now the development council had the last word. It was presided over by Khalifa, Zeid's eldest son, Hamdan was a member, the other sixteen were an assortment of merchants, of whom, it was rumoured, half could read and write. A sample of their deliberations was that of sewage disposal, now that work on the main sewage treatment plant had been suspended. After two hours discussion it was decided that sewage disposal would be the responsibility of each householder.

So I drove to Al Ain with little hope of resolving the situation - unless I could get Zeid's ear. I looked forward to telling him what I had learned from Dr Keilani on my way back through Beirut: namely that two Lebanese companies were proposing to build private hospitals in Abu Dhabi 'in view of the poor hospital facilities existing there'. I had Kim McManus with me. Her morale needed boosting, something I tried to do on the journey. This suffered a set back when we reached the check post at Sa'ad, about twenty kilometres out of Al Ain, where I waved at the policeman and drove past in my smart government limo. Fifty yards further on and 'Bang!' he loosed off at me with his rifle. I halted abruptly and reversed at high speed to the barrier. There I learned that, during my absence of leave, Khalifa - as deputy ruler - had made a rule that the drivers of government cars which failed to stop at check points should be arrested. This was because some government driver had 'gone ape' on the way to Dubai and sold the vehicle! I confessed my crime while Kim waited in the car; and noted a yellow Mercedes taxi without number plates steaming past with seven passengers in it. I kept quiet and was then escorted to Al Ain police station - where I made a suitably dramatic announcement as to who I was! This caused some consternation; and minutes later Tahnoon, Hamdan's brother and governor of Al Ain - was on the 'phone and asking me if I was all right.

Unfortunately Kim went to see Sheikha Fatima, Sheik Zeid's No. 1 wife, with one of the Arab nurses and had just finished her indignant description of the event when Zeid walked in - he of course nearly died laughing when he heard what had happened! I must in future write a letter to myself permitting me to use my own government car to drive to Al Ain and then get a pass from public security which would be valid for seven days... I decided to use an unmarked taxi.

I admit that on our return journey in the evening Kim and I were ushered through the Sa'ad check point by a police guard of honour; but it was cold comfort, for I had failed to get a positive answer from Zeid about Al Ain Hospital. He had hidden behind the development council. Was he getting his own back on me for the medical recruiting committee?

"It will be their decision - I only have to sign it."

Things were approaching a crisis; or so it seemed to us in government service. Dismissals were in the air. Abdul Shakoor followed Sunni Binagar back to Sudan, and it was clear that any project with which he had been implicated was scrutinised for evidence of corruption. Alas these included the hospitals. I always thought he had been as honest as any man could have been in his position. Victor Hashem, the owner of Atto Company who were doing the civil works for the Al Ain Hospital advised me to be patient.

There were rumours that none of us would get paid the following month. A British team of auditors from Whinny Murray were appointed to investigate government expenditure. Even medical treatment was curtailed as we were not allowed to buy medicines from the local agents: one in particular, Rasul Jishi from Bahrain, had helped us out of many sticky problems, but now Rashid Aweida, his local Abu Dhabi partner, had decided to take 75% of the profits - for doing very little. So this was a blow to Rasul. Then daily paid staff were not paid - and walked out. I lost 167 from the health department, and Harold Wynn's postal service collapsed.

Attendance at the hospital doubled. I estimated 90% were malingerers. The development council decided that all Tb cases were to be sent to India for treatment, having decided Abu Dhabi was being 'ripped off' by the sanatoria in Lebanon. I doubt if this was true, Keilani kept quite a tight hold on them. What he couldn't control was the money spent by the 'attendants' who insisted on staying up there.

Several expatriate staff now lost their jobs and in the midst of this Dr Rahim, who had been in Karachi for medical treatment, returned looking worse than when he went. If a medical board found him unfit the embargo on recruiting new staff would leave us with yet another gap - better half a doctor than none?

By now I was working by instinct rather than coherent thought and wondering how long it would be before I was terminated. (Nine out of the original twelve directors had already departed.) But HMG might get there first!

Zeid had decided that he needed to ingratiate himself with the ruler of Ras Al Khaimah, who was showing signs of succumbing to Egyptian flattery at a time when the future of a United Trucial Coast was in the balance. Therefore he decided to build a clinic for him at a small, isolated fishing village called Bukha; and told me to get on with it. So off I went in an ADDF helicopter and landed at Ras Al Khaimah to present my - or rather Zeid's - credentials to the ruler. While there I witnessed an embarrassing scene which demonstrated that Zeid's fears were not imaginary. The ruler had a defence force, so as to 'keep up with the Jones'. We used to say that each of the Trucial states had to have its own airport, cement factory, defence force, harbour and radio station to be able to look its neighbour in the face.

A young British major marched in, saluted the ruler and gave a brief report, in Arabic. Behind him were two Egyptian officers who took a pace forward to flank him. One shouted an order; the three about turned and marched out - the impression was clearly intended to show that the OC was under close arrest!

We flew on and landed at the village. I had a surveyor and civil engineer from PWD with me and it did not take long to agree a site and services with the local mukhtar. We left, loaded with tea, dates and 'Brownie points' from the locals.

But when we landed back at Abu Dhabi I was in trouble. There was a message telling me to report to Her Majesty's political agent, whatever the hour. And Jim Treadwell got down to business before even offering me a drink. I had noticed a slightly sinister individual lurking on the edge of the crowd in Bukha, with a black and green 'schmarg' partially covering his face - virtually diagnostic of an English officer masquerading as a local Arab. It soon transpired he was a member of the Sultan of Oman's Intelligence Service, who had radioed my arrival back to his HQ in Muscat as soon as I arrived.

It transpired that I had landed in the Sultanate of Muscat and Oman and that Bukha did not belong to Ras Al Khaimah after all. Well, I left that to the political agents to sort out; but I will say that next day Jim accompanied me to Hamdan and explained that I was not allowed to visit Bukha again without a visa from Muscat; and that perhaps Sheikh Shakhbut would appreciate a clinic there, but that it was not to be built for the ruler of Ras Al Khaimah. Ah... even without gunboats we still had some clout in Arabia.

Time was running out. I was no longer responsible for medical services in the ADDF, but I still interfered whenever I could! I had left Corporal Ali Raschid in charge, an ex-Trucial Scout 'medic' who had made an excellent job of things before a British doctor, Peter Flamanck, arrived. I was also able to get my deputy chief pharmacist, Bassam Abu Ghazaleh, transferred to ADDF, which gave him a securer future. But a major coup was to see that Charles Wontner's Royal Guard had their own MO. This was one of the Egyptian MO's who had arrived 'in bulk' from Cairo, Nabil Sabbagh, a Roman Catholic, whose wife Marie-Therese celebrated National Day by giving birth to a daughter in Cairo! She duly benefited from Zeid's munificence.

We became friends; and later Nabil was to tell me how, before leaving Cairo, an intelligence officer had briefed him to watch a certain doctor Peter Horniblow who had been an active terrorist in the Yemen some years earlier. That was my 'five minutes of fame' of which, until then, I had been unaware.

It was late in the autumn that I had another experience with ADDF. Binnie was still in England, Kathy had not yet returned and Pereira had an afternoon off when I had a visit from two Arab ladies, Sue and Munira, members of the sophisticated Jordanian 'expat community'. They mingled with the British community and the Abu Dhabian ruling family on more than equal terms - in fact they were slightly patronising to both! I for one could hardly blame them, coming as they did from wealthy Palestinian families dispossessed by the Israelis and their British 'allies'.

Their visit was not unexpected, as a young British officer in the ADDF had preceded it by a few minutes. Munira and he were on close terms and Sue took me aside and said: "Listen! That young man's a criminal!"

As he was on secondment from the Black Watch I was prepared to believe her. It transpired that he and a colleague were planning to steal the payroll of their regiment, then stationed on the western frontier, and amounting to some BD14,000. I knew that this was an unhappy regiment, in fact there had been a minor mutiny not long ago, and it seemed likely that a new CO would be appointed. I dismissed the story as yet another 'Walter Mittyism' - one of the problems with an army which has never seen action, and is unlikely to in the foreseeable future, is that imagination runs riot.

But... the next thing I heard was that the payroll <u>had</u> been stolen and that the 'usual suspect' had been arrested, i.e. the Pakistani pay clerk. I decided to keep 'shtum' until John Paley had returned from leave. When I rather diffidently told him my story - which, in Binnie's absence, had discreditable connotations! - he acted quickly. SIB officers flew in and within days the case was closed. The two officers in question had departed on leave immediately after the theft but were soon tracked down; and all but BD1500 was recovered.

Poor John - when he reported the incident to Zeid, the latter looked at him sadly and said: "Is there nobody left I can trust?"

The heat of the summer was fading and Binnie was due back, having been actively house-hunting in England, and the days of 'pseudo-bachelordom', which Jim Timms and I had been enjoying were coming to an end. Our final fling was on a dhow trip, organised by Joe Yachi, an Iraqi émigré of the 'old regime', whose Swiss wife was also on vacation. In addition to several other Arabs and their wives we had Bilho and Zara with us. Joe was a Christian -

in fact his father had been Archbishop of the Orthodox Church in Iraq - so there was no shortage of alcohol. So much so that all the girls got slewed. One Lebanese wife started fingering Zara - who clearly did not enjoy it! (Thus exploding a theory held by certain uncharitable members of the expatriate community.) She followed this up by attacking me in the water, perhaps to prove her point. Then Bilho got carried away by the current and screamed to me to rescue her. All this makes it sound as if I was the 'catch of the season!' Alas, I was aware that all this was part of the great game, both girls were out to snare Joe. I was just bait. Meanwhile Kathy was having a great time with the other children on board. Such was expatriate life when the wives were away.

Time was definitely running out... Eric Thompson was finding the stress of the financial turmoil too much, resigned, and was replaced by John Butter, who arrived with his wife Joyce, an artist.[1] His arrival helped cool down the financial inferno, and thereafter the ship of state floated on a more even keel. But not before we were told that Sheikh Raschid Al Maktoum of Dubai had offered Zeid to buy Abu Dhabi for BD450,000, but that Zeid had turned down the offer unless he accepted all the expired letters of credit as well!

Work started on the Al Ain Hospital and as we entered the 1970s, solid progress was under way. We even added a VIP ward to the Abu Dhabi Hospital. But I confess most of my planning at this stage was for an expedition to the Karakorum, which I was planning with Philippa Treadwell.

---

[1] John had served both before and after World War II in the Indian Civil Service, one of the happy band who had ruled India with tact, diplomacy and sheer hard work, occasionally augmented with a gun. To hear John, the dignified man of financial probity, recall: "Knocking over a 'badmash' at 50 yards with a bullet from my Colt 45 and see him cartwheel to a halt was really satisfying," was yet another surreal experience. After Partition he had gone to Kenya and rose to be Jomo Kenyatta's Finance Minister. By now it was time to move on, hence his arrival in Abu Dhabi; although they kept their home in Nairobi.

22
A Hike in Chitral

Tony Streather had inspired me with such tales of derring-do in the Chitral Scouts as to make me want to visit that part of north west Pakistan. He, alas, was soldiering in Northern Ireland so couldn't join us. Furthermore his wife Sue might have demurred as she recalled his discreditable tales of Kalash maidens being brought to the Officers' Mess and scrubbed by the mess sergeant before being produced as the after dinner 'sweet'. (See later for the joint research that Philippa and I carried out on the Kalash!)

I had great hopes that Jawed would be able to accompany us. We had remained in touch since he and his wife Kauser had stayed with us in Harley Street in 1966, when he was attending the Army College at Shrivenham. He was now on the staff of GHQ in 'Pindi and not enjoying it. Sadly, his CO refused him permission to accompany us as liaison officer; such fraternising with the former imperial power was frowned on at that time.

There was a lot of planning to do and I recall with affection how dear Mrs Todd kept the wires humming between London, Abu Dhabi and Karachi, where the splendid Ahmed Jaffer was our 'go between'. Together with Ahmed Suwaidi, who was President of the Emiri Court they oiled wheels for our visit. Hamdan lent me a Land Rover and his under-secretary Hamid bin Sultan, who was also the local agent for the United Bank of Pakistan, ensured that they too gave us their support. Never has an expedition, albeit of only two people, set off better armed!

Our actual start was not auspicious. We left for Dubai by car and half way there had a puncture. The car actually belonged to an SAS officer charged with training the Royal Guard and it was his driver - who found that the wheel nuts were rusted on; and the spare tyre was the wrong size. Who cares who wins? Well we got to the airport, as our plane landed, with black smoke pouring from the spare tyre, which was rubbing against the body work.

But thereafter everything ran smoothly. Our reception committee at Karachi would have suited minor royalty; we never saw an official and were ensconced in the Metropole Hotel within minutes. One can get a taste for this sort of thing! We had an hour to freshen up, then were off for cocktails with the Inspector General of Police. Next day, more cocktails, a visit to the Golf Club with one Raschid Habib - who owned the bank of the same name - and the wedding of Major General Mohammed Yusuf's son to Nafeesa Hamid. And this was meant to be a mountaineering expedition? But Ahmed Jaffer was such a superb host, neither of us could complain.

Philippa went up to Lahore next day. She and Jim had been there with the

High Commission at the end of the 1950s, and she had friends she wanted to see. I remained in Karachi where Ahmed Jaffer had arranged for me to meet with the doyen of the medical profession and indulge in a little pro-Zeid propaganda! Then on to the Yacht Club and a sail in one of their 'tomtits' which brought back happy memories. But there was no rest. On to the rowing club where I met Z. A. Bhutto, who lost interest in me once he learned my political views!

Meanwhile, thanks to Ahmed and the United Bank, our kit from the UK and the Land Rover were married up and, with driver Mohammed and mechanic Suleiman, set off for the 1,000 mile drive to 'Pindi. I had a last lunch with Zara's sister, husband and gorgeous sixteen-year-old daughter and then it was farewell and away to 'Pindi by air, where Jawed met me, resplendent in service dress and sporting parachute wings. Our meeting was dampened by the news that his boss would not let him accompany us, even on holiday.

We went to Flashman's, which had had a real face-lift since Binnie and I last stayed there in 1962. There were fitted carpets and central air-conditioning, together with a veranda big enough to stack our kit. Philippa was still in Lahore so that night I dined with Jawed, and Gabby, who was with us on Khinyang Chish in 1962. Khurschid and Sid Durrani, alas, were stationed away from 'Pindi. It was sad enough, just the three of us, remembering Jimmy and Dick. Later Kauser and Gabby's new young wife joined us. Gabby, like Sid, had been in the Special Service Group in the 1965 war against India: and had got a bullet through his chest that had somehow passed between his lung and liver without killing him. He confirmed that Sid had been parachuted straight into the arms of an Indian brigade; and had suffered torture during his four month's imprisonment. Even so the Indians were still happy to let him go, he was such a bloody nuisance to them!

Next day Philippa arrived, looking like the wreck of the *Hesperus*, so I sent her off to the Intercontinental Hotel to have her hair done at expedition expense. The hairdresser was a Lebanese girl, so Philippa sauntered out with a 'Beirut bouffon'. Jawed arrived with 2,000 rupees... in one rupee notes! Useful for paying porters but I estimated we would need an extra porter to carry them. Philippa bought all our pots and pans in the bazaar for Rs.147, while I bought 1,000 aspirin tablets and 1,000 cascara tablets for the princely sum of Rs.12 - just less than £1 - so that I could do my 'great white physician from over the water' act.

We were finally ready for the off so, waving Jawed and Kauser *au revoir* we set off for Malakand, in dull, still and hazy weather. Next day we went on to Dir, when I took over the driving from Mohammed - having worked for Hamdan on shooting expeditions in Sind, he had never seen a mountain road. I noticed the battery wasn't charging so our start the next day was delayed while the armature was rewound and new brushes fitted. It was now I realised that 'Sheikh Hamdan's new 6-cylinder Land Rover', as described to my by UBL in Karachi, was in fact a clapped out 4-cylinder job. But I mustn't complain. What did piss me off was the fact that they had indeed fitted us up with five new tyres... but they were balloon tyres for desert travel. Not the best thing for mountain tracks.

Next day we went on to Lowari Top, the gateway to Chitral, an 11,000 foot pass to which I drove with the engine complaining at the cold, rarefied air after days grinding through insufferable heat. It was only 7am when we finally stalled near the summit. It was bitterly cold and we were all still in shirts and slacks. Inevitably we stopped at the narrowest part of the jeep track where there was no room to pass. We hunted in our rucksacks for wind-proofs. At least the view was wonderful - thick forests rising almost to the top of the pass, plumes of snow whirling from the peaks on either side of us and spring flowers breaking through the lingering snow patches.

Mohammed had the bonnet up and was... tinkering. Then we heard it - the whine of a straining engine getting louder until a jeep burst into sight with some ten passengers hanging on. Bonnet to bonnet we faced each other - impasse but also our salvation. The driver, a ferocious looking Pathan, leapt out of his jeep, thrust his head under our bonnet, produced sandpaper, a shred of silver cigarette paper, a screwdriver - and hey presto! The points were adjusted, the distributor closed, and the engine burst into life. Mohammed backed us to a point where the track widened a little, where we watched aghast as the jeep rocketed past on the slope above us at an angle of 45 degrees.

I cannot recall a word being spoken or a smile exchanged during this inci-dent. On to Chitral via Drosh, where we spent a night as guests of the Chitral Scouts. Their adjutant, Captain Saadullah, a Bengali, rhapsodised with us about the beauty of Chitral; then, after several drams of malt whisky, became maudlin and confessed he just wished he was back amongst the fleshpots of Chittagong. But he was a kind host. The experience underlined the enor-mous gap that existed across India; it was probably not his fault that he had been transferred from Bengal to the Afghan border. Next day we went on to Chitral where we stayed in a neat and clean civil rest house set among lawns, flowers, tall trees and with a wonderful view of Tirich Mir, looking like a giant molar tooth.

We spent two days getting 'geared up' and engaging one Abdul Sumat as guide and interpreter. He was a Chitrali but had served in the old Indian Army, hence was fluent in English and Urdu as well as his own tongue. The leader of a previous Norwegian expedition, Arne Naess, had described him as: "Capable, conscientious and cunning." We never found where this latter talent lay. He was the soul of honesty, hardworking and, apart from a patho-logical hatred of opening tins, a first class camp boss.

Next day Jawed and Kauser turned up, the former having told his boss a pack of lies and gone to the extent of driving south from 'Pindi until he was sure he was not being followed! We had to hire two jeeps now, as the track north of Chitral became so narrow that our Land Rover, with its balloon tyres, would not be able to negotiate the bends. We reached Parpish, 40 miles north, that evening and camped under a huge chinar tree on the lawn of the guest house - the latter being a tip. Next morning we set off with packhorse and six coolies for the village of Barum, where Abdul Sumat recruited two high altitude porters, Abdul Karim and Yacoob Khan.

The following day we started a delightful two day trek and, as is right and proper we paid in advance for our subsequent delight with a hot and thirsty flog up a precipice. After that the slope relented and we had a gorgeous trudge up to the end of the valley where we camped again under chinar trees. I reflected how much more attractive this country was compared with the dreary slogs through Baltistan and Nagar ten years previously. However the people were the same, goitrous and malnourished, but unfailingly helpful and kind. We drank ice-cold water from the silt-laden mountain streams, which once again did us no harm!

Next day we rambled up a precipitous path alongside a cunningly built irrigation stream, carved in places out of solid rock, until the last village with its green fields and poplars had been left behind. Then the days of wine and roses were over and we flogged up the Barroom Glacier for our last three hours until we reached the grove of stunted trees the locals called Shoker Shal (the Sugar Stall) but christened 'The Idyllen' by the Norwegians twenty years previously.

Kauser was exhausted and frightened. She was 23 and this was her first time in the mountains. Until she climbed the stairs to our flat in Harley Street four years earlier I don't suppose she had ever put one foot above the other! We were surrounded by peaks of 17-20,000 feet, with the towering mass of Tirich Mir itself above us. She gave Jawed some stick! We'd had to cross three landslides, ankle twisting and knee wrenching they were too, and she clearly blamed Jawed for their presence. But she also found the wildness and remoteness of the place too much and insisted on going back down at once, with the other five porters who had carried our kit up from Parpish. Jawed did not demur. I know he wanted to visit one of the Kaffir valleys and he only had five days before he was due back in GHQ. It was good of them to have come so far just to be with us.

Idyllen by name and nature; but there was little point in staying there once we had drunk our fill of the view, for it was a base camp for Tirich Mir itself and nothing else. We decided to have a rest day and then climb the ridge behind us which provided us with even more stunning views of the mountain. We put a tent at 14,000 feet, which Karim and Yacoob carried up for us. They descended and we had a wonderful sunset behind Tirich, which Philippa photographed. (An enlargement of this is still my favourite mountain photograph and hangs in my 'studio'.)

Alas, at 4am it began to snow. At 6am we brewed up, cooked sausage, bacon and beans and took a dim view of the weather. By 8.30am we decided to have a go and set off through the murk. Two hours later Philippa called out that the steps I was kicking in the snow were filling up before she could reach them. We were at 17,000 feet, and I could see the ridge cornice just twenty feet above me... all around a 'white out'. Reluctantly we descended. Yacoob and Karim were at the tent so, after a quick brew, we descended and reached Idyllen late that afternoon in pouring rain. Sumat assured me that this sort of thing never happened in Chitral in June. I seem to have a knack of causing climatic miracles! Everything was sodden. We polished off the rest of the whisky, heated a gallon of soup and crawled into our wet sleeping bags with a couple of 'Nembutals' apiece.

Next morning the clouds had gone and the sun shone from a cloudless sky for the rest of our stay in Chitral. Oh ye of little faith. We spent a few days exploring the glacier. These mountains are newcomers in the earth's history, still raw and jagged, so that little snow clings to their lower slopes. Only above 20,000 feet, where ice is eternal, are their outlines softened.

We decided to leave Idyllen and camp south of Tirich where there was a peak, Ausher, or 'Little Tirich' as we called it because it was of a similar out-line to its giant neighbour, which we thought might 'go'. We found a pleasant meadow above the Awir Glacier, then next morning set off with Yacoob and Karim to set up camp one, again on a lovely meadow at 15,000 feet, sur-rounded by snow but with a stream running through the middle and a fringe of iris, buttercups and miniature primroses on the banks. While we gazed and lazed, our two porters burned up our reserves of primus fuel to make chapat-tis.

The next day's climb was hardly one for the record book. There was rock, a snow-filled couloir, and ice, all tackled under a cloudless sky. Shortly after noon I led up a cornice to a rock peak shaped like a crocus. The summit, would you believe? Of course not. We could see the world and 400 yards away, at the end of a knife-edged ridge, the west peak of Ausher, 350 feet higher.

We settled for a first ascent of Ausher East. There was only room for two of us on top. We left our beautiful eyrie after half an hour and descended with care. Nevertheless as we crossed the top of the couloir Yacoob slipped and fell a couple of hundred feet before blessedly somersaulting to a stop in soft snow just above its lip. I had turned to take a photograph of Philippa just as he fell; no doubt he looked at the print I sent him later and reckoned that was one of his nine lives saved.

That night at our base camp we ate a stewed goat I had bought for Rs.27, in case we had had reason to celebrate: served me right, it was disgusting and I had to surreptitiously slip away and empty our plates behind a rock. Yacoob and Karim gnawed away happily with another porter who had joined us. He had a transistor radio, a serpent in Eden, but it did bring us news of the Conservative victory in the UK election. This was a surprise to us, we had been out of touch with British politics for some time. Our only worry was that some gung-ho foreign secretary would reverse the Labour Party's deci-sion to quit the Gulf.

Our walk out took us over the Awir Pass, about 15,000 feet, from where we had a wonderful view of the western Karakorum; Nanga Parbat, Haramosh and Rakaposhi, all over 25,000 feet, standing out like giant sentries along the eastern horizon. We camped among yellow roses the first night. The second day was an easy stroll downhill. The people in this valley were Ismailis and some four years earlier the Aga Khan announced he was going to visit them so the villagers had rallied round and started building a jeep track. When it was two thirds finished he cancelled his visit.

Talking of which my own arse-ache recurred. I had been troubled by external piles before and had found that a primitive form of cryothermy worked a treat - namely, choosing a secluded part of a glacier, removing one's pants and then sitting on the ice, cheeks well apart, until one literally had a numb bum. I suspect army loo paper from the compo packs was to blame; anyway the Awir Glacier treatment worked.

That evening we camped near a river that had reputedly been stocked with trout in the past. Philippa had a crude rod; we never sniffed a trout but caught a couple of grey, perch-like, fish that we subsequently fried in compo margarine. They tasted like wet cotton wool.

Jawed had arranged for a jeep to take us the last twelve miles to Chitral, where we duly arrived after an exciting drive, with a broken clutch and one flat tyre. Next day we set off to visit the Kaffirs.

⫷ ⫷ ⫷ ⫷ ⫷ ⫷ ⫷ ⫷ ⫷ ⫷ ⫷ ⫷ ⫷

Much has been written about these people; and much of it is rubbish. According to Sir George Robertson in Hastings' *Encyclopaedia of Religious Ethics*, writing in the 19th century, there were two types: the Kati or Red Kaffirs, who were tall, fair and pale-eyed; and the Kalash or Black Kaffirs, olive-skinned and black haired. The Kati tended to be headmen, priests and medicine men: thus possibly descendants of the Bactrian colonists with a proportion of Greek blood, inherited from Alexander the Great's soldiers. How they survived for the next thousand years is not known; but they almost certainly chose the rich alluvial plains alongside the Indus, until they were forced to flee into the mountains by the forces of Islam. Once there they imposed their authority on the local aboriginal population; and then left them to their own devices. Hence 'Kaffirs', or unbelievers. By the late 19th century their religion was a form of polytheism, with Irma, the supreme creator, who had fathered many lesser gods. Religious observances were of a two kinds, ritual dance and animal sacrifice. Their days as an independent tribal group in the valleys of the Hindu Kush were numbered. In 1895, Abdul Rahman Khan, Emir of Afghanistan, felt strongly enough to subdue and/or convert them to Islam. Sadly the attempt ended in a massacre. Kaffiristan became Nuristan, the land of light. The few survivors withdrew into three remote valleys.

We had to hire a jeep as Mohammed and Suleiman had gone off to 'Pindi, having taken the precaution of immobilising the Land Rover by taking the rotor arm with them; and these don't grow on trees in Chitral. We reached

Ayun that evening and camped outside the rest house, built on a bluff over the river and facing straight at Tirich Mir. (The building itself had fallen down.) It was the most beautiful campsite I have ever known.

In the morning we were back on our feet again and, accompanied by a new guide, Ghazi, a friend of Sumat's, and two porters, we toiled up 4,000 feet in the heat until reaching the blessed shade of pine trees where we collapsed on the soft forest floor and inhaled resin. Our mountain travel had rendered us very fit and I cannot recall even being thirsty! Then down 3,000 feet into the

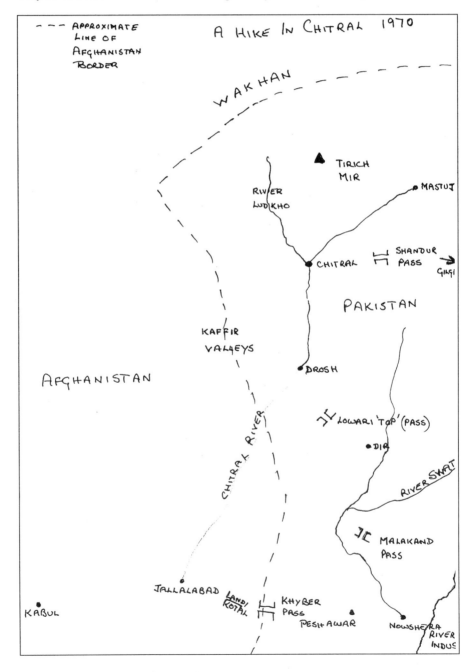

Rumbhur Valley. This, together with Bomboret and Birir further south, was the homeland of the Kaffir survivors.

We reached the village of Baladash. The cemetery was sadly neglected but there were still a number of carved wooden 'headstones' to be seen - crude figures in what we assumed to be Bactrian dress - Turkoman helmets, tunics, crossed webbing and daggers. Ghazi showed us what he called the Boy Virgin's Temple. The décor certainly suggested a decadent polytheism - there were holly, runic crosses, animal heads and orthodox swastikas, i.e. symbols of light rather than the Nazi variety. Perhaps the attempt to follow so many spiritual paths had backfired as Ghazi said few people followed them; and most, albeit with some reluctance, accepted Islam.

We were then shown the 'Bashali' house, where menstruating women must stay during their periods and throughout their pregnancies, but there were only two women there so we decided that was another aspect of their religion the people had abandoned. When we came out we were treated to a 'ritual dance'. By this time a group of unpleasant Pakistani youths had turned up by jeep from Bomboret, they were drunk and made obscene gestures at the Kalash girls.

The dance routine was that I had grown to expect anywhere east of Suez - one two three hop, shuffle shuffle hop hop; but they were worth studying if only for their clothes which did indeed indicate an exotic past. They wore robes like that of the Franciscans, of brown wool, with belts of the same material. On their heads they wore a coif of goat's hair decorated with cowry shells - and remember - the nearest beach was the shore of the Arabian Sea. A hood covered this partly, and this was crowned by a purple pom-pom. Their hair was plaited and came down to their waists. They were indescribably dirty - which is perhaps why they are known as the Kalash (Black) Kaffirs. Two men provided the music with drums - which the Pakistanis augmented with sticks and spoiled the rhythm: we were glad when they wandered off.

We left too, saddened more than interested by what we had seen. Civilisation, as practised by the youth of Karachi, would soon complete the disintegration of Kalash culture.

❦ ❦ ❦ ❦ ❦ ❦ ❦ ❦ ❦ ❦ ❦ ❦ ❦

Sumat, Mohammed and Suleiman were waiting at Ayun with our tarted-up Land Rover, resplendent with five new heavy-duty tyres, new plus, distributor and fan belt. We set off for 'Pindi, and apart from the worst night of our lives in the rest house at Malakand - which involved broken water pipes, bats, cockroaches and centipedes - we had an uneventful trip back to 'Pindi.

There a telegram from Binnie was waiting at Flashman's: "Advise you return Abu Dhabi soonest." This put a dampener on the trip; which was worsened by Jawed asking me to fix a job in the Abu Dhabi government for a nephew of his who was in trouble with the police for theft and drug-taking...

east is east and west is west when it comes to helping friends.

Jawed and I parted, our relationship strained. I was not to know this was the last time we would meet. A few months later he was killed in East Pakistan, shot by his own men when he tried to stop them, Punjabis, from running amok and killing a crowd of rioting Bengalis. I lost a friend and Kauser a husband. It was to be 30 years before we met again. She was still a widow, living with her two sons and daughter.

Before leaving Pakistan I called on the Under Secretary of Health, whom I had met during previous recruiting tours and put it to him that, as my days in Abu Dhabi were probably numbered, perhaps I could spend a year or so working as a doctor in the Northern Areas, e.g. Gilgit or Skardu. I will always respect him for his direct reply.

"My dear chap - it would cost me my job if I gave a work permit to a British doctor."

❖ ❖ ❖ ❖ ❖ ❖ ❖ ❖ ❖ ❖ ❖ ❖ ❖

Philippa and I flew back to Dubai where we were met by Jim and Binnie and driven to Abu Dhabi. It was July and perishingly hot.

My fears were justified. My relations with Zeid, while always unpredictable, had worsened since he had consulted me earlier in the year about Sheikha Fatima's health. Summoned to the desert one Friday, we sat in the sand and, like an idiot, I gave him my personal opinion. I really don't think I was trying to impress him, I had genuinely come to like as well as admire him for the way he kept his cool under increasing and often unbearable pressures. But of course I should have followed the fundamental rule - 'If it's family, get a second opinion.'

It was six months before I summoned help from Harley Street, and by then it was too late - for me at any rate. Furthermore during the months of financial uncertainty that began in the summer of 1969, heads had fallen among government officials: in fact, I was the only white face left of the original directors appointed in 1966 - apart from the military. I had begun to resemble the proverbial 'sore thumb'.

But before the inevitable denouement, world events intervened. These began, as far as I was concerned, with what might be termed 'local unrest'. To be more precise feuding in the ruling family. This time it seemed serious enough to report to the Political Residency in Bahrain. (Summer leave had, as usual, decimated the staff of the Political Agency in Abu Dhabi.) Also, I wanted to visit England for some pressing family matters - Binnie and Kathy were already there on leave. So on 8 September I took a local flight up to Bahrain having booked an onward flight next day on the BOAC flight from Bombay to London. Having delivered my news to a somewhat disinterested residency official I went to Manama airport early next day where I bumped into Abdul Jalil, whose father was the Abu Dhabian partner of Middle East Airlines.

"Where are you going, Doctor?" he cried.

"London," I replied.

"On what flight?"

"BOAC, of course!" I replied cheerfully, knowing that his father's great friend and business rival was the agent for that airline.

"And I'm paying for my own ticket!"

"Then you are travelling tourist class?"

"Of course," I answered.

"Then you must transfer at once to MEA and I will see you are upgraded to first class, and you can at least travel with me to Beirut," he said, somewhat imperiously, I thought. (He had been educated at Millfield.)

I didn't need too much persuading; and so it was a few hours later we were circling over Beirut waiting permission to land. We waited a long time and eventually the news spread through the cabin that an airliner had been hi-jacked and was being re-fuelled in Beirut. Eventually we saw it take off and head east. Before we got permission to land we were told this was the BOAC VC10 en route to London from Bombay, which had been hi-jacked after taking of from Bahrain.

It was in fact the fourth airliner to be hi-jacked since 6 September by the PLFP, one Swiss and one US having already been forced down at Dawson Field, the other, another US Jumbo was flown to Cairo and blown up after the passengers and crew had got out. Dawson Field, as it was called after the RAF's last CO in the Levant, was an emergency landing strip some 25 miles north east of Amman.

After what seemed the proverbial age we landed. An impassive Abdul Jalil thanked me for my company and saw me on to my London connection. I owed him one; otherwise I'd have spent an uncomfortable few weeks as a hostage. I later learned that it was almost common knowledge down the Gulf that the hi-jack of a BOAC flight was imminent. Either British intelligence was asleep or it had been decided that as Pax Britannica no longer applied on land or sea, it might as well not apply in the air either.

23
INSURRECTION ARAB STYLE

A week later I was back in Abu Dhabi, having put Kathy into her prep school at Lavant House, a traumatic experience for us all. Fortunately the school matron, Beulah Barnes, was the widow of a man I had known in the Kuwait Oil Company, so we knew she had a kind heart to hand.[1]

In Abu Dhabi all talk was about the impending civil war in Jordan. The Palestinians were pressuring Zeid to help and he certainly donated a lot of money. The war erupted with a vengeance on 17 September when King Hussein was finally forced to send in his armour. A grinding battle went on for days and stories began to circulate of 'ten thousand dead on the streets of Amman'.[2]

Some bright spark in the palace suggested to Zeid that Abu Dhabi should send a medical mission to care for the victims, as there was already an ICRC Mission preparing to leave Switzerland. 'Horrenblor' was summoned.

The upshot was that on 24 September a De Havilland 'Caribou' of the Abu Dhabi Air Wing, piloted by Captains Les Brown and 'Spike' Marie, took off before dawn for Amman. On board, in addition to myself, were an Indian anaesthetist and three nursing orderlies. I had not exactly been overwhelmed by volunteers for the mission, and ended up with a Somali, a Pakistani and Fouad Sakr, the sole Palestinian. We were carrying two hundredweight of medical kit and a long-wheel base Land Rover belonging to the ADDF which contained, in addition to our personal kit, limited to ten kilos each on my orders, jerry cans of water and petrol. We also had our passports and vaccination certificates. I had been long enough in the Middle East to know that whatever the crisis, somewhere there is always an obstructive minor official just waiting to put a spoke into our wheels! John Butter had also armed me with $10,000 in sticky greenbacks. Impartial care was our aim; to be shot at by both sides our expectation. Binnie had been an absolute brick during the whole build up, advising me to return in one piece, when all around her people were telling me she was mad to let me go - apart from Charles Wontner, who had very decently added to our team an Abu Dhabian gunslinger called Eissa as a personal bodyguard.

We re-fuelled in Kuwait, without problem but, delayed by the refusal of Air Traffic Control in Damascus to approve our flight plan, it was dark again by the time Les and Spike decided to 'go for it'. Near Damascus the controllers, xenophobic at the best of times, began to screech at us - what was an Arab military transport plane flown by pilots who only spoke English doing on an unscheduled flight in the middle of the night? Les replied: "This is Red Cross

[1] Ted her husband, had broken down in the desert and died of thirst. He and his companion had committed the cardinal sin of leaving their vehicle. When found, the radiator was still full of water.

[2] See later.

flight triple X on a mercy mission from Abu Dhabi to Amman. Over and out."

I was crouching between the pilots and he turned to me and said: "We now have radio failure."

We dived down and levelled off a few hundred feet above the rolling brown desert. The sky was lightening to the east and then in front we saw a pillar of black smoke about 40 miles away rising into the still air. Spike shouted: "If that's Amman we've got just about enough fuel to make it."

Away to port the wreckage of the three jet airlines came into view as we passed Dawson Field. The Fedayeen had blown these up some ten days earlier. Soon we swept under the black shroud of smoke enveloping Amman and over the airport. The control tower was deserted. Les shrugged, and put our overloaded aircraft down on the runway. We rumbled to a halt outside the main hangar. After eight hours flying the silence was a pleasure; but wen we opened the doors to sniff the morning air we heard the 'dawn chorus'. Despite a week's fighting Amman was not as dead as it had seemed from the air. There was the flat thump of rockets, and then machine guns tore the air. We scrambled out. A few men emerged from the hangar, scratching themselves sleepily and gazing at us without expression. We hadn't expected anyone to kiss our feet, but some interest would have been welcome.

I walked over to a small office alongside the hangar where I found two Swiss members of the ICRC. They weren't too pleased to see me either until I explained I wanted neither beer nor breakfast. They had been there for two days, living on bully beef and water, charged with unloading relief supplies from incoming aircraft. Already they had managed to pile up an impressive mass of stores; but their immediate problem was how to distribute them before they were stolen. Martial law had been declared but the army, after the intense fighting of the past few days, was having difficulty even in administering itself. One of the Swiss then told me that the army had however promised to send men and lorries that day, and they would soon empty the airport. (I decided to keep our supplies on our Land Rover at this news.)

In theory the supplies should be delivered to ICRC headquarters, which had been established in a private hospital, owned by Dr Muashir, about eight miles away on Jebel Hussein.

The rest of the team had unloaded the aircraft while I had been talking to the Swiss and the pilots had managed to get some fuel from a friendly officer in the Royal Jordanian Air Force. They were anxious to get out before someone lobbed a mortar shell at them - the indiscriminate firing was increasing hourly - so who could blame them? I slipped Spike $1,000 and off they went to Beirut, promising to return in a few days to see how we were. I felt as if my umbilical artery had been cut as they droned off to the north west.

I decided I needed a 'visitation' before I made the next decision. It came in the shape of George, an engineer of Jordanian Airlines, who had spent the last week camping in his workshop. I learned that a cousin of his, the Director of Army Medical Services no less, was in a hospital nearby, and he would be happy to guide us there. (Fortunately all Arabs tend to have several hundred cousins.) But this certainly seemed a better option than driving across eight miles of war-torn Amman to Jebel Hussein - at least until we learned how the land lay.

So off we drove, trusting the Red Crescents painted on our vehicle would deter the more homicidal snipers, past the bullet-riddled sign 'Welcome to Amman'.

The streets were ominously empty. That's the time to get worried, I had been taught. The shops were shuttered, the pavements littered with broken glass and telephone wires. After a mile I turned a corner to find a tank blocking the road. I jerked to a halt just as its gunner fired a shell into a house barely 50 yards away. The effect was unimpressive, apart from the shattering noise; the shell passed straight through the house and exploded about a mile away. George thought he knew the tank commander and beckoned me to proceed. This I did, with a glassy smile that would have done credit to visiting royalty and I received a friendly wave in return. We turned into the army hospital as the tank rumbled off to hunt more snipers.

The usual crowd outside any Arab hospital gave us tea, then ushered us into the director's office. A full general, he was grave and polite, and drank glass after glass of water before asking us how he could help. (I was irresistibly reminded of Harpo Marx in A Night at the Opera when he impersonated the pilot who had just flown the Atlantic and was at a loss for words.) The tank firing shell after shell into neighbouring houses interrupted further conversation. Finally I was able to explain whom we represented and why we had come. He looked at me, pity mingled with amazement, but Arab courtesy outweighed everything and he announced he would have us escorted to Muashir's hospital: "Where we would be safe and comfortable and amongst friends."

I knew it would be pointless to protest so I thanked him effusively. As we rose to leave the ICRC delegation entered. We sat down again after introductions. The three of them were tired and baffled.

War has changed since the Battle of Solferino, when dead and wounded lay on the open field selected for slaughter by the opposing commanders. By the terms of their Convention the Swiss would offer aid to the victims of both sides, who in turn would support the medical teams. But in Amman, no civil services were functioning, the Army was busy looking after itself; and no one knew who was leading the Fedayeen. So what could the Swiss do? There were fine sentiments expressed by both sides. But they knew these were irrelevant. Arabia was winning again.

I learned of the remarkable response of the League of Red Cross Nations to the ICRC's call for help and decided it must already be 'standing room only' in Muashir Hospital: and British, French and American teams hadn't even arrived yet! Already I began to suspect there might soon be more doctors and nurses than wounded in Amman.

George took us back to his workshops where he insisted that red crosses replace our carefully painted red crescents. (Both sides had abused the signs, the commandos were using ambulances to bring ammunition down from their stockpiles at Dawson Field, while I saw with my own eyes an army gun carrier sporting red crescents alongside its machine gun.) We helped unload a Yugoslavian relief plane while we waited for the paint to dry. Then George proudly produced our gleaming white Land Rover with no less than seven red crosses on it.

As we got ready to drive off, two C130s roared overhead. Firing to the south was heavy as the army battled to crush the Fedayeen's stronghold in Ashrafia. As the first giant transport floated down onto the runway a mortar shell burst in front of it. The pilot coolly braked through the smoke. We waited tensely to see if the second aircraft would get the same reception. It did, but incredibly the gunners had lost the range and a salvo of bombs exploded beyond the runway. It was a warning that the lunatic fringe of the Fedayeen still had the upper hand.

I walked over to greet the shaken pilot of the first aircraft. The aircraft was unmarked so I spoke in English: "Gosh! Well done! That was a close shave!"

I understood enough of his explosive retort to appreciate this was no time to promote *l'entente cordiale*. The French had arrived.

George took us round the ring road to Jebel Hussein, judging it to be safer than a direct route through the city. Once there our chattering ceased as we passed derelict cars, all riddled with bullets. Fighting had been in progress sporadically since June. George pointed out a ruined house which had been Yasser Arafat's HQ before he had been shot out of it a few days earlier. In nearby Place Maxime the damage was even worse, fires still smouldering. There were no civilians in sight, only wary soldiers. The smell of death, both human and animal, was overpowering.

We turned into Muashir Hospital. The whole population of Amman, other than military, seemed to have gathered in the forecourt - suppliants, wounded, officials and the merely inquisitive kept up a curiously monotonous babble. On top of the steps stood Dr Muashir himself, who bore a remarkable resemblance to Bob Hope. He was surveying the scene with apparent equanimity. His staff had been treating victims of the fighting for days but now he had to cope with the influx of enthusiastic Red Cross doctors, all determined to make their presence felt and inevitably ruining hospital routine. One visiting surgeon had already managed to take ten hours over an exploratory operation, thereby using up all the anaesthetic gas available.

Our arrival went almost unnoticed, which scarcely mattered, as it would have been a waste of time to try and get any sense out of anyone in the atmosphere of restrained hysteria that prevailed. It was pure chance that I heard a Swiss surgeon, in full theatre garb, demanding of anyone who would listen why he could not move into an empty school down the road? I nudged George and we were off.

We found the École des Frères apparently deserted, but slipped into an open door at the back. Down the dark passage came a priest bearing a lantern.

Another surprise, he greeted me in a soft Dublin accent. He took us to Brother Edmond, head of the school. For the first time since we had landed we were welcomed enthusiastically! The poor man had been offering his premises to the authorities for days without success. Our group moved in and within two hours we had emptied five classrooms, erected 50 stretcher beds - borrowed from the Swiss - and set up our HQ in a sixth. I ran back to Muashir and told him we were 'in business'. Within minutes the first of the overflow were straggling in. By the following night our beds were full: wounded soldiers and Fedayeen we placed in two rooms at opposite ends of the corridor, separated by three rooms occupied by civilian men, women and children. While we attended to their medical needs, a handful of priests and nuns managed to feed and wash the patients, us, and themselves and keep the place clean - all with a few buckets of water; until Brother Edmond managed to produce a water tanker, apparently out of thin air.

That first night the nuns showed their mettle by producing an excellent supper from our dry rations. Boosted by this (and a large Scotch from my hip flask) I walked back to Muashir's Hospital, Eissa shadowing me - if a man in a gleaming white dishdash and white headdress could be termed a shadow. But as I had opted for a white bush jacket and trousers myself I could hardly complain that he had made us a sitting target - or, even a walking one in this case. I was more worried that we would be jumped by the military when I would be pushed to explain why a Bedu with a Biretta was escorting me.

At the hospital the milling crowd was larger. I heard that the Fedayeen had released 32 passengers off the TWA Boeing they had hijacked nearly three weeks earlier. They'd been turned loose in the streets of Amman but no one knew where. My informant, Abdul, pointed out a small group of Anglo-American diplomats keeping their cool under a barrage of questions from the President of TWA. As I watched, a bland gentleman with a stick joined them.

"The Egyptian Ambassador!" hissed Abdul.

Wrong, in fact he was the Egyptian second secretary, ie. intelligence officer, whom I later knew as Yusuf. This looked promising -and it was. Yusuf knew where the hostages were, and they were very tired of walking. The immediate problem was to find sufficient transport to pick them up. ICRC, now charged with collecting them, had only a twelve seater bus and a small car.

I piped up: "My Land Rover will hold twelve at a pinch."

The senior ICRC official looked pleased. "But who will drive?" he asked.

"Well, I've been driving it so far," I answered.

"Impossible!" he retorted, "you're not a delegate!"

At which point everybody shouted at him at once, the TWA President loudest at the thought of yet more delay in the release of his passengers. The Swiss weakened, then turned to me again.

"You realise there will be danger?" he asked solemnly. I nodded, just as solemnly. He nodded twice more then drew a brassard 'Comite International de la Croix Rouge' from his pocket and pinned it on my jacket. (I still have it.)

"Destin," he shrugged. Fame at last, I thought.

We were off. I collected the Land Rover and Eissa who snuck in beside me and followed the two Red Cross vehicles. At first we rushed through the streets, all lights blazing, until we reached Jebel Amman. Here an army tank commander who was both nervous and hostile stopped us. Yusuf pacified him and we crawled on down into the valley with sidelights only. It was nearly 9pm and both sides, aware that something was afoot, were jumpy. From behind us the army launched a salvo of rockets into the hillside oppo- site while the Fedayeen responded with a shower of tracer. It was all com- fortably above our heads, but I confess to feeling exhilarated by it. This, I later reflected, was how ignorant men welcomed war as a 'thrill'... and I was ashamed.

Flares now lit up a gruesome scene. Glass crunched under our wheels, then sickly stench of death mingled with the smoke. We passed a dead donkey, four legs held rigid in the air by his distended abdomen. Then an overturned bus blocked our way. Two villains with long hair, beards and sheepskin jack- ets darted out of the shadows and spoke with Yusuf. We were guided through a gap, then waved to a halt. I could see gunmen peering down at us from first floor windows.

Several voices were raised at once. "Switch off your engines!" "Leave your engines running!" "Switch on your headlights!" "Turn your lights off!"

I looked at Yusuf who shrugged. I compromised by turning my engine off but leaving my sidelights on. Yusuf grinned at me. I got out and sat on the kerb to await events. I had decided long ago that we should have left Arabia to the Egyptians. Above me I could hear two of the Fedayeen talking excit- edly, but in a language I didn't recognise.

"Was it true," I murmured, "that some of Castro's men had enlisted with the Fedayeen?" Yusuf shrugged his shoulders again.

Suddenly, figures burst out of the darkness beside us. It was the hostages, scrambling out of cellar. Eissa greeted them with a big grin. They looked worried at the sight of him but a Fedayeen urged them aboard with his gun butt. I leapt aboard, to find a Rabbi in the seat next to me.

"Good evening," he said conversationally, "Do you have a banana?"

I was non-plussed, and said I was sorry. At that moment there was a loud bang behind us, where an army shell had landed short. Behind me a voice cried out: "Hey! This truck ain't safe! It's got no sides! I'm getting out!"

"Pipe down, sonny," a second voice drawled, "it'll take more than canvas sides to save us if we're hit."

"No! No! I gotta get out - stop the driver!" shrieked the first, and the next moment I was seized round the neck and jerked off my seat. I clawed at the arm but then I heard a dull smack of bone against bone and the grip relaxed.

"I said pipe down sonny - OK let's go."

I raised a limp hand and off we drove. Soon we were back, unharmed, at Muashir Hospital. The hostages sprang out with cries of thanks and scurried inside. Only the Rabbi and a burly Texan who grinned and rubbed his knuckles stayed to shake my hand. I missed the party and went to bed.

Next morning I found an American surgeon had been sent to join us by the American ambassador who had told him: "Join those Aboo Derbians, they're the only guys who seem to know what's happening round here." Dan was employed at the Baptist Mission Hospital in Ajlun normally but thanks to the fighting in the forests nearby had been unable to return there once the fighting had started and was 'raring to go'. Actually he was a damned good surgeon and made our small team that much more effective. But I was still worried about the 20,000 wounded that were meant to be lying in the streets; especially as our beds were already full. I happened to catch a Jordanian doctor, visiting Brother Edmond, who undertook to take me to Ashrafiya where thousands of casualties were reported.

It was an opportunity to distribute some of the Red Cross rations that had been stacking up at Muashir Hospital, so Eissa and I loaded up the Land Rover with as many Red Cross food parcels as we could cram in. The Jordanian doctor sat beside me and, with Eissa crouching between us, we set off on the ring road.

At the bottom of a hill we saw a crowd of civilians beside the road and I halted. Eissa and the doctor began to hand out parcels. Next minute we were overwhelmed as people appeared from nowhere - one particularly fat slob clambered into the back of the vehicle and was cramming food into his mouth with one hand and stuffing parcels down his shirt with the other. I turned round and pushed him back into the road where he landed with a satisfying thud. I shouted: "Yaller!" and drove off, calling to Eissa, "Just throw the parcels out the back!"

He did so as we drove smartly away. It was a lesson I should have learned before - never stop to distribute food to hungry people but keep moving!

When we got to the camp it was difficult to tell how many of the shacks had fallen down and how many had been knocked down. There were dead animals, wrecked cars, bullet holes through shop shutters, but no sign on the 'indiscriminate shelling' that had been reported: wounded there were none. The only sick we saw was a young man clutching his stomach in an alley, his trousers round his ankles. My companion sniffed and said:"Dysentery!"

It began to look as if sanitary inspectors would be needed more than surgeons. Back at the school we learned that ICRC delegates had tried to enter Ashrafiya but had got caught in crossfire. There was little sense in repeating a further approach by the 'front door'. If there were a back door, one man would have the key - Yusuf. I found him without much difficulty and he provided me with a guide.

Next morning we entered Ashrafiya from the south, without seeing a single armed man. But here there was none of the relaxed atmosphere that we had met on Jebel Hussein the previous morning. The people were sullen and hostile, nerves stretched taut by days and nights of shelling. Already embittered by more than twenty years of incarceration in refugee camps, where they had been treated as little more than political pawns by the major powers, these Palestinians had tasted seven intoxicating days of power when they had held the world's attention by their defiance. Now, they had lost. They faced the outcome of their defeat with fear. My guide, a Fedayeen himself, looked as anxious as I felt; for he too knew the volatile nature of his countryman; and how easily he would cease to be a hero of the revolution, and become instead the mad dog who had brought destruction on their heads.

I counted six wrecked tanks on the perimeter of the camp. Clearly King Hussein had paid dearly for committing his armour to street fighting. But their shells had been ineffective, passing straight through the flimsy walls of the shacks while the occupants sheltered safely in the concrete cellars beneath. Clearly preparations had been in hand for recent events, and the PLO's announcement that the camp had been razed to the ground, rebounded against them.

At Ashrafiya Hospital it was a different story. The shells had torn huge holes in the concrete walls of this modern 500-bed building. It had been a strong point for the Fedayeen, which the army had eventually stormed, and, it was said, bayoneted 70 wounded. The destruction inside the hospital was indeed dreadful but when I clambered through the wreckage in wards and corridors I could find no trace of blood. It must have been pretty gentle bayoneting. A very gallant Arab doctor, who, with four orderlies, was trying to restore some sort off order amidst the tangled bedding and furniture, accompanied me. Flies were pouring in through the shell holes and settling on the rotting food left by the soldiers when they had withdrawn the previous evening, under the terms of the cease fire: they now rested in the shade of their tanks, just 50 yards behind the hospital. I told the doctor that I access to ICRC supplies and I'd bring him whatever he wanted.

"Disinfectant... disinfectant... and more disinfectant!" was his cry.

We returned to Muashir Hospital. The atmosphere was tense. The president of TWA was on the prowl again; six of his passengers were still missing. The diplomats and Yusuf were again in a huddle. I offered my Land Rover again, but this time it was declined. Yusuf saw my disappointment, and motioned me to wait. When the party broke up, he invited me to join him in the large car the Arab League Cease-Fire Committee had lent him. I found myself sitting next to an extremely tough looking Palestinian, in an advanced state of nervous exhaustion, who clearly resented my presence. Yusuf referred to him by his code name, Abu Jihad. I settled myself as far into the corner of the back seat as I could and asked where we were going.[1]

"To Irbid, dear chap," cried Yusuf, in his best upper class English. Meantime Eissa was struggling to get into the car with me.

"Oh dear, it's Lawrence's bodyguard," said Yusuf, whose Egyptian humour never faltered. He spoke kindly to Eissa, who nodded, smiled at me, salaamed and walked away.

"You're a clever bastard," I couldn't help saying, then remembered my manners enough to say: "Oh, and my deepest sympathies on the loss of your presi-

---

[1] He was in fact a senior PLF member, who was to die in the army's final assault on the last remaining Fedayeen stronghold near Jerash in the summer of 1972.

dent," for we had heard that Gamal Abdul Nasser had died that very day. Yusuf inclined his head and was silent. It was indeed a tragic loss for his country.

Off we drove. I pondered on our destination. Irbid is the northernmost town in the kingdom. I had assumed we would be going to Jerash, which was the Fedayeen's main stronghold. Passing the last army outposts on the outskirts of the city we descended into the Suweileh Valley where there is a post-1947 refugee camp. The few civilians waved when they saw the green flag of the cease-fire committee on our car and the ICRC jeep behind us. Even here they had had enough of the fighting. We drove slowly, our driver skirting every mark on the road that might conceal a mine. We reached a bridge. As a self-appointed demolitions 'expert', thanks to the patient instruction of Ken Cross in 21 SAS, I viewed the incompetent attempt to destroy it with contempt: I suspect a vast amount of explosive had been wasted. All that happened was for the whole centre span to drop about six inches. Abu Jihad got out, two guards appeared at once and waved us forward.

Soon we were passing through the Roman arch into Jerash. Few inhabitants were visible, but commandos were much in evidence, swaggering around and shouting defiance, a characteristic of Arabs in defeat. A nervous café owner served us cold drinks. Then we were on our way again, across the high deserted plateau until we reached a row of tanks, their guns pointing north against any further Syrian attempt to come to the aid of the Fedayeen in Jerash. The soldiers grimly waved us on.

I turned to Abu Jihad, whose face was if anything grimmer: "You'll have to live with them again."

He shook his head violently: "Never! Not after what they have done to us!"

"Then perhaps their children and yours?" I countered. He shrugged his shoulders.

Another few miles and we reached the Fedayeen post on the outskirts of Irbid, still under their control. Burned cars, barbed wires and tangled telephone wires formed the backdrop. A solemn child, staggering under the weight of a sub-machine gun, guided us to a house in the centre of town. Here, the inhabitants were clearly not in favour of the revolutionary regime.

"We have been loyal to our King! Now let him send us food!" was one cry we heard.

"Bastards! Traitors!" Abu Jihad ground the words through his teeth. Since they were not Palestinians this hardly seemed fair; but some of them were actually amused at the way the Fedayeen were 'cheeking the bosses'.

An older commando with a mouthful of gold teeth invited us to tea and led us into a house with a narrow corridor, at the end of which he flung open a door. There stood six pale men in black suits, crisp white shirts and dark ties; each clasping a brief case. For fully five seconds no one spoke. I felt rising panic - Mertre! It was a trap, now we were going to become hostages! I turned to the nearest Swiss and asked nervously: "Er, I don't think these are the people we've come to collect, do you?"

"No," he muttered, "I think these are the heads of the commandos."

"The hell we are!" burst out the tallest, "We're the TWA hostages!"

Next minute we were all shaking hands. I introduced the Swiss team leader who cried: "Now we've found you we can all go home!"

He'd reckoned without Yusuf who had just burst into the room.

"No! No! No! This is not the way at all!"

We were duly chastened as he lectured us on the agreement reached between the Palestinian Resistance Movement (a new one on me), the Arab Peace Committee (another new one) and the ICRC - who clearly knew nothing about it - which stated that the hostages must undertake to tell the true story of the Palestinian tragedy and how well they had been treated during their captivity. The hostages agreed at once; although I doubted whether the message would ever reach the people of America - three of the six hostages were American Jews with dual nationality.

The drive back to Amman was uneventful. The six hostages squeezed into the ICRC jeep while I stretched out in the back of the saloon. I hoped they couldn't see me. On Jebel Hussein we stopped to let Abu Jihad slip out into the darkness, just as a black Mercedes swept past, King Hussein clearly visible in the back. Yusuf failed to see the funny side of this incident. I was glad to get my head down that night.

⋖⊱ ⋖⊱ ⋖⊱ ⋖⊱ ⋖⊱ ⋖⊱ ⋖⊱ ⋖⊱ ⋖⊱ ⋖⊱ ⋖⊱ ⋖⊱ ⋖⊱

I had not been impressed by the activities of the ICRC to date but the arrival of a new head of mission, a Danish doctor called Rafft, signalled an improvement. Next morning I took him up to Ashrafiya. The atmosphere was still tense but the army was recovering its damaged tanks and Fedayeen were distributing food from government lorries. In the hospital the doctor I had met earlier had managed to get two wards open; but where were the wounded? I suggested the three of us should go to the local Fedayeen HQ and find out. There we were told that the wounded were still too frightened to leave their homes. There were plenty of fighters lounging around and I suggested some of them should accompany the doctor back to the hospital and help in clearing up the mess. Eventually I learned that six did but the doctor soon kicked them out, as they were so lazy.

Outside the hospital Rafft and I sought the mass grave which had been dug by the roadside. We counted 127 bodies in this, the only mass grave I found. We recalled tales of the 15-20,000 dead that were meant to have strewn the streets of Amman. A young doctor arrived and asked if we could help bring some more bodies up the hill in our Land Rover. I accompanied him and found four more bodies partially buried under a wall. We asked for help from the onlookers, only two agreed, and the rest just held their noses. Certainly the stench was bad as they had been killed some days before and the bodies were distended and green. I lifted one corpse by his boot - and his leg came with it. It was enough for me. I turned to the crowd of some 200 able-bodied onlookers and shouted: "You can clear up your own f......g mess!"

I drove off indignantly, only to be deflated by the roars of appreciative laughter that followed my outburst. Never lose your temper with an Arab.

Amman was coming back to life. By early October ICRC had 800 beds available and only 401 registered patients. It was time to go. I persuaded Brother Edmonde to accept a gift of $2,000 on behalf of Sheikh Zeid. Eissa was bored and was taking pot shots at the pigeons in the school grounds. There was a last promise to fulfil. Dan was anxious to return to his hospital in Ajlun so I agreed to take him, having filled our Land Rover with supplies that the Swiss team had donated. Our last patient was a little girl who had lost her parents and her right arm in the fighting. Brother Edmonde found a Jordanian called Abdulla who was ready to adopt her. We piled them both aboard and set off for Abdulla's home, where no less than nine other children, his own, ran out to greet us. One look at their joyous faces as they embraced their new little sister was enough to satisfy us. I gave this great Samaritan $300 on behalf of Sheikh Zeid and we drove off northwards, feeling uplifted for the first time in days.

Our way took us through Jerash, where the people were still sullen and hostile, then through the wooded hills leading to Ajlun, where I had first walked over 20 years before. On the left we passed the Valley of Dibbeen, (the Two Wolves) where the fanatic Fedayeen had established their training camps three years earlier in the aftermath of the disastrous Six Day War, and recruits had accepted death in the course of their training as part of the price of waging Holy War against Israel.[1]

❧ ❧ ❧ ❧ ❧ ❧ ❧ ❧ ❧ ❧ ❧ ❧ ❧

I remember an Arab folk story. A field mouse came to a river it wanted to cross. There was a scorpion on the bank.

"Will you give me a ride across?" asked the mouse.

"If you wish," the scorpion answered. Half way across the scorpion began to sink. It stung the mouse.

"Now we shall both drown!" cried the dying mouse.

"I can't help that," said the scorpion as they sank, "I'm an Arab."

---

[1] Another nine months were to pass before the shells of the Jordan Army splintered these woods as they finished the destruction of the Palestinian guerrillas that had started in September in Amman.

24
HAIL AND FAREWELL

Spike Marie and Les Brown collected us and we flew to Beirut, where we indulged in some well-deserved rest and relaxation before returning to Abu Dhabi. Not everyone shared the heroes welcome we thought was our due. For instance Tug Wilson was more than a bit narked when we descended from our 'Caribou' to reveal an empty hold.

"Where the hell's my Land Rover?" he demanded.

"Sorry Tug," I said shamefacedly, "I presented it to the Palestinian Red Crescent before we left... it was a bit beat up," I ended lamely.

It had in fact been about the last thing I'd done before leaving Amman and I did at least have a letter of thanks addressed to Zeid in my pocket. Meanwhile the CO of the Air Wing, 'Twinkle' Storey, was gazing in horror at the stained and chipped aircraft and the oil dripping from the starboard engine. The two pilots tried to explain that service facilities were limited in Amman and that they'd put in an excessive number of hours in the air. One day, when they had very decently returned to Amman to see how we were getting on, they had been persuaded by the ICRC to take a crowd of so-called 'refugees' to Beirut and had been kept circling around the airport until they'd run out of fuel - whereupon they had put the aircraft down without permission: after which they had been denied service facilities at the airport since they were 'military'.

Back at the hospital little had changed. Jock Gardiner, the senior dental officer, had acted for me and warned me there was trouble afoot in the outpatients department. He had taken a new Egyptian doctor, Ibrahim Sami, on a tour of the hospital and when they had reached the OPD, Jock had introduced him to Dr Mohammed, acting medical officer in charge, in the absence of Rahim who was on sick leave. Ibrahim's eyebrows had shot up but he said nothing at the time.

Later, back in my office, he told Jock that 'Doctor' Mohammed was in fact a dispenser from a government clinic in Cairo. A shame really as he was doing a good job! The day after my return he appeared in my office in tears and begged me to take him with me to England when I went - which he implied would be soon. When I found an advertisement for the post of Director of Health for the Government of Abu Dhabi in the current British Medical Journal I realised he knew something I didn't. Later the same morning when I was doing my weekly ward round, an ashen-faced Indian clerk appeared and handed me a letter. It was in the customary Arabic/English format and informed me that: "Due to a reorganisation of the health ministry my services would no longer be required with effect from 1 October," ie. a few days

I decided to do a Sir Francis Drake and continued with my ward round. Then I drove into the town to the bookshop, which Binnie had opened with Derry Clements, Arthur's wife, and gave her the news. She found it difficult to take in. That evening I went to see Hamdan in his Palace. He was clearly embarrassed but shrugged his shoulders and said: "What can I do? It is Zeid's order."

When I did see Zeid a day or two later in his majlis, he greeted me cheerfully and asked me what my plans were! A less pleasant episode was the telephone call I had from the DMS in Bahrain, a local of Persian descent called Kanoo, who could hardly keep the exultation out of his voice as he suggested we could meet in London.

In fact we were treated very decently after that first blow. We stayed on in our house for a further three months. I even took delivery of my new ministry car, and was allowed to use it. During this time Binnie wrapped up her share in the bookshop. I started studying the radiology journals and taking vigorous walks along the Corniche every morning - when the buses taking the hospital staff to work would hoot gaily and the occupants wave their greetings. In the afternoons I would sail every possible day and amassed enough points to win the Helmsman's Trophy. In fact it was an enjoyable life for a bit! To give them their due I was also paid every penny I was owed. But a job I could not organise. Campbell Golding had retired from the Middlesex and there was no rush to employ me.

Our personal effects were shipped from Dubai and we prepared to leave in January. Before that I met my successor, Dr Boak from England, a surgeon in fact. Duncan Hamilton was also on the way out, but Boak told me he could find no fault with his care of surgical patients. Pierre Fahmy had acted up on my retirement and was clearly glad to see another 'fall guy' in place![1]

One of our more pleasant duties before we left was to see Charles Wonter marrying Georgina Fraser in our Anglican Church. We then meandered home via Iran, where we stayed with Chet and Martha in Teheran. Then to Beirut where we met up with Charles and George on the second half of their honeymoon. Egypt had been pretty grotty for them - the country was still reeling after Nasser's death - so we were pleased they could share the delights of Lebanon with us. For tourists at least, the country was at its apogee, this was 1971 and it would be another few years before the first shudders of impending disaster struck. We ate, drank and made merry; so apparently did the Lebanese. They were certainly making money. We drove into the mountains several times: my most lasting impression being the day spent in and around the great Crusader castle of Krak des Chevaliers. Ah! Earth's glories fade and pass away... Israel please note.

---

[1] In fact, Boak lasted only a few weeks in post; Fahmy was re-appointed but lasted only until a senior Scots doctor arrived to take over. He resigned after three months. Ibrahim Sami took over, then he was sacked and within six months of my departure - four years to the day after I had started my contract - Harry Napier took over as director of health, a post he held for a year or two. Sadly, on his retirement he developed Parkinson's Disease and died, possibly by his own hand, after a bachelor lifetime. A brave and good friend.

25
A Year in England - Less a Month in Ethiopia

So back to 72 Harley Street. It was mid-February by the time we arrived and it took another two months for me to find a job. Colonial re-treads, I learned for the first time, were not readily employed. I was suspected of irresponsibility, alcoholism, even homosexuality. But I finally got a post as a senior registrar at St Helier's Hospital, Carshalton, where I was first accused of anti-Semitism, latterly of racism!

St Helier's was one of those triumphs of hospital planning for which we have to thank the NHS. An imposing white pile, in the style of London University's Senate House, it had been built with non-sulphate resistant cement. As it was just a few miles from Epsom, home of the Salts, this seems remiss. As it started to collapse, a simple if dramatic remedy was applied - sulphate-resistant cement was pumped into the basement. This caused a certain re-arrangement of the hospital's services, but at least it stopped falling down.

It was also close to Sutton Station so while London's commuters fought their way into the city each morning, I took a tube to Victoria then joined a nearly empty train to Sutton, and reversed the procedure each evening.

There were three consultant radiologists on the staff. One of them, a flamboyant character called David Symers, had no qualms about admitting he was in radiology for private practice: but he pulled his NHS weight and taught me more than the other two put together. The latter did not speak to each other, a not uncommon situation in the medical profession. One, Morris Johnson, was head of department. He was friendly and easy going; nevertheless it was with him I clashed.

During our morning coffee break I read out a press release stating that 6,530 Iraqis had been admitted to hospital during the previous year after eating seed grain protected by a methyl mercury fungicide. 459 had died, despite repeated warnings that the seed was for sowing and not consumption. As it had been supplied by the US I commented: "The warnings were probably written in Hebrew -the Americans don't believe the Arabs can read or write."

David Symers guffawed: "Watch it Philip, you're not in Arabia now!"

I saw Morris shift uncomfortably, then get up and leave the room. David watched him go, then turned to me and remarked: "That was a pretty tactless thing to say in front of a Jew."

I followed him out to his office, intending to apologise - it had not occurred to me that he was a Jew. But it was too late. He asked me to leave his office and thereafter our relationship was, to say the least, frosty.

More trouble came to pass when Ministry of Health officials came on an inspection visit. One of the radiographers was a Ghanaian whom I called 'Okee'. He was a good worker who had already served several years in the medical branch of the RAF and we got on splendidly, sharing a slightly warped send of humour. We traded on our respective colonial backgrounds, to the bafflement of the other staff. He also had a lovely wife, as tall as he and with a splendid figure. She danced divinely.

One morning we were due to work on a screening list. I arrived early, before the first patient was ready, and I walked into the room, ready to start our usual banter: "Good morning you black bastard - how are you?"

This usually met with a reply such as: "Just waiting to kiss your shoes, bwana."

But this morning he shook his head anxiously and put his finger to his lips. As I rambled on, he desperately pointed behind the door through which I had entered. I peaked round and saw two men with 'civil servant' written all over them. There was an uncomfortable silence until I said: "Good morning, can I help?"

They muttered a reply and walked out. Okee and I started our morning list. Later that afternoon one of the secretaries put her head round the door of the office where I was reporting and said: "The hospital secretary wants to see you - now."

When I reached his office I found the two men I had met that morning standing, one each side, behind him as he sat at his desk. He didn't waste any time: "You met Mr X and Mr Y this morning. They overheard you insult Mr Okee, actually calling him a black bastard. I must say I am surprised at a doctor of your experience behaving like this. What have you got to say for yourself?"

I mumbled that I was sorry. I knew it was impossible to explain a relationship such as ours to tight arsed Home Counties officials. He went on: "I've asked Mr Okee to come here and if you apologise and shake hands with him in front of us we'll consider the matter closed."

A moment later his secretary appeared with Okee in tow, and the matter further explained to him. Okee looked suitably grave then turned to me. I wrung his hand harder than was necessary and said how sorry I was. Everyone else beamed and Okee and I slipped out. Once in the corridor with the door shut behind us, then as if at a signal, we flung our arms around each other and snorted with suppressed laughter.

Unfortunately the door opened at that moment and, still entwined, we turned to see three wide-eyed men gazing at us in amazement. We made off as fast as we could. There was another satisfactory sequel to that affair.

Come the hospital Christmas dance, which Binnie had no wish to attend, Okee was on duty so I took his wife, who, as I have already recorded, danced divinely. She also had a wicked sense of humour and insisted I should introduce her to the Hospital Secretary during the course of the evening. I did so; he shook her hand gravely but again looked nonplussed when she said: "My husband doesn't usually allow me to go out with white trash, but he thinks this one's safe." She then completed her act by rolling her eyes at me provocatively and murmuring: "If only he knew..." Dear Friends, you added real colour to that boring year back in England.

❧ ❧ ❧ ❧ ❧ ❧ ❧ ❧ ❧ ❧ ❧ ❧ ❧

It was the turn of the other Disturbing Influence in my life to re-appear. Tony Streather asked me if I could join the John Hunt Exploration Group as medical officer for an Endeavour Training expedition to the Simien Mountains of Ethiopia for a month.

A word about these organisations - Endeavour Training was an offshoot of the National Association of Youth Clubs, and was the brain child of Dick Allcock, a man dedicated to enhancing the lives of young people and a committed Christian. Lord Hunt, as Sir John became, had been the inspiration behind the exploration group. Other mountaineers like Tony and George Lowe had been recruited to help set up expeditions for young people in search of adventure and 'character building', as Dr Arnold might have called it. Ethiopia had been chosen for the latest foray.

I got a month's leave and mid-January found me in the belly of an RAF Hercules waiting to take off from Lyneham for the long flight to Addis Ababa. The hold of a C130 cannot be recommended for comfort; and the noise of four Pratt & Whitney engines is deafening. Along with me were a dozen other senior members and an equal number of youngsters, aged from 17 to 25. The same number of young ladies flew out on a commercial airline.

We reached Addis Ababa the following afternoon and set up camp at the Wingate Secondary School, founded in memory of the late General Orde Wingate who helped liberate Ethiopia from the Italians early in World War II, prior to his death in Burma. The school staff was British, including the bursar, who was a friend of Tony's. We had three days to wait until the ladies arrived, which gave us a chance to see the city.

Among the sights was a huge modern hospital, the Princess Zahia Hospital, built and equipped by the Swedes. Unfortunately, the annual running costs of this prestigious project absorbed over half off the annual health budget! At the hospital I tracked down Charles Leithead from Liverpool, who had directed our research into heat illness many years before in Ahmadi. We reminisced about the film he had helped direct, *Sweat without Tears*, which had 'starred' Dr John Dilley and myself, and had become obligatory viewing for tanker crews and others setting out for the Persian Gulf back in the 1950s. Charles was now professor of tropical medicine at the university.

I was also introduced to the local bread, *injara*, which I disliked: as it was the basis of our diet for the next three weeks it was not surprising that I lost weight.

We set off by bus for the Simien Mountains. Near Addis, the impact of the short-lived Italian Occupation was impressive - roads, woods and farms reminiscent of Tuscany. After three days we abandoned the bus and loaded our kit onto mules, which proceeded to take off in all directions, in true Himalayan style. Soon civilisation faded and we were in a mountain wilderness, whose few inhabitants faced a life of poverty exacerbated by absentee landlords.

We set up camp on the Geech Plateau, high, dry and windy. The group, more than 50 strong and now including eight Ethiopian students from the school, split up into smaller parties and carried out mountain climbing, flora and fauna study, and exploration.

I set up a medical tent. My first patients were a woman with a compound fracture of the tibia and a boy with a finger sloughing off. Plaster, antibiotics and prayer were offered. Only one of our lads had altitude sickness and as we were only at about 12,000 feet I decided to let him acclimatise in camp - which he duly did.

Mr Ulrich Muller, from Switzerland, was the National Park warden. He and his wife had their house nearby. Frau Muller, a laboratory technician, had instituted a daily clinic outside their house. I decided to augment this and persuaded two 20-year-old girls, Jean Strettle, a clerk from Pilkingtons, and Sarah Deery, an air cartographer of the WRAF, to try their hands at nursing. They shone! Mary Thompson, another secretary, tried her hand, but threw up at the sight of the sloughing finger. No shame, what a world it would be if we could all accept putrefaction with equanimity.

Meanwhile, other members were repairing mule tracks which suffered from erosion, largely due to horizontal ploughing. They also searched for ibex and foxes, helped repair huts and established radio contact with the outlying parties. Tony took a group up the highest mountain in Ethiopia.

Joe Brown, Britain's leading rock climber, was there with his wife Val. Poor Joe came unstuck. He was demonstrating rock climbing techniques when, as he put it: "Something went wrong. I raised my left foot to armpit level and pushed myself up and something went 'twang!' in my back."

Now Joe is somewhat anthropoidal - his hands come down below his knees when he's erect and his lower legs are longer than his thighs. I can hardly get a foot up to my armpit level even lying on my back! Let alone exert enough strength to raise myself up a rock face. We got him up the cliff and as he lay there with pains shooting down the back of his left leg, it didn't need a genius to diagnose a prolapsed lumbar disc. I gave him a shot of pethidine and waited to see how he would respond to heat and analgesia. He didn't. This was no place to hang around and after a day or two it was clear he should be back in Addis. We had a mountain stretcher as part of our kit and next morning all activity came to a halt as first four, then six of us, struggled to carry him up the ridge to the nearest road head. Joe rocked from side to side but hung on grimly and gamely. I supervised the operation... and after about twenty minutes concluded that the journey would take three days. However, before I could make the necessary arrangements for rations for the stretcher party, fate intervened.

Two of our local Simien porters, who had been watching our antics with incredulity, sprang forward. One took the front two poles, the other the back, and in one movement, lifted Joe on to their heads - and trotted off up the slope. For three days, read four hours. It was one of life's more humbling moments.

Joe and Val got safely back to the UK where Joe subsequently underwent surgery and made a complete recovery. Meanwhile Tony had asked me to take a party of eight to search for an ancient church, allegedly hewn out of a rock face.

❧ ❧ ❧ ❧ ❧ ❧ ❧ ❧ ❧ ❧ ❧ ❧ ❧

The Abyssinians, or Habashis as they are known among the Arabs, have been Christians since the earliest times. In chapter eight of the Acts of the Apostles, there is the description of how the Ethiopian eunuch, a man of great authority under Candace, Queen of Ethiopia, was baptised by the Apostle Philip, and 'went on his way rejoicing'. Ethiopians to this day believe that their royal house are directly descended from the son of Solomon and the Queen of Sheba. After the rise of Islam the Ethiopian Church was cut off from both Rome and Orthodox churches so it developed along its own lines.

Between the 11th and 15th centuries it had been the custom to carve their churches from rock faces; and an Italian guide book of 1938 reported the presence of two such churches in the region of Derasghie, some two or three days walk from our present camp. One was dedicated to St Gabriel, the other to Our Saviour. Our contacts in Addis had told Tony this was unlikely, in fact there were no ancient churches in the area. Tony, being an explorer after my own heart told me: "Go ahead Philip, prove 'em wrong!"

I compromised by planning a circular route via Chenek, returning via a direct but precipitous route when our mules would be less laden; at least we'd have adventurous travel if the church proved a myth.

It took three days to reach Derasghie. Several of the party developed diarrhoea and vomiting and our guides had only the vaguest knowledge of the route - and the time taken to complete stages: so what's new? Westerners learn the hard way that travelling in the east is not the same as being on a guided tour of the Lake District. Our journey took us across lobelia-strewn slopes, snow-covered passes, and cold camps. The porters were half-frozen and seldom stirred until 10am. The final day, however, found us striding across an open plain with Derasghie always in view on a wooded hilltop; and never getting any closer. As Bridget Kennedy, group secretary said, medieval pilgrims must have felt like us as they flogged up to Jerusalem from the coast.

But at last we arrived. Inevitably the entire village came and squatted around our campsite. We learned there was a rock hewn church some three hours walk away, but that we would need permission from Addis Ababa before a guide would be permitted to take us there. I recall flashing some money and the problem was solved. A villager called Fusar agreed to take us next day.

He duly turned up at 10am and announced we would have to run to reach the village of Serabar, near where the church was situated, and get back that day. In fact, we spent nine hours 'on the hoof', over the very rock country we encountered after dropping off the Simien plateau. While descending a rocky mule track, Alan Cass, the *Daily Express* reporter who was with us, slipped and sprained his ankle. One of the girls, Sue Wheeler, offered to stay and escort him back to Derasghie. A noble gesture, sacrificing the chance of seeing the church, which by now as acquiring a mystic aura for us all.[1]

We struggled up and down a series of precipitous wooded ridges until at last Fusar pointed down and across at the base of yet another 1,000 foot slope in front of us and said: "There is the church!"

I could see only a cliff face. We sweated down the hill and were faced with a low wall in front of the next cliff, with a gate in it. We walked through and there was a small, newly built stone church with a thatched roof... Eureka? Fusar stood proudly beside it. To say we were overwhelmed with disappointment is to put it mildly. We walked on to the foot of the cliff and sat in

---

[1] When we met by chance some years later in Oman I was able to tell her how she had become a heroine in Kathy's eyes when I told her the tale.

the shade. Fusar went to get us water. I don't know who it was but one of the party wandered along the foot of the cliff and disappeared. We ran after him when we heard his cry: "Here it is!"

Round the corner was a hollow and there was a church cut out of the orange-pink sandstone. This was the Church of Belegzebeher, the 'Church of God'. When Fusar came back with the water he could not understand why we were excited about this old cave when he had shown us the smart new church behind the wall.

Belegzebeher comprises a portico of four large arches with carved crosses on the pillars, behind which is the 'body' of the church, its roof supported by six huge pillars, and about 100 square metres in size.

Tradition says it was cut out by King Lalibela (1150-1220) but subsequently John Buxton, after studying the photographs and sketches we provided, concluded it was in fact more probably a Tigrean church of the 14-15th century. This news came too late to upset us very much!

Fusar now got into a panic about our return as he said there would be 'shifta' (bandits) around after dark. This was all we needed. We set off up and down the ridges separating us from the escarpment which we finally reached after dark; then strode across the plateau following Fusar's shining white 'shamma' as it streamed behind him in the icy wind. Several of the party were in tears when we finally reached Derasghie - where I for one drank eight mugs of tea. Alan and Sue congratulated us; and I felt Sue's wet cheek when I gave her a big hug for her selfless behaviour. I tried to tell her that it was a far, far better thing she'd done, etc., and prayed this did not sound too pompous. For us it had been a fine adventure.

Next morning we attended the Church of St Maryam at the invitation of the chief priest, who showed us the crown of the Emperor Theodore, a magnificent creation of gold and silver. He was crowned here in 1855, about the time the church had been built. It was a circular wooden building, surmounted by an impressive gold cross. The roof was made of corrugated iron. This sacrilege had been committed only the year before, according to the priest, by a group of 'white people'. One can only seethe at their lack of sensitivity.

Our return journey outshone all others for incompetence. We strolled back across the Simien Plateau to the point where the path dropped into a valley. Whereupon our muleteers all started to shout and point in different directions. We had at least 'walked onto' the German map I had (the only one of the district) and it was clear we wouldn't be back at Geech by the following night, even if we took a straight line across country! We were now short of food and water. So there was nothing for it but to find a campsite near water. I was glad I had told Tony that we would return via Chenek as I knew he planned to withdraw from Geech base camp the next day; and there was a good chance we could intercept them.

My luck changed. We struck camp early and headed straight for Chenek, ignoring the complaints of the muleteers. Towards midday we saw a party converging on ours some miles across the valley. It was Tony taking the base camp party to Chenek. He greeted me cheerfully: "Thought we'd run into each other!"

As they were carrying the 'unexpired portion of the rations' they soon learned how glad we were to see them!

⋘ ⋘ ⋘ ⋘ ⋘ ⋘ ⋘ ⋘ ⋘ ⋘ ⋘ ⋘ ⋘

It was time for me to rejoin the NHS and return to looking through people rather than at them. My medical presence had been worthwhile. Rigorous pre-expedition medicals for all the British members had paid off. They acclimatised to the altitude well. Gastrointestinal upsets were unusually widespread and rather more severe than the usual 'runs' encountered on foreign travel. I suspected a viral origin as all the attacks lasted 24-48 hours, were preceded by nausea for 6-8 hours, followed by bouts of violent vomiting, and varying amounts of diarrhoea. Then there was a day of malaise when fluid balance was restored with copious draughts of water flavoured with lemonade powder, 'jungle juice', to which I added salt. Cases continued sporadically throughout the expedition, Tony being the last victim in Axum, during our return to Addis. Trauma cases were mild - apart from Joe's back.

Among the locals the picture was depressingly similar to remote Himalayan villages and our treatment of chronic skin sepsis did more good for local relations than achieve much curative effect. I was interested to learn that the local cure for tapeworm was crushed flowers of the cousus tree. On my return to England I found that an infusion of this flower was still recorded as an anti-helminthic in the British Pharmacopoeia until 1908, when extract of male fern replaced it as the drug of choice. Finally I had my customary moment of dental glory when I extracted a broken canine root that had been festering for two years from one of the game warden's scouts. After a struggle, retained pus duly gushed forth, and next morning there was a surprisingly clean socket on view. Father would have been proud of me.

I flew back via Al Italia. There was an interesting postscript to this flight; I had paid for the ticket with an American Express card in Addis. Six months later the company were threatening me with prosecution for failing to settle a substantial bill in US dollars. It took a referral to Houston before the company could appreciate the difference in value between the US and the Ethiopian dollar.

⋘ ⋘ ⋘ ⋘ ⋘ ⋘ ⋘ ⋘ ⋘ ⋘ ⋘ ⋘ ⋘

Back in Harley Street the next nine months passed in preparation for the final FRCR examination. When the time came, I failed. My year's appointment as a senior registrar at St Helier's ended in the summer and I undertook a series of locum consultant appointments around southern England. The diploma in medical radio-diagnosis was sufficient for these, the FRCR having not yet 'come into its own'.

But already the lure of Arabia was dangling before us again. Dr Asim Al Jamali, of whom I have written when he was serving HMG as senior medical officer for the Trucial States, was now Minister of Health in Muscat. He had been summoned by the new Sultan, Qabbous, as soon as his father, Said bin Taimur, had been flown into exile by the RAF, following the palace coup in July 1970.

I had got on very well with Asim when he was in Dubai. In many ways he had an easier job than I since he enjoyed the direct support of HMG. We had coordinated public health measures and I enjoyed both his company and advice, even if, during the chaotic days of 1969 - when relations between Zeid and the Al Maktoums were at a low ebb - Zeid had forbidden me to have anything to do with him. This meant Asim and I had to have secret meetings in the desert beyond the Muqta Bridge in order to coordinate our activities. Now he had sent a message asking me to manage the new central hospital, Al Nahdha, or 'the Dawn', which had in fact been built by Said bin Taimur but never commissioned.

Again, one came to realise that, as in Abu Dhabi, most of the development that took place in the first few years after the palace coups had in fact been instigated by the previous reactionary rulers.

I had no wish to get into medical management again. I guessed it would only be a matter of time before I trod on some worthy's toes and found myself on the next plane back to England. I had cast my lot into the field of diagnostic radiology and that is where I wanted to stay. So I signalled that I would be only too happy to join him in Oman; and would be glad to provide him with a radiological service. The offer was accepted gracefully, but I could sense disappointment. I think he hoped to change my mind when I got there.

Before leaving St Helier's Hospital I had managed to do the health service of Oman a real favour. I was introduced to the night superintendent, Pam Jago, as one who shared a common Middle East background - she had worked in Saudi Arabia - but also because she had accepted a post as matron in Abu Dhabi. (I had received my OBE by now, for 'services in Abu Dhabi', and some of the St Helier's staff considered this reflected glory on them!) Now, I confess that I was still smarting a bit from the treatment I had received from Abu Dhabi, fair though it was, and lost no time in persuading Pam that Oman was the place for us. She took my advice; and subsequently arrived in Oman four days before us and became the first British matron in Rostaq; the beginning of a decade of dedicated service to the people in the interior of Oman. This was also recognised by HMG who awarded her an MBE.

So when August came we packed up at Harley Street and moved ourselves down to Somerset where Bin's parents had bought a house and orchard on the Fosse Way, in a small village not far north of Yeovil. It had a barn large enough to take our furniture. As we had a couple of months to spare I went down to Yeovil one day and introduced myself to the radiologist, a genial Irishman called Martin Barry. He had been in this single-handed post for about fifteen years and my offer to do a few weeks as a locum was grasped as a straw by a drowning man! Thus began a happy relationship with a hospital that was to last intermittently for 30 years.

I spent two or three weeks getting accustomed to the rather more pedestrian ways of the NHS in Somerset. One of my duties was to cross the border into Dorset and do a screening session at a hospital in Sherborne. Here there was a splendid radiographer of the old school called Jack Durrant, whose father had been there before him; and whose son was to follow him into radiography - through, perhaps fortunately, in view of the hazards of radiation to the family genes, he chose to go into the commercial side of the profession.

There was an occasion when I was called upon to do a barium meal examination on a Dorset farmer, who had never been in a hospital before. The lights were dimmed; Jack thrust a glass of the barium liquid into his hand and barked: "Drink one mouthful - now!"

The excitement was too much for this sturdy son of the soil. Instead of watching a column of contrast run down into the patient's stomach, the whole screen brightened and the image disappeared as the poor man slumped to the floor in a dead faint.

"Quick! Lights!" I shouted in a panic. Next minute I saw to my horror Jack crouching on the floor with the farmer's head cradled in his lap, slapping him hard on the temple and crying: "Wake up Albert - you're alright!"

He duly came to despite this assault but opted to postpone the examination until he felt better. After he'd left the room I asked: "Mr Durrant what on earth do you think you were doing? He might have fractured his skull when he fell!"

"No, no," replied Jack, "these Dorset farmers are tough. When they faint they think their brain has turned round inside their skull so they can't see out of their orbits. Once he felt me slapping him he knew I was turning his brain back so that his eyes could see out again!"

I realised that I would have a lot to learn if ever I was to practice radiology back in England.

The time came for our departure and I routed us via Bahrain, from where we were able to visit Chester and Martha, who had by now returned to Riyadh. On our arrival there we were both stunned by the progress that had been made in the seven years we had been away. Feisal's accession to the throne in 1964 had clearly borne fruit. Chester and Martha had a new multistorey house with large front garden in a new suburb, of a standard such that his visiting boss from Washington was heard to say: "Huh! And they call this a hardship post!"

To be honest, in many ways it still was, even if you had access to the PX, Aramco, and other US government outlets. The cold hand of Wahabism was still paramount in the society in which perforce they had to live. We left with the firm intention of seeing them both in Muscat.

26
THE SULTANATE OF OMAN

We landed in late autumn on the new runway at Sib, which had just been commissioned; thus avoiding the hazards of the old runway where the wreck of a Gulf Air Dakota still lay as a memorial to the hazards of landing in the narrow Ruwi Valley. Although Qabbous had been in power for over two years by now, progress had been slower than that of Abu Dhabi. Not only was oil revenue less but also there been some in-fighting among the family during the first year or so and only now were a plethora of plans beginning to unfold. Again, though, as in Abu Dhabi, much of the groundwork has been achieved, however sluggishly, under Said bin Taimur.

The health service was a case in point. I have already mentioned Al Nahdha Hospital and it was there that Binnie and I went to live. One of the first things that happened after the coup was the realisation that doctors and nurses needed somewhere to live! So a block of flats had been constructed at the west end of the compound and a nurses' home backing onto the southern hillside - the hospital itself standing in the narrow valley that leads out of Ruwi to the Battna coast beyond.

Like much built in Oman at this time, a British architect called John Harris was responsible. He had been the 'man on the spot' before the coup and his firm had benefited, both then and subsequently. He had already won international prizes for hospital design, e.g. in Qatar, but I often wished he'd had to work in them! Among his idiosyncrasies was to make the hospital entrance as inconspicuous as possible. Thus, in my early days I was always finding people wandering around, trying to find their way in. Another was to avoid ay discussion of drainage or sewage disposal. "The Arabs don't like to talk about such things," he would say.

So when we moved into a ground floor flat it was not surprising to find the drains blocked! Each of the six flats flowed into a soak-away pit behind the building; and the rocky soil was hardly conducive to drainage. Furthermore a Dutch administrator had occupied the flat previously and left it in a filthy condition. Binnie wept when she saw the inside of the fridge. After the relatively luxurious life we had lived in Abu Dhabi and nearly two years slaving away in London, this was a let down. That night we went to the Al Falaj Hotel, the only 'western' hotel in the capital area at that time. We received a call from David Phillips and his wife Kate; he was setting up the British Council offices in Muttrah and had been there a few months. David, as a bachelor in Saudi Arabia, had been a regular visitor to our house and Kathy's first boyfriend. When we got there we were delighted to find that Joe Zenakis was the manager. We had known him in our early days in Abu Dhabi when he had been managing the Bustan Hotel in Dubai, a welcome watering hole after the long drive across the desert in order to buy food and furniture.

Here he was again, coping with faulty drains, intermittent electricity and water and unexpected palace guests. Complaints ran off his back like water off a duck. I remember some time later visiting Sir Gawain Bell when he was staying there; we had known him when he was Political Agent in Kuwait. As the power failed, he muttered: "Really! This is the worst hotel in the Gulf!"

"Oh no sahib, this is the worst hotel in the world!" piped up the Indian servant who was in the room at the time.

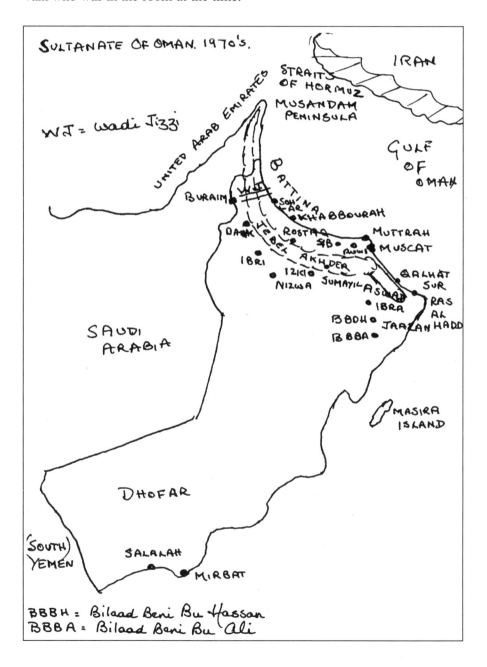

Dear Joe, he did his best under nigh on impossible conditions and I trust he enjoyed a well-earned retirement back in Greece.

Rumours of our disenchantment may have reached Asim for soon an order reached me that we were both to join his entourage on a tour of the interior. There followed a wonderful five days as our little convoy travelled along the length of the Battna coast. We diverted south into the Jebel Akhder to visit the new district hospital at Rostaq; and there we found Pam Jago, just installed as matron. She was longing for a shower! And we promised her one just as soon as we got back - providing the water was 'on'.

There were six new district hospitals, each of 50 beds, nearing completion at this time. They were built by a Swedish-Dutch consortium, Skanska of Stockholm and Philips of Eindhoven, with civil works being provided by Costains of the UK. These were 'turn key' contracts with their own power and water supplied and more successful than such 'deals' usually are, largely because of the sophistication of the parties involved. Too often they are foisted on governments either incapable or unwilling to address their real needs. Those in politically sensitive areas were commissioned early. Thus Nizwa, on the edge of the Jebel Akhder where the 1958 insurrection had broken out, was first, followed by Rostaq, on the north side of the mountain. Buraimi would be next, and it was there we were now heading. Buraimi was in fact less than a mile from Abu Dhabi's Al Ain Hospital and clinics, and Zeid had already offered free medical treatment to Omani citizens; but political sensitivity has several facets!

We had taken the scenic route. Soon one would drive along a smart new coastal road to Sohar that Costains would build, then drive up a metalled road through the Wadi Jizzi to reach Buraimi. But now we turned south before that at Al Khabbourah, where there was an agricultural and public health project under way, with the help of Durham University and the Save the Children Fund. From here we wound up the rugged but beautiful Wadi Hawasna. I remember kingfishers sparkling over the pools alongside the track. We spent the next night in Wadi Dank, where the old clinic had recently been washed away in a flash flood and the Pakistani doctor in charge was trying to look unconcerned - either because he wanted to give the impression that he was used to this sort of thing, or that he might be blamed for it.

Next day we reached Buraimi and saw the hospital duly signed for by Dr Asim. It was strange being so close to Al Ain again and we could not resist slipping over the border to the Al Ain Hilton, new since our day, and now a welcome source of gin and tonic for the thirsty traveller.

Next day we set off for Nizwa on our return journey. On the way we stopped at Ibri, where oil exploration had begun, in the country of the Duru tribe. Said bin Taimur had built a hospital for them as a sweetener at a place called Tanam, some miles to the south, another design by John Harris, and it had cost the proverbial 'bomb', largely because Said had insisted it be built in the middle of a wadi. Not unreasonably Harris said that if that was the case the building must be raised on concrete foundations at least six feet above the ground in case of flooding. What it must have cost to drag all that cement across the desert I dread to think.

Then on to Nizwa, where the hospital was functioning and I saw one of the Philips x-ray apparatus working under the care of a competent Indian technician. The medical officer in charge was a charismatic Indian Muslim called Muhammad Al Ghose who showed off the new mosque beside the hospital that his staff had volunteered to build in their spare time. Well, there wasn't much recreational activity available so the more power to them for their efforts. Next day we drove down the wadi to Sumayil where another district hospital was approaching completion; and so back to Ruwi.

Our attitude to Oman had certainly lightened and I for one was actually looking forward to the challenge of developing radiology across the country! Everywhere we met not only enthusiasm but, as often as not, understanding of the difficulties involved in introducing the 20th century to a Koranic, even Biblical, land. Charles Doughty warned me never to expect thanks from Arabia; I had learned in addition that your best intentions could be either thwarted or misinterpreted: but there came an evening in that same wadi when Binnie and I stopped for a cold beer and to dabble our feet in the stream. We looked at each other and one said to the other, I've forgotten which: "You know, I think I'm going to enjoy living in Oman."

The feeling was mutual. The next six years were the best we spent in Arabia.

❦ ❦ ❦ ❦ ❦ ❦ ❦ ❦ ❦ ❦ ❦ ❦ ❦

In 1971 there had been just 20 dispensaries in the whole country plus three hospitals, and two of these were run by the Reformed Church of America, who had been present in Oman since the beginning of the century. Staffed by American surgeons and sisters, often of Dutch descent, (the church itself was originally the Dutch Reformed Church), they had provided the only western-style medical care in the country. There was also a small hospital in Salalah, built by Said Taimur, and designed for him by a passing Italian motorcycle engineer... well, he was known for his parsimony.

By the time we arrived there were six new hospitals, seven health centres and fourteen dispensaries under construction. However the only x-ray apparatus were in one of the Mission hospitals in Muttra, the other in Salalah. So initially I had time to stand and stare.

❦ ❦ ❦ ❦ ❦ ❦ ❦ ❦ ❦ ❦ ❦ ❦ ❦

I decided to start in Salalah. Thanks to the Sultan's Air Force, I was able to hitch a ride in one of their Viscounts and arrived one morning to be met by an old friend, Assad Al Shanfari, who had worked as a technician for the Getty Oil Company in the Kuwait Neutral Zone. Not the world's greatest radiographer, he had a bright student under his care, another local, whose mother was

---

[1] When I last heard of him in 2002 he was the finance director for the Ministry of Health in Dhofar Province, responsible for a budget of some 10,000,000 riyals a year.

a Jebali. This was Amer Ahmed Farah, who was destined for greater things.[1]

Dhofar is the south-eastern province of Oman, mostly a high dry plateau but there is a fertile coastal strip where it looks as if a giant has taken a bite out of the Jebel. Facing the Indian Ocean, with no land between it and Antarctica, it is the only place in the Arabian Peninsula exposed to the monsoon. Thus, each summer a blanket of mist and drizzle descends over hill and plain, while the rest of the country bakes. It is not surprising that the ruling family still opt to live there when possible. The 'wali', ie. provincial governor, Sheikh Bureik, was an enlightened and ambitious man who encouraged development after the sterile years of Said bin Taimur's rule.

Agriculture was a favoured project and a British couple, Mike and Robin Butler, soon became friends. Mike had been a British soldier in Aden and had achieved fame by taking a convoy of army trucks up the Jebel while the British Army was still in Aden, the first wheeled vehicles to make it to the top. Mike, now a civilian and en route to becoming a farmer back in England, was having a last 'colonial fling' at running the government farms on the plains, while Robin worked as a secretary in Sheikh Bureik's office. The Dhofaris were no more averse to physical labour than other Arabs! So there came the day when Robin, David Phillips, and myself, harvested the wheat on Salalah Plain.

"All is safely gathered in", we sang as we worked; and wondered whether an announcement to the effect that this success was due to the efforts of three expatriates, due to the idleness of the locals, would get us imprisoned rather than just deported. Discretion won.

With its palm trees, sandy beaches and teeming bird life I had to look for excuses to visit the small hospital, and its even smaller x-ray department. The war seemed very far away, apart from the distant crump of shells and the whine of the Sultan's Jet Provosts taking off from the nearby airfield on their way for another strike.

The senior medical officer, Dr Mohammed Mughairi, was a Zanzibari, who had struggled on after the 1964 Revolution, trying to maintain health services on Pemba Island; but anti-Arab feeling became too much and he and his wife returned to their roots. Alas, like so many returned colonials they found it difficult to adjust to life in Oman. Their hearts, especially hers, remained in Africa. Mohammed wrote poetry, of a romantic nature, in English; and had an English sense of humour. Later, when the great Qabbous Hospital had been built outside the town, he would write, as though for Vogue magazine, of the fashion parade that took place daily in the women's outpatient department. These were early days and patients still had to learn how to use a hospital. In the meantime attendance at the hospital was a way of filling the long hours. X-rays were, unfortunately, extremely popular - both with doctors and patients. The former were harassed by the latter, and the former knew that reaching for the magic green form requesting an x-ray examination would (a) make the latter happy and (b) get the latter out of the room. Prior to the appointment of another radiologist in 1975, I would sometimes find myself faced with a list of over 30 barium meals to perform on my monthly visit!

One woman confessed to having had five barium meals during the space of one year, by seeing five different doctors and trotting out the symptoms and signs she had learned would exact a Pavlovian reflex and a request for a barium meal. Needless to say, all were normal. Other requests were equally irritating, e.g. "Headache. X-ray chest please." I was tempted to report in the words of an Indian colleague I had known in England: "No headache seen in chest."

(And before some smart arsed clinician declares it would be reasonable to exclude a primary lung tumour, may I point out these were usually healthy young adults looking for time off work!)

'Check up' was another English term that had slipped painlessly into the Anglo-Indian vocabulary and was the justification for many unnecessary requests to get a patient out of the doctor's hair.

Visits to Salalah became exhausting and it was on returning from one of these that I had my first meeting with His Majesty Sultan Qabbous. I had gone into the department at Al Nahdha Hospital in the early evening. I had noticed an unusual quiet in the corridors but having taken a short cut through the kitchen had not seen the fleet of cars outside the front that marked his presence. I was walking back from my office when I saw the royal entourage approaching; and slipped behind one of the double doors in a side corridor.

Unfortunately this was the door through which he chose to turn; and a royal guard pushed it back, hard. It struck my nose a stunning blow and blood dripped down on to my white shirt. The party passed up to the end of the corridor while His Majesty made a cursory inspection of each room, before wheeling around and returning. I perforce remained behind the door, only partially hidden. For a fleeting second our eyes met. Without a flicker of emotion he strode past, and the rest of the party took their cue from him and walked past without a glance while the blood dripped down on to my sandals. I would be interested to know what protocol would have had me do.

Meanwhile hospitals and clinics were springing up like weeds - perhaps I should say flowers - all over north Oman. Most of these developments were successful and provided basic health care to a population who had never before received anything other than the attentions of the local bone setter or herbalist; but sometimes schemes backfired.

Way out in the north east of the country near Ras Al Hadd, the furthermost tip of the Arabian Peninsula, was the port of Sur, and its wild hinterland, the Ja'alan. Sur was a harsh place, at the end of the line, which I find encourages sullen no hopers who do not welcome visitors. They had a history of violence and non-cooperation with the capital. It is not surprising that the perpetrators of an attempted coup the year we arrived were imprisoned near there while their fates were decided. I would visit the new district hospital monthly and it was there that I came into contact with the local bone setter.

My colleagues regarded them as pests, but I had learned that they had a practical knowledge of local herbs; and certain of them were remarkably skillful at setting fractures. Their main defect is a total ignorance of pathology.

On this occasion I had examined a boy who had a fracture through a huge but apparently benign bone cyst in the upper end of his tibia. It was soon clear that the father wanted nothing more to do with our hospital, once he had the x-ray in his hands.[1]

However I thought that the lad would need the cyst packing with bone chips if it was to heal satisfactorily, so I went down with father and son to the village bone setter to make my case. Soon this became a general debate, the whole village joining in! The bone setter listened quietly then set about kneading the leg until it was straight - apparently without pain as the boy made not a sound. Then he bound palm leaves around it.

"Fine," I said, "until he puts weight on it - the bone is weakest at that point."

The bone setter looked at me pityingly: "I will not allow him to put weight on it for several weeks; and by that time the blood will have dried and filled the hole with pannus." (I understand this to mean fibrous tissue.)

Fifteen love to the bone setter I thought. But before I could go on he added: "You know, if you had been any good as a doctor you would have got a job in London."

Game, set and match, I decided.

I mentioned earlier that sometimes our schemes backfired. A classic example was in the Ja'alan, the hinterland of Sur. There live two tribes, the Beni bu Ali and the Beni bu Hassan. They enjoy a comfortable enmity across the intervening six miles of desert with looting and pillage as time-honoured customs. Once, in the 19th century, they had united to massacre a force of British Indian soldiers who had rashly landed on their coast, then returned to their old feuding. Now it was time to bring health to the people. I was still carrying a torch and determined that this time we should get it right.

Back in Muscat the DMS, a Dutchman called Will Gitzels, and also a missionary in the health field, agreed to give me my head. I suspect Dr Asim smiled sadly to himself when I told him of my plans.

This was to be more than just a please the people centre. As the blessings of western know how were limited, there must be access for all for prophylactic injections - always wildly popular - minor surgery, x-rays and microscopy to spot the wicked falciparum, the main cause of malaria locally.

The first cloud soon appeared on the horizon. The track would have to detour around the date palms of an intransigent elder of the Bu Ali; and pass over a belt of soft shifting sand. The contract price rose and the project was put on hold. The Bu Hassan complained that it was my fault. The Bu Ali were offended and held a public meeting. Then the foundations of the new centre were overturned one night. I was summoned to the Ministry and advised to leave well alone!

The outcome was predictable. Some years later each tribe had its own muddy, fly-infested clinic with its operating room and broken fly screen door ajar. Small x-ray machines seldom worked as the generators were out of order as often as not: and a languid orderly spread hepatitis among the vil-

[1] In the early days my x-ray filing system was simple but effective - give the precious x-ray to the patient for safe-keeping and impress upon him the importance of bringing it to the hospital whenever he attended in future.

But whereas I could shrug this off as 'not my fault old boy', a critical situation arose in the x-ray department in Sur that had me somewhere between hopping mad and scared witless. In the early days, when both shipping and air freight deliveries were erratic, we sometimes got caught without films. I had learned the trick of having chest x-rays taken on four films, each 12" x 10", if supplies of 17" x 14" films ran out. Chest x-rays were, of course, our bread and butter; and the demand for these examinations was seemingly insatiable. On one occasions Sur ran out of almost all films, without telling me back in Muscat. The doctors got together and came up with a splendid wheeze. They would write our request forms with the code word 'drama' written in one corner. In the x-ray department the radiographer, a bright lad from Kerala, south India, called John Abraham who knew his job and did as he was told, placed the patients behind the x-ray screen, peered at the affected part or organ, then wrote a report, telling the patient to wait outside. John then slipped into the store, grabbed an x-ray envelope and film off the shelf where in-patient films were stored, gave it to the patient, who trotted off happily back to the doctor, clutching the precious film in one hand and John's report in the other. I found out about this when I made a surprise visit. The doctors were unrepentant - it got the patient out of the room and anyhow, if he were really ill, he would be admitted. But what scared me was that the wretched John had collected fifteen times the permitted monthly dose of radiation, although apparently without ill effect by the time I left. I opted to draw a veil over the event, and was serenaded that night in my room in the guest villa by a choir of the Church of South Indian members, ie., most of the staff, singing doleful hymns of repentance. I was moved.

Was John dedicated or just scared? His work was faultless, under normal

Oman, 1977/8, Turtle Beach, Ras Al Hadd.

Was John dedicated or just scared? His work was faultless, under normal working conditions... but then, no one will ever compare his work to the young Swiss lady radiographer I'd met in the Red Cross Hospital in Yemen during the civil war.

I cannot leave Sur and the Ja'alan without recalling our discovery of a beach nearby which we christened, for reasons that will become obvious, 'Turtle Beach'. It was a very special beach. Over half a dozen years we managed to keep it secret from all but a trusted few. This proprietary instinct was probably unwarranted as it lay over 200 miles east of Muscat and even on the black arteries spreading across eastern Oman it took all of a day to drive there. To you, dear reader, suffice it to say that it lies south of Ras al Hadd, the easternmost tip of the Arabian Peninsula that points across the Indian Ocean to Karachi; and from where in World War II, the RAF flew its 'Liberators' to protect the seaways from Japanese submarines.

Discovering it was a fluke; but then, when the earth's surface is increasingly covered with humans, any discovery of solitude is a fluke. We were led there by John Jennings, at that time head of exploration for PDO.[1] An enthusiastic archaeologist, he had aroused our interest with tales of copper vessels, flint arrowheads, etc., on the hills south of Sur. After visiting the site, and as is inevitable for amateurs, finding the artifacts themselves pretty disappointing, there had been discussion as to where to camp for the night. I have one of those splendid photographs, four men on a rock, each pointing to a different point of the compass. John however had seen the sea... and led us to this deserted beach below rocky cliffs with no land between us and India.

That night we sat round a campfire. In the surrounding darkness we became aware of movement, nothing alarming, more like mice. I think it was Philippa who shone a torch and we saw a crowd of baby turtles heading towards the light of our fire. Thus we learned we were on a breeding beach and that when the turtles hatch they are conditioned to move towards light - which, unless wretched humans have invaded the hatchery - will be the band of light over the sea's horizon, be it moonlit or overcast. Well... we avoided an ecological disaster, first kicking the fire out, then grabbing buckets and bowls, filling them with sea water, picking up the scurrying creatures and dumping them beyond the breakers. It was nearly midnight when we turned in.

On another occasion our arrival coincided with the actual laying of the eggs. The big loggerheads showed no fear of us but waddled up the beach, dug a hole with their rear flippers then squatted and delivered several eggs into the hole. They then swept sand over the eggs and lumbered back into the sea.

On a subsequent visit to 'our' beach we found that the gently shelving shoreline had been eroded and a steep bank formed, apparently too steep for the turtles to negotiate. At any rate, we never saw them again.

---

[1] John was to go on to become head of Shell UK.

27
WE GROW ROOTS

As sure as night follows day, problems increase with development. As we struggled with erratic power supplies, water shortages, mechanical breakdowns, and Murphy's Law, bureaucracy reared its head. In 1974 the first Sultanic Decree was issued. In itself it was perfectly reasonable. Faced with the flood of immigrant labour and the high risk of infectious diseases they brought with them, it was stated that everyone must have a chest x-ray before starting work. The Sultan's advisers were smart enough to realise it was no good asking immigrants to produce chest x-rays on entering the country. If they knew they had active TB, they'd simply acquire a clean film. Shades of the smallpox scams in Kuwait and Abu Dhabi.

We had just three x-ray machines in the capital area; and now every contractor descended on me demanding chest x-rays for all their labourers - preferably yesterday as they had tight contracts to fulfil and no labourer could commence work without my magic report saying 'chest clear'. Ministry of Labour officials, anxious to flex their muscles like all good civil servants, would see to that.

I had, perforce, to resort to screening - that is to say, I sat in front of an intensifying screen while man after man was ushered behind it. I then switched on the x-ray tube behind him. I could move the screen horizontally and vertically, thus I was able to view the heart and lungs, in the same way you have seen patients swallowing barium for stomach examinations. I wore lead protective clothing, nevertheless as each examination took half a minute, I picked up a lot of x-irradiation. However my film badge did not 'go into the red'.

Of course had this situation arisen in England one would have simply reverted to the old, by then, mass miniature radiography system, developed in the days when open TB was commonplace. This custom-built mini apparatus could race through a crowd faster than I could screen them, producing miniature chest x-rays on a roll of film providing 100 exposures. But we didn't have one. Nevertheless, I applied the same diagnostic protocol. I was not sitting there trying to make a diagnosis, as soon as I saw an abnormality the man was marched off for a standard x-ray plate.

There were in fact surprisingly few 'casualties', those who had made the trip to Oman had been through a better recruitment process than those we had encountered in Kuwait 25 years earlier.

I did not see why the companies should get this service scot free, so made a private arrangement with each of them. I charged a nominal fee; the ministry got half; I got the rest and split it with the x-ray staff. That way no one had a grouse!

At this point it is worth mentioning that salaries in Oman were not compa-rable to those in the rest of the Gulf. I was paid 400 Omani Riyals a month as a specialist (this had risen to 600 by the time I left) and in those days the riyal was slightly stronger than the pound sterling - and grew stronger as the years passed. There was no income tax, our accommodation was free, but, sensibly, we were charged for power and water. In a country where these were at a premium it was only sensible to make people economise. I knew Indian staff who would live by the light of a 15-watt bulb!

But we weren't comfortably off. The ministry provided me with a soft top Land Rover, good old 477, I still miss her, and Binnie drove a small white Honda - in which she bravely taught Khattack to drive! Raham Zed Khattack, or whom more later, was my x-ray engineer. The sight of a fierce tribal Pathan submitting to instruction by a woman was something to behold. I could have sold tickets; but Binnie was always kind enough to take him on deserted roads for his early lessons.

Otherwise we had a restricted lifestyle, initially at least Binnie was the cook-bearer; and by the time we had paid Kathy's boarding school fees in England there wasn't much left. Of course, we had learned that every time one moved post the salary one received in the first year melted. And we had now moved post five times - and house ten times - in our first ten years of marriage.

Thus the chance of making a little on the side was attractive. I did not have to resist bribery as I had done in Abu Dhabi; I was now in too lowly a posi-tion for such approaches. But when I found a growing mass of old x-ray films filling valuable space - some of them were twenty years old and from the American Mission Hospital - and doing nothing save gather dust, silver recovery came to mind.[1]

Back then old films were heavily coated with silver halide - and that spelled money! I cleared the idea with the ministry, then had words with Peter Felton,[2] the SAF movements officer. Sure enough there was a civilian char-ter aircraft returning empty to the UK after delivering material for SAF. The crew were happy to carry the x-rays for free in their empty hold, and so one morning Khattack and I, grinning happily, watched a 'Skymaster' lumbering along the tarmac at Sib en route to the UK with stacks of our old films on board. There, a truck would be waiting to carry them off to the factory in Shropshire where the silver would be recovered, and the company would then pay us handsomely.

Alas, there was silence. Suffice it to say that the next news I heard was that the company had gone bankrupt; and nobody knew where our load of x-rays had gone. We never found out either. I have often thought I was born to lose money.

---

[1] This was before the time when the US entrepreneur Nelson Bunker Hunt went out to try and capture the world's silver market - and nearly succeeded! One result of that upheaval was that the companies like Kodak were forced to reduce the amount of silver in the film emulsion in order to keep costs down.

[2] Peter later married Pam Jago: and sadly died in their retirement home in Spain many years later.

Raham Zed Khattack, x-ray engineer extraordinary.

Earlier I mentioned breakdowns. In the developing world at that time it was not uncommon for 90% of x-ray apparatus to be out of action. The fact that in Oman they weren't was due to two factors. The first was that all our equipment came from one company (Philips of Eindhoven), hence we had a service agreement with them. There was a Dutch engineer actually resident in Dubai, who could be with us in a short time. On one occasion, a very short time!

We had just installed our first big screening unit in Al Nahdha Hospital and hit a snag that same evening. The Dutch engineer had returned to Dubai that afternoon. I rang him, full of apologies.

"No matter. Now I shall show your ministry what a service contract with Philips means!" he announced.

He happened to have a private pilot's licence and his own aircraft. About an hour later I was stunned to receive a call in our flat from the Omani immigration officer at Sib Airport.

"Dr Philip, we have a Dutchman here without a visa who has just landed in his own aircraft. He says he works for you. Is there any reason why we should not deport him?"

I had to think fast. Dr Asim I knew was out of the country. The next call to Said Shaksi, the under secretary, was answered by his wife, another highly educated Zanzibari lady who suggested I ring 'my friend' in immigration.

"Who was that?" I answered, somewhat nonplussed.

"Why, your fellow Englishman of course!" I could almost hear the sneer on her face! She was a splendid lady, but racism is not confined to whites.

The penny dropped. Immigration control was in the hands of Jack Richmond, ex-Hong Kong police border control, and thus used to dealing with hordes of incomers. Jack reigned supreme in his department. The possession of almost any document with his signature in his chosen green ink was literally a passport to travel. Thus, I acquired such a laissez passer, drove to the airport and was back at the hospital within the hour. At 2am I watched the intrepid Nooitgedacht take off on his return flight to Dubai, his work complete.

Such panic calls grew less with the arrival of Raham Zed Khattack. Fortune had smiled on me again. One day Chuck Pringle, the local manager of Costains, rang me: "Hi Philip - guess what? I've just discovered one of the new electricians recruited from Pakistan is in fact an x-ray technician. Could you use him?"

Could I! I believe it was typical of the attitude of the British in Oman at this time, it was early 1973, that someone as senior as that could still put the interests of Oman so high on the agenda, despite the hassle that it caused him. I met Khattack, took to him at once and began the tortuous business of getting him released from Costains, sent back to Pakistan, recruited again by the Ministry of Health and allowed back into Oman. I needed Jack Richmond's help on this occasion too!

Once he arrived he set about setting up a routine maintenance programme, a workshop and, most important, a spare parts store. Nooitgedacht's somewhat 'gung ho' behaviour must have been costing Philips, for he was replaced soon after his mercy flight into Sib by another Dutchman, Henk Zonnevjille, who became quite a friend and support for Khattack. In fact, he arranged for him to be sent to Holland for three months to undergo higher training on x-ray plant. Thereafter, we had no serious breakdown lasting more than 24 hours anywhere in Oman. Once he received a call he would set off in his Land Rover anywhere in the interior - and fix it. I was glad Binnie had taught him to drive - it was a proud day for her when he passed his driving test! But money was less important in a country where one could fulfil so many dreams.

So after getting all this expensive kit up and running, what did we do with it? Well, our problems were pretty basic. Radiology had no part to play in the battle against malaria, sadly prevalent along the Battna coast, as well as in the interior. I summed it up as 'Tb and trauma'. Tb was common among the locals but we did not have the money, as in Abu Dhabi, to send patients off to sanatoria overseas. Initially, we did have our own small Tb hospital, situated in Wadi Uday behind Al Nahdha Hospital, but this closed in the fullness of time as standards of living rose and with them, the public's health. Treatment in the early days was therefore largely 'on the hoof' with frequent radiological checks on progress.

Trauma varied. It was mostly in the interior and seasonal. In the summer people fell out of palm trees when harvesting dates: in the winter, they fell down wells. This of course was to change once the roads developed and cars started to crash into one another.

As the Ministry of Health's facilities improved, PDO were quick to close down their own hospital, always an expensive luxury to maintain as I had learned in Saudi Arabia with Aramco. Their hospital was handed over to us and became a surgical hospital. It was not satisfactory, having medicine and ophthalmology in Al Nahdha, and surgery two or three miles away outside the PDO compound at Mina Al Fahal; but it was the best we could do until the main capital area hospital was built later.

Fortune smiled on us again. When the new Qabbous Hospital was built in Salalah the same year it again was a turn key project. This accelerated programme caught me at least with my pants down for I had already ordered a large x-ray screening unit, for installation in the old hospital, where it lay, still in its packing case. Thanks to SOAF, we were able to fly it back north and it replaced the old Watson machine in the PDO Hospital - which Khattack unceremoniously dumped in a nearby Wadi!

28
OMAN BECOMES HOME

L ife had settled down in more ways than one and money seemed less important in a place where one could fulfil so many dreams. Dr Asim was about to leave the Ministry of Health, to become Minister without Portfolio, thus readily available for the Sultan as a 'trouble shooter'. Before he left he kindly sanctioned the purchase of a villa for us, in a new development outside Ruwi called Medinat Al Qabbous. We'd been in the hospital flat for well over a year and were getting tired of blocked drains. Also, Binnie wanted a garden. What she got was half an acre of rock-strewn sand on a steep slope; but by assiduous digging of a 'falaj' system i.e. water channels spreading between the rocks, she was able to grow a pleasing mixture of desert plants and shrubs over the next few years.

Medinat Qabbous was a cantonment of villas for foreigners built by Taylor Woodrow Towell, the latter being their local partner in Oman. Rumour had it that the development, some seventy houses, was originally planned for the Al Garve but TW failed to get the contract. Probably untrue but certainly the villas would not have looked out of place on a Mediterranean shore. My main complaint was that the roof was only about ten centimetres thick, hence we baked in the summer unless we ran the air conditioners all the time. This, apparently, was what rich expats were expected to do. Expats we might have been but rich we weren't! So we slopped a few buckets of whitewash on the roof which reflected some of the heat off the black asphalt.

As a matter of interest, the Ministry of Health purchased that three roomed villa for 35,000 Omani Riyals. After we left they sold it for more than 100,000 ROs. I calculate my total salary over the six years we served there did not exceed 40,000 ROs - so I was indeed a profitable servant!

But it was good to be able to invite visitors in the cooler weather. Jim and Judy Johnson stayed several times, so did their children, Lottie and Rupert. Lottie and her girlfriend Sarah were popular in a bachelor-driven society, especially with the military, and I had to be avuncular on mess nights... threatening to come and collect them - the crowning insult for the young! Rupert had an unpremeditated adventure, which he blamed on me, when I got him a lift one day up to the Saiq airstrip on Jebel Akhder. Here he was abandoned by the pilot, who was tasked to go somewhere else, and left to find his own way down. He did, of course, being a Rupert of initiative and charm.[1]

Chet and Martha were due to visit while we were still in the flat but when the time came, Chet was forbidden to travel to a 'British zone of influence' by his regional boss.

"Hey! The Brits won't mind! But you know those Ay-rabs, they'll go ape

---

[1] He was at Bristol University at the time and deep into self-sufficiency. For instance, he decided it was wasteful to use a tea bag for just one infusion so took to pegging them out to dry on the clothes line: until Binnie one day showed him flies crawling over them!

if they think we're dropping a spook amongst them!"

So Martha came alone and she and Binnie cleared the Muttrah suq together. She also managed to look as if she owned the Political Agency when we were invited there for drinks one evening... not her fault, Martha is an imposing six footer, even draped over the balcony, and the Political Agent and his wife at that time were 'vertically challenged'.

Visitors in the cool season meant... camping. In these early post-colonial days the British still behaved as if they were in India when it came to recreation - picnics and amateur dramatics headed the list of activities.

Binnie's talent for organising camping trips became famous. (The time came when she was tasked with taking a royal party into the desert.) I had learned from the earliest days in Arabia never to let on I was a doctor when travelling. Quite early on in Oman this policy backfired on me - as so many things did!

We were in Wadi Beni Khalid, east of Sur. The wadi ran south, its winter flood water expiring in the Wahiba sands. We had chosen to go there one weekend with Terry Clarke and John Shipman, professional Arabists from the Political Agency, and Romilly David, a Welsh Guardsman seconded to SAF, whom I had lined up as a prospective husband for Lottie! (She wasn't with us.)

There were apocryphal tales of caves leading into paradise... well, this was a magic land. We stopped near the entrance into the wadi where we intended to ask advice from the locals. Inevitably the first question from them was: "Is one of you a doctor?"

The party was well briefed. Nevertheless, some glanced sheepishly at me.

"No, no! I am an engineer!" I said cheerfully.

"Ah!" was the response, "Just what we need! We have a problem with the road over the hill there."

Protesting weakly, I was dragged off while the others chortled. I managed to bluff my way out of that particular situation.

We did find the caves and indeed crawled into them; but the large empty chambers devoid of life save for an underground stream, were not my idea of paradise. Perhaps the cool and water were for the Arab.

Another key to the good life came my way when we were invited to join the PDO Club. In accordance with oil company policy of integrating with the community, two doctors were offered membership.

I was one; the other was Dr Mohammed Sultan, medical superintendent of Al Nahdha Hospital. He had forgiven me for declining the offer of this post before I ever came to Oman! It was a thankless task: but now we got on famously - although Mohammed got on with everyone famously. He was an Adeni, the son of the director of Aden Airways, and had trained as a doctor at Trinity College, Dublin. He was rather more British than the British. He had worked as a doctor for the colonial administration but after the British withdrawal in 1967, had made his way to Oman, thanks to his father-in-law, an American trained dental surgeon, whose daughter Nasreen he had married.

Her father, Dr Kharusi, was a Zanzibari but with roots firmly in Oman - indeed his family takes their name from a major wadi on the north side of Jebel Akhder! He now headed the dental department in Al Nahdha Hospital.

Mohammed was thrilled at the invitation for, despite being a good Muslim, he was also a playboy. The restaurant, dance floor and cinema in the PDO compound were the breath of life to him. I, on the other hand, saw the invitation as the opportunity to sail again.

And I did. The yacht club on the shores of Mina al Fahal Bay had half a dozen 'Fireflies' and thereafter rarely an evening passed without my slipping down for a quick sail. Most members were Dutch; one of them, Marijke, became my regular crew for weekend racing. We seldom won but she was good company and managed to keep laughing when we capsized - which we did fairly regular. The club house was a popular spot for the Dutch, who consumed large quantities of Heineken's beer and listened to deafening music of the 'Oompah, Oompah' variety - music for planting tulips by, as one British member called it. But my first love remained the mountains; and so began my *affaire de coeur* with Jebel Akhder. A brief description is necessary.

❦ ❦ ❦ ❦ ❦ ❦ ❦ ❦ ❦ ❦ ❦ ❦ ❦

Jebel Akhder forms the spine of North Oman, more than 200 miles long, 6-10,000 feet in height, extending as a shallow crescent from the Musandam Peninsula in the north west before plunging into Wadi Sumayil, where it radiates into several spurs. These continue in a more easterly direction, Jebel Aswad being the most prominent, before flattening out towards the Indian Ocean: Wadi Sumayil thus divides the country into north western and eastern halves. Numerous fertile valleys that run down to the sea intersect it. Some say that they give rise to its name the 'Green Mountain'. Some 40 tracks, from north and south, lead to the crest: this is arid for much of the year, although when we were on it in February 1975 there was enough snow to make snowballs!

The mountain is made of limestone and sandstone overlying conglomerate, crushed into a rugged mass by conflicting pressures and often tilted at alarming angles. In general the north side is steep, the south slopes gently down towards the desert. Its highest point is Jebel Shams, a little over 10,000 feet.

My appetite to explore had been whetted by our first trip with Dr Asim when we circumnavigated the entire range, so I was delighted when a party from PDO, led by Ross Urquhart, their chief engineer, asked me to join them, just two months after our arrival. He provided transport around to the south side where we parked in Wadi Ghul, just beyond the mountain village of Al Hamra - a picturesque village, *trop touristique*, and thus soon to suffer incursions by foreign visitors, much to the annoyance of the villagers.

From there we set off at dawn the next day up the south flank of the mountain. I was in poor shape, rapidly dehydrated, and soon had to give up. The rest of the party got to the summit and returned before nightfall, having found a measly couple of gallons of dirty water in a rock pool. Otherwise they would have been in trouble too. But it was the north side of the mountain that offered both a challenge and beauty. I knew that George Band, then with PDO, and David Insall, then with SAF, had made an attempt a couple of months earlier, but had run out of time - and water. Then two months after my abortive visit, Martin Robb and Romilly David from SAF had led a party to the summit from the north, but had been forced round to the south east to reach the summit.

However they had cracked the water problem. Approaching from Rostaq via the lush Wadi Sahtan they had found a local guide, Saud bin Annas al Abri, in the highest village. He had led them up to a cave, Kef Saab al Naar, the 'Cave of Fire', which contained ample fresh water.

So in November 1973, a party of seven of us - Ruth Hawley, allowed out by Donald, then the British Ambassador, Ross Urquhart, Dave and Kate Phillips from the British Council, Berj and Suzy Aprahamian, staying with us on a visit from Abu Dhabi, and myself set off for a summit bid. We drove to Al Hub and hired Saud bin Annas to guide us. Next day we climbed to about 6,000 feet where Saud showed us a fresh water spring called Ain Habne. Nearby were the ruins of a small mosque, Masjid ma'Ullah. This was an idyllic spot, flat enough to lay out our mattresses and surrounded by euphorbia and juniper trees. Soon we had a fire going and slept comfortably.

Next day we came to grips with the mountain. Instead of a ramble up gently inclined donkey tracks, surrounded by grass and low scrub, Saud led us into a steep wadi and then out onto a fairly hairy traverse. This discouraged the Phillips and Aprahamians, who opted to descend to Ain Habne. Ruth, Ross and I pressed on with Saud, who by now had tied small rubber pads to his bare feet. We reached a col, Aqbat Azukia, by noon and Saudi indicated we should camp here.

Martin Robb had told us that SAF had used this airy spot as a camp, approached from the south, and we were glad of the stone walls they had built to shelter themselves from the cold wind, and now us.

At this point it is worth explaining that what we called Jebel Shams, or the 'Mountain of the Sun', stretches for some miles along the crest; but there are four prominent features worthy of the name of peaks.

Take Shams One first, because we thought it was the highest, (10,019 feet). A mile or so east of this is Shams Three, below which we were camped on the col. It is a prominent bluff that appears to the unwary onlooker from the north to be the true summit. In fact it is only about 9,000 feet, the lowest of the four. To the north west is Shams Two, about a couple of miles away and almost the same height. (In fact it was over 25 years later that it was finally proved that it was twelve feet higher than Shams One!)

Finally there is a further peak, Shams Four, lying half a mile north of Shams Two, so called because it was the last one we climbed, over fifteen years later.

On the prominent bluff of Shams Three I made a somewhat deflating dis-

Summit of Shams One, looking north, left to right, Ross Urquhart, Lady Ruth Hawley and Saud Bin Anaas Al Abri.

after a snack, decided to push on and reconnoitre Shams Three by myself. I started to scramble up the cliff but soon reached a point where it would be stupid to continue both unsupported and without protection. Just one more stretch around the sharp edge... and behold! I found myself clutching a rusty iron peg hammered into a crack.

Now, no Jebali in his right mind would have climbed this face... so who had? I concluded that it must have been a relic of the Jebel War of 1958, left there by the SAS. Later I spoke with Johnny Cooper, then commanding SAFTR after his Yemen adventures; and who had commanded 'A' Squadron of 22 SAS on the north side of the Jebel in 1958 and subsequently became self-styled 'Lord of the Green Mountain' - in succession to the rebel Suleiman bin Himayr who had fled to Saudi Arabia after his defeat! Johnny told me that men of the regiment had gone rock climbing in this area after the successful conclusion of the campaign; but he knew of no party that had 'claimed' the summit.

So... perhaps we were the first? I returned to the Aqbat, convinced that we were not equipped to tackle 'Shams Three' *direttissimo*. By now we were thinking of dinner and needed water.

"Ma fee Mushkilla!" cried Saud. Odd to think that that infuriating phrase 'no problem' has now entered the English language and is repeated as a parrot-like response to each and any question. Saud led us down a track to the north and in ten minutes showed us a vertical crack in the rock.

"Kef Saab Al Naar!" said Saud proudly. I crawled into a dank, dark, tunnel, then fell with a sickening thud into a blessedly shallow hole. Eventually we came to a turgid pool in the floor of the tunnel, from which we drank - and then, to Saud's horror, washed. We were not impressed by this source of and then, to Saud's horror, washed. We were not impressed by this source of fresh water. But Saud urged us on, until my torch revealed an astonishing waterfall of glistening stalactites in front of us as the tunnel widened into a chamber. Beneath them in the chamber floor was a deep fissure containing as much as 600 gallons of cold, clean water.

We returned refreshed to our camp, and hunkered down behind the stone walls as the now bitter wind whipped over the darkened col. Ruth was a great quartermistress! She fed us on smoked oysters and oxtail soup, followed by smoked sausages and tortellini... only Saud did not ask for seconds. We crawled into our sleeping bags. The mist thickened, the wind howled, and it sounded as if half the mountain was collapsing.

"Only the wind," announced Saud placidly. Dawn seemed a long time coming; and when it did, the mist dripped from very twig and nose.[1]

A brisk breakfast of tea, 'khubs' and jam, and we were off, past the cave, in the steps of the nimble, barefoot, Saud. Soon he turned off the track and scrambled up a steep gully. This opened out on to a scree slope beneath a steep rock face, probably about 60 degrees, certainly enough to make us rope up. Even Saud tied his rubber pads on again. At the top we found ourselves on a broad ledge. Saud set off eastwards and within a few minutes he turned to me in triumph.

"The top!" he cried. Unfortunately it was the wrong one. I reflected on the number of wrong peaks I had 'summitted' and added this one to the list. We were on 'Shams Three'. (Shades of yet another 'ascent of Rum Doodle'.) It was about nine o'clock and our companions down at Masjid Ma'Ullah, who had their binoculars trained on the promontory, waved enthusiastically. Behind us, and perhaps a thousand feet higher, was Shams One, hidden from

Aqbat Azukia.

[1] Later I learned that this mist was the fountain of life for the Green Mountain, the vegetation having learned to live by foliar drinking, ie. absorbing mist through leaves, in the absence of any significant precipitation.

their view. I asked Saud if there was a route there.

"Ma fee tareek!" he cried cheerfully. I decided, wrongly, that what he meant was that he had never been there. What was the point when one had such a splendid view and grass for the asking all around us? I recall being cross. I stalked off westwards with him muttering beside me. We contoured for an hour, by which time 'Shams One' was only about 300 feet above us; but its slopes were vertical and we were not ready for the technical climbing involved. We continued westwards, the cliffs above us getting lower, but the escarpment we were on becoming steeper. After another hour we came to a fault in the vertical cliff. With total lack of good practice, we jammed a big tree trunk into the crack and scrambled up it. Ruth led us out on the cliff top so it is only right that this became known as 'Ruth's Col' for the aficionados of Jebel Shams - or 'Ruth's cleavage' among her friends, since it was a very steep and narrow ravine!

We paused long enough to gaze at the great isolated bulk of Jebel Khorr, rising to the south, a splendid 'exotic' deposited by the continental drift, then scrambled back eastwards, and were soon on the top of Shams One.

The air was cool and sweet and there on a small cairn the empty Moet and Chandon bottle left by Martin Robb, Romilly David and the other members of Muscat Regiment the previous spring. However, they had not climbed our north face route - as I shall make clear! It was now that Saud chose to recall there was a short cut back to the Aqbat.

"Lead on," I said. We returned to Ruth's Col, then backtracked below the cliffs to Shams Three but, instead of a laborious descent of the north east route we had ascended, he led us down a valley to the south east. This narrowed into a ravine down which we slid with varying degrees of ill-temper until we reached a gentle slope that led back to the Aqbat - in less than half the time we had taken on the ascent. Saud now admitted that this was the only route he had known leading to Shams One. So I claimed a first for the north face - certainly Ruth was the first woman! We collected our rucksacks and descended to camp one at Ain Habne where Berj, Suzy, David and Kate, had kindly barbecued a goat they had bought off a passing herdsman. Next day we went back to Al Hub and home.

I shall not bore you with detailed descriptions of another nine visits to Jebel Akhder during the next decade! These included a last great trek, with donkeys, from Wadi Sumayil in the east to Jebel Shams, then down to Wadi Sahtan in the west; and a north to south crossing via the Persian Steps. We camped under the stars on the trek. One night I spotted a satellite passing overhead and tried to explain to our donkey men this was an 'automatic star' for communications, an example of western know how. I probably sounded patronising. If so I was soon put in my place.

One of them piped up: "Yes, and there'll be another in about 40 minutes. That one's Russian."

The Persian Steps produced no problems, other than their origin. The 19th century explorer, S. P. Miles wrote of: "the unsurpassed skill shown by those who completed them."

Certainly the placing of the huge slabs up the pass so as to reinforce the precipitous edge of the track was stunning. Miles himself tried to find out who had built them and failed. He wrote: "This it prompts me to consider that it is of Persian origin and work."

Another story we heard was the name arose from a mistranslation of 'fars' (Persian) for 'faris', Arabic for a knight or noble rider, who had presumably fallen there. Miles wrote: "It can only evoke from me my greatest admiration and respect."

Perhaps I may be forgiven for a description of my last visit to Jebel Akhder? This was in 1982. Dr Mubarak Al Khaddouri, who showed me equal kindness, had succeeded Dr Asim as Minister of Health. I had already left Oman four years previously, yet every year he would authorise a two week visit for me, all expenses paid, nominally to advise on health matters. He was aware that I would push off to the mountains as soon as I decently could! (He had already authorised three months leave for me to go to Everest in 1976.)

The WHO representative, Dr Adriano Paltrinieri, had been there for some years and we had already shared some mountain adventures. Adriano had fought the Germans as a teenage Italian partisan and had led an adventurous life ever since. Also working in North Oman was Dr Hugh Morris, who was charged with establishing GP surgeries in the interior. Hugh had been in Salalah as medical superintendent of the new Qabbous Hospital before I'd left, and I would stay with him and his wife Miranda on my visits. Miranda had achieved fame not only as an Arabist, but also for here research into the dialects of Eastern Arabia. She fell in love with the Island of Socotra!

Erik Bennett, retired from the RAF as an Air Vice-Marshall, had stayed on to command SOAF. He now repaid the hospitality Binnie had showed him when he first arrived, friendless, in 1974, but armed with an introduction from Jim Johnson. Until he infiltrated the higher echelons of Omani society he would call on many an evening and join us for supper.

He authorised a helicopter to take the three of us to a 'bowl' at 8,700 feet above a vertical cliff 4,000 feet high - unequalled anywhere on the north face of Jebel Akhder, in Arabia, or perhaps even Europe.

Adriano and I had discovered this cliff on our 1981 visit when we had summoned Saud bin Annas to help us again. Our target was Shams Two - from the north of course. We left his house in Madruj and climbed for three hours, then started on a traverse that took us up beautifully carved orange and black steps leading into a huge cirque with a vertical cliff 1,500 feet above us, and another 3,000 feet below! It was indeed airy! Alas, all that Saud could tell us was that this magical path was 'very old'. It took us just fifteen minutes to walk round to a terrace that eventually led east to the summit of Shams Two.

Steep 200 foot cliffs enclosed this terrace, the only exit being a narrow wadi that drops away to the south. Its floor was covered with rank grass, low scrub, euphorbia and large junipers, some 30 feet high.

The summit of Shams One from the SE

There was no water, and this was why we had to resort to the unsporting use of a helicopter. We had three four and a half gallon jerry cans aboard when Flight Lieutenant Jonathan Palmer put us down one afternoon in March. We hoped that the helicopter's rotors caused the biting cold wind: alas, we were wrong, it persisted long after the aircraft disappeared down the wadi. We were spoiled by 120 kilos of kit and clothing. We established camp; even so the cold was more than we had bargained for. Our object was to explore the west end of Jebel Akhder, and 'knock off' Shams Four while we were there.

I had undertaken to do the catering, something which I had always delegated in the past - usually to Binnie. So the fare was spartan, some would even say squalid. We slept fitfully in the cold, Adriano resorting to gymnastics in his sleeping bag to ward off the cold! He had very decently surrendered his two man tent to Hugh and I.

At 6.30am I produced a Levantine breakfast of coffee, 'khubs', cheese and olives - the latter were a disaster - I'd bought the kind used by American hostesses for stuffing at cocktail parties. Adriano saved the morning. I had served him, an Italian, tinned macaroni for supper the night before; but he had forgiven me. He now produced French loaves and plum jam from his personal cold box.

Discouraged by my culinary failure the other two opted to depart for Shams four without a packed lunch, nor any water for that matter. It seemed a reasonable decision at the time; we should be back within three hours...

We did in fact climb the peak in an hour; and were rewarded by the greatest view in 'my' world, from Madruj nestling beneath us to the far horizon where the Gulf met the sky. On either side we saw water in the wadis, perhaps for the first time since 1977.

And so to our second blunder of the day, my breakfast being the first. Exhilarated by height and sun, we charged off down the north west slope to see what adventures might befall us. We found exotic-looking gems (probably worthless) embedded in stones, live silver fish (can they live anywhere?), a few lizards, and - despite the delayed spring weather - dwarf primulas nestling in a crevice. Soon we had descended 4,000 feet! In a wadi were several burned junipers; and some sangars nearby; possibly relics of the Jebel War of the 1950s?

We had forgotten lesson one on the Jebel - where is the water? Adriano found some damp earth below a cliff, dug a few inches, and there was enough water to lap. Then we shared our emergency rations, two tangerines and two lumps of cheese. After some discussion, i.e. an argument that I lost, the other two decided to return to camp, by a circular route that took them south and then north up towards Shams One. After an hour I felt exhausted, and nauseated - classic signs of dehydration. Hugh had twisted his knee and was hobbling. Only Adriano, iron man of the Piedmont, was going well. We found a pool of disgusting red water, from which only I was brave enough to drink. It was growing dark as we laboured up towards Shams One when Hugh spotted a stick pointing down into the shadows. It was one of the rare signposts on this part of the mountain and led westwards, down a precipitous track into the wadi, then up the other side. From the top we could see a flat rock, tantalisingly close, which we knew was just above our camp. With lightened hearts we strode on, and nearly fell into another wadi. Even in the semi-darkness it was gruesomely familiar. It was the one running south from Shams Two; and it was deep. Wearily I turned north and started up the wadi edge.

It seemed that we would have to climb another peak. But Adriano was made of sterner stuff than I was. He plunged straight over the side of the wadi and disappeared into the dark. Nervously we followed... By instinct he had found a path; or at least an apology for one. Then grace, from whom we did not deserve such luck, brought us to a terrace with dead trees. We stopped. I may not have had a torch but at least I had matches. Soon we had a huge fire going and in the warmth I slept. Then the moon rose and the indefatigable Adriano decided to go on. I'm afraid I slept again, but awoke as it grew colder. I looked across at Hugh huddling by the fire.

Then I became aware of another presence, behind my right shoulder. I have enough Highland blood, on my mother's side, to have experienced such presences, both before and since. It was comforting. I had no wish to look over my shoulder to see what or who was there. Despite there being no physical relief, I knew we were no longer in danger. On other occasions I have been aware that dehydration and/or hypoxia were factors. But I record it as testimony.

Another hour passed. A light appeared on the opposite side of the wadi. In the moonlight, now rested, Hugh and I scrambled down and up towards the light. There we found an exhausted Adriano. The poor man had lost his way and had been forced into yet another wadi before reaching our camp. There he had rested a bare ten minutes, drinking water and eating bananas, before setting off back, armed with torches, beer and chocolate. Hugh and I gorged and felt life flow back into us. Bravo Adriano! I can't say he saved our lives - but he did save us from further acute discomfort!

We reached camp and crawled into sleeping bags with more water and biscuits. We were not yet out of the wood; the wind rose, high clouds and low mist scurried across the moon. It began to rain. Our tent was pitched in a stream bed and Hugh, aware of the hazard of flash floods, opted to move out and join Adriano who was under a tree. I weighed up the odds and decided to stay put. After an hour the rain stopped and utter stillness descended... It was the calm before the storm. Gusts of wind grew stronger and stronger. As the sky lightened the tent blew down. Dawn was hard and grey with a watery sun.

Leaving our heavy kit near the LZ we moved the rest to a narrow terrace under a cliff, clearly much used by the wild donkeys of the Jebel, (descendants of those imported from Africa for the Jebel War). It was protected from the weather by the huge overhanging lip of a waterfall - now dry. It was fortunate indeed as soon it began to rain again and continued for the next twelve hours. We were shivering in a clammy mist. Not what we expected in spring-time in Oman.

Plans for day two, a walk to Shams Two, were shelved. The day passed, night fell and with it came a break in the clouds and moonlight. We consoled ourselves with two thoughts - one, that we had covered more ground than we had ever intended the previous day and two, how wonderful for Oman was the gentle but relentless downpour! We rose before dawn and carried our kit to the LZ. Another high front was rushing in from the north and it was still bitterly cold. We listened anxiously for an engine. It came, and with a comforting thump, thump, thump, our Bell 205 swept in over Shams Four. Hugh emptied out the last jerry can of water as it touched down. We boarded quickly and Jonathan flew us low over the lip of the bowl for one last stomach-churning look down the 4,000 foot vertical cliff into Wadi Sahtan.

Half an hour later we landed at Sib and stepped out into a hot house, peeling off sweaters that had been barely adequate to repel the cold just minutes before.

29

SALAD DAYS (WITH A VISIT TO EVEREST)

By the mid-70s Oman had become the nearest thing to home that Binnie and I had experienced since we had married. Kathy too, she had felt the first wrench of leaving for boarding school before she was 8 whilst we were still in Abu Dhabi. Now, as a teenager, she had sun and sea, parties and picnics, to her heart's content during school holidays. Jim and Judy became more and more frequent visitors as Jim, still playing hooky from Lloyds, was up to his neck in security affairs.There was talk of them moving out to Oman on a permanent basis at one time, when Jim was being considered for the post of Defence Secretary. But Judy confided to me that it was too late for her to become a 'Sandgirl' in a post-Colonial environment and that she preferred the environs of Sloane Avenue and its cultural hinterland. After all, she had worked at the Royal Opera House before marrying Jim. So there was a happy compromise - they visited us frequently in the cool weather - until it was darkened by her illness.

But this was yet to come and meanwhile we enjoyed Lotus Eating in the desert and the mountains, on the beaches and on the sea. Our first home leave together was not until late in 1974. We celebrated this by being chased out of North Cyprus when the Turks invaded. We had flown there on our way home - fortunately, Kathy had stayed with her grandparents when the summer term ended - and were smartening up our villa which had been empty for some time.

On the day that the Greeks tried to take over the island we were actually on our way to the airport to fly home. Firing had broken out as we drove through the city but we got to the airport to be told that it was closed. We did a smart about turn and headed back for Kyrenia by the back streets. There was quite a lot of firing going on, although as with most civil insurrections it seemed that no-one on the ground actually knew what was going on, but, as I said to Binnie: "It's when it gets quiet that it's time to get worried!"

At that moment, of course, all firing ceased and a deathly hush descended on the streets. I hit the floorboard of our hired car and high-tailed it back to Kyrenia. We stopped outside a café on the harbour front and hurried in, encouraged by more shots from the other side of the harbour.

"Keep inside!" announced the proprietor. "How would you like your coffee?"

I got the impression most of the Greeks knew what was happening but chose to play dumb. Eventually a policeman arrived and told us we could now go home. This was all very well; we'd already shut up our house. We decided to dump ourselves on Arthur and Derry Clements, our friends from Abu Dhabi, who were in their villa further along the coast. We drove there, being stopped frequently at roadblocks manned by, what I can only term as, irregulars or Greek bandits. However, they let us through.

Derry and Arthur were excited to hear news of the uprising and made us welcome. That night we sat and watched the crest of the Kyrenia Range ablaze from end to end - the shepherds taking advantage of the breakdown in law and order to indulge in the time-honoured pastime of burning down the forest, thus ensuring luxurious grass for their goats to rip up next season.

After a couple of days the situation stabilised enough for us to return to the airport 'on spec', to see if there were any planes leaving for U.K. We found a BEA flight due to leave for London via Athens. At this point I discovered that I'd left our passports back at the house. Leaving Bin to plead with BEA I drove back faster than was safe, collected them from a bemused Derry, and was back in time for us to catch the flight - having only busted through one roadblock shouting: "I'm English!" A ploy which still worked. It was a drive worthy of Jonathan Mansel! (For those who are aficionados of Dornford Yates.) The aircraft was full of British holiday makers who sat calmly throughout the flight and then burst into a fine display of hysterics for the benefit of the press when we disembarked at Heathrow.

By then, Binnie's parents had moved to Somerset where, on our arrival, we were treated to a fine display of insouciance from Kathy: "What kept you?" I wasn't sure whether to be angry or flattered.

Whilst in England we attended the christening of the Hawley son and heir and brother for Sara, Caroline and Susan. I joined Sir Geoffrey Arthur and John Shipman as one of Christopher's godfathers. Ruth had celebrated the nationalisation of the PDO Hospital by giving birth to Christopher the following day. Quite a PR coup for the Sultan as well! Following the return of mother and child to the Embassy I had declared Christopher right as rain. Fortunately, Ruth ignored me, flew home with him and a few days later he underwent surgery in Great Ormond Street Hospital. (Well, in my defence Christopher, you <u>did</u> develop signs of the lesion far too soon after you were born!) The Hawleys left early in 1975 - and were replaced by the Treadwells. My oldest - or rather, longest standing - climbing buddy was back!

The fighting in Dhofar peaked in 1975. War, war, more war.

The large number of British officers hanging around the periphery of this war went on to prove the adage that in peacetime it is women who become hysterical. In war time, men. The old sweats amongst the contract officers curled their lips in disdain and said: "Huh! They should have been here a few years ago when there was some real fighting." Certainly the casualty rate was falling as the Sultan's increased weaponry made its mark.

While I still used to lie under the palm trees and listen to the war, I did come up against a problem on my visits to the south. The 'Adoo' had started using plastic mines that could make just as much mess of the unlucky man who trod on one as a traditional metal one. They were a special problem for the surgeons called upon to remove fragments from the eyes as they were non-opaque to conventional x-rays. So I visited Moorfields Hospital when I was in London, and explained the situation to the x-ray staff. They came up with a simple but effective solution - place two, not one, films in the cassette. (This is the metal case that protects the film from light before it is exposed.) The first film acted as a filter, thus rendering the plastic fragment relatively more opaque; they became just visible on the distal film.

We used this technique on several patients before hostilities ended. But whether the eye surgeons found them useful, alas, I don't know. They were flown to the R.A.F. Hospital in Cyprus for surgery, and I never had any feed-back. But at least I knew that soldiers we were referring did have intra-ocular fragments.

That was the second war we had seen in these so-called peaceful times. But worse was to come.

In 1975 I visited Beirut. It was by no means the first time, since we were married there in 1961, and it was only to be expected that I visited the St. George Club, where we had had our reception. The club had moved with the times, Harry Carpenter was still secretary but it was no longer a British bastion. It was summer and one could enjoy the view over sea and city from the rooftop bar. One day after lunch we were drinking our coffee and brandy when a Christian Lebanese in our group looked at his watch, yawned and said he must be going. It was 3.30pm.

He said: "The Muslim children will be leaving their school soon." Innocently, I asked why that was important. "Oh I like to fire mortar bombs at the gates, one can be sure of getting a few parents as well at this time." was the astonishing reply.

Those few words encapsulated the horrors of the civil war that would engulf this beautiful country for the next decade. The following morning I watched a further outrage. I had gone to visit a doctor friend, a Muslim this time, and was in his apartment overlooking the Rue Hamra. We had gone to the roof where two armed men lay, their weapons at their sides.

"These are my guards!" my friend said cheerfully. Then turned to them and continued: "Anything to report?"

"The Christians are getting nosy," said one, and turned to my friend, "shall I show him?"

My friend shrugged his shoulders and grimaced. Without another word the guard shouldered his rifle and fired at a man crossing the road, who dropped and lay where he had fallen. Eventually two passers by scurried out and dragged him into a shop door. I looked on in horror and left as soon as I could - no 'decently' about it. I wondered how long it would take me to become like them in such a situation.

To happier subjects. I have already mentioned the disturbing influences in my life, eg, Jim Johnson. But there was the other, though perhaps less potentially dangerous! Tony Streather! I received a message from him asking would I like to join a Joint British-Nepalese Services Expedition to Mount

Everest in 1976 as a medical officer? How could I say no? Not for the last time, Binnie said: "Of course you must go! You'll be safe with Tony." Whilst I believe Sue had told Tony: "You'd better take Philip along with you to look after you."

And so it came about that I sought an appointment with Dr. Mubarak Khaddouri, my Minister. He, bless his heart, granted me three months' leave of absence. (Later he told me: "There was little point in my refusing your request - you'd have resigned if I hadn't - I knew your record!") Which still didn't stop me being forever grateful to him. Neither Binnie nor I had any wish to leave Oman at that stage.

⋘⊳ ⋘⊳ ⋘⊳ ⋘⊳ ⋘⊳ ⋘⊳ ⋘⊳ ⋘⊳ ⋘⊳ ⋘⊳ ⋘⊳ ⋘⊳ ⋘⊳

And so it was that on 4 March, 1976, I found myself boarding a RAF VC10 in Bahrain, bound for Hong Kong, then at the height of its Colonial prosperity. On my arrival I was met by a young Sapper officer who thrust half a dozen bottles of Tio Pepe in my arms as the Nepalese were trying to charge 500% duty on expedition booze, so we were all required to carry some! It was reassuring to be back in military hands!

I have already described, in some detail, two Himalayan expeditions, and as this was only the third out of fifteen - I'll keep it short! The story has been well told by Jon Fleming and Ronnie Faux in *Soldiers on Everest*. I had trained quite hard on Jebel Akhder the previous winter so the fifteen day approach march to Thyangboche was not too arduous. My medical 'oppo', Dick Hardy, thought along similar lines when it came to medication... minimalist! At this stage of the expedition we were armed with Kleenex and Lomotil. He had been on Nuptse the previous year, as had many members of the present expedition, when there had been loss of life. Now there were signs of divided loyalties amongst them and us, ie, the Nuptse party which had been led by Jon Fleming - now deputy leader of this party - and felt he had been usurped by Tony Streather; and the new boys. This was my third expedition with Tony and I made it clear to all and sundry that, however good a chap Jon was, I would support Tony 100%. Happily, Tony's firm, low-key leadership won everybody round.

I shared a tent with a Sapper, Meryon Bridges, whom I described on my diary as "suave and articulate." Later, he and his wife Suzy became great friends and it showed how accurate was my original assessment of him! My other walking companion was Ronnie Faux, the *Times* correspondent. My description of him was less polite! But he and his wife, Fanny, also became family friends. (I shall confine myself to remarking that he could play each of the Goons in turn, while his imitation of a German officer was much better than mine. For example, he would appear at breakfast and bark: "Achtung! Zis morgen all the peaks will fall in facing me!" Well, at 16,000 feet it was hilarious.)

We had a lot of our kit flown up to an airstrip near Thyangboche; it was cheaper than hiring more porters. There, I also received a letter from Kathy, posted in Sherborne just six days earlier. It started: "Dear Daddy. I hope you are well and that nothing fatal has happened to you so far."

While there we took the opportunity of visiting the Japanese Everest View Hotel. Oh dear, what a disaster. Despite charging $65 a night, it was losing money hand over fist. Not surprising as it had oil-fired central heating and no water - both had to be flown in! We took coffee on the terrace and admired the view. There were no guests at the time, just the resident Japanese doctor who had gone mad. When guests did arrive, he would lurk near the reception desk and, as they booked in, thrust injections of 'Lasix' (used for treating altitude-induced pulmonary oedema) into their rear ends, straight through their clothing!

The end came when he burst into the room of a perfectly fit American tourist one night, jammed an oxygen mask over his face and shouted at the night porter to hold him down while he thrust an IV drip into his arm. The manager persuaded all the staff to sign a circular saying he was mad - but he pre-empted further action by walking out.

We acclimatised at Pheriche, at a height of some 15,000 feet, where I was course officer for the National Yak Race. Quite a riot, despite there being only five runners, with their crazy Tibetan riders. I was also course bookie and had to divide the first prize between Jon Fleming and Mike Kefford - confusing the issue, one of them backing the rider, the other the owner. I joined the survivors of the Nuptse disaster on an acclimatisation hike to their base camp, where they laid a memorial to their lost friends. I noted that those who had a good cry at the time came back refreshed.

Next, Nigel Gifford, Bassant (one of our Gurkhas), and I climbed Island Peak, some 19,000 feet. It started to snow on the top so we struggled down a gully, which had taken us ten minutes to negotiate on the way up and two

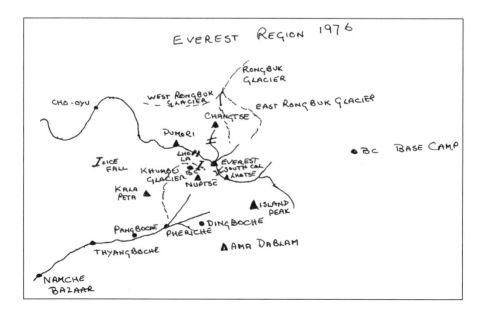

hours on the way down!

By early April we were at base camp and my beard was coming along nicely. It was grey and Ronnie said I looked like Spike Milligan. We wired ourselves in, a necessary precaution against trekkers who tend to regard expedition base camps as a cut-price supermarket. A pleasant surprise was the cleanliness of the site. For this we had to thank a party of altruistic Americans who had taken it upon themselves to clear the rubbish en route to the mountain. I shared a tent with Tony from now on, a relief as I was exhausted by the constant breast-beating amongst the Nuptse gang. Apart from their relative youth, I was beginning to find my role as group therapist exhausting!

From our tent you could look east straight up the icefall, steeper than I had expected, and to the west at the Lo La Pass. From this, in 1921, Mallory had looked down at the Khumbu Icefall and pronounced it 'probably impassable'. So it remained until 1952 when Eric Shipton looked at it again and decided it might go. In 1962, Chinese soldiers sat on it and watched the Indian Expedition below - it's only about 1,000 feet above base camp - until BeeGee, who was now our liaison officer, and was the same to the Indians then - climbed up and told them to "Piss off"! It was not until 1986, on Brummie's expedition to the North East Ridge, that I had the chance to do the same - look down at base camp I mean.[1]

Meanwhile, Dick had led the SAS contingent - Brummie Stokes, Bronco Lane, and Steve Johnson - up the icefall and had roped it - a very creditable effort in the poor weather we had had until now.

I set up my medical tent, and started on the usual gory task of all doctors in the Himalayas - extracting Sherpas' teeth! Also, poor Captain Dougie Wheelan blew an inguinal hernia after his efforts, and I had no choice but to send him back to the Gurkha depot at Dhahran where he could have it surgically repaired. Rotten luck for a potential summiteer. I also had to put Ronnie Faux in a neck collar after traction. He was convinced I intended to strangle him, but when I assured him I would put inches on his height he was satisfied.

Now that all 2,000 vertical and 10,000 or so horizontal feet of the icefall were roped I started carrying loads up to camp one. This meant a 5am start, but the route between seracs and across crevasses was truly breathtaking, in every sense, and I did it a dozen times all told. Eight thousand feet of rope were used, with ladders and ice pitons, to make it as safe as possible for porters. Bronco and Brummie gave me a hero's welcome, on an occasion when they were resting at base camp, for being the slowest porter on the mountain.

In mid-April tragedy struck. Terry Thompson of the Royal Marines died at camp two after falling into a crevasse. John Peacock brought me the news in my medical tent. After telling me to sit down, he said: "Philip I'm terribly sorry but T...y has been killed." It took me another minute to get it into my thick head that it was Terry and not Tony who was dead. Still the shock was terrible. Tony even submitted to being given sleeping tablets that night, he was so upset.

[1] Poor Beegee later developed an infected pilonidal cyst that I had to drain under a general anaesthetic administered by Dick Hardie.

An attempt to recover Terry's body was made by Henry Day and an Alouette III helicopter, of the Royal Nepalese Air Force, flown by the almost legendary French pilot, Commandant Pierre Lefrocq, and Michel, his engineer. They landed near base camp in high wind and under the shadow of Everest thrown on to high streaked cirrus cloud, coloured green and red in the dawn light. We loaded Henry aboard, complete with crampons and bone dome. He had been so nervous the night before when he learned it was to be a Nepalese pilot that I'd had to give him Lomotil! He was reassured by Pierre's arrival. They climbed up to 22,000 feet, then descended into the Western Cwm.

Next thing we saw was the Alouette being catapulted over the edge of the icefall! Landing was out of the question. Pierre said that as they approached camp two he was using maximum power and lift, - and registering rate three descent at the same time. A very pale trio landed nearby. Pierre tried once more without success, but managed to give Henry an unofficial view of Everest's North Face, ie, from Tibet. Tony radioed camp two that Terry must perforce be buried in the Western Cwm.

The drag of building up advanced base camp (ABC), formerly camp two, continued. Soft snow balled up under your crampons until you were about seven feet high; whereupon you rolled slowly over. The Western Cwm looked like a flag-bedecked old people's home in some places, thanks to previous expeditions; the Japanese ladies' expedition who were in front of us and the remains of a failed Spanish expedition.

On the medical front, Dougie Wheelan had returned from Dhahran armed with a clean bill of health from the surgeons, and had started to carry a load up the icefall the same morning and - out popped his hernia again. This really knocked the stuffing out of him, not surprisingly. Then BeeGee, whose abscess had settled satisfactorily after drainage, developed dental neuralgia, associated with a badly impacted wisdom tooth. He'd slipped through the pre-expedition medical net. Dental problems have always loomed large at high altitude, though usually due to leaky fillings. Anyway, I had to pack him off back to Khatmandu.

Base camp visitors will always be a pain for expeditions. We had a large but polite notice requesting them to keep away as we were busy climbing a mountain... the meaning however was clear - "Piss off!" There were still alarms and excursions however. One day we had to chase after a bunch of American hippies who thought it would be fun to climb the icefall...

But two visitors we did welcome, John and Eileen Jackson. He had just retired from running the Mountain Centre at Plas-y-Brenin and they were spending nine months wandering in the Himalayas. John had been on Kanchenjunga with Tony in 1955 and to see the two of them meet up again was heart-warming. He did much to restore his morale. These grand Lancastrians did much to cheer all of us up; Terry's death still hung over us like a cloud.

Base camp was becoming tedious. One day I persuaded Ronnie and Meryon to become tourists. Ronnie had recovered from an acute attack of D&V - he had appeared one dawn clad only in cap comforter and duvet jacket, an apparition that would have, in normal times, reduced me to helpless laughter, but under the circumstances only induced sympathy for someone squirting at both ends on snow and in sub-zero temperatures. Now he'd recovered. Meryon on the other hand was exhausted after twelve days carrying in the Western Cwm and severely depressed at what he regarded as a military assault on a mountain deserving a more reverential approach. Nevertheless, we thumped off down the glacier after a 5am breakfast to Gorek Shep, whilst the trekkers were still abed. By 10am we were on the top of Kalapetar, a trekkers' peak on the side of the beautiful Pumori. From here we had a wonderful view of the top 5,000 feet of Everest, straight up the west ridge, thus allowing views of the north col, the north east ridge with its first and second steps, the south west face and across to the south col. We were humbled.

On our descent Pierre came roaring in to evacuate BeeGee, landing on a frozen lake. He also took Tim King who had severe chest problems. What a debt we owed that pilot.

I think the three of us benefited from our away day. Next day I did my last carry up the icefall. I'd reached double figures and had lugged two and a half hundredweight of kit up to camp one. I went with Ronnie who was grumbling because what he had written in the *Times* had upset some buffers in the MOD who had contacted his editor, to say: "His articles are offensive to those who can read between the lines." And, he'd mentioned that there were SAS men on the expedition. So he'd decided to get lost for a few days, after sending a blistering article to his editor, inviting his critics to come out and join us. What the silly ass had also done was to carry a 40 pound load up the icefall. This was too much for his torn neck muscles and his blinding headache soon recurred. I got him back to our tent and gave him a load of analgesics.

Two days later I was back sharing a tent with Tony in ABC at 22,000 feet. Despite being early May the temperature dropped to −30C at night and I couldn't write to Bin as my pen had frozen. Spring had not yet come to Everest this year, but the view was breathtaking.

The head of the western cwm, topped by the south col was about three kilometres away. On our left was the south west face of Everest, chocolate brown in colour beneath the snow and ice. On the right the Nuptse face, *café au lait* in colour. It was like being in a cathedral. But in every Eden there is a serpent! On the south west face we could see the bedraggled tents of an expedition from the previous year, whose filth in their ABC nearby defied description.

A previous expedition also caused us botheration when it came to paying our high altitude porters. We had settled for Rs30 a day, but one Sherpa let on that they had been paid Rs300 for a special effort! Talk about spoiling the market.

For the most part our eyes were on Lhotse, which forms the head of the Cwm. On its face we could see our climbers crawling up to the higher camps.

The long winter meant that winds of 50 knots persisted on the south col itself. Several climbers, like Ivor Helberg and Nigel Gifford, were knackered after their efforts on Lhotse face and had to descend, as did Ronnie, still holding his head, and Dougie Wheelan, coughing horribly, who had come up to ABC with me. The weather was bad. The Sherpa cooks had succumbed to the altitude and I had perforce to cook curried chicken and rice one evening for fifteen climbers. (I must be honest, I found one Sherpa who could work a pressure cooker and hence boiled the rice.) Just to add to our difficulties a serac collapsed in the icefall; thus we were cut off from base camp for 56 hours, while the icefall gang worked like Trojans to get the route reopened. Up at camp four, Steve Johnson had an unexpected visitor in the shape of a three-quarter hundredweight lump of ice through his tent roof. Fortunately, he was sitting at the other end at the time.

Once the icefall reopened we were hit by a severe storm and the Sherpas scattered their loads all over the western cwm before making a dash for camp. It was a miserable group of climbers who gathered in the mess tent - more like an igloo with a tarpaulin over the top - that night. Tony saved the day with an inspired ten-minute pep talk to climbers and Sherpas alike. Even the weather was listening. The blizzard stopped and next morning the Sherpas scurried back down the cwm to collect their loads. Another serac fell in the icefall, this time however the right way up, so one could walk across it and the sun shone.

To celebrate, and to avoid having to cook again, I joined Tony on an old man's carry to camp three, ie, we took a couple of oxygen bottles. But when we got there I found poor Bassant, the Gurkha NCO who had looked after me on Island Peak, lying in agony with three strangulated piles. He later admitted he had been suffering for days but was too ashamed to admit to, what was in his eyes, such a shameful condition. I recalled that piles, for the Arabs, were equally disastrous as they were thought to be the cause of impotence.

Brummie subsequently described the ensuing operation - at 23,000 feet a world record I think - in his book *Soldiers and Sherpas*. It showed how he got the worst of the deal. A shower of pus in his face when I took the somewhat desperate step of incising them in turn and releasing the trapped faeco-purulent contents. I then rammed a shell dressing up his backside and started to pray. Under normal circumstances, death from haemorrhage was the likeliest outcome. I spent a sleepless night but my prayers were answered. Next day Henry stretchered him down to ABC with the help of three others.

We were building up for the summit bid. I had become, by default, expedition meteorologist and watched the weather anxiously, as well as trying to relate the radio forecasts we were receiving from Khatmandu to conditions on the ground. These were sometimes, well, fanciful. Tempers were frayed and efficiency dropped, doubtless as the result of prolonged hypoxia. For instance, oxygen bottles got left behind when they were urgently needed at camp four.

By 14 May Brummie and Bronco were at 27,500 feet, having established camp six on the site of the American 1963 trans-summit expedition. At 11pm a blizzard sprang up. Snug in our Whillan's box Tony and I had a sleepless night.

"This couldn't have happened at a crueller time," was Tony's comment. It lasted until next morning, and then it snowed until mid-afternoon when the sun shone. The night was calm and the next day (16 May) we presumed Brummie and Bronco were on their way to the summit while a support party - Pat Gunson, John Scott, Phil Neame and Steve Johnson - moved up to camp six. Then it began to snow again. Radio contact was intermittent and it wasn't until 7.30 that evening that Phil Neame got back to camp five to say that there was no sign of Brummie and Bronco.

We had another miserable night, despite having taken Mogadons. Tony looked like a ghost: not another Haramosh for him I prayed. But a radio call at 7.15am seemed to confirm our worst fears, there was no sign of them. Two hours later I left to descend with Tim King, still having breathing difficulties, while we heard that John Scott and Pat Gunson were climbing, albeit slowly in the thick new snow, up to camp six. It was a still and beautiful morning, a cloistered calm in the cathedral. It was also intensely hot and Tim and I staggered through the soft snow to camp one - I weakened enough to unload my day pack onto a porter!

Then Peter Page, one of the 'icefall heroes' who had remained there, keeping the route open throughout the expedition, appeared out of his tent and announced with all the aplomb of a BBC news reporter that Brummie and Bronco had reached the summit 48 hours earlier. Forced to bivouac above their camp because they were caught by darkness they were even now approaching camp five, assisted by John and Pat who had abandoned their own summit bid. We wept and hugged each other, in my case almost as much for Tony's sake as for Brummie and Bronco. I knew what he had been through. After drinking five pints of 'Rise and Shine' we continued through thick luminous mist to base camp. The lower icefall was unrecognisable, the silence uncanny. Then Dougie appeared with a shout - Brummie and Bronco were asleep in camp five, both badly frost bitten and Brummie snow-blind, but alive!

After that, as the saying goes, it was all downhill. On the way out Tony and I stayed with Terry Bowring, DA in Khatmandu, and nursed Brummie and Bronco, ie, kept them from getting into too much trouble! With padded boots they were able to bicycle around and I made them go to church to give thanks for their survival. Apart from applying dressings to their frost-bitten extremities, whisky remained the best medication. Bassant had been evacuated by helicopter from base camp and was in hospital in Dharhan. I flew back to Muscat via Hong Kong and Bahrain, courtesy of Transport Command, and by 29 May was back home in Oman.

30
LAST YEARS IN OMAN AND A FIRST TRIP TO TURKEY

To arrive back in Oman in the height of the hot weather, some seven days after descending from 22,000 feet in the western cwm of Mount Everest was asking for trouble. It was not long in coming! I had slipped back into my role of roving radiologist and was en route - as I recalled later - for Sumayil.

Somewhere on the airport road I became aware that (a) I had no idea who I was, (b) where I was, and (c) where I was going. Self preservation still ruled and I drew into the roadside and switched off the engine. There were no 'nasties', like loss of bladder control. Gradually memory returned. There was no fear, just mild curiosity. Logic intervened; I opened my briefcase and found some notes on Sumayil Hospital. It seemed reasonable to suppose that was where I was going. So I did, and I was expected. The whole episode had not lasted longer than twenty minutes.

Later that summer I returned to England for a short spell of leave and consulted Michael Ward, now a consultant surgeon, who had been on Everest with John Hunt in 1953. He checked me over and suggested that I had suffered a series of micro-emboli in the brain. As my haemoglobin at the time had been 16.6 grams it seemed probable. My heart would have been pushing blood as thick as tomato ketchup around my body!

Bin saw me settled in and advised our Indian house boy, Xavier, to look after me while she took a trip around Yemen with Fiona Fraser.[1] This was an adventure in those days. They saw the site of the Marib Dam - disappointing - and the suqs of Sana'a - exciting - thanks to their host Hugh Leach, first secretary in the British Embassy. Hugh, always a stickler for protocol, insisted on sleeping in a tent in his garden while the ladies were there!

I was ready for a quiet life - for a bit! I had managed to recruit another two radiologists, from Egypt and India, who looked after Khoula Hospital and Salalah respectively. The days of pounding round the country trying to report on every x-ray that had been taken were over. In the south, the war too was virtually over and my trips few and far between.

On one occasion I was on an SOAF Viscount which had been taken over by the Sultan to fly VIPs to Salalah for the official opening of the new hospital. On board was Richard Lea, doing a spell with the research department - as the internal security department was known - but a long-serving SAS officer when wearing his other hat. According to him - and I confess I had forgotten the incident - I left the plane first, turned to Jim Treadwell, HM's Ambassador, and said: "Be a good chap and carry my bag Jim. See you

---

[1] Khattack also rallied round and fed me at what we called 'Pathan number one' restaurant in Ruwi.

later!" Then stepped into a brand new Mercedes 300, which had been sent to me. Wildly improbable as it sounds, there was a possible explanation for this 'stylish behaviour', as Richard subsequently put it! In my pocket I had a vital spare part for the Philips' x-ray super screening apparatus which we had installed, and was to be part of the show for Sultan Qabbous. Without it the apparatus was defunct. Panic-stricken messages between Muscat and Salalah were responsible for my presence in Salalah, and every precaution had been taken to obviate any delay on my part! Also I knew that Jim was going to stay in the health ministry guesthouse with me that night.

Philips still had a European engineer stationed in Dubai at the time; he was now in Salalah for the big event. We saw the machine up and running and then breathed again. Karl was German, rather than Dutch, and a very typical example of that race! Hardworking but humourless, obsessional about his work and intolerant of other's weaknesses. He also happened to have been born in Chile in 1946... which made me ponder on his father's activities under the Third Reich.

It so happened that two days later we were due to fly back to Muscat and as the SOAF flights were busy ferrying VIPs back - and Karl wasn't one of them - he had taken the precaution of booking himself on a Gulf Air flight. When we went to check him in at the civil terminal we met up with a young American Peace Corps volunteer who was teaching our nurses. Jack was a likeable young Californian and I am still grateful to him for presenting me with a US Army sleeping bag when he returned to the States - the epitome of comfort and warmth!

Karl got to the head of the queue; and then this being Arabia, he was told that he did not have a seat. Muscat had not made a reservation. Karl drew himself upright and exploded: "I have here an endorsed ticket for this flight and I demand a seat - NOW!"

The poor Indian clerk wilted. Then came an American voice with a German accent behind me: "Furthermore, if I don't get it, the Fuhrer will be very displeased!" I regret - slightly - collapsing with laughter. Karl looked baffled. Without further ado I grabbed his kit and dragged him round to the SOAF check-in where I begged the duty officer to let him fly with me on a Skyvan which I knew was headed north, in order to avoid an incident. We got aboard and had a long tedious flight back. Karl hardly ever spoke to me again.

The winter months passed pleasantly. The Johnsons came to stay; it seemed Judy was 'out of the woods' medically. I began to think of the future. Whilst it seemed probable that, in my low-profile job as a radiologist I was unlikely to offend any of the Great and Good amongst the Omanis, I was nearly 50. There was still a chance of landing a consultant post back in England in my particular field - had it been in main stream clinical medicine I would have been written off as too old. But there was a dearth of radiologists. As 1977 wore on I began to make noises to Martin Barry, the radiologist in Yeovil, whom I knew was going to retire in 1978; and to Sir Howard

Middlemiss, professor of radiology in Bristol and doyen of tropical radiology. In fact I invited him to stay, knowing what an inveterate traveller he was!

Among memorable events in our last year was a dhow trip to Qalhat, way down the coast towards Sur, organised by Chuck Pringle, still managing Costains in Oman, where his company flourished - with or without Margaret Thatcher's intervention! Nine of us - the Treadwells included - set out one Wednesday afternoon from Muttrah Harbour in Chuck's splendid motorised dhow commanded by Salim bin Afeef. What followed was a gastronomic as well as geographic feast. We cruised to the east past Muscat Harbour, then down the coast beneath forbidding cliffs for an hour and a half, before anchoring in Bandar Khayran. A land-locked bay, excellent for swimming, followed by 'authentic' Cornish pasties!

After dark our voyage continued eastwards. At dawn we passed Tiwi, a dramatic wadi falling into the sea, which connects with the Wadi Beni Khalid where we had searched for paradise! Nine hours after leaving Bandar Khayran we dropped anchor at Qalhat. "The elusive Qalhat," Ian Skeet[1] had called it. Certainly, its former glories had passed away. Marco Polo had raved about it in the 14th century as a great commercial port with its imports from India and export of horses. Fifty years later Ibn Batuta was equally enthusiastic, especially about its fine Persian mosque. Then tragedy; first a geographical earthquake, then a human one in the shape of a depredatory - as usual - visit from the Portuguese invader Albuquerque, who completed its destruction.

We dropped anchor outside the shallow 'khor' (inlet) and looked askance at this historic site. On the right a square tower with a domed roof and what looked like a Nissen hut. These were all that remained of the once mighty Qalhat. Later, ashore, we found the Nissen hut was in fact a huge cistern. We looked around the stony ground and saw a million pottery fragments amongst the foundations of long-vanished buildings. Across the khor, an uninspiring shallow tongue of water stuck into the rocky beach that disappeared into a cleft in the mountains, lay the modern fishing village, stuck on to the side of the wadi. And a few miles away to the east lay the thriving town of Sur; to the west, Muscat.

Why, therefore, did Qalhat ever flourish? Ian Skeet deduced that in times past Qalhat had fresh water and Sur didn't; and the khor at Qalhat was deep whilst that at Sur was silted up. Centuries passed and these attributes swapped hands. Today the French contractor who built the road to Sur has lifted anything of archaeological value that was there in his day. The ruins were depressing and served to remind us of our own mortality! But we were revived when we returned aboard and lunched off 'terrine au Chuck', followed by chicken and salad, Stilton, and a refreshing dry white wine. Then we set off back to Tiwi, where we anchored late in the afternoon and Chuck excelled himself with roast beef marinated in barbecue sauce, then grilled 'en populate' - I think!

Next morning, we swam and then paddled up the creek lined with palm

[1] Ian was manager, PDO, in the 60s.

trees to the pools below the village of Ghayl Asshaab, the aptly named place of the steep ravine. Like so many of these coastal villages the people were friendly, the children bright and amusing.

After a nourishing lunch of grilled crayfish - thanks to our local fishermen - we set off back to Muscat in wroughty weather. An ever increasing swell from the north east, but Salim kept quietly confident, while we gazed over the stern and tried to kid ourselves it was really as calm as the wake we left behind us! We reached Muscat safely in the dark. It had been a great trip.

Towards the end of June I took a couple of weeks local leave while Binnie was away. Money was, as usual, a bit tight, so, through the good offices of Peter Felton, I managed to hitch a lift on a freight plane returning to UK from Karachi via Muscat. The trouble about such flights is they are unpredictable. I hung around at home for three days, then received a call and reached the airport just in time to board. We then proceeded to fly to Karachi instead of westwards, night-stopped and flew back to Muscat next day! However, beggars can't be choosers, etc. As I was the only passenger I sat in the navigator's seat and, as the captain pointed out to me, soon realised this was the only way to fly!

The one refuelling stop was in Istanbul, where I disembarked and met up with Philippa. We stayed with John Jennings in his beautiful house on the shore of the Bosporus.[1] The object of this visit was for the three of us to join up with Philippa's cousin, Sidney Nowill, and two stalwart ladies - Elizabeth Parry, a producer of operas in England, and Dorothea, Countess Gravina, English widow of an Italian Count, both long-time members of the Ladies Alpine Club. Then we planned to climb a 12,926 foot peak in the Anadolou Daglari Mountains in North Turkey - in Lazistan, to be more precise.

I have already promised not to describe any more amateur mountain adventures. I remember *The Ascent of Rum Doodle!* And that was written as long ago as 1956! So I shall keep the climbing details on this trip to a minimum.

Lazistan does not rank amongst the more notorious 'stans', but it is significantly more civilised than some, and yet retains a romantic remoteness. Sidney and the two ladies were already in the north and John set off in a huge de Soto 4x4 truck, brightly painted in Shell colours, on a combined inspection and PR tour of the north. Philippa and I had a spare day so we visited Scutari and saw the hospital where Florence Nightingale had worked, the enormous statue erected in her memory, and the Crimean War cemetery for those she hadn't been able to nurse back to health.

Next day we flew to Trabizond. No sign of the Towers - but then the airport lies to the east of the town. It was 22 June and although not actually raining one could not but help notice the muddy water swirling miles out into the Black Sea from the streams rushing down from the mountains behind us. The prevailing wind on this coast is from the north, making it a lee shore for yachtsmen, already discouraged by the heavy rainfall that ensues.

John arrived in his campaign bus; we loaded our kit and set off for Cayali, where we met the others and enjoyed a superb shish kebab in the Husref

---

[1] John had been appointed general manager of Shell (Turkey) after completing his tour with PDO in Oman.

Salim Bin Afeef (left)

south into the mountains alongside a rushing torrent and in pouring rain to Aydar. The 28 mile trip took two and a half hours. Aydar, at 3,871 feet, was as neat and tidy as any Swiss mountain village and the Kachgar Hotel, where we stayed the night, as clean.

As we stood and watched the relentless rain *mein host* told us that it rains every day of the year in this valley! One result, apart from the raging torrent in the valley bed, is that the trees are enormous - over 40 deciduous varieties, like sweet chestnuts and beech. Higher up are the conifers, in which the Lazis have their beehives; while down the valley near the coast hazelnuts and the tea gardens that bring wealth to the area. The Turks are every bit as fanatical tea drinkers as the British.

Next morning we continued our drive up the valley to lower Khadron village where we left our vehicles and loaded our kit onto five horses. The villagers were neat, clean and polite, while the children were so well dressed as to make me wonder whether they had been expecting royalty! But no, I was told, they are... good children.

The valley gradually widened out and after a three and a half hour walk we reached the site of our base camp. The walk, I said to anyone who was listening, reminded me of the route from Pheriche to Island Peak near Everest, with its walls of yellow rhododendrons. Well, one is allowed to show off sometimes amongst friends? The rain had relented but through the mist and cloud we could see a be-fanged monster that we were told was our target!

"Trust me," said Sidney.

Well, he was the expert and had decided that Kachgar Dag (13,000ft) was a suitable peak for 50-year-olds plus - and I do mean plus in some instances - climbers!

a suitable peak for 50-year-olds plus - and I do mean plus in some instances - climbers!

We were in an amphitheatre above upper Khadron village, at about 9,800 feet, where the inhabitants were again clean, well dressed and friendly. The surroundings were certainly more Swiss than Himalayan. Our camp lay on the east side of the main valley. Opposite us was a glacier that descended from the peak. It still looked ferocious through the swirling mist.

We slept early. I was conscious of the fact that Sidney was not quite up to speed with expedition catering. In fact I crawled into my sleeping bag feeling decidedly peckish. Perhaps the superb efforts of the Army Catering Corps on Everest and Ruth Hawley's imaginative menus on the Jebel Akhder had spoiled me. Anyway I slept well and awoke at first light with that delicious feeling that I could doze for another three hours. It was a fine clear morning and Kachgar looked positively benign. Perhaps Sidney was right after all. After a meagre breakfast of tea and a boiled egg, John, Sidney, Dorothea and I set off on a recce. How Dorothea moved with her arthritic knees I shall never know. But move she did with never a word of complaint.

We left Philippa and Elizabeth to guard our tents as the villagers of upper Khadron had decided to graze their bulls in our amphitheatre. It was soon clear that the glacier was an autostrade that led to a recessed col from which there was easy access to the summit. The weather began to close in about 11.30am, so we returned to camp where I was glad to find that Philippa had sorted out the rations as well as beating off the bulls.

It began to hail and then rain. This lasted for three days and nights. Further description is unnecessary. There was no dry clothing left. But after 48 hours Sidney decided that we should go for it - reveille at 2.30am to be exact. I tried to persuade him to postpone the climb for another 24 hours but he was adamant. After Turkish porridge - not one of the country's greatest

Chuck's dhow

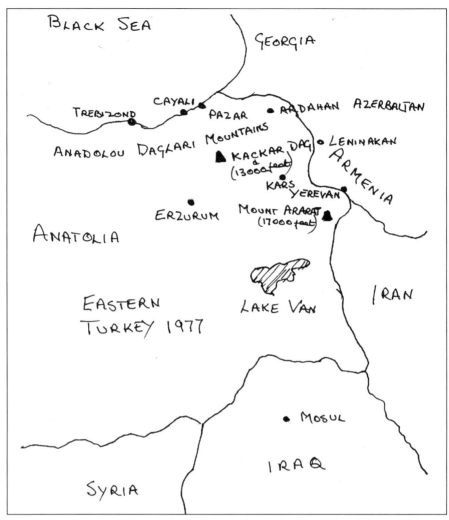

culinary successes - we set off.

Sidney went galloping off in the dim light and soon we caught up to find him blundering around looking for Dorothea. After a delay we found her; and the rain stopped. A wet mist gradually cleared, we roped up, ascended the glacier and by 8.45am were on the col. From there it should have been a stroll to the summit - but it wasn't. There was a narrow snow bridge. I attempted to traverse this and sank up to my crotch in new snow. Sidney announced he was blown. He would wait for me. I decided I was too old to be a peak bagger. I also thought it was the gracious thing to do. We wouldn't have been there without Sidney and his command of the Turkish language.

We descended through a thick yellow mist. The others had descended earlier and were resting. But, apart from John, they were knackered: and his knee was playing up. The two of us prepared ham and pea soup. It was so salty as to be undrinkable. As Jon Fleming would have said, it was time for 'a courageous decision'.

I was the only fit member of the party, and cold, wet, and tired. But this sort of thing had happened before; and I drew strength from it. I chucked out the soup, washed the congealed breakfast porridge bowl (yukk!), got water, a stove going and prepared goulash. It tasted quite good. At least the others ate it. Having washed up and made a sick round of the others I retired to my wet sleeping bag and decided it had been a good day after all!

Next day the sun shone and we dried out - usually the best day on any expedition. But I noticed that our campsite appeared to be 180 feet higher than on the day we arrived, ie, the barometer had dropped like a stone. Sidney, as ever, had a tortuous explanation instead of the obvious - that it might presage a temperature rise! Of course it didn't. Next day he awoke John and I at 4 am, and we set off for the mountain again. A fine dawn but there was high cirrus coming from the north. When we reached the foot of the glacier the party split, the ladies going to the west lower col while we three chaps went for the summit. At 7.05am we reached the col after a splendid unroped climb and we looked set for a record ascent.

At 7.10 a blizzard hit us - from the south! We cowered for an hour behind rocks, while some very distressed snow cocks and a huge Taurus partridge whizzed past us in search of shelter. *Alors...*

We descended the glacier snout, fresh snow already balling up under our crampons. John and I opted for a last throw, at the east col, while Sidney opted to wait for us. We flogged up a couloir, changing the lead every 50 steps, and even then were exhausted when we finally reached the lip. We were rewarded by a dramatic view across Anatolia under a stormy sky with Ararat on the distant horizon. Kachgar Dag was wreathed in snow and cloud. We were 650 feet below it.

We descended through persistent rain and had another sodden night. Next morning Sidney produced 'halvah' (grease!) for breakfast! Our horses arrived two hours early, so we packed and bade farewell to a lovely if wet campsite. At lower Khadron John and I climbed aboard the Land Rover with the bulk of the kit and descended to Ayder where John's Shell truck was waiting. After numerous delays, false alarms, missed RVs, interspersed with excellent Turkish meals, ie, a traveller's life, we got John off to Istanbul and,

Armenian Church near Ardahan

thanks to Sidney's undoubted skills as a negotiator, the rest of us were off on a three day tour of eastern Turkey in a comfortable Peugeot 504.

We drove up wet valleys with their giant dripping ferns to the Russian frontier: This was country where the border changed 'at shift of sword and sword.' Thus, we crossed iron Russian bridges, passed ruined Armenian castles, villages and Turkish 'caravanserais'. Here the people had none of the grace of Lazis. They were dirty, corrupt, even the trainee harlots coarse. War may bring out the best in people but the aftermath does the opposite. Yet the wild gardens grew beans, pomegranates, apples and maize. In one village there was a ruined Armenian bathhouse, destroyed, we were told, in the fighting after World War I. It did not appear that the inhabitants had washed since! To be fair to the Turkish authorities the people were being moved from their squalid ruins to some red brick army barracks down the valley.

It was with some relief that we crossed a high pass, still in the pouring rain, through pine forests, and down to Ardahan, approaching the town through lush meadows alive with lupins and other wild flowers. So we came to the Anatolian plains. It was a different world. Stone houses with stone chimneys, grass roofs where storks had their nests, and no windows, surrounded by cattle and wild horses. It had been raining for three months. Everywhere we stopped the food was uniformly excellent.

We travelled on to Kars, where we needed a new tyre. Here there is a wonderful citadel, legacy of this disputed territory. The railway line to Russia starts from here, up to Leninakan. We found a comfortable hotel, called Bal, (honey), where we were able to dry our tents and sleeping bags for the first time.

Philippa and I shared a room, as she would not sleep by herself in Turkey; and I suspect Sidney snored worse than I did. Next day we drove on to Erzurum, which was dreary - such a disappointment - I was hoping to see Sandy Arbuthnot lurking on a street corner. We watched the ladies beating their carpets and washing their hair at the same time in the river. Although not overtly offensive, one sensed their hostility. The presence of seven army camps on the outskirts could not have been soothing. Low hills, desert and volcanic towers surrounding them. How could the Armenians believe they had been dispossessed of a second Garden of Eden? Not this part of Asia!

Back to Trabizond from where we flew in our different directions. I went back to John Jennings and waited for my freighter back to Oman... and waited... and waited. Eventually John took the initiative, and I came back from a sail up the Bosporus one afternoon to find him waving an air ticket to Muscat via Teheran next day! House guests and fish etc. He had been a good host and, among other kindnesses, had taken us to see a performance of *Hamlet* by the visiting Royal Shakespeare Company in a Roman amphitheatre on the shores of the Bosporus, with Derek Jacobi in the role. Thank you John.

So I flew home on a Panam flight to Teheran. A memorable moment was the pilot's announcement as we approached the Iranian border: "If passengers will look out of the port windows you'll see Mount Ay-rat, where Noah parked his arse after the flood!"

I hoped his dyslexia didn't extend to the rest of his map reading.

31
HOME VIA THE HIMALAYAS

Our last winter in Oman flew by. Weekend after weekend we camped; or I climbed, with Philippa and Adriano Paltrinieri as often as not. Jim and Judy came to stay, as did Fiona. Jim's 'business' with the Sultan flourished and, partly as a result, our social life flourished! Work proceeded smoothly and I managed to persuade another British radiologist, Iain Morle, to replace me in due course. (Sadly he did not thank me for it, or enjoy the experience very much.)

I was sad to be leaving, and so was Binnie, but with her unquestioning acceptance of <u>major</u> decisions in our joint lives she accepted it without demur. (The same cannot be said for lesser decisions!)

Dr Mubarak Khaddouri was kindness itself, threw a huge farewell party for me and presented me with a superb silver coffee-pot made in Nizwa. Jim and Philippa also gave us a rousing send off, accepting our guest list in toto - so as we could avoid the endless, repetitive, round of parties that precede most expatriates' departures. My staff presented me with a fine brass clock, (they knew English customs!), which still hangs on my study wall.

We said goodbye to our little house and moved into the Al Falaj Hotel, now boasting a tower block, for our last few days. Then we departed for India. Our household effects were packed and dispatched by truck, all the way overland to England - apart from the Channel crossing.

Binnie joined a group of friends from the British Embassy and spent the next month in Kashmir, while I met up with a party of sappers, led by Henry Day, in an attempt on Trisul 2, a 23,360 foot peak in the Garhwal Himalayas. Henry had kindly invited me to join him as MO for his party. Now I have already given blow by blow descriptions of three expeditions to the Himalayas. I was actually lucky enough to visit them fifteen times in all! So I shall henceforth write only about what one might term Himalayan highlights.

This expedition was a happy one. No one got hurt and Henry himself reached within 200 feet of the summit, going solo by then, before deciding to be a responsible husband and father and turning back. I had set my heart on seeing Nanda Devi since 1963, when I had purchased a painting of the mountain from Dr T. Howard Somervell, David's father, at an Alpine Club Exhibition. To tell the truth, he was quite loath to part with it! But he recalled that I had prepared supper for him in the Hornli Hut on the Matterhorn many years previously and decided, on balance, that I deserved first refusal! He had painted it in 1931 when he and his wife were on holiday with Hugh Ruttledge and his wife in the Garhwal. It is a lovely painting, albeit somewhat fanciful, as THS was the first to admit. There is such a thing as artistic licence - even nature can be improved upon at times. It has hung on my wall for 40 years, and is still a constant source of pleasure.

I also knew that Eric Shipton had made a survey of Nanda Devi in 1936, towards the end of which he had crossed an unnamed col leading from the Ronti Glacier into the Nanda Kini Valley - where we planned to have our base camp. What I did not know, until we returned to England later, was how he had reached the Ronti Glacier from the Rishi Ganga, the great gorge that leads through the Outer Sanctuary into the Nanda Devi Basin. Had I done so we would have missed a fine mountain journey!

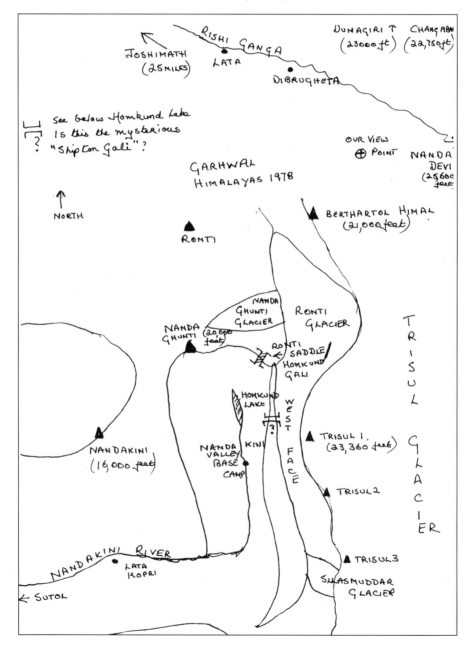

There was a col above our base camp. Messrs Ruttledge and Longstaff had seen it in 1927, when they were looking for a route into the Nanda Devi Basin, but bad weather stopped them crossing it. They called it Ronti Saddle. Meanwhile Indian pilgrims have since named it Homkund Gali. Homkund, a nearby lake, is an object of Hindu pilgrimage. We subsequently passed this at the beginning of our journey, a few miles up the Nanda Kini valley from our base camp. It is only a few feet deep and surprisingly warm, considering how close it lies to the glacier snout. But nothing is simple in the Himalayas.

When we started upon our ascent of Trisul we climbed a steep gully on the east side of the Nanda Kini valley to establish our camp one. This we pitched at the head of the Ronti Glacier which lies to the east and parallel to Nanda Kini - but much higher. Indian pilgrims called the top of this gully Shipton Gali. Some mystery surrounds it - Shipton clearly stated that he descended from the Ronti Glacier to the Nanda Kini valley in 1936 and it is the only link between the two. No one records having descended it until we arrived in 1978. But Shipton described his route as: "Presenting no difficulties what-soever." Either a typical understatement, or perhaps snow conditions were better later in the year than when we used it as a porter route and it had become a wet and slippery stone chute that we had to rope much of the way!

So it was that, in late June, as the Trisul climbers returned to base camp, four of us prepared to retrace Shipton's route. The four were Pat Gunson, who had been on Everest in 1976, with Corporals Tony Swierzy and Len Atkinson, and myself. Tony went into the SAS and sadly was killed six years later on the north face of Everest. Pat still lives in the Lake District. I have lost touch with Len. They were good companions.

One of my last efforts at base camp was to ensure all the rubbish was burned. We built an impressive pile. I then doused it with surplus fuel from our stoves. Unfortunately I had never observed the effect of lighting naphtha in the open at high altitude. The effect was truly impressive. The bulk of the rubbish rose in the air in a mushroom cloud reminiscent of Hiroshima, then was deposited around us in an area of several hundred square feet. It took the rest of the day to gather it up again.

Next morning, bright and early, we set off for the Ronti Saddle. From the very outset we were aware that we were not following in *In the Steps of Shipton*, the title of a lecture I gave to the Alpine Club later that year, but we'd had enough of the gully leading to Shipton Gali. We took two porters, Nirman and Worr Singh, cousins from Sutul, and proven high altitude porters. They opted to wear boots while the rest of us had crampons on right from the start.

Henry came along to see us safely over the top and together we enjoyed an pleasant tramp to the col. We were impressed by the steep slope beneath us; but we managed to kick step the first few hundred feet before glissading to the glacier another thousand below. Here we encountered the usual rock shambles that occur where glaciers meet, the Ronti on our right, the Nanda Ghunti on our left. We then scrambled up onto the east lateral moraine of the Ronti, below the cliffs of Bertaholi Himal. We bounded happily down this until we came to a re-entrant on our right. This looked a logical place from which Shipton would have debouched onto the Ronti glacier - remember we were _re_-tracing his steps, ie, backtracking. There was a grassy terrace, a nearby stream, alpine accentors observing us and three goats that trotted off. It would have been a crime not to have camped here!

Next day we flogged up the side of the re-entrant, then into a rock-filled gully to a col from which we hoped to see Nanda Devi. We couldn't... but we could see Kamet to the west and behind us a tiny white banner hanging below the east ridge of Nanda Ghunti - the Ronti Saddle that we had crossed.

The sun had done its worst and we struggled across a snow slope, then down to another valley floor, where we spent an uncomfortable night. I had encouraged the others to travel light. Here we were on ice, and I was the only person to have brought an inflatable mattress and a high altitude sleeping bag. The remarks of my companions were not very complimentary: "Bloody poofter!" was one of them.

They were rewarded later when I discovered there is an amazing amount of oil in a tin of mackerel, heedlessly opened at 16,000 feet. It erupted like an aerosol spray and drenched me. I emitted a healthy tang of the sea for several days thereafter.

Next morning we set off up the gully beyond our camp, its head sheathed in ice. We made good time; except for Nirman and Worr who, without crampons, had to struggle up loose rock on the side, gaining three feet and losing two at a time. Once more we hoped to see Nanda Devi from the col. And this time we did. The two young sappers had raced ahead of me, front-pointing up the ice - a new fangled technique for this middle-aged climber, who was still cutting steps, very elegantly, mind you. Their cries of delight were justified. There, due east, was the huge bulk of Nanda Devi. The west ridge and peak were superimposed, obscuring the east peak. We were at 18,000 feet, enjoying a view of the mountain that I suppose no one - excluding Shipton? - had ever seen before.

We spent an hour on the col, revelling in our good fortune - and praising the Lord who had made these hills. The eastern horizon was a mountain showcase - Dunagiri, Changabang and Rishikot to the north. In front the west rim of the Nanda Devi basin hung like a huge stage curtain. On our right the east ridge of Bertaholi Himal fell gradually into the gorge beneath. And, to cap it all, there was visible assurance that a clear route lay before us.

Finally we tore ourselves away and glissaded down the snow to the valley floor. We lunched at the site of the Bertaholi Himal base camp. Dr Longstaff had named this Juniper Camp in 1907 on his epic climb of Trisul from the east. We were among dwarf pines, azaleas - and litter.

Our return to Joshimath was down the well-trodden path of the Rishi Ganga. We passed through Dibrugheta, where I was impressed by the sight of a woman on her haunches managing to piss against a wall some three feet away! In the book of Samuel, David swears to kill, "Any of these mothers' sons ranged against him who pisseth against the wall." It seems unfair that she would have suffered the same fate as the men!

We also passed some 80 porters en route to Nanda Devi to re-supply an American party on Nanda Devi. There was still concern throughout north India following the disappearance of a nuclear-powered listening device that the Americans had planted some years before on the east face of the mountain to monitor Chinese activity in Tibet. The fear was that the waters of the Rishi Ganga would become contaminated by radioactive material - and thus spread down the Ganges across India. The porters had a military escort and I unwittingly caused a stir by mentioning to the officer in charge that we were part of a British Army Expedition - and that I was a radiologist. The officer sprang to his feet with an abrupt apology, and presumably the telephone wires to Delhi were soon humming. As we were blissfully unaware of the scare at the time, our *sang froid* was probably the reason we were let go on our way unhindered, but back in Islamabad we learned the authorities were scared the British were interfering and were checking up on the Yanks! Personally, I never thought Anglo-American relations with Pakistan stood much chance after the American militarists renamed Probyn's Horse the Fifth Cavalry. (At least it wasn't the Seventh - Custer's Last Command!)

We had been lucky so far, now the rain returned and it was not until the evening of the following day that it relented and we camped in a golden haze. In the clear dawn next morning we gazed back at Trisul and again saw the white banner that was the Ronti Saddle! It looked only slightly smaller than when we had last seen it a week before! Until then we had basked in the amazed disbelief that greeted news of our epic crossing from the Nanda Kini valley. Now we felt a bit deflated!

We'd hoped to catch a bus for the last part of our journey but the last one of the day swept past us, without an inch of room; an accurate statement for those who know the almost infinite capacity of Indian buses to transport both humans and animals!

We did manage a short hitch in an Indian Army lorry but otherwise we tramped the last fifteen miles to Joshimath in the dark. There we sealed our return to civilisation by getting sucked into the crowd leaving the late show at the garrison cinema. By now mildly hysterical we started comparing imaginary opinions on the film. This caused the crowd to shrink back from us in silence; or was it the combination of our bedraggled appearance and smell?[1]

We reassembled in the Indian Army Sappers' Mess at Roorkee and made our various ways home. Binnie was already there and we were reunited under the roof of her parents' house at Lydford-on-Fosse in Somerset. Thanks to Martin Barry I already had a post as locum consultant radiologist in the county, based in Yeovil, but with sessions in Taunton and a weekly visit to the Bristol Royal Infirmary where Howard Middlemiss, the much-travelled professor of radiology, had dumped me on one of his colleagues, Dr

[1] An afternoon spent in the Alpine Club library after my return showed we had retraced only the last part of Shipton's journey. He had climbed into the Ronti glacier from the Rishi Ganga much further west than we had.

Frank Ross, in order to acquire a knowledge of the relatively new discipline of diagnostic ultrasound. After an initial display of petulance at being put upon yet again with one of Howard's colonial retreads - the first time I had heard this name - Frank proceeded to be an enthusiastic and pragmatic teacher of this exciting and operator-dependant subject.

Soon we were busy enough. In November we bought our new home in a small village in North Somerset, thanks to the encouragement and assistance of my old friend, Tony Arnott, home from abroad and once more practising as a surveyor. The house had been sold at auction in 1957 for £2,650 to a retired headmaster from Surrey, and by 1978 needed a lot of work doing to it!

Martin, who was due to retire in 1979, had finally got agreement to have a second consultant radiologist based in Yeovil District Hospital. The post was advertised and I was appointed in February of that year. Thus began what proved to be the happiest fourteen years of my professional life.

Not that it seemed so at the outset! It was not only the 'winter of discontent', but a bitterly cold one. We wondered what the hell we had done by coming home! Also, these were the glory days of the NHS unions when their 'hit squads' squatted in the hospitals: when porters decided which patients to take to theatre: and medical staff were offered cheese sandwiches or nothing in the hospital canteen. (Although one of the kindly serving staff once whispered to me: "Come back when they've gone love, I'll get you some bacon and eggs.")

In retrospect, I think most of this trouble was due to the class war, although the protagonists were fighting it on out-dated concepts. For example, that year, of some 45 consultant staff at the hospital, only two had been to public schools: yet to hear the grumbling that went on, one would have thought that consultants had bought their appointments in much the same way that sprigs of the aristocracy had bought commissions in the army in the previous century.

I was acutely conscious of my neo-colonial background and ready to hold my peace at clinical conferences. Also to expect far higher standards of care and skill amongst the medical and nursing staff than I had experienced during my twenty-odd years of service in the sands. Gradually I became aware that this was not so; that the diagnostic skills of my erstwhile Arab and Indo-Pakistani colleagues were, in many cases, superior to those I encountered in the UK. Whilst we had lacked the presence of English ward sisters, by now a disappearing breed thanks to the Salmon Report, the devotion of the Indian Christian nurses in the Arabian Gulf was certainly not exceeded back in England.

The same applied to hospital administration. I was reminded of a comment by a former member of the ICS: "The standards of administration in the Bengal Secretariat in the 1940s was significantly better than that of the Civil Service in England."

Eventually, I achieved a balance. I decided I'd better look to my own laurels unless I wanted to be left behind! I took advantage of the post-graduate education that was to hand, after years of reading the professional journals as the only way of keeping up to date. I should not have been surprised to find that my administrative experience, albeit in a neo-colonial environment, was to lead me into the field of NHS management. This could hardly be described as a cut and thrust business. Indeed, it was too overtly chummy for its own good in many cases. But it did allow me to witness some bizarre events.

Once I attended a meeting in Shepton Mallet to discuss the future of hospital services. I was charged to promote the concept of these services being initially shared with Wells, some six miles to the west; and then a new community hospital being built at Croscombe, half way between the two. Uproar ensued, and I was howled down. Later, when sinking a therapeutic gin and tonic in a nearby pub, two of the local councillors came in.

"Have a drink, no hard feelings!" said I, thinking that perhaps something could be salvaged from the debacle. Gingerly, I got round to asking why the adamant rejection of our proposal?

"Ah! You wouldn't understand," cried one. "They killed six of our men!"

Silently I cursed myself for making the elementary mistake of not doing my homework. Whatever had caused this animosity I should have known about it. I mumbled condolences. The one who had spoken went to the gents.

His companion looked at me quizzically. "No," he said slowly, "I suppose you couldn't be expected to have known - but it was a wicked ambush, innocent men seeking fodder for their animals. We knew they had more than enough in Croscombe - but then they were damned King's men!"

It took me several more minutes to deduce he was describing an event that had taken place during the Civil War.

On another occasion I was doing a radiology session in the hospital at Bridgwater, and chatting with the sister-in-charge of outpatients when I saw her eyes dart over my shoulder and suddenly narrow.

"Excuse me," she muttered, and pushed past me.

I heard those stentorian tones, reminiscent of Hattie Jacques at her best, ordering a family of four to follow her into an adjoining room; and admonishing them to stay there until she called - and no one else! A group of commandos would have obeyed. She turned to me.

"What was that about, Sister?" I enquired in my innocence.

"Huh! Those were Dryers - and right behind you are the Thompson family. Thank goodness they didn't see each other! No! Don't turn round!"

I duly froze. "And...?" I asked tentatively.

"Oh there's always trouble when those families are here. Back in Monmouth's time, the Dryers let on that the Thompsons were hiding some of his men after the defeat at Sedgemoor. The King's men took them away and Jeffreys hanged them! And two of the Thompsons for good measure! They've been rowing ever since."

I reflected on the Beni Bu Ali and the Beni Bu Hassan; and decided that life in Somerset was not going to be that different after all.

ABBREVIATIONS

ABC - Advanced Base Camp
ADC - Aide de Camp
ADDF - Abu Dhabi Defence Force
ADMA - Abu Dhabi Marine Areas
ADMS - Asst. Director Medical Services
ADPC - Abu Dhabi Petroleum Company
ALAF - Arab Legion Air Force
AMA - Army Mountaineering Association
APC - Analgesic tablets
ARAMCO - Arab-American Oil Company
ATS - Auxiliary Territorial Service (now Womens Royal Army Corps)
BACSA - British Association for Cemeteries in South Asia
BCCI - Bank Credit & Commercial International
BD - Bahrain Dinar
BMJ - British Medical Journal
BOAC - British Overseas Airways Corporation (now BA)
BP - British Petroleum
CIA - Central Intelligence Agency
C-in-C - Commander in Chief
CMO - Chief Medical Officer
CMS - Christian Missionary Society
CO - Commanding Officer
CT - Computerised Tomography
DA - Defence Attaché
DDT - anti-malarial chemical
DH - de Havilland
DMRD - Diploma in Medical radio-diagnosis
DMS - Director of Medical Services
DRS - Desert Reconnaissance Squadron
FRCR - Fellow Royal College Of Radiologists
GHQ - General Headquarters
GP - General Practitioner
HMG - Her Majesty's Government
ICRC - International Committee of the Red Cross
ICS - Indian Civil Service
IMS - Indian Medical Service
IPC - Iraq Petroleum Company
KD - Kuwait Dinar
KOC - Kuwait Oil Company
LZ - Landing Zone
MBBS - Bachelor Medicine, Bachelor Surgery
MBE - Member of the Order of the British Empire
MEA - Middle East Airlines

MO - Medical Officer
MOD - Ministry of Defence
NHS - National Health Service
NLF - National Liberation Front
NWFP - North West Frontier Province
OBE - Officer of the Order of the British Empire
OC - Officer Commanding
OPD - Out Patients' Department
PAF - Pakistan Air Force
PDO - Petroleum Development Oman (Shell)
PFC - Private First Class
PIA - Pakistan International Airlines
PLF - Palestinian Liberation Front
PLFP - Popular Liberation Front for Palestine
PLO - Palestinian Liberation Organisation
PNS - Pakistan Naval Service
PR - Political Resident
PWD - Public Works Department
PX - US Forces shop, (equivalent to NAAFI)
RADC - Royal Army Dental Corps
RAF - Royal Air Force
RAMC - Royal Army Medical Corps
RASC - Royal Army Service Corps
RDF - Radio Direction Finding (beacon)
REME - Royal Electrical and Mechanical Engineers
RMA - Royal Military Academy, Sandhurst
RSM - Regimental Sergeant Major
SAF - Sultans Armed Forces
SAFTR - Sultans Armed Forces Training Regiment
SIB - Special Intelligence Branch
SMO - Senior Medical Officer
SNOPGY - Senior Naval Officer Persian Gulf
SOAF - Sultan of Oman's Air Force
TA - Territorial Army
TJFF - Trans-Jordan Frontier Force
TWA - Transworld Airlines
UAR - United Arab Republic
UBL - United Bank Limited
USAF - United States Air Force
USMAG - United States Military Aid Group
WAAC - Women's Army Auxiliary Corps
WHO - World Health Organisation
WO - Warrant Officer
WAAF - Women's Auxiliary Air Force (became WRAF)

INDEX

Acknowledgements

I would like to express my thanks to Hugh Leach and St. John Armitage for their help with the T. E. Lawrence photographs.

MORE BOOKS FROM HAYLOFT

The Maddison Line, Roy Maddison
(£10, ISBN 1 9045240 6 0)

A Herdwick County Cook Book, Hugh & Therese Southgate
(Hardback, £19.95, ISBN 0 9540711 8 2)
(Paperback, £14.95, ISBN 0 9540711 7 4)

The Long Day Done, Jeremy Rowan-Robinson
(£9.50, ISBN 1 9045240 4 4)

From the High Pennines, Marmaduke Alderson
(£10, ISBN 1 9045240 7 9)

Pashler's Lane, A Clare Childhood, Elizabeth Holdgate
(£10, ISBN 0 9542072 0 3)

Odd Corners in Appleby, Gareth Hayes
(£8.50, ISBN 1 9045240 0 1)

The Ghastlies, Trix Jones and Shane Surgey
(£3.99, ISBN 1 9045240 4 4)

A Journey of Soles, Lands End to John O'Groats, Kathy Trimmer
(£9.50, 1 9045240 5 2)

*Changing the Face of Carlisle, The Life and Times of Percy Dalton, City
Engineer and Surveyor, 1926-1949,* Marie K. Dickens
(£8, ISBN 0 9540711 9 0)

*From Clogs and Wellies to Shiny Shoes, A Windermere Lad's Memories of
South Lakeland,* Miles R. M. Bolton
(£12.50, ISBN 1 9045240 2 8)

A History of Kaber, Helen McDonald and Christine Dowson,
(£8, ISBN 0 9540711 6 6)

The Gifkin Gofkins, Irene Brenan
(£2.50, ISBN 1 9045240 1 X)

*A Dream Come True, the Life and Times of a Lake District National Park
Ranger,* David Birkett
(£5.50, ISBN 0 9540711 5 8)

Gone to Blazes, Life as a Cumbrian Fireman, David Stubbings
(£9.95, ISBN 0 9540711 4 X)

Changing Times, The Millennium Story of Bolton, Barbara Cotton
(£12.50, ISBN 0 9540711 3 1)

*Better by Far a Cumberland Hussar, A History of the Westmorland and
Cumberland Yeomanry,* Colin Bardgett
(Hardback, £26.95, ISBN 0 9540711 2 3)
(Paperback, £16.95, ISBN 0 9540711 1 5)

Northern Warrior, the Story of Sir Andreas de Harcla, Adrian Rogan
(£8.95, ISBN 0 9523282 8 3)

Military Mountaineering, A History of Services Expeditions, 1945-2000,
Retd. SAS Major Bronco Lane
(Hardback, £25.95, ISBN 0 9523282 1 6)
(Paperback, £17.95, ISBN 0 9523282 6 7)

2041 - The Voyage South, Robert Swan
(£8.95, 0 9523282 7 5)

Yows & Cows, A Bit of Westmorland Wit, Mike Sanderson
(£7.95, ISBN 0 9523282 0 8)

Riding the Stang, Dawn Robertson
(£9.99, ISBN 0 9523282 2 4)

Secrets and Legends of Old Westmorland, Peter Koronka and Dawn Robertson
(Hardback, £17.95, ISBN 0 9523282 4 0)
(Paperback, £11.95, ISBN 0 9523282 9 1)

The Irish Influence, Migrant Workers in Northern England, Harold Slight
(£4.95, 0 9523282 5 9)

Soldiers and Sherpas, A Taste for Adventure, Brummie Stokes.
(£19.95, 0 9541551 0 6)

North Country Tapestry, Sylvia Mary McCosh
(£10, 0 9518690 0 0)

Between Two Gardens, The Diary of two Border Gardens,
Sylvia Mary McCosh
(£5.95, 0 9008111 7 X)

A Riot of Thorn & Leaf, Dulcie Matthews
(£7.95, ISBN 0 9540711 0 7)

Dacre Castle, A short history of the Castle and the Dacre Family,
E. H. A. Stretton
(£5.50, 0 9518690 1 9)

Little Ireland, Memories of a Cleator Childhood, Sean Close
(£7.95, ISBN 0 9540673 0 4)

A Slip from Grace, More tales from Little Ireland, Sean Close
(£9.99, ISBN 0 9540673 1 2)

Isaac's Tea Trail, Roger Morris (£2)

Antarctica Unveiled, Scott's First Expedition and the Quest for the Unknown Continent, David E. Yelverton
(£25.99, 0 8708158 2 2)

You can order any of our books by writing to:
Hayloft Publishing,
South Stainmore, Kirkby Stephen,
Cumbria, CA17 4EU, UK.
Please enclose a cheque plus £2 for UK postage and packing.
or telephone: +44 (0)17683) 42300
For more information see: www.hayloft.org.uk